Grave Error

How The Media Misled Us (and the Truth about Residential Schools)

Edited by

C.P. Champion and Tom Flanagan

Cover photo credit: Deschâtelets-NDC Priest with Kamloops IRS students, Missionnaires Oblats de Marie Immaculée, with permission.

Edited by Dr. C.P. Champion, PhD, FRCGS, and Dr. Tom Flanagan, PhD, FRSC.

First edition 2023

Published by True North and Dorchester Books.

Contents

Preface

Conrad Black

Never in my lifetime, which is now barely on the right side of 80 years, have I known of a book which was as profoundly needed for the restoration of sobriety in public discourse in Canada as this one. *Grave Error: How the Media Misled Us (and the Truth about Residential Schools)*, edited by C.P. Champion and Tom Flanagan, is a collection of rigorously researched and written aspects of the current controversy, raging under the misapplied heading of "Reconciliation," about the history of the relations of Canadian native people with the government of Canada.

The saga recalls the famous book of Charles McKay published in England in 1841 under the title *Memoirs of Extraordinary Popular Delusions*. Subsequent editions extended the title to include "the Madness of Crowds," which was subdivided into National Delusions, Peculiar Follies, and Philosophical Delusions, constituting a virtual encyclopedia of tremendous waves of false belief in fraudulent or spurious financial projects, individual charlatans in many fields, irrational behavioural fads, and other aberrant conduct. It began with three of the most notorious financial scams in history: the 18th century stampede to invest in fanciful notions of development along the Mississippi River, the infamous South Sea Bubble in the 18th century, and the 17th century Dutch Tulip Mania, in which the value placed on an individual tulip growing in a small pot of earth was the current equivalent of $25,000. McKay canvassed a wide range of pseudo-religious swindlers, outright thieves, frequent instances of misinformed public sentiment causing acts of violence over alleged abuses, and even the Thugs of India.

Among the practices excoriated by MacKay were alchemy, unsubstantiated economic speculation, tales of ghosts, absurd speculation about the influence of politics and religion on beards and vice versa, and fake medical cures. Unfortunately, the current popular conceptions of the grievances of native people in Canada are not misplaced under such a title; and unlike MacKay's infamous examples of frenzied mass departures from common sense and rational thinking, in the current hysteria of confected national guilt over the official Canadian conduct towards the native people, the government of Canada is one of the principal carriers and propagators of the terribly destructive virus of insane misconceptions on the subject. The present federal government has done great damage to the very necessary rational discussion of all the problems of native policy by legitimizing and declining to offer any legal or public relations defence against escalating and profoundly false allegations that constitute blood libels against the British and French founding peoples of this country.

Almost every reasonably informed person in Canada is aware of at least the outline of the native grievances against the Europeans and their descendants in this country. The Canadian policy towards the native people until the last 40 years had been to promote their assimilation, as with immigrants from civilizations that do not speak either of our official languages. The assumption was that this would best serve the interests of the natives, as it would enable them to participate fully in the life of the country and achieve higher education levels, have greater access to public health services, and enable them to be thoroughly competitive in the workplace in the economic life of Canada. There was undoubtedly a good deal of condescension and implicit disparagement of the absence of a written language in the rudimentary native cultures and of their languishing in a Stone Age economy at the time of the arrival of the Europeans just before and in the early decades of the 16th century.

But official intentions were benign. The much-maligned Sir John A. Macdonald, the principal founder of Canadian Confederation and the first prime minister, gave the native people the right to vote and had his allies among the First Nations who were helpful in defeating the uprisings led by Louis Riel; and he remained loyal to chiefs who had been helpful to him, including Crowfoot. Seeing the violence across the United States as the settlers moved west, Macdonald required that treaties be negotiated assuring adequate territory for the natives to live their nomadic lives and to avoid armed confrontations between natives and settlers. These treaties should all now be renegotiated in favour of the natives but not without some recognition that they spared a great deal of bloodshed and sorrow to both the Aboriginal inhabitants and the newly arriving settlers. Yet Macdonald has been severely traduced and only sketchily defended, despite his incomparable role in the founding of Canada and its political institutions.

In the conspicuous and shameful absence of any effort by the government of Canada to shape this urgent political debate over what has gone wrong and how things can be put right on the basis of historic facts, the European settlers in this country and their dependents have been represented by the government of Canada itself before the whole world, and including in the United Nations, as guilty of some form of genocide. This is a monstrous falsehood. It might usefully be noticed that there is no historical precedent for attempted genocide causing the population of the targeted minority to rise as the population of the native peoples did in this country from approximately 125,000 at the time of Confederation in 1867 to 1.8 million today.

As the editors of this book, C. P. Champion and Tom Flanagan, summarize in their postscript, it is widely believed, even by informed people in Canada, that there were "thousands of missing children," who were ripped from the arms of their parents and forced to attend residential schools, where many of them were murdered after being hideously abused, and were buried in unmarked graves on a scale that constitutes genocide. It is also widely believed that most native children attended the schools, and the schools were entirely bad and were devoted altogether to this instruction of Indian culture and language.

All these widely held beliefs are wholly or largely unfounded, as the precise and learned analyses in this book demonstrate conclusively. No unmarked graves of native children have been found. All students at the Indian Residential Schools were scrupulously accounted for and in many cases were pressed upon the schools by their parents to deliver them from the poverty and illiteracy of native life. The objective was to qualify the native children in English or French but absolutely not to deprive them of, or cause them to be embarrassed about, their Indigenous culture. Undoubtedly, there were many nasty and terrible incidents, but this was contrary to official policy; to some extent abuses occur in all schools.

This monstrous campaign of defamation against the residential schools and the native policy of the Canadian government generally has been, as the authors remark, undertaken in the interests of "reconciliation." This is the development or restoration of good relations between parties in dispute and it requires both a will to be reconciled, and a desire to ascertain the facts in an attitude of forgiveness and goodwill. The so-called reconciliation process which the present federal government is pursuing with the native peoples is based on the 94 recommendations of the 2015 Report of the Truth and Reconciliation Commission. Every one of those recommendations is a denunciation of the motives, competence, or integrity of the government of Canada and by extension of the non-native majority of the Canadian people. Since such a comprehensive indictment of the people of Canada is unjustified, it is going to be impossible to achieve reconciliation by the wholly inappropriate process of one side hurling righteous damnations at the other side, granting the other side no goodwill or benign intent, and crediting them with absolutely nothing positive or even defensible in their conduct, and endlessly demanding humbling acts of guilt and shame accompanied by vertiginous reparations.

The native peoples themselves and their institutions have already received $4.7 trillion in promises and, as to a large part of that, of actual delivery of reparations. They have no natural entitlement to anything more than that and they do have the duty of accepting indisputable facts in their own history even if they are unflattering to them and dilute somewhat the strictures of demonization that they have applied to non-Aboriginal Canadians, a nationality that has earned and enjoys a reputation throughout the world as a civilized and generous people. The only demand not yet made by the aggrieved natives is that Canada accept that its conduct toward the First Nations of Canada has been morally indistinguishable from that of Hitler and Stalin toward Poland: that we are invaders who must withdraw.

Up to now, almost all the Canadian media have fallen in with the false narrative and contributed to the madness of Canada's response to Aboriginal questions. I can only wish for the widest possible sale and positive critical treatment for this timely, scholarly, and irrefutable compendium of relevant facts. There will be no reconciliation and there will be no resolution of these problems if one side requires as a precondition to any progress the acceptance of a false and defamatory version of a very important part of Canadian history.

Introduction

C.P. Champion and Tom Flanagan

This book is a response to the moral panic unleashed on May 27, 2021, when the Chief of the Tk'emlúps te Secwépemc or Kamloops Indian Band announced that ground penetrating radar (GPR) had located the remains of 215 "missing children" in an apple orchard.[1] These were allegedly "undocumented deaths" from the Kamloops Indian Residential School, which had closed 52 years earlier. The young anthropologist who conducted the GPR search later added a note of caution that only forensic investigation could confirm that these were indeed burials,[2] but the moral panic was already under way.[3] Politicians and media precipitately seized on the first announcement, and "mass unmarked graves" and "burials of missing children" became the storyline that quickly ricocheted around Canada and indeed much of the world. Meanwhile several other First Nations that had at one time hosted residential schools quickly hired their own anthropologists armed with GPR and announced similar discoveries.[4]

Canadian Prime Minister Justin Trudeau set the tone of the public response on May 30 by ordering Canadian flags to be flown at half-mast on all federal buildings to honour the "215 children whose lives were taken at the Kamloops residential school,"[5] thus elevating the possible burials to the status of victims of foul play and making Canada sound like a charnel house of murdered children. Unprecedented in Canadian history, flags remained at half-mast until Remembrance Day, November 11, and were

---

[1] Office of the Chief, "For Immediate Release," May 5, 2021.

[2] Michael Potestio, "Number of probable graves near former residential school pegged at 200," *Kamloops This Week*, July 16, 2021.

[3] Frances Widdowson, "Billy Remembers," The American Conservative, February 15, 2022.

[4] 'The truth is finally being revealed': Manitoba grand chiefs react to Cowessess announcement (aptnnews.ca); Canada residential school: 182 human remains discovered in unmarked graves near former St. Eugene's Mission School - CNN; Potential graves discovered at B.C. residential school | CTV News.

[5] Trudeau asks for lowered flags to honour dead residential schoolchildren | The Star.

returned to normal height only after the Assembly of First Nations gave its OK.[6]

Sixty-eight Christian churches were vandalized or burnt to the ground during this period — the majority of the latter were Roman Catholic — a number that reached 83 by the summer of 2023.[7] Many of these were historic church buildings, priceless heritage still used and revered by native people, 27% of whom declared themselves Catholic in the 2021 Census.[8] The pretext for arson and vandalism was that the Kamloops Indian Residential School had been run by a Catholic religious order, as had 43% of residential schools.[9] Think of the outrage in the media if that many synagogues or mosques had been vandalized and burned. Yet the attacks on 83 Christian churches passed with only mild criticism and even with approbation in online comment sections. One U.S. Roman Catholic commentator said the attacks were nothing less than hate-based "terrorism," predicated on "fabrications" that were intended to "demonize Christians."[10]

An article in the *New York Times* was typical of media commentary about the unmarked graves. It was first published under the headline "Horrible History: Mass Grave of Indigenous Children Reported in Canada" on May 28 and updated on October 5 under the same title. "For decades," the article said, "most Indigenous children in Canada were taken from their families and forced into boarding schools. A large number never returned home, their families given only vague explanations, or none at all."[11]

---

[6] Canadian flags to be raised after Remembrance Day | CTV News.

[7] UPDATE: A map of the 83 churches that have been vandalized or burned since the residential schools announcement | True North (tnc.news).

[8] "The proportion of Catholics varies from one Indigenous group to another: 31.6% among Métis, 24.5% among First Nations and 17.4% among Inuit. Meanwhile, the share of Anglicans (37.4%) is much higher among Inuit than among the entire Indigenous population (6.1%)." Statistics Canada, *The Daily*, October 26, 2022.

[9] Rodney A. Clifton and Mark DeWolf, eds., *From Truth Comes Reconciliation* (Winnipeg, MB: Frontier Centre for Public Policy, 2021), p. 34.

[10] Matt Walsh, "Canada's 'Mass Graves' Hoax Is Yet Another Fabricated Narrative To Demonize Christians," "The Matt Walsh Show," E1209, *The Daily Wire*, August 21, 2023.

[11] Cited in J. Rouillard, "In Kamloops, Not One Body Has Been Found" *The Dorchester Review*.

The discovery of the so-called unmarked graves was chosen by Canadian newspaper editors as the "news story of the year."[12] And the World Press Photo of the Year award went to "a haunting image of red dresses hung on crosses along a roadside, with a rainbow in the background, commemorating children who died at a residential school created to assimilate Indigenous children in Canada."[13]

Yet all the major elements of the story are either false or highly exaggerated.

At her original press conference, the Chief of the Kamloops Band claimed to have discovered unmarked graves, and the media, politicians, and even Pope Francis ran with the story without waiting for proof.[14] No unmarked graves have been discovered at Kamloops or elsewhere — not one. As of early August 2023, there had been 20 announcements of soil "anomalies" discovered by GPR near residential schools across Canada; but most have not been excavated, so what, if anything, lies beneath the surface remains unknown. In the few cases where excavations have taken place, no burials related to residential schools have been found.[15]

Most recently, the Minegoziibe Anishinabe First Nation undertook a four-week excavation in the basement of a church that had been built on the site of the Pine Creek Residential School. In spite of a lot of local lore about secret burials in the church basement, the chief had to announce that careful work by archeologists from Brandon University had turned up no remains.[16] In some cases, GPR research has been conducted in whole or in part on known community cemeteries located near the sites of residential

---

12 Canadian Press names Kamloops unmarked graves discovery Canada's news story of the year | CBC News.

13 Haunting Canada boarding school shot wins World Press Photo - ABC News (go.com).

14 Zoe Demarco, "Pope addresses 'shocking discovery' of 215 children buried at BC residential school," Daily Hive News, June 6, 2021.

15 "Canadian Indian residential school gravesites," Wikipedia.

16 Kelly Geraldine Malone, "No evidence of human remains found beneath church at Pine Creek Residential School site," Canadian Press, August 18, 2023.

schools.[17] It would hardly be surprising to find burial sites in a cemetery. But again, since excavations have not been conducted, it is not known whether these potential unmarked graves contain the bodies of children, let alone students from residential schools. Media have generally failed to differentiate between claimed burial sites at schools and known but neglected cemeteries, further confusing the public reception of harrowing allegations.

The truth is that there are no "missing children." This concept was invented by the Truth and Reconciliation Commission (TRC), whose members spoke at various times of 2,800 or 4,200 Indian children who were sent to residential schools but never returned to their parents.[18] Indeed, some children died at residential schools of diseases such as tuberculosis, just as they did in their home communities. And the fate of some children may have been forgotten with the passage of generations — forgotten by their own families, that is. But "forgotten" is not "missing." The myth of missing students arose from a failure of TRC researchers to cross-reference the vast number of historical documents about residential schools and the children who attended them. The documentation exists, but the TRC did not avail themselves of it.

In the moral panic, the "unmarked graves" are presumed to be populated by the "missing children" who died at residential school. Lurid tales of torture and murder, of babies thrown into the furnace and hanging from meat hooks, make the stories more appalling.[19] It is another example of the "Extraordinary Popular Delusions and the Madness of Crowds" chronicled in 1841 by the Scottish journalist Charles Mackay.[20] Delusions based on little or no solid evidence became widely believed and resulted in widespread action, like the persecution of witches or speculation in tulip bulbs. Eventually they burned themselves out, though sometimes not

[17] Catholic Church providing $70,000 to identify unmarked graves in Cowessess Cemetery | CTV News; All Indigenous Communities | St. Eugene Resort (steugene.ca).

[18] Children who never returned from residential school commemorated in Quebec | CBC News.

[19] The False Narrative of Residential School Burials – The Dorchester Review; Billy Remembers - The American Conservative.

[20] Charles Mackay, *Extraordinary Popular Delusions and the Madness in Crowds*, Barnes & Noble, 1994. Cf. 1852 edition available at Project Gutenberg.

before enormous damage was done. The contemporary moral panic over unmarked graves and missing children shows that the "madness of crowds" is still with us, even in our supposedly more rational age.[21]

The notion of missing children, like the other delusions of earlier moral panics, cannot stand up to critical scrutiny. Indian parents, like other parents, loved their children and certainly would have noticed if they went away to school and never came back. Yet no inquiries about missing Indian children were ever filed with the police or other authorities — even though there are several documented parents' complaints about harsh discipline which were addressed by school authorities in favour of the parents.[22] Children were carefully followed in the residential school system. As in schools all over the world, each child received a number upon admission for keeping track of clothing and other possessions.

The federal Department of Indian Affairs also kept close track of students because it paid a per capita subsidy to the schools. It reviewed admission records meticulously because it didn't want to pay for the white and Métis students who sometimes got into the residential schools, which were supposed to be only for Indians. On the other side, the residential schools were equally motivated to keep track of students because their income depended on the per capita subsidies. If students disappeared, their subsidy would have decreased.

Media stories about Indian residential schools are almost always accompanied by the frightening claim that 150,000 students were "forced to attend" these schools, but that claim is misleading at best.[23] Scholars generally agree that more students attended day schools on Indian reserves than went away to residential schools. Children were not required to go to residential school unless no day school was available. Moreover, a large number didn't go to any school at all. It wasn't until 1920 that attendance at either day school or residential school was made compulsory for Indian

---

[21] A recent study is Douglas Murray, *The Madness of Crowds: Gender, Race and Identity* (Bloomsbury Continuum, 2021) free download at Internet Archive.

[22] See chapter by Rodney Clifton in this volume.

[23] "They Were Not Forced" – The Dorchester Review, online April 21, 2022; in print: Nina Green, Brian Giesbrecht, and Tom Flanagan, "They Were Not Forced," *The Dorchester Review*, Vol. 13, No. 1, Spring-Summer 2023, pp. 49-56.

children, and in practice, enforcement was often lax.[24] It was estimated in 1944 that upwards of 40% of Indian children were not in any kind of school.[25]

For students who did attend residential school, an application form signed by a parent or other guardian was required. Many of these forms still exist and can be seen in online government archives.[26] The simple truth is that many Indian parents saw the residential schools as the best option available for their children. Cree artist Kent Monkman's painting, "The Scream,"[27] showing missionaries and Mounted Policemen snatching infants from the arms of their Indian mothers at gunpoint, is a fever dream of the imagination — not even close to an accurate depiction of historical reality, not even taken metaphorically.

How could the moral panic about unmarked graves, with its attendant legends of missing children ripped from the arms of their mothers, have gained such wide currency among political, media, and educational elites? Why was the rational discovery and analysis of the facts swept aside by a wave of emotion and revulsion against the alleged perpetrators? One answer is that the alleged perpetrators were Christian clergy and teachers, and part of the revulsion is a type of anti-Christian backlash, or what Philip Jenkins has called "the new anti-Catholicism."[28] The Prime Minister seemed to allude to this when he said the church-burnings were "understandable." Another explanation is that the indulgence of moral panic serves perfectly the progressive or "woke" narrative of white supremacy, a version of Canadian history in which the white majority flourished only by oppressing racial minorities, above all Indigenous

---

[24] Ibid.

[25] The misleading claim that 150,000 Indigenous children were forced to attend residential schools, True North (tnc.news), December 19, 2021.

[26] Example application for admission, https://central.bac-lac.gc.ca/.item/?op=img&app=microform&id=c-7925-009

[27] "The Scream" - Kent Monkman - Google Arts & Culture.

[28] Philip Jenkins, *The New Anti-Catholicism: The Last Acceptable Prejudice* (Oxford, 2003).

people.[29] But there is also a specific etiology of the unmarked grave narrative.

Prior to 1990, residential schools enjoyed largely favourable coverage in the media, with many positive testimonials from students who had attended them. Indeed, alumni of the residential schools made up most of the emerging First Nations elite. Middle-class Indigenous people almost always credited residential schools with their success in life. But then Manitoba regional chief Phil Fontaine spoke, on a popular Canadian Broadcasting Corporation television show hosted by Barbara Frum, about how he had suffered sexual abuse at a residential school.[30] After that, things went south quickly. The Royal Commission on Aboriginal Peoples wrote critically about the schools,[31] two historians published influential books,[32] and lawyers launched multiple class actions on behalf of residential school "survivors," claiming damages for physical and sexual abuse, as well as loss of language and culture at the schools.[33]

Rather than contest these lawsuits in court, the Liberal government of Paul Martin negotiated a settlement in 2005, which was accepted shortly afterwards by the newly elected Conservative government of Stephen Harper.[34] Ultimately about $5 billion in compensation was paid to about

---

[29] Tom Flanagan, "Progressive Identity Politics: The New Gnosticism" | C2C Journal.

[30] Phil Fontaine's lifelong mission to get a papal apology delayed, but not over | Radio-Canada.ca, December 13, 2021.

[31] Royal Commission on Aboriginal Peoples (1991-1996) - Residential Schools - LibGuides at Coast Mountain College.

[32] Shingwauk's Vision: A History of Native Residential Schools : Miller, J.R.: Books - Amazon; A National Crime: The Canadian Government and the Residential School System: Milloy, John S.: 9780887556463: Books - Amazon.ca.

[33] Fiscal Explosion: Federal Spending on Indigenous Programs, 2015–2022 Federal Spending on Indigenous Programs, 2015–2022 (fraserinstitute.org).

[34] Indian Residential Schools Settlement Agreement (rcaanc-cirnac.gc.ca).

80,000 claimants,[35] and in 2008 Prime Minister Harper gave a public apology for the existence of residential schools.[36]

Mr. Harper might have thought that the compensation payments and his apology would be the end of the story,[37] but instead it became the beginning of a new chapter.[38] The Truth and Reconciliation Commission that he appointed took off in its own direction after the initial set of commissioners resigned and had to be replaced on fairly short notice.[39] The TRC held emotional public hearings around the country at which "survivors" were invited to tell their stories without fact-checking or cross-examination.[40] Most had already made claims for financial compensation in which the amount paid was proportional to the degree of sexual and physical abuse suffered, again without fact-checking or cross-examination. The TRC concluded in 2015 that the residential schools amounted to "cultural genocide."[41]

Cultural genocide is a metaphor, an emotive term for assimilation or integration of an ethnic minority into an encompassing society. The next step, it turned out, was to start speaking with increasing boldness of a literal, physical genocide involving real deaths. In 2019, Prime Minister Trudeau had already begun to adopt genocide terminology in the wake of the Final Report of the National Inquiry into Murdered and Missing

---

[35] Statistics on the Implementation of the Indian Residential Schools Settlement Agreement (rcaanc-cirnac.gc.ca).

[36] Statement of apology to former students of Indian Residential Schools (rcaanc-cirnac.gc.ca).

[37] The "genocide" that failed | C2C Journal.

[38] Tom Flanagan, "Ten Years of Aboriginal Policy," (series "How Good Was Harper?" *The Dorchester Review*, Vol. 7 No. 2, Autumn/Winter 2017, pp. 57-61.

[39] Bill Curry, "Two remaining Truth and Reconciliation commissioners resign," *The Globe and Mail*, January 31, 2009.

[40] Rodney A. Clifton and Mark DeWolf, eds., *From Truth Comes Reconciliation* (Winnipeg, MB: Frontier Centre for Public Policy, 2021), p. 173.

[41] "Canada guilty of cultural genocide against Indigenous peoples: TRC," APTN National News, June 2, 2015.

Indigenous Women and Girls, launched in 2016.[42] Now the new claims about missing children, unmarked burials, and even "mass graves" reinforced a literal genocide scenario. In summer 2022, Pope Francis made a visit to Canada, after which he also started using the G-word. "I didn't use the word genocide because it didn't come to mind but I described genocide," he said on his way back to Rome.[43] In the autumn of that year, the House of Commons gave apparent "unanimous consent" to a previously rejected motion "that what happened in residential schools was a genocide."[44] Such a resolution has no legal impact, and was brought forward in the disorderly atmosphere that follows the end of Question Period when many MPs are exiting or moving around the House,[45] but it has reinforced the genocide narrative in the eyes of the media and public opinion. If a tale is supported, or accepted, by all parties in the House of Commons, many voters will say: can it be false?

Unfortunately, yes. It is a strange genocide in which the target population has increased rather than decreased. It is estimated that in 1867, Canada's population included 100,000 to 125,000 Indians, about 10,000 Métis, and 2,000 Inuit.[46] Yet the 2021 census counted about 1.8 million Indigenous people,[47] an increase of 1,200 percent in just over 150 years. But the point of genocide claims is not historical accuracy; it is to enable use of a word with maximum emotive effect. The 20th century saw genuine physical genocides of Armenians, Jews, Ukrainians, and Rwandans, in which millions of people were slaughtered. Canada's House of Commons in February 2021 unanimously passed a motion, M-62, saying "China's treatment of the Uighur Muslim minority in the Xinjiang region constitutes

---

[42] Catharine Tunney, Trudeau says deaths and disappearances of Indigenous women and girls amount to 'genocide' | CBC News, June 4, 2019.

[43] Ka'nhehsí:io Deer, Pope says genocide took place at Canada's residential schools | CBC News, July 30, 2022.

[44] Richard Raycraft, MPs back motion calling on government to recognize residential schools program as genocide | CBC News, October 27, 2022.

[45] House of Commons *Debates*, 119, October 27, 2022, time-stamp between 15:10 and 15:15.

[46] Demography of Indigenous Peoples in Canada | The Canadian Encyclopedia.

[47] "Indigenous peoples" – 2021 Census promotional material (statcan.gc.ca).

genocide."[48] However affixing the label of genocide to Canadian Indian policy is a way of transferring the emotions of horror and righteous anger to the residential school situation. It is based on unconfirmed, uncorroborated reports, selective manipulation of historical evidence, and what is essentially a caricature of Indian residential schools.

With the G-word comes a family of D-words and political neologisms — denial, denialism, denialists — that are also being used to prop up the genocide narrative. The D-words had been appropriately invoked to describe the authors of books such as *Did Six Million Really Die?* and *The Hoax of the Twentieth Century,*[49] who argued that Jews were only incidental casualties of the Second World War, not the target of attempts to eliminate them as a race. But Holocaust Denialism, as it came to be called, had to devise a bizarre conspiracy theory, maintaining that the mountain of physical and documentary evidence proving the existence of the Holocaust had been invented by the governments of the United States, the United Kingdom, and the Soviet Union, acting in concert under the secret control of an international Jewish conspiracy first unveiled in *The Protocols of the Elders of Zion.*

The situation with Indian Residential Schools is entirely different. There is no physical or documentary evidence of mass murder, or indeed of any murder. Holocaust Deniers attempt to ignore or minimize obvious evidence of mass murder, whereas those who are accused of Residential School "denialism" are merely demanding to see evidence, any evidence, of murder associated with the schools. Those who question Canada's unsubstantiated genocide are asking, like the little boy in the Hans Christian Anderson fairy tale, "Where are the emperor's new clothes?"

The most common explanations for the absence of evidence are that excavating alleged potential burial sites would violate Indigenous spiritual sensibilities, and that both physical and documentary evidence have been covered up through the collusion of school, church, police, and government authorities. The court of public opinion should not judge on

---

[48] "Canada's parliament passes motion saying China's treatment of Uighurs is genocide," Reuters, February 22, 2021.

[49] *Did Six Million Really Die? The Truth at Last* (1974), cf. Did Six Million Really Die? - Wikipedia; and Arthur Butz, *The Hoax of the Twentieth Century* (Historical Review Press, 1976).

such convenient rationalizations but should demand actual evidence — and a lot of it — because genocide is the most serious allegation one can make.

Perhaps sensing the weakness of their evidence-free position, purveyors of the IRS-as-genocide narrative are beginning to double down, demanding that criticism of their assertions be made illegal. First was Winnipeg NDP MP Leah Gazan, who introduced the House of Commons resolution declaring IRS to be genocidal. According to a February 18, 2023, report by the CBC,

> NDP MP Leah Gazan, who got the House of Commons last October to unanimously recognize that genocide occurred at residential schools, now wants to take the issue a step further by drafting legislation to outlaw attempts to deny that genocide and make false assertions about residential schools. "Denying genocide is a form of hate speech," said Gazan, who represents the riding of Winnipeg Centre. "That kind of speech is violent and re-traumatizes those who attended residential school."[50]

Marc Miller, then Minister of Crown-Indigenous Relations, immediately supported Gazan's proposal: "Residential school denialism attempts to hide the horrors that took place in these institutions," his office said.[51] The endorsement was important, because Miller went to school with Justin Trudeau and is reportedly a close friend.[52]

Even more significant was a statement by David Lametti, then the Minister of Justice, that he was "open" to considering "legal mechanisms as a way to combat residential school denialism," as recommended by Kimberly

[50] NDP MP calls for hate speech law to combat residential school 'denialism' | CBC News.

[51] Ibid.

[52] Daniel Leblanc, "How Trudeau's high-school friend plans to win back a Liberal stronghold," *Globe and Mail*, April 5, 2014.

Murray, Independent Special Interlocutor on Unmarked Graves.[53] Any legislation of this type would be drafted by the Department of Justice, so the Minister's endorsement must be considered significant.

Both Miller and Lametti were shuffled out of their positions on July 26, 2023. That may mean that Prime Minister Trudeau is backing away from a proposal sure to be criticized as contrary to the right of free expression embedded in section 2 of the Canadian Charter of Rights and Freedoms. Or maybe not. We may learn more if and when mandate letters are posted for the new ministers of Justice and of Crown-Indigenous Relations.[54]

Canada, then, is already very far down the path not just of accepting, but of legally entrenching, a narrative for which no serious evidence has been proffered — that both Catholic and Protestant missionaries tortured and killed thousands of Indian children, then hid their bodies in secret burials, often pressing other Indian children into service to dig the graves; and that generations of religious authorities, police officials, civil servants, and elected politicians have prevented the truth from coming out. This book is an attempt to appeal for rationality and truth amid a moral panic of stories about Canada that are so implausible that they should not be believed without convincing evidence.

The contributors include retired judges, lawyers, professors, journalists, and others who have had careers in researching and evaluating evidence. It is no accident that most are retired, because that gives them some protection against attempts to silence them as "deniers." In the words of Janis Joplin, "Freedom's just another word for nothin' left to lose."

Several of the contributors, as well as others who have helped research and edit these publications, even if their names are not listed as authors, had for many years been writing for major metropolitan dailies, national magazines, academic journals, university presses, and commercial publishers. However, we quickly learned that the corporate, legacy or mainstream media, religious leaders, and political figures have little desire

---

[53] Canada should consider legal solution to fight residential school denialism: report (msn.com), Canadian Press, June 16, 2023.

[54] "Mandate Letters," Prime Minister of Canada (pm.gc.ca). At the time of writing (September 2023) the letters following the 2023 cabinet shuffle had not yet been posted.

to stand up to the narrative flow of a moral panic. We thus wrote about residential schools mainly in specialized journals such as *The Dorchester Review* in print and online; online media such as *C2C Journal*, *True North*, and *Western Standard*; and online journals such as *Quillette*, *Unherd*, and *History Reclaimed*, whose raison d'être is to challenge conventional wisdom. We owe a debt of gratitude to all the editors who risked publishing our controversial material.

Publication in online journals has allowed us to raise basic questions before a world audience about the now-dominant Canadian narrative of unmarked graves, missing children, and genocidal missionaries. Publication in book format will make it easier for readers to appreciate that these questions are not just isolated queries or knee-jerk dismissals — but constitute a powerful, research- and fact-based indictment of the moral panic over residential schools. We also hope that the book will enjoy a degree of permanence, remaining in library collections for future readers to discover. That used to mean walking through stacks of books, now it is more likely to mean digital browsing in an online library catalogue, but the discovery process is similar.

There is a certain amount of repetition in these chapters because they were written at different times for different audiences, but we wanted to bring the book out before the Government of Canada can make good on its eerie speculation about criminalizing divergence of opinion about historical issues. There is also some disagreement among the authors about details, which is to be expected in discussion of such an explosive topic, where new information and opinions are constantly coming to the fore. Also, some of these seeming disagreements stem from editors with deadlines, who wanted authors to pull a few punches. But all authors in this collection agree on the main point: that *no persuasive evidence has yet been offered by anyone* for the existence of unmarked graves, missing children, murder, or genocide in residential schools.

The reader will see that the contributions in this book focus on three main topics: the weakness of factual claims about unmarked graves and missing children, the irresponsible treatment of these subjects in the legacy media, and the wild exaggeration of judgments about the residential schools. We do not deny the faults of the residential schools — though these faults, too, have been exaggerated with unreliable evidence. But we do want criticism to be factually based and offered with an awareness of what was possible and practical at the time — in other words, sound history, not anachronistic denunciation. And we want Canadians to examine and consider the mountain of publicly available factual evidence that requires significant effort to assimilate, but which was omitted by the TRC and ignored by the media.

Chapter One

In Kamloops, Not One Body Has Been Found

Jacques Rouillard

After more than two years of recrimination and denunciation, where are the remains of the children buried at the Kamloops Indian Residential School?

In 2022, the World Press Photo Organization bestowed its top award to a Canadian photograph featured in the *New York Times*.[55] The image depicted young girls' orange and ochre dresses suspended on crosses, symbolic representation of the mistreatment endured by Indigenous mothers and the suffering endured by students of the Kamloops residential school. This photograph gained prominence during the summer of 2021, thanks to a controversy stemming from the radar scanning of a portion of the site, located in the interior of British Columbia, where the school operated from 1890 to 1978.

The "confirmation of the remains of 215 children who were students at the Kamloops Residential School" was first reported on May 27, 2021 by *Tk'emlúps te secwépemc* First Nation Chief Rosanne Casimir.[56] The discovery followed surveys led by an anthropologist who found depressions and abnormalities in the soil of an apple orchard near the school while using ground-penetrating radar (GPR). According to Chief Casimir, these "missing children" represent "undocumented deaths" and their presence has long been "knowledge" in the community. Some children, she said, "were as young as three years old." The findings are

---

[55] Ian Austen, "'Horrible History': Mass Grave of Indigenous Children Reported in Canada," *New York Times*, May 28, 2021; World Press Photo 2022 Contest Winners, online.

[56] This chapter is an updated and substantially expanded article published online in January 2022 and in print in *The Dorchester Review*, 12: 1, Spring/Summer 2022, pp. 27-36. I thank Shannon Lee Mannion for her remarks and helping with the translation, and C.P. Champion and Tom Flanagan their careful editing. On the Kamloops "discovery" itself, see the excellent and informative research work of Nina Green: *Kamloops. Indian Residential School* on her website, and Nina Green, "The Kamloops 'Discovery': A Fact-Check Two Years Later," *The Dorchester Review* online, June 23, 2023.

only "preliminary" and a comprehensive report would be provided by the anthropologist the following month.[57]

Ground-penetrating radar technology does not directly identify human remains. Instead, it emits high-frequency pulses that reveal soil disruptions, indicating variations between surrounding earth and a specific location. While these disruptions could point to burial sites, they could also signify various other structures like rocks, tree stumps, or even variations in ground composition.[58]

At a July 15, 2021 press conference, further details emerged. The name of the anthropologist involved became known: Sarah Beaulieu, a young instructor in Anthropology and Sociology at the University of the Fraser Valley since 2018. She narrowed down the potential discovery from 215 to 200, probably due to past excavations in the same apple orchard by an archeologist in the late 1990s and early 2000s, of which she had been unaware. These earlier searches were related to investigating patterns of long-term land use by Indigenous peoples and had nothing to do with finding potential bodies.

Beaulieu did not repeat the Band Council's claim that children's remains were found. She was more cautious, merely stating that she had found "probable burials" and "targets of interest." Having "barely scratched the surface" covering just under two acres, she found many disturbances in the ground, but ruled out anomalies such as root systems, metal, and stones. The "disruptions picked up by the radar," she said, led her to conclude that the sites "have multiple signatures that present like burials."

She also referred to the previous discovery of a child's tooth — which was eventually revealed to be not of human origin — and to a juvenile rib found by a tourist in the early 2000s whose human origin was never tested

---

[57] Tk'emlúps te secwépemc (Kamloops Indian Band), "Remains of Children of Kamloops Residential School Discovered," May 27, 2021; Courtney Dickson, Bridgette Watson, "Remains of 215 children found buried at former B.C. residential school, First Nation says," CBC News, May 27, 2021, Updated: May 29, 2021.

[58] Diane Peters, "How Radar Is Helping Track Down Lost Indigenous Grave Sites," May 28, 2022; Kisha Supernant, *Archaeological Remote Sensing: Unmarked graves*, transcript, Canadian Archeological Association/Association Canadienne d'archéologie, Institute of Prairie and Indigenous Archeology, University of Alberta.

and whose whereabouts have since become unknown. The stories of "knowledge keepers" (elderly Aboriginal people) recall, she said, that "children as young as six years old were woken [sic] in the night to dig holes for burials in the apple orchard."[59]

However, Beaulieu couldn't definitively confirm the "probable burials" without "forensic investigation involving excavation." The press release of the Indian Band reiterated the same view: "definitive results come from forensic investigation with excavation."[60] Finally, due to the comprehensive nature of Beaulieu's extensive presentation, a community spokesman said that the full report "cannot" be released to the media. For Chief Casimir, it remained uncertain whether excavation would occur.

In the press release, the Band Council announced its intention to engage with the B.C. Coroner about the findings. The Coroner's Office was indeed contacted to ascertain whether technology is available to answer questions related to remains' age, cause of death, and how the process of finding such answers would be done. The Office issued a statement that it will continue to work with the First Nation.[61] In fact no further requests were made by the Council to the Coroner's Office.

The "discovery" should also, in the normal course of events, have prompted the Council to request the assistance of the Royal Canadian Mounted Police (RCMP) to launch an immediate investigation. But again, this was not the path that was followed.

---

[59] Jana G. Pruden and Mike Hager, "Anthropologist explains how she concluded 200 children were buried at the Kamloops Residential School," *Globe and Mail*, Jul. 15, 2021, Updated: Jul. 16, 2021; Michael Potestio, "Number of probable graves near former residential school pegged at 200," *Kamloops.This Week*, Jul 16, 2021; Frances Widdowson, "Billy Remembers," *The American Conservative*, February 15, 2022. The July 15 press conference can be viewed on YouTube: *B.C. First Nation releases report on unmarked graves discovered in Kamloops*, July 15, 2021. The part where Sarah Beaulieu gives her presentation can also be found at: *CTV News*, Vancouver.

[60] Tk'emlúps te secwépemc, Press Release, "Kamloops Indian Residential School missing children's findings but a fraction of investigation and work need [sic] to bring peace to families and communities," July 15, 2021.

[61] "BC Coroners Service issues statement on the burial site found at former residential school," *Kamloops This Week*, May 28, 2021.

Panic Without Evidence

The alleged Kamloops discovery in 2021 triggered a swift reaction across Canada and internationally. Only three days after the *preliminary* assessment of May 27 and before any report became public, Prime Minister Justin Trudeau accepted Chief Casimir's account of murders and hidden burials and — just like that — referred on Twitter to "a dark and shameful chapter" in Canadian history.[62]

Former British Columbia Premier John Horgan, likewise, said he was "horrified and heartbroken" to learn of a burial site with 215 children — he, too, had no confirmation that this was true — which highlighted the violence and damage done by the residential school system.[63] Several Aboriginal communities and media outlets then followed up with references to unmarked graves around other residential schools.

In June, prompted by the "revelations," hundreds of people rallied and marched in cities across Canada to "honour the lives of the 215 Indigenous children" whose remains had been "discovered." Spontaneously, clusters of children's shoes and orange shirts and other paraphernalia were placed on church steps in many cities or on the steps of legislatures in memory of the alleged victims.

The reaction became so intense that, in many locations, it reached a level of anger rarely seen in Canada: no less than 83 churches were burned down, vandalized, or desecrated.[64] Many were burned and completely destroyed. Prime Minister Trudeau was rather tolerant about these abuses: "It is unacceptable and wrong that acts of vandalism and arson are being seen across the country, including against Catholic churches," but he added

---

[62] Justin Trudeau, *Twitter*, May 28, 2021.

[63] Canadian Press, "B.C. premier 'horrified' at discovery of remains at Kamloops residential school site," May 28, 2021.

[64] Cosmin Dzsurdzsa, "A map of the 83 churches that have been vandalized or burned since the residential school announcement," *True North*, January 16, 2023.

that these events are "real and fully understandable, given the shameful history that we are all becoming more and more aware of."[65]

Again, Trudeau made these statements without any factual confirmation and without waiting for Dr. Beaulieu's actual report, which to this day has never been released.

Statues of prominent figures in Canadian history were spray-painted and pulled down in retaliation for what protestors had convinced themselves was the fate of many children. At a rally in Toronto, the statue of Egerton Ryerson, who "left an indelible mark on Canada's education system" in the mid-19th century, was vandalized and splattered with red paint because he was referred to as an "architect" of the residential school system.[66] The statue of Queen Victoria in Winnipeg was defaced and pulled down. Montreal's statue of Sir John A. Macdonald, Canada's first prime minister, was also knocked down by "anti-racists" in August 2020. His detached bronze head symbolically rolled on the ground.[67] Some observers hailed all of this as the beginning of a new chapter in Canadian history that will start the process of decolonization — almost giving the appearance that the announcement had been seized upon and exploited by a wider, organized political movement.

Important symbolic decisions by the Canadian government immediately followed. On May 30, flags were lowered on all federal buildings "in memory of the Indigenous children who were sent to residential schools, for those who never returned home, and in honour of the families whose lives were forever changed."[68] This action is significant in two ways: the government admitted that children were buried near the residential schools,

---

[65] CTV News, YouTube, "'Unacceptable and wrong': PM Trudeau condemns church vandalism."

[66] "Ryerson statue honouring architect of Canada's residential school system vandalized again," *CP24*, June 1, 2021.

[67] A first report from an *ad hoc* committee set up by the City of Montreal advocated in November 2022 that the statue should not be reinstated because of his "assimilative and genocidal policies he implemented against Aboriginal peoples and the discriminatory acts he perpetrated against several groups of people," Jeanne Corriveau, "Pas de retour en vue pour la statue de John A. Macdonald," *Le Devoir*, 22 novembre 2022).

[68] Government of Canada, Joint Statement by Canadian Heritage and Crown-Indigenous Relations and Northern Affairs Canada as the National Flag of Canada Returns to Full-Mast at Sunset on Sunday, November 7, 2021.

and it abdicated the decision to raise the flags to the Assembly of First Nations.[69]

The Canadian flag is among the "paramount symbols" of the Canadian nation, and yet the government permitted an interest group to determine its position on the national mast. The government did not stipulate when the flags could be raised, so they remained at half-mast for the longest period of time in Canada's history, more than five months. It was finally decided they would be raised on November 9 so that they could be lowered again (as is traditional) on Remembrance Day, November 11, and then subsequently raised.[70]

Just a week following the emergence of the Kamloops story, Ottawa on September 21 swiftly introduced a new federal holiday to be known as the National Day for Truth and Reconciliation, to honour the memory of the "missing" children and "survivors" of residential schools. The new statutory holiday, which will take place on September 30 each year, was designated for federal government employees and federally-regulated workplaces across Canada.

In a statement issued on September 30, 2021, Prime Minister Trudeau purported to acknowledge that

> at least 150,000 Indigenous children from across the country were forcibly separated from their families and their communities. Children were brought to residential schools where many were abused in addition to being removed from their culture, languages, and traditions. It is also a day to remember the many children who never returned home, as well as an opportunity for everyone to learn more, and to affirm the need for reconciliation and thereby committing ourselves to the work ahead.[71]

---

[69] Government of Canada, *Rules for half-masting the National Flag of Canada*; Olivia Stefanovich, "Flags will remain at half-mast until agreement is reached with Indigenous leaders: Trudeau," *CBC News*, September 10, 2021.

[70] Government of Canada, *Rules for half-masting*.

[71] Prime Minister of Canada, Justin Trudeau, *Statement by the Prime Minister on the National Day for Truth and Reconciliation*, September 30, 2021, Ottawa.

In June 2021, Trudeau professed himself "deeply disappointed" in the Catholic Church and the Supreme Pontiff for not acknowledging their "responsibility" and "culpability" in the Government of Canada's residential school system.[72] He endorsed the term "survivors" for former students, a term that drew parallels to the language used to describe victims of Nazi concentration camps, indicating the perceived gravity of their experiences.

Compensation for "Day Scholars"

Subsequently, in response to the preliminary report of the alleged discovery of 215 remains, the federal government reversed its stance and opted to provide compensation to Aboriginal individuals who attended Indian Residential Schools (IRS) by day from 1951 to 1992. These were students that did not board (stay overnight) at a school and who in fact returned home daily after class. The students who stayed overnight at the schools had been financially compensated through a settlement agreement in 2006.

The compensation for day-school scholars was not for abuse at school, but because, allegedly, they suffered the same eradication of Aboriginal language and culture as had residential school students. Again these consequences of their education were simply assumed and declared, rather than proven. For example, one of the plaintiffs, Diena Jules, who attended as a Day Scholar at Kamloops IRS for five years, going home at the end of every school day, claims that she "became disconnected with my family and community" as a result. "I lost language, my cultural pride and my own identity."[73] Stories like hers were simply accepted unquestioningly as truthful representations of educational experience.

---

[72] Arvin Joaquin, "Trudeau calls on Catholic Church to take responsibility for residential schools," *The Canadian Press, CTV News*, June 4, 2021.

[73] Theresa Wright, "Settlement reached on residential school 'day scholars' class-action lawsuit," *The Canadian Press, CTV News*, June 9, 2021.

In previous years, the federal government denied, for example, any legal responsibility in 2019 court filings. The loss of language and culture, the lawyers then argued, was an "unavoidable implication of children being educated in English or taught the Christian doctrine." They admitted that the schools were meant to "assimilate" Indigenous people, but denied the federal government of that era "sought to destroy the ability [...] to speak their Indigenous language or to lose the customs or traditions of their culture." Those languages and cultures were also eroded by "historical, personal and society circumstances" and by interactions between "Indigenous communities and the dominant culture," along with urbanization.[74]

However, several days after the alleged discovery of the remains of 215 children, the federal government reversed its stance and accepted responsibility for the loss of Aboriginal language and culture. To teach Indigenous children the public-school curriculum taught to other Canadians, it transpires, was wrong. Teaching Indigenous children how to speak, read, and write in English or French, and how to use numbers, conflicted with Aboriginal values. Ottawa's reversal implies, as stipulated by Aboriginal leaders, that it would have been better to keep young natives illiterate.

But it should be pointed out that Aboriginal languages before European contact had no formal writing system and that there were numerous Indigenous languages across Canada. It was Christian missionaries who developed written syllabic language and dictionaries that helped to preserve Aboriginal languages.

The June 9, 2021 settlement included individual compensation of $10,000 for the first year attended, but not the $3000 extra for each subsequent year received by students who stayed overnight. An extra $50 million was added for the Day Scholars Revitalization Fund to support healing, wellness, education, language, culture, heritage, and commemorations for

---

[74] John Barrera, "Ottawa says it's not liable for cultural damage caused by Kamloops residential school: court documents," *CBC News*, June 2, 2021.

survivors and descendants.[75] This settlement also proved lucrative for law firms, resulting in $9.6 million in legal fees for past work and settlement implementation. A new item was introduced that had not appeared in the 2016 IRS agreement: a settlement package containing compensation for *heirs* of day scholars who died after May 30, 2005 without having received their compensation.

The claims process, initiated in January 2022 and closing in October 2023, encompassed day scholars from 71 industrial schools. Claimants were not required to provide supporting documentation for attendance but instead filled out survivor claim forms which were deemed sufficient. Additionally, a list of 24 schools was established for day students, necessitating sworn declarations confirming their status and nighttime residence.[76] By December 2022, the fund had received 11,453 claims and paid out to 3,735 claimants.[77] The overall cost to the government remains uncertain due to ongoing claims, but estimates suggest the program may ultimately reach an expenditure of approximately $200 million.

The RCMP Bows Out

In Kamloops, the local Royal Canadian Mounted Police (RCMP) detachment launched an investigation in early June 2021 following the news of the discovery of children's remains.[78] Given the gravity of the allegations, police involvement was to be expected. Police visited the site and consulted the Kamloops First Nation. They also met with

---

[75] Renée Lilley, "Federal Court approves residential school day scholars' settlement," *CBC News*, Oct 01, 2021; Renée Lilley, "Residential school day scholars can now apply for compensation under the settlement," *CBC News*, January 5, 2022.

[76] *Gottfriedson Indian Residential School Day Scholars settlement claims process now open*, Canada, Crown-Indigenous Relations and Northern Affairs Canada, January 4, 2022.

[77] Deloitte, *Class Action Matters, Indian Residential Schools Day Scholars Class Action, Claims Administration*.

[78] Kristy Kirdup and Mike Hager, "RCMP investigating former residential school site in Kamloops, B.C.," *CBC News*, June 3, 2021, Updated June 4, 2021. Cf. Brian Giesbrecht, "The RCMP Failed Canadians at Kamloops," *The Epoch Times*, July 12, 2023.

anthropologist Sarah Beaulieu, who was "quite scared" by the approach taken by the RCMP, according to Murray Sinclair, the former senator and chairman of the Truth and Reconciliation Commission. Before a House of Commons committee, he criticized what he called the "typical heavy-handed" way in which the Mounties were "simply intimidating people rather than helping them." He suggested that the RCMP should focus on obtaining relevant documents from the schools that could shed light on the deaths, rather than "pursuing those who are revealing the information."[79]

Following Sinclair's criticism, the RCMP investigation was halted at the government's request, possibly due to connections in the Prime Minister's Office. The RCMP's officer in charge stated that they would take guidance from First Nation community leaders to determine the next steps, "while at the same time being supportive, respectful, and culturally sensitive to the Indigenous communities that are impacted." Chief Casimir was more decisive: she claimed that the RCMP had thereby acknowledged that her Nation "will be leading the investigation."[80] That, of course, meant that the Kamloops Indian Band would conduct its own criminal investigation into a significant criminal allegation — an unprecedented move in Canadian criminal history. Since then, there has been no excavation, and no proper investigation by the RCMP.

This trend of Indigenous communities conducting their own amateur criminal investigations in cases involving alleged graves of murder victims near residential schools has persisted.

Indeed, during a search undertaken at the Kuper Island Residential School in British Columbia in December 2021, a *Globe and Mail* reporter asked if the RCMP would conduct a criminal investigation if unmarked graves were found in other locations. The spokeswoman, Robin Percival, RCMP's Executive Assistant to the Executive Director of Public Affairs, responded in the same way as the police did in Kamloops: "Any support undertaken

---

[79] Kirdup and Hager, "RCMP investigating," *Globe and Mail*, June 3, Updated June 4, 2021. "RCMP investigating former residential school site in Kamloops, B.C.," *CBC News*, June 3, 2021, Updated June 4, 2021.

[80] Alyse Kotyk and Andrew Weichel, "RCMP investigating B.C. residential school site after discovery of children's remains," CTVNews, June 3, 2021; Glenda Luymes, "Kamloops residential school will not be torn down: chief," *Vancouver Sun*, June 4, 2021.

by the RCMP would be Indigenous-led, community-based, survivor-centric, and culturally sensitive."[81]

This acquiescence in amateur crime detection is apparently now the policy of the RCMP, in the name of being "respectful."[82]

However, this approach raises concerns about the RCMP's abdication of its duty as a national police force. Allowing non-police entities to investigate serious allegations of crime — in potentially a hundred locations across the country — creates a de facto parallel system of policing. The abdication is even more pronounced given that these are cases in which a party or parties stand to gain financially and politically from announced findings. It is puzzling that the media have not scrutinized this apparent relinquishment of responsibility by the RCMP and its implications for public trust in policing. Will political parties or even biker organizations be the next non-police entities permitted to investigate for themselves?

False Reports

In the aftermath of unverified claims about Kamloops, several media outlets repeated and amplified the story by alleging that the bodies of 215 children had been *found*, that "thousands" of children had "gone missing" from residential schools, and that parents had not been informed. The undisturbed sites were even portrayed as "mass graves" where bodies were dumped in a jumble.

This supposed "news" spread widely, tarnishing Canada's self-image and its international reputation. Even the *New York Times*, traditionally a reliable news source, deviated from its historic standards. Just one day after the initial "discovery," an article entitled "Horrible History: Mass Grave of Indigenous Children Reported in Canada" painted a grim picture. It claimed that "for decades, most Indigenous children in Canada were taken from their families and forced into boarding schools. A large number

---

[81] Patrick White, "What a long-forgotten B.C. RCMP task force uncovered about residential school abuses," *Globe and Mail*, December 13, 2021.

[82] Kotyk and Weichel, "RCMP investigating B.C. residential school site," CTVNews, June 3, 2021

never returned home, their families given only vague explanations, or none at all." The Indigenous community "has found evidence of what happened to some of its missing children: a mass grave containing the remains of 215 children on the grounds of a former residential school." [83]

These baseless reports prompted the Office of the United Nations High Commissioner for Human Rights to allege "a large-scale human rights violation." The UN urged Canadian authorities and the Catholic Church to conduct "thorough investigations into the discovery of a mass grave containing the remains of over 200 children." Again, all of this was said before even a single verified body had been exhumed.[84] Likewise, without providing evidence, Amnesty International demanded that the persons and institutions responsible for the "remains" "found" in Kamloops be prosecuted.[85]

Ironically, of all countries, China, known for its extensive human rights violations, used the United Nations Human Rights Council in June to call for an investigation into wrongs done to Indigenous people in Canada. This demand occurred just before Canadian officials readied themselves to address a statement to allow the UN human rights chief access into Xinjiang to investigate the unlawful detention of over one million Uyghur people, a large Muslim minority that suffers under Chinese rule. Trudeau responded by contrasting Canada's federally appointed Truth and Reconciliation Commission with China's refusal to acknowledge its own problems.[86]

Apologies continued to come from the alleged perpetrators of the "crime" of unmarked graves: governments, religious communities, and the Canadian Conference of Catholic Bishops. Pope Francis expressed his

---

[83] Ian Austen, "'Horrible History': Mass Grave of Indigenous Children Reported in Canada," *New York Times*, May 28, 2021, updated October 5, 2021.

[84] United Nations Human Right, Office of the High Commissioner, "UN experts call on Canada, Holy See to investigate mass grave at Indigenous school," Geneva, June 4, 2021.

[85] Amnesty International, "Letter to Prime Minister Justin Trudeau," June 14, 2021.

[86] Adam Taylor, "China calls for Canada human rights inquiry, pre-empting demand for investigation into abuse of Uyghurs," *Washington Post*, June 22, 2021; David Ljunggren, Stephanie Nebehay, "Canada's Trudeau angrily questions China seeking probe of Indigenous children's remains," *Reuters*, June 22, 2021.

distress in June, citing "the shocking discovery in Canada of the remains of 215 children" at Kamloops.[87] In a remarkable gesture, he pledged to visit Canada, an undertaking that was realized in July 2022. Meanwhile, Aboriginal leaders are seeking a formal apology from the Pontiff, and figures like Rosanne Casimir have called for the church to offer greater compensation to "survivors."[88]

International Involvement

On June 4, 2021, the Southern Chiefs Organization, a group that purports to speak for 34 First Nations in Manitoba, called for international intervention, asserting that,

> the unsurprising discovery of 215 precious children buried in a mass grave at the Kamloops residential school site is absolute and further proof of the genocide and crimes against humanity that Canada committed, kept silent on, and tried to cover up for generations [...] the churches are parties to the genocide as they worked to fulfill the government of Canada's policies, intended to "Kill the Indian in the Child."[89]

By coincidence, at the same time, 15 lawyers from across Canada submitted a substantial document of 14 pages highlighting the alleged "mass grave" to the International Criminal Court (ICC) in The Hague. This extraordinary move was an attempt to prompt an investigation into the Government of Canada and the Holy See for their potential roles in "crimes against humanity." These lawyers, acting "in the name of the Aboriginal people of Canada, and all people of Canada," sought assurance

---

[87] Linda Bordoni, "Pope expresses shock for Canadian Residential School discovery and prays for healing," *Vatican News*, June 6, 2021.

[88] Brooklyn Neustaeter, "Indigenous leaders call for apology, compensation from Pope amid possible Canadian visit," CTV News, October 27, 2021.

[89] Southern Chiefs' Organization Inc., "Southern Chiefs' Organization Statement on Former TRC Chair Murray Sinclair's Calls to Conduct an Investigation into Residential School Burial Sites," *SCO News*, June 4, 2021.

that those responsible for these alleged crimes would face prosecution.[90] However, the world court in November 2021 refused to open a preliminary investigation, stating that the primary responsibility for prosecuting such crimes rests with the Canadian government, which has declined to do so. Furthermore, since the alleged deaths occurred before Canada ratified the crimes against humanity law on July 1, 2002, the ICC deemed itself without jurisdiction over alleged crimes committed before that date. [91]

Four months later, the Assembly of First Nations passed a resolution stating that the Kamloops "mass grave" was a manifestation of a broader "pattern of genocide." They demanded that Canada and the churches be held accountable for "potential breaches of humanitarian and human rights law." To shed light, they called for a Special Rapporteur on the Rights of Indigenous Peoples of the United Nations Human Rights Council (UNHRC) to be sent to Canada to investigate the "overall human-rights situation" of Indigenous people in light of the discoveries of unmarked graves near former residential schools.[92]

In the following months, RoseAnne Archibald, the Assembly of First Nations National Chief, asked the UNHRC to launch an investigation into Canada's possible human rights violations in respect of residential schools. Her plea, she claimed, stemmed from a lack of confidence in Canadian investigators, given the alleged involvement of the RCMP in the "forced" separation of Indigenous children from their families for attendance at residential schools. In response, Canadian Justice Minister David Lametti — once again based on activists' assertions, not evidence — affirmed his full cooperation with any UNHRC investigation.[93]

---

[90] Karim Khan, K.C. Chief Prosecutor to Khan, International Criminal Court, The Hague, The Netherlands, June 3, 2021; News staff, "Lawyer wants criminal investigation into Kamloops residential school," Edmonton, CityNews, June 3, 2021.

[91] Michael Melanson and Nina Green, Canada's "'Genocide' — Case Closed?" *The Dorchester Review*, October 27, 2022; Jeremy Appel, "ICC Turns Down Lawyers' Request to Investigate Residential Schools," *Toronto Star*, November 19, 2021.

[92] Assembly of First Nations, *2021 Annual General Assembly Resolutions Update Report for the December 2021 Special Chiefs Assembly*, December 2021, pp. 1-3.

[93] Olivia Stefanovich, "AFN national chief asks UN to investigate Canada's role in residential schools," CBC News, April 25, 2022.

In April 2022, Chief Archibald made a three-day trip to the United Nations Permanent Forum on Indigenous Issues in New York. Her mission was to appeal directly to Francisco Calí Tzay, the special rapporteur on the rights of Indigenous Peoples, to visit Canada and investigate the deaths of these innocent children. "We're seeking remedies for human rights violations," she said, "including genocide." Calí Tzay, however, stated that a formal invitation, preferably from Prime Minister Justin Trudeau, was essential for his intervention, as he lacked the authority for investigation "in terms of documentation or study." [94] He added that "Special rapporteurs do not have a mandate to launch a full-fledged investigation akin to a prosecutor, nor do they have the authority to conduct criminal prosecutions" on crimes related to the unmarked graves. [95]

The Canadian government invited Mr. Calí Tzay to come to Canada in March 2023 for a ten-day visit to five provinces. During his visit, he met with Indigenous leaders, federal ministers, senators, and human rights advocates, among others. [96] As his visit concluded, Calí Tzay delivered a preliminary report describing the cultural, economic, and social problems faced by Aboriginal communities and reiterated their concerns and their claims. He pointed out the alleged discovery of 215 unmarked graves and the negative legacies of residential schools to which many children were sent but from which they are said never to have returned. He said the impact of these schools lingers to this day, perpetuating human rights violations and causing an over-representation of Indigenous peoples in the child welfare and criminal justice systems.

Calí Tzay's report insisted that the Government fully embrace the recommendations of the Truth and Reconciliation Commission. "True reconciliation can only be achieved by respecting existing treaties and

---

[94] Shari Narine, "AFN wants meeting with Trudeau to formalize invitation for UN special rapporteur," May 5, 2022, Windspeaker.com.

[95] Patrick White, "UN special rapporteur planning trip to Canada to examine 'human-rights situation' of Indigenous people," *The Globe and Mail*, May 26, 2022.

[96] Brett Forester, "Guatemalan expert's Canada visit ends, report expected in September," CBC News, Mar 10, 2023.

providing restitution and compensation for the loss of lands, territories and resources," he said.[97]

Soil Disturbances

By failing to point out that the Kamloops "discoveries" are only speculative, and that no remains have yet been found, governments and media have given great credence to what is in reality a thesis: the *thesis* of the "disappearance" of children from residential schools.

What once began as allegations of "cultural genocide" endorsed by the Truth and Reconciliation Commission (TRC), has now evolved into the realm of "physical genocide," a conclusion that the TRC explicitly rejected in its own report.[98] This shift in narrative relies solely on indications of soil abnormalities that could easily be attributed to factors such as root movements or other causes.

Anthropologist Scott Hamilton, who worked on residential school cemeteries for the TRC between 2013 and 2015, underscores the need for caution when interpreting ground-penetrating radar findings. His subject is not newly alleged burial sites, but long-known and neglected cemetery sites. Hamilton emphasizes that over time soil may have changed owing to sedimentary texture, cultural impacts, obstructions, or other variables. He concludes that the effectiveness of ground-penetrating radar relies on supplementary measures such as "post-survey inspection of the ground surface, supplemental investigation with a metal detector or soil probe, or test excavation." [99]

---

[97] José Francisco Calí-Tzay, United Nations Special Rapporteur on the Rights of Indigenous Peoples. *Visit to Canada. United Nations Special Rights Procedure, End of Mission Statement*, March 1-10, 2023.

[98] The Truth and Reconciliation Commission of Canada, *Honouring the Truth, Reconciling for the Future. Summary of the Final Report of the Truth and Reconciliation Commission of Canada*, 2015, p. 1.

[99] Dr. Scott Hamilton, "Where are the Children buried?" Dept. of Anthropology, Lakehead University, c. 2015, National Centre for Truth and Reconciliation Reports, pp. 36, 38.

Adding complexity to the Kamloops imbroglio is the fact that the school's apple orchard is situated on soil that has been perturbed by decades of agricultural and horticultural activity. The field has been extensively plowed to provide the school with grain and vegetables, leading to a multitude of inconsistencies in soil layers that hinder precise grave identification. Also, trenches were dug and one crossed the orchard at a depth of 3.6 feet to accommodate a sewage disposal system established in 1924 and subsequently upgraded in 1937-1938.[100] Even though these disused trenches remain under the surface, their presence apparently escaped the notice of Dr. Sarah Beaulieu.[101] Furthermore, archaeologists from Simon Fraser University conducted inspections and monitored construction activities between 1983 and 2004, covering roughly 30% of the orchard. Their extensive efforts yielded no traces of graves or human remains.[102]

It's pertinent to mention that the Kamloops revelations are not isolated instances in which ground radar has been utilized to infer the potential presence of children's remains. A similar initiative began at Manitoba's Brandon Residential School in 2012, which operated from 1895 to 1972. This endeavor resumed in 2019, combining archival research with survivor interviews. The unearthing of "215 children" in Kamloops during June 2021 rekindled the Brandon effort. The team drew on the insights of elders, refining their search to encompass 104 graves spanning three cemeteries — locations where of course the dead are supposed to be buried. Nonetheless, the supervising anthropologist admits that ground-penetrating radar "can

---

[100] W. C. Warren, *Report on suggested repairs and improvements to the sewage disposal system*, Kamloops Residential School, Kamloops Agency, Library and Archives Canada, Department of Indian Affairs, Headquarters central registry system: engineering and construction file series – 15090, RG 10, lac_reel_c15090, 161919, C-15090, 1577508; E.H. Tredecroft, Report Re: *Construction of sewage disposal plant at the Kamloops industrial school*, Jan. 20, 1926, Library and Archives Canada, Department of Indian Affairs, RG 10, vol. 6450, File 882-9, part 2.

[101] Nina Green provides a thorough analysis of the impact of the sewage system under the title, *Kamloops. Indian Residential School*.

[102] Kam Res, architect (a pseudonym), "Graves in the Apple Orchard: Contextualizing and questioning the claims."

detect anomalies in the soil, but it cannot confirm a grave's existence unless the soil is peeled away."[103]

"Missing" Children

In its 2015 Report, the Truth and Reconciliation Commission identified a total of 3,200 child deaths across all residential schools from 1867 to 2000. It was able to determine the location of death of 1,241 children whose names are on record: 443 died in a hospital or sanatorium, 423 in school infirmaries, 300 at their home, 75 in a non-residential school.[104] But, surprisingly, the TRC was unable to provide names for one-third of the children (32%), and for *half* of them (49%), the cause of death remained unknown.[105] Why is a significant number of residential school students labelled "nameless" (1,161)?

In reality, residential school principals each trimester reported the names of students attending, in order to secure government funding, and they were required to detail the names of deceased students. All were counted in the *Report* as named residential school students. But the Commission decided that it would also include *unnamed* students in the total count of student deaths, a matter that borders on speculation. These 569 unnamed students primarily died in school infirmaries (409) or at their home (118) during the year they left the school.[106] What is the source of information for these unnamed students?

According to the Report of the Commission (vol. 4), there are "significant limitations" in the data they have used to compile residential school deaths. These limitations have led the Commission to include in their death

---

[103] Ian Froese, "Team investigating Brandon's former residential school for grave turns to elderly people for clues," *CBC News*, June 20, 2021.

[104] Final Report of the Truth and Reconciliation Commission of Canada, vol. 4, *Canada's Residential Schools: Missing Children and Unmarked Burials* (Montreal & Kingston: McGill-Queen's University Press, 2015), p. 21.

[105] Ibid., p. 1.

[106] Ibid., p. 21.

toll, without identification, students whose death the principals h[...]
reported in previous years. Thus the cumulative count may be inf[...]
students for whom they have not included names, dates, or cause[...]
death.[107] Indeed the Commission has acknowledged that some of the deaths
recorded in the Named Register might also be included in the Unnamed
Register.[108] Therefore, it is possible that certain deceased students are
counted twice: once in the trimester report by the principals with names,
and *again* in the general compilation without names.

The report ultimately conveyed that its data are incomplete and further
investigation is necessary to adhere to the criteria for including deceased
students in the sub-registers, whether named or unnamed. The National
Centre for Truth and Reconciliation (NCTR) was tasked with this
assignment and is supposed to create a National Residential School
Student Death Register using various information sources.[109]

The lack of information and the use of a biassed methodology greatly
inflates the count of missing students and creates confusion surrounding
their deaths. Their approach lends credence to the assumption that many
unnamed students vanished without their parents' being informed, and that
some schools might have buried them in mass graves. The supposed
existence of these unknown students has prompted a series of ground
penetrating radar searches near other residential schools, announced to the
media at regular intervals, presumably to keep speculative allegations in
the news, as if real children's bodies were actually involved.

It is likely that the TRC's methodological gap stems from figures from the
years preceding 1950. That is because the Commission's recorded death
rate in residential schools from 1921 to 1950 (named and unnamed deaths)
is twice as high as that of Canadian youth in the general population aged
five to fourteen for the same years over the same period. On average, this
mortality rate equated to about four deaths per year for every 1,000 youths

---

[107] Ibid., pp. 7-8.

[108] Ibid., p. 7.

[109] Ibid., p. 8.

attending the schools. Their deaths were mainly attributed to tuberculosis and influenza, when the Commission could ascertain the cause.[110]

It is important to highlight that the school mortality rate for those years may have been no higher than on reserves. In his annual report for 1906, Dr. Peter Bryce, the chief medical officer for Indian Affairs, observed that "the Indian population of Canada has a mortality rate of more than double that of the whole population, and in some provinces more than three times." He observed a cycle of disease in which infants and children were infected at home and sent to residential schools, where they subsequently infected other children. The ones infected at school were "sent home when too ill to remain at school, or because of being a danger to the other scholars, and have conveyed the disease to houses previously free."[111]

A historical study by Michelle Robinson highlighted that "the problem of tuberculosis among school children could not be separated from that among children in the home, since almost every child being admitted to school seemed to carry the disease either in a latent or acute form."[112] As is well-known, the immune system of Aboriginal people of the plains, already more vulnerable to infectious diseases than that of Europeans, was further weakened by hunger and malnutrition due to economic hardships resulting from the disappearance of buffalo and the decline of the fur trade.

In later years, spanning from 1950 to 1965, the situation improved notably in residential schools. The mortality rate aligned with the Canadian average for youth aged five to fourteen.[113] This decrease can be attributed to the administration of vaccines, mirroring the practice in other Canadian

---

[110] Ibid., pp. 22-23.

[111] *Annual Report of the Department of Indian Affairs*, 1906, pp. 274–275, in the Truth and Reconciliation Commission of Canada, *Honouring the Truth, Reconciling for the Future. Summary of the Final Report of the Truth and Reconciliation Commission of Canada*, pp. 95-96.

[112] LAC, RG 10, volume 3957, file 140, 754-1, "Recommendations Based on Conclusions from the Investigation of 243 Indian School Children," Bryce to Pedley, November 5, 1909, p. 1, cited in Michelle M. Robinson, *Dying to learn: infectious disease and death among the children in Southern Alberta's Indian Residential Schools, 1889-1920*, Master's Thesis, Laurentian University, 2008, 65.

[113] *Annual Report*, 1906, pp. 274–275, in TRC, *Honouring the Truth, Reconciling for the Future. Summary*, pp. 19, 22.

schools. It's plausible that children received vaccinations more promptly at school compared to on reserves.

Based on incomplete information the TRC drew some unfounded and illogical inferences. It concluded that it was not "common practice throughout most of the history of the schools to return the remains to the communities of origin," and that "no one would have bothered to count the number of dead or record their burial sites." The TRC Report also states that "many students who went to residential school never returned," that they were lost to their families forever, and that "their parents were often uninformed of their sickness and death."[114] These statements based on either unspecified sources or so-called "deficient" records, have carried considerable weight with the media, especially coming from the well-funded and ostensibly credible TRC.

The Oblates of Mary Immaculate

Established in 1890 on the leadership of Shuswap Chief Louis Clexlixqen, the Kamloops residential school operated until 1969, overseen by successive generations of priests and brothers of the Oblates of Mary Immaculate (OMI), as well as numerous teachers from the Sisters of St. Anne from the province of Quebec. From its opening to the Second World War, annual enrollment was around 60 students, increasing to approximately 400 between 1946 and 1967.[115] The Kamloops IRS drew students from various small bands in the region. In 1936, the school was managed by five Oblate Fathers, two Oblate brothers, and eight Sisters of Saint Anne. By 1960, these numbers had shifted to five Fathers, three Brothers, and ten Sisters.[116]

The Oblates were the most successful Christian congregation in Northwest Canada, overseeing 39 of the 45 Catholic residential schools that served

---

[114] Ibid., p. 4.

[115] NCTR Archives, NAR-NCTR-128 Kamloops Residential School Narrative.

[116] Ibid., pp. 625, 788.

diverse populations including white, Amerindian, Métis, and Inuit. Their missionary efforts commenced in the Northwest in 1845, with 273 members already operating in the area during the later decades of the 19th century. Of these, 238 originated from France and 82 from Quebec.[117] The proportion of members coming from French Canada was even greater in the first half of the 20th century when they established missions and administered residential schools across Manitoba, Saskatchewan, Alberta, and British Columbia. In 1931, there were 111 Oblate missionaries from Quebec working outside Quebec, mostly in Western Canada.[118]

The Sisters of St. Anne of Montreal, founded in Quebec in 1850, were well-represented in B.C. where they were engaged in education (managing 14 schools) and healthcare (operating five hospitals) for both Indigenous and non-Indigenous communities. They established a boarding school for young girls of multiple nationalities and denominations in Victoria in 1858. They also played a role in five Indian Residential Schools in B.C. These were at the following locations: Cowichan (1864-1964), Mission City (1867-1984), Kamloops (1890-1970), Kuper Island (1891-1974), and Duncan (1940-1969). In 1900, out of the 100 sisters working in B.C., 65 were French Canadians from Quebec, a number that rose to 106 out of 285 sisters in 1958. Their commitment required leaving their families without the prospect of reunion, and adapting to an English setting. They brought many traditions from Quebec, where they were involved in girls' and boys' schools, municipal schools, home schools, teacher training colleges, and higher education.[119] Their missionary efforts extended to Yukon, Alaska, the United States, Japan, Chile, Cameroon, and Haiti.

Originating in France in 1816, the Oblates belonged to a wider missionary congregation around the world. As with Protestant missionaries, their objectives encompassed integrating Indigenous people into European ways of life and, fundamentally, converting them to Christianity or deepening

---

[117] *The Oblate Assault on Canada's Northwest* (Ottawa: University of Ottawa Press, 1995), p. 206.

[118] Jean Hamelin et Nicole Gagnon, *Histoire du catholicisme québécois. Le XXe siècle*, Tome 1, 1898-1940 (Montréal: Boréal Express, 1984), p. 156.

[119] Louise Roy, *Les Sœurs de Sainte-Anne, Un siècle d'histoire,* tome II, 1900-1950, (Montréal: Éditions Paulines, 1992), pp. 305, 315.

their understanding of the faith their family had already embraced. The Oblates' success was often attributed to their adherence to vows of poverty, chastity, and obedience, which facilitated permanent residence in remote missions for little or no pay. In reality, the Oblates forged strong connections with Indigenous people through their willingness to learn native languages, a requirement *mandated* by their Order. In contrast, many Protestant missionaries entered and exited the country with only a knowledge of English.[120]

As noted by historian Henri Goulet in his work on Quebec residential schools, proficiency in Indigenous languages was considered, "a primary condition for the success of their work." [121] The Oblates' publications in native languages were predicated on the notion that highlighting positive aspects of Indigenous culture would ease the transition to modern society. Father Jean-Marie Raphaël Le Jeune, for example, who arrived from France and was assigned to Kamloops in 1882, epitomized this approach. He mastered the Chinook jargon ("*Chinuk Wawa*"), a pidgin blend of Nootka, French, and English that originated during the fur trade and was adopted by the Oblates to communicate with Amerindians. Proficiency in this language was crucial for gaining their respect, converting them to Catholicism, or better educating them in the faith.

Father Le Jeune adapted the pronunciation of Chinook jargon words into a written form using a shorthand method from France. He imparted this knowledge to fellow Oblates and to Chief Louis Clexlixqen. In 1891, he even launched a periodical titled *Kamloops Wawa* ("Echoes of Kamloops") written in both Chinook jargon and English. It was regularly published until 1904 and intermittently until 1917. Father Le Jeune also authored pamphlets and educational books in English to further these efforts. Alongside Chief Clexlixqen and another chief, he embarked on a journey to Europe to showcase their expertise. During this trip, they were received

---

[120] Ibid., pp. 227-230.

[121] Henri Goulet, *Histoire des pensionnats indiens catholiques au Québec. Le rôle déterminant des pères oblats* (Montréal: Presses de l'Université de Montréal, 2016), pp. 182-183, 205-207.

by King Edward VII at Buckingham Palace and by Pope Pius X at the Vatican.[122]

The TRC Report acknowledged that several Oblates were skilled linguists who developed their grammars and written dictionaries to preserve Indigenous languages. Thanks to these priests and brothers, written syllabic languages and dictionaries were created, preventing the extinction of those languages. However, these impressive achievements are interpreted cynically in the TRC Report — not as a show of respect for Aboriginal culture but rather as a tool to undermine it and to challenge their pre-Christian spirituality, supposedly intact.

More generally, the Report characterizes the residential school system as being "founded on a racist belief that European civilization and the Christian religion were superior to Aboriginal culture, which was viewed as primitive and brutal."[123] These are rather broad brushstrokes for such a large and variegated catalogue of hundreds, perhaps thousands, of clerical and lay staff over more than a century of history. The record surely demands a more differentiated and nuanced approach rather than the simplistic demonization invoked by the presumptuous use of the scare-word "racist." Certainly a scholarly, accurate, and compassionate account of the devoted, remote, and nowadays utterly thankless service and sacrifices made by teachers and staff remains to be written.

Poor Research

One factor contributing to the markedly critical tone of the TRC Report is that the researchers consulted religious communities' archives but didn't adequately incorporate them into their analysis. Remarkably, the references predominantly revolve around government archives, largely disregarding

---

[122] Lynn Blake, Jean-Marie-Raphaël Le Jeune, *Dictionary of Canadian Biography,* vol. 15 (1921-1930); Harold Gurney, *The Work of Reverend Father J.M.R. Le Jeune, O. M. I.,* U.B.C. M.A. Thesis, 1948.

[123] *Final Report of the Truth and Reconciliation Commission of Canada,* vol. 1, *Canada's Residential Schools: History,* Part 1, pp. 94-97, 164-165.

the plethora of written documentation supplied by religious congregations. Despite the current blame directed towards these congregations, and allegations of withholding or refusing to release records, the congratulations actually provided the Commission with all the necessary records. It's worth noting that certain documents, underutilized by the TRC, are available to the public in provincial archives, and other researchers have made use of them.

The *Chronicles* maintained by nuns and the *Codices* of the Oblates offer significant insights into Roman Catholic residential schools. Eloi DeGrace, a retired archivist for the Roman Catholic Archdiocese in Edmonton, transcribed the sisters' *Chronicles* in French and English from five Alberta residential schools spanning from the late 19th century to the 1960s.[124] These include the Sisters of Providence at Cluny, the Sisters of Charity (Grey Nuns) at Cardston, and the Sisters of the Assumption of the Blessed Virgin at Delmas, Hobbema, and Onion Lake. These orders were founded in Quebec, and many nuns were French-speaking and taught in French, at least until the First World War. DeGrace summarized their role by stating:

> The Sisters were more than just teachers. They cared for the students as if they were their own children. [...] They noted in their chronicles everything that was wrong with the children in the school. They were close to the seriously ill children and wrote down the names of those who died at school, at home or in the hospital. They were so attached to their students that chronicle writers often noted the names of "former students" who had died; the Sisters were always near grieving families.[125]

This perspective aligns with the findings of Nina Green, who reviewed the *Chronicles* and their reports of daily school events. These records provide a unique understanding of life in residential schools, as the sisters resided full-time with the children. Ms Green emphasized that the sisters transcended their role as teachers, deeply caring for the children as if they

---

[124] Provincial Archives of Alberta, Missionary Oblates of Mary Immaculate (1842-1980), PAA, PR, 1971.0220. See Staff chronicles on Nina Green *Indian Residential School Records*.

[125] Eloi DeGrace, *Residential Schools Chronicles and Codices, 1894-1972*, Staff Chronicles online, February 14, 2022.

were their own. The *Chronicles* refer to the students as "our dear children," "our dear pupils," and "dear little ones," and their parents were similarly addressed as "our dear Indians to whom we so much desire to do good."[126] Publishing the sisters' *Chronicles* could potentially rectify misconceptions and restore the reputation of these often-forgotten and much-defamed missionaries. These individuals dedicated their lives to service far from their families and places of origin to better the lives of Indigenous youth. Their success is reinforced by testimony from former students and alumni attending reunions years after graduation.

To gain a more comprehensive insight into life at a boarding school, it is worth examining the *Chronicles* of St. Mary's Indian Residential School of Alberta (Cardston). The school is situated on the South Blood Reserve in Alberta, positioned roughly midway between Cardston and Standoff. This Roman Catholic school was managed by the Sisters of Charity (Grey Nuns of Montreal) from 1898 to 1966 and then by the OMI until 1973.[127]

The *Chronicles* were authored by nuns in French. In the 1920s, the school had an enrollment of around 120 students, rising to 300 by the 1950s. The *Chronicles* record important daily events in all aspects of life related to education, religious events, recreational activities, and so on. Parents were welcome at the school and attended many student performances. Given the TRC Report's overwhelming depiction of residential schools as a horror story, specific attention may be paid to medical care and child mortality.

Detailed records were kept on illnesses at school and the names of deceased children. A doctor was summoned whenever a student fell seriously ill, and when necessary immediate hospitalization occurred. Starting in 1919, annual medical examinations were conducted, and from 1927 these were mandatory prior to admission. The 1930s saw efforts to combat tuberculosis through vaccination, with the vaccine being administered as early as 1931. After the Second World War, vaccinations

---

[126] Nina Green, "Our Dear Children": Sisters' Chronicles of Indian Residential School," *The Dorchester Review* online, April 1, 2022.

[127] *Indian Residential School Records*, Staff Chronicles, cf. "Cardston-Alberta."

and lung examinations became routine, and X-rays were taken annually from 1933. Dental check-ups, including extractions and fillings, were introduced in the early 1930s, and ocular examinations were conducted yearly from the same period to prevent trachoma.

The *Chronicles* meticulously document the names and dates of student deaths, often accompanied by the cause, such as influenza, tuberculosis, smallpox, and scrofula. From 1898 to 1967, there were 46 reported student deaths at school, in hospitals, or at home (only six after 1940 and six due to a single epidemic in 1920). This death rate appears within the norm considering the student population, averaging one per year before 1940. Deceased children were buried in the Roman Catholic Blood Reserve Cemetery. Contrary to media myth, the funerals were not secretive affairs: children attended them either at the sisters' chapel or the mission church. Contrary to unsubstantiated allegations, there is no evidence of "missing" children and no evidence of any resort to unmarked graves.

To have access to the *Chronicles* of the Sisters of St. Anne from Kamloops residential school would be revealing. It's likely they contain similar information to that found in the Cardston reports. Such records could be instrumental in comprehending the dynamic between the administration of the Oblates, the sisters, and the students in Kamloops. The Order of St. Anne submitted its B.C. *Chronicles* to the TRC Commission in 2012, and they are likely stored at the National Centre for Truth and Reconciliation (NCTR) in Winnipeg. Although an agreement has been reached to digitize these and transfer them to the Royal B.C. Museum, they are not yet accessible to researchers or the public.[128]

The imputation of *secrecy* must therefore, at least in the interim, belong to the NCTR, not the religious orders.

The hope is that the Centre will make such records available soon, because they can shed light on the bizarre and unlikely allegations against the Oblates and the Orders of St. Anne who dedicated their lives to the children and families of Kamloops residential school.

---

[128] Darryl Dyck, "Order of nuns that staffed residential schools to pass records to Royal B.C. Museum," Canadian Press, *Victoria News*, June 2, 2022.

Kamloops School Deaths

Consulting the sisters' *Chronicles* could play a crucial role in identifying the children who were allegedly lost at the Kamloops residential school, as requested by Chief Casimir with ostensible sincerity.[129] The so-called Memorial Register of the NCTR has officially documented the names of 51 children who died between 1915 and 1964 at the school or within a year after leaving.[130] These names were primarily derived from the *Quarterly Returns* submitted by the school principal to the Department of Indian Affairs.

However, private researchers, without any of the infrastructure or public funding that has been provided to the NCTR, have found a great deal of information on these children in records in Library and Archives Canada, as well as death certificates held by the British Columbia Archives online Genealogy resource, which was either ignored or not utilized by NCTR researchers.[131]

By combining these two sources, a comprehensive understanding of the deaths of at least 35 out of the 49 students (excluding duplicates) listed by the NCTR has been obtained. Of these, 17 died in hospitals and eight on their respective reserves due to illness or accident. In four cases there was an autopsy, and in seven a coroner's inquest. Regarding burial sites, 24 children were interred in their home reserve cemeteries, and four were buried at the Kamloops reserve cemetery. For the remaining 49 children, information is either missing or requires the complete death certificate from B.C. Vital Statistics for a fee of $50 each. Still, these findings contrast significantly with the unfounded claims that authorities ignored or concealed children's deaths, that parents were uninformed, and that

---

[129] Tk'emlúps te secwépemc, Press Release, "KIRS missing children findings but a fraction of investigation and work need to bring peace to families and communities," July 15, 2021.

[130] *National Student Memorial Register of National Centre for Truth and Reconciliation.*

[131] B.C. Archives, Genealogy, General Search. All of these certificates in the B.C. Archives were checked, cf. Genealogy, General Research Copies of death certificates, available on Nina Green's website at Kamloops IRS Death Records. Cf. Library and Archives Canada, School Files Series - 1879-1953 (RG10), Indian and Inuit Affairs Program School Files Series, 1879-1953 (RG10-B-3-d), LAC c-8770, no. 829; LAC c-8773, no. 1323. Copy of quarterly returns for Kamloops (1943-1944) at Kamloops-Quarterly-Returns.

remains were never returned home. In reality, most parents were informed, and most deceased children were returned home.

According to the TRC's "Missing Children" report, in the early 20th century, Indian Affairs established a policy for the burial of students who died at residential schools. The policy is outlined in an undated memorandum by J. D. McLean, the departmental secretary from 1897 to 1933:

> Funeral expenses are met from Relief Vote [federal monies set aside for welfare-related expenses], if a pupil of an Indian residential school dies elsewhere than at the school, and provided the parents or guardians are unable to pay the costs of burial. When a pupil dies at a residential school, it is considered by this department that the school authorities should be responsible for the expenses. Occasionally, the Department has paid the cost of transporting the body from the school to the home of the parents, when the parents have refused to permit burial at the school.[132]

For these early years, the TRC Report concludes that Christian burial was the norm at most schools since they were part of a larger church mission that might include a church, missionary accommodations, a farm, and a cemetery. "The church was intended to serve as a place of worship for both residential school students and for adults from the surrounding region employed in operational services and custodial care. In the same way, the cemetery might serve as a place of burial for students who died at school, members of the local community, and the missionaries themselves."[133] This is exemplified by the Marieval residential school, as outlined below.

From 1935 onwards, Indian Affairs instituted a specific procedure for handling student deaths. The principal was required to inform the departmental agent, who formed an inquiry committee with the principal

---

[132] Final Report of the Truth and Reconciliation Commission of Canada, vol. 4, p. 118.

[133] Ibid., p. 119.

and the doctor who diagnosed the death. Parents were informed of the investigation and had the option to attend and provide statements.[134]

For example, Kathleen Michel, 14 years old, fell ill on April 25, 1937, and received treatment from a school nurse before being taken to the Royal Inland Hospital of Kamloops on May 1. She died two days later of acute nephritis with contributing factors of measles and cardiac dysfunction. The doctor's report found no inadequacies in the care provided at school. The father was informed of the investigation but chose not to attend. Unfortunately, the inquiry memorandum did not specify her place of burial.[135]

Significantly, the Kamloops residential school is strategically located at the heart of the *Kamloops Reserve* itself, a fact that is overlooked in media reports. A Catholic cemetery near St. Joseph's Church is in close proximity to the residential school. Given this context, is it credible that the remains of 215 children were buried clandestinely in a mass grave, on the reserve itself, without any response from the band council until the summer of 2021?

Yet Chief Casimir asserts that a certain gnostic "knowledge" of the alleged presence of children's remains has been present within the community for an extended period — in spite of the fact that such "knowing" has nowhere been mentioned until the past couple of years.

Aboriginal families are presumably as concerned about the fate of their children as any other community. The question arises: why did parents, siblings, family members, and leaders remain silent? Why did the elders, supposed to hold the community's memory, never mention the names of missing children who supposedly did not return home?

Additionally, is it plausible that religious communities dedicated to high moral standards could conspire to commit heinous crimes without any dissent or a single whistleblower? How can one accept the idea that the

[134] Ibid., p. 9.

[135] Pensionnat Kamloops, Kathleen Michel, Library and Archives Canada, School Files Series - 1879-1953 (RG10), LAC C-8773-01350.

Sisters of St. Anne, who knew generations of students, could be complicit in such repugnant crimes? There were significantly more sisters at the school than Oblate priests and brothers, with nuns primarily responsible for teaching and Oblates for administration. The same order of Sisters also worked in various social and charitable initiatives in Quebec, including orphanages, but never faced such accusations there.

The school's proximity to the city of Kamloops further diminishes the likelihood of unreported or concealed events. Agents of the Department of Indian Affairs closely monitored school activities and would have swiftly responded to any news or rumours of missing or deceased children. As archivist Eloi DeGrace observes, extensive oversight made it nearly *impossible* for a child to go missing:

> There was a school registry. The government knew who was attending the school [...] there were many inspections of all kinds during the year. School inspectors, doctors, nurses, reserve agents, agency inspectors, reserve inspectors, Ottawa officials visited the school, sometimes several times during the year. If there was a single student missing, it would have come out.[136]

And as retired Manitoba Provincial Court Judge Brian Giesbrecht wrote, "is it even remotely possible that thousands of parents of any race or ethnic group would simply accept the fact that their children had gone to live in a boarding school, and never returned? Would not any parent be alarmed, and demand to know where their child was? For heaven's sakes, are Indigenous parents houseplants?"[137]

Finally, as we have seen, the Province of British Columbia mandated the completion of a death certificate for all deceased individuals. At the turn of the 20th century, B.C. was not the wild west. Today, researchers seeking death certificates for children who attended the Kamloops residential school can access them by searching names and dates of death on the B.C.

---

[136] Email from Eloi DeGrace in the author's possession, January 26, 2022.

[137] Brian Giesbrecht, "Are There Really Thousands of Missing Indigenous Children?" *Frontier Centre for Public Policy*, October 21, 2021.

Genealogical Records website, and similar research avenues exist in other provinces.

The chosen approach raises the question of why such research is not pursued instead of employing ground penetrating radar to search for alleged remains. GPR is an inherently ambiguous method, in sharp contrast to data sitting unread in archival records.

The Compliant Media

On January 13, 2022, the CBC broadcast an extensive documentary about the "traumatic discovery of what is believed to be children's graves" near the former Kamloops residential school. The documentary featured interviews with nine "survivors" of the school, some of whom emotionally recounted stories of pits or caves behind the school where children were ostensibly buried. These accounts, unlikely on the fact of it, suggested that leaving the school equated to being "dead and buried." They claimed to have heard that the orchard was not to be walked in because there were dead bodies there. It was alleged that a furnace in the basement was used to dispose of children's bodies, the implication being that they sought to conceal evidence of foul play. The furnace story is an even more outlandish claim that, suspiciously, has suddenly cropped up for the first time at other school locations since then.

The only two "survivors" who claimed to have witnessed anything were scarcely credible: one said he saw four boys hanging by the neck in a barn, and the other saw blood-stained clothing in the furnace room that, it was implied, suggested a miscarriage or abortion. The host of the *Fifth Estate*, a program that normally makes a point of investigating in depth, did not ask any probing questions about these highly unlikely claims. The tone and flow of the documentary suggest that all the stories are simply to be believed without corroborating evidence.[138]

---

[138] Fifth Estate, *The Reckoning: Secrets unearthed by Tk'emlúps te Secwépemc*, broadcast January 13, 2022, on YouTube.

According to Frances Widdowson, a former professor at Mount Royal University in Calgary, these fantasy stories of buried children were first raised in 1998 by Kevin Annett, a defrocked clergyman who had been expelled from ministry by the United Church of Canada in 1995 for spreading conspiracy theories. He subsequently made a career of seeding or encouraging among Aboriginal leaders the allegation of the existence of mass Indigenous graves.[139] His book *Hidden No Longer. Genocide in Canada, Past and Present*, published in September 2010, contains a list of supposed mass graves at former Indian residential schools. One is related to the Kamloops Industrial School (i.e. the residential school) with supposed guidance as to where the mass grave is located: "Mass grave south of school, adjacent to and amidst the orchard. Numerous burials witnessed there."[140] Whether or not he was the first to invent the story, or heard it from others, is not recorded. What is clear is that Annett either planted or reinforced in the "memory" of Indigenous people around Kamloops the belief that numerous children's bodies were clandestinely buried in an orchard.

Tracing the allegations back, the story was told in Kamloops in 2008, when a local newspaper, *Kamloops This Week*, referred to Annett's claims that the land surrounding the residential school is full of the remains of dead children and that "eyewitnesses witnessed several burials in the land adjacent to the old residential school and the surrounding orchard." Also quoted in the article is the communications director for the Archdiocese of Vancouver, who denied allegations of a deliberate plan to perpetrate "genocide" against the First Nations. He added that neither Annett nor anyone in Kamloops brought the allegations to the RCMP, and Annett refused numerous invitations offered by several archdiocesan officials to meet and discuss his allegations.[141]

---

[139] Widdowson, "Billy Remembers," loc cit.; Mike Milne, "Reconciled to Hard Truths," United Church Observer, May 5, 2008.

[140] Kevin Annett, *Hidden No Longer. Genocide in Canada, Past and Present*, International Tribunal into Crimes of Church and State (Canada), 347.

[141] Cassidy Olivier, "Burial ground — or bogus?" *Kamloops This Week*, April 24, 2008.

It is significant, too, that claims of children buried in the orchard contradict the accounts of 45 published interviews conducted with former students, both girls and boys, who attended the school from the 1940s to the 1960s. These are lengthy taped interviews in which students freely recount their residential school experiences. Thirteen interviews were conducted by ethnologist Celia Haig-Brown in 1985 and 1986, and thirty-two under the auspices of the *Secwepemc Cultural Education Society* in the 1990s.[142] These facts again make subsequent claims by the Kamloops Band highly unlikely and, according to ordinary common sense, suspicious as to provenance and motive.

While not all of their experiences at the school were positive, none of the published interviews make any reference to graves in the orchard. Only one student mentioned being prohibited from going to the orchard, stating, "I heard stories, but not until I was older, that we shouldn't go down there alone."[143] The reason for this prohibition remains uncertain, with suggestions that it might relate to the behaviour of boys or activities deemed inappropriate. Oddly enough, very similar suspicions have arisen, again involving fruit orchards, at other schools such as at the Sandy Bay residential school in Manitoba and the Mohawk Institute in Brantford, Ontario. However, ground-penetrating radar searches conducted in Brantford in 2011 and 2022 yielded no findings.

Regardless, the burials of 215 students, in the unlikely event that they occurred, would certainly have caught the imagination of students who lived all day in close proximity and would have become a story etched in their memory and perpetuated from cohort to cohort. However, none of the 45 students interviewed who lived in the residence mentioned such graves. It wasn't until 2021 that the story was revealed, albeit without any names of missing children.

In this context, the account of Emma Baker, an alumna of the Kamloops residential school, is revealing. At 84 years of age, in May 2021, she

---

[142] Secwepemc Cultural Education Society. *Behind Closed Doors: Stories from the Kamloops Indian Residential School* (Penticton: Theytus, 2006); Celia Haig-Brown, *Resistance and Renewal: Surviving the Indian Residential School* (Vancouver: Arsenal Pulp Press, 1988).

[143] Secwepemc Cultural Education Society. *Behind Closed Doors*, p. 146.

disclosed to a reporter that she and her friends made up stories about graves in the apple orchard during their attendance at the elementary school from 1952 to 1956 and later at the high school level. She noted: "There were rumours of a graveyard, but nobody seemed to know where it was and we didn't even know if it was true."[144] These word-of-mouth rumours shared among children, like any oral tradition in any culture, are subject to the distortion of the feelings and opinions of those who pass them on.

There are obvious problems with relying on oral testimonies rather than facts to find the truth. "A tale grows with the telling" is an old idiom.

A year after the rumour of 215 unmarked graves, Chief Rosanne Casimir announced plans for new research using ground-penetrating radar over a broader field area, rather than excavation. "No consensus," she said, "has emerged among survivors, with some seeing exhumation as a process that could help lay victims properly to rest, while others want them left undisturbed."[145] When questioned about police involvement, Chief Casimir revealed that the RCMP and the B.C. Coroners Service were informed shortly after the initial discovery in May, although details on this matter were not provided. She also mentioned the formation of a technical task force comprising professors, technical archeologists, and ground-penetrating radar experts.

A day later, the Prime Minister met with Casimir and council members at an evening ceremony. "It was a difficult year for survivors and their families," Mr. Trudeau said. "It was a difficult year for Canadians as well. We have a long path ahead of us for reconciliation."[146]

Despite this, no further research took place on the orchard site over the summer, and no action was taken for the second anniversary of the graves

---

[144] Alissa Thibault, "Calls for accountability over Kamloops residential school discovery," CTV News, May 29, 2021, Updated May 30, 2021.

[145] Dirk Meissner, "Work to exhume remains at former Kamloops residential school could begin soon, chief says," *The* Canadian Press, May 20, 2022.

[146] Dirk Meissner, "Trudeau faces chants, pounding drums as he walks through the crowd at Kamloops memorial, the Canadian Press," CTV News, May 24, 2022.

or possible remains. Nonetheless, reports of remains "found" in Kamloops continue to make headlines in the media.

Marieval Residential School

We can close with an examination of another "nameless burial" site near a residential school, specifically the Cowessess (Marieval) First Nation in Saskatchewan. This site also created shock waves in June 2021 following the Kamloops revelation. Opening in 1899 in a remote area, the school was overseen by the O.M.I. and the Sisters of St. Joseph of St. Hyacinthe in Quebec. The use of ground-penetrating radar in this case yielded the discovery of 751 well-arranged graves, which, as duly noted by a *CBC News* reporter, is, in fact, the Catholic *cemetery* of the Mission of the Immaculate Heart of Mary in Marieval.

Records of baptisms, marriages, and burials from 1885 to 1933 confirm the presence of graves in the cemetery, including those of children who died at the Marieval Residential School. However, the cemetery also contains the graves of many non-Indigenous adults and children under the age of five from the surrounding area. Residents Pearl Lerat and Linda Whiteman, who attended Marieval during the late 1940s to mid-1950s, pointed out that the cemetery encompasses the resting place of not only local First Nations individuals but also whites and natives from outside the community, reflecting a diverse mix of backgrounds. According to nearby residents, crosses and headstones once adorned the graves, until the 1960s when they were ostensibly removed because the cemetery was in "terrible shape."[147]

Chief Cadmus Delorme of the Cowessess First Nation confirmed that this site is not a mass grave but rather consists of unmarked graves. While not all unmarked graves necessarily belong to children, oral stories within the Cowessess First Nation mention both children and adults being interred there, including individuals from nearby towns and the church community.

---

[147] Jorge Barrera, "Catholic register, survivors offer clues to who may be buried in cemetery next to Marieval residential school," CBC News, July 20, 2021.

Some of the remains discovered were "maybe people who attended the church or were from nearby towns." [148] No excavation has taken place.

As reported first by *La Presse* and in the *Toronto Star*, J.R. Miller of the University of Saskatchewan believes the remains of children discovered in Marieval and Kamloops were buried in accordance with Catholic rites, marked by wooden crosses that deteriorated over time. Brian Gettler of the University of Toronto confirms that the wooden cross was a typical marker for Catholic burials, particularly for those of limited means.[149] Interestingly, photographs from July 2013 show that the crosses and headstones at the Marieval cemetery adjacent to the school did not disappear in the 1960s. They still stood behind the Church, which later burned down, likely due to arson.

The TRC Report, too, states that churchyards often served as a place of worship and burial for students who died at school, as well as for members of the local community and missionaries. Due to the abandonment and neglect of such cemeteries when the government and Aboriginal communities assumed control in the 1970s, following the schools' closure, these sites were forgotten. Cemetery perimeters eroded, fences vanished, and wooden crosses decayed.[150] As a result, locating these sites or repurposing them became challenging. The Commission rightly proposed that they be documented, maintained, and protected in line with Indigenous Christians' cultural traditions to this day.

The Quest for Suspected Graves

The revelations in Kamloops and Marieval have ignited a moral panic among the public (Canadian and Aboriginal), among news consumers, and

---

[148] Bryan Eneas, "Sask. First Nation announces discovery of 751 unmarked graves near former residential school," CBC News, June 24, 2021.

[149] Mathieu Perreault, "Religious orders in residential schools is a 'Quebecois' story," *La Presse* and *Toronto Star*, July 2, 2021.

[150] *Final Report of the Truth and Reconciliation Commission of Canada*, vol. 4, pp. 125-134.

Aboriginal leaders, concerning the alleged existence of children's graves near other residential schools across Canada.

This has led to discussions about a possible broad conspiracy by religious orders to conceal the supposed deaths. As a result, searches using ground-penetrating radar have been initiated by Aboriginal communities around numerous residential schools across the country, and even at hospitals.

The Canadian government allocated $27 million to Aboriginal communities in June 2021 to "identify and delineate burial sites, and return remains home if desired." In August, an additional $83 million was announced, dedicated to locating supposed burial sites and commemorating the children who are presumed to have lost their lives in residential schools.[151] A swift distribution of $116.8 million went to the 70 Residential Schools Missing Children Communities program over four years. All that without true evidence of the existence of real burials at any school, apart from cemeteries already known.

The Prime Minister explained that "determining where and how many more Indigenous children's remains may be buried in this country is an important part of discovering the truth." Then-Crown-Indigenous Relations Minister Marc Miller clarified that the federal government wouldn't unilaterally initiate excavations, as some communities consider these former residential school sites to be sacred ground. He emphasized that, even though some people may perceive these sites as crime scenes, the government does not intend to involve itself in the investigation of burial sites. The exercise must be led by Indigenous communities to respect their cultural ways of laying the dead to rest.[152] In this process, the Canadian government decided it has no authority over First Nations to ask for excavations, but only to finance costly searches for graves that are only presumed to exist.

---

[151] "Government of Canada enhances support to Indigenous communities to respond to and heal from the ongoing impacts of residential schools," News Release, Government of Canada, August 10, 2021.

[152] Rachel Aiello, "$27M will soon be available to communities to help locate children who died at residential schools: feds," CTV News, June 2, 2021.

In spite of all these government and Indigenous measures, in reality there is a viable method to uncover the fate of children who died in residential schools.

This involves gathering their names from the NCTR's Memorial Register and cross-referencing them with provincial death registers. Independent researcher Nina Green has, to date, revealed details of student deaths at 47 residential schools, primarily in B.C. but also in Saskatchewan, Alberta, Manitoba, and Ontario.

Green's findings indicate that most of the approximately 500 deaths at these schools did not occur at the schools themselves, but in hospitals under medical supervision.[153] Death certificates, often signed by parents, physicians, or Indian Affairs officers, confirm that most were interred in cemeteries on their reserves.

Once again, the assertion that a significant number of residential school children disappeared without a trace turns out to be baseless.

The Pine Creek Excavation

On August 15, 2022, representatives of the Pine Creek First Nation in Manitoba made a request to the RCMP to investigate 14 ground anomalies under the basement of Our Lady of Seven Sorrows Catholic Church, on the grounds of a former residential school. The Pine Creek Indian Residential School operated from 1890 to 1969 in Camperville, Manitoba, along the shores of Lake Winnipegosis.

A substantial four-story stone building constructed in 1911, the school was entirely demolished in 1972-73, purportedly due to the deeply painful history associated with it for Anishinaabe children and families. The remains of the large stone mission school were returned to the lake so that

---

[153] Nina Green, *Indian Residential Schools Records*, Residential Schools - Death Records.

the water will heal the pain and suffering of the community.[154] Throughout its existence, francophones were very much in evidence at this school: the principals and assistant principals had French names and were members of the O.M.I.[155] Much of the teaching was done by the Missionary Oblate Sisters of the Sacred Heart and Mary Immaculate.

In 2021, the community received $332,500 from the federal government for research purposes.[156] Research was conducted by a private contractor starting in May 2022, prior to RCMP involvement. Using ground-penetrating radar, 71 anomalies were found on the grounds in the vicinity of the church, near the cemetery and the old residential school.

However, the community's focus rested primarily on 14 anomalies directly underneath the church where two ground-penetrating radar scans had been conducted. They revealed features at depths ranging from three to four feet, findings that align with similar ground searches of unmarked burials in Canada and other regions.[157] In addition, Chief Derek Nepinak opined that "to bury remains under a building suggests a dark and sinister intent that cannot be unaddressed as we expose the truth of what happened in our homeland.[158]

Accordingly the Chief, along with Council members and Elders, sought assistance from the RCMP to conduct an investigation. But by July 2023, after a year of interviews, inquiries, speculation, and repeated sinister

---

[154] Georgina Nepinak, *Mina'igoziibiing: A History of the Anishinaabeg of Pine Creek First Nation in Manitoba*, Master's Thesis, Brandon University, Manitoba, May 2013, p. 282.

[155] NCTR Archives, NAR-NCTR-042, *Pine Creek Residential School Narrative*.

[156] Canada, *Residential Schools Missing Children Community Support Funding Recipients,* Crown-Indigenous Relations and Northern Affairs Canada, 2021.

[157] "RCMP investigate after search of western Manitoba residential school site discovers possible unmarked graves," CBC News, October 14, 2022; Chief Derek Nepinak, Minegoziibe Anishinabe announcement on the findings of an excavation of 14 reflections under the Catholic Church in Pine Creek, via Facebook.

[158] "Western Manitoba First Nation set to start search of church site for potential unmarked graves," Canadian Press, July 20, 2023.

insinuations delivered in the media, the RCMP failed to uncover any evidence of criminal activity.[159]

Not wishing to drop the matter after investing so much energy in the pursuit, the Band Council initiated efforts to excavate the anomalies. This marked the first such action since the reports from Kamloops, where no digging has been done in the two years since. Instead of asking the RCMP to execute the excavation, the Council enlisted a research team from Brandon University, which includes an anthropologist, students, and local experts. It was proposed that if unmarked graves were discovered, they would follow up with carbon dating, DNA testing, and the school's student registry to identify the (presumed) "remains." The excavation of these anomalies was expected to span around a month.[160]

In August 2023, the Chief Derek Nepinak, sad and perplexed, announced in direct video that no bodies were found in the basement.[161]

It is significant to refer back to what residents said before they were forced to admit there was nothing there. Local resident Brenda Catcheway, who has been part of the search since it first began, claims that her grandmother hesitated to send her to day school, "because of the horrors she faced at the residential school," adding, "I used to just think she was telling me scary stories, but I think we're coming down to the truth that she was telling me real stories."[162] This statement offers a glimpse into the depth of emotional involvement in the search, the prevailing belief in the crime committed by priests and nuns, and that excavation will certainly reveal the bodies of children. However, whatever the outcome of the search, the grievances are

---

[159] Superintendent Rob Lasson, Officer in Charge of Major Crime Services, Manitoba RCMP, Update – Manitoba, "RCMP begins investigation into reflections detected in Minegoziibe Anishinabe (Pine Creek First Nation)," Winnipeg, Manitoba, July 21, 2023.

[160] Chelsea Kemp, "Manitoba community gathers to prepare for church basement excavation of possible unmarked graves," CBC News, July 25, 2023.

[161] "Chief says excavation of Manitoba church basement found no evidence of human remains," Canadian Press, August 18, 2023.

[162] Chelsea Kemp, "Manitoba community gathers to prepare for church basement excavation of possible unmarked graves," CBC News, July 25, 2023.

so entrenched in the minds of the community that their opinion is unlikely to change even if nothing is discovered.

The decision by the Council to proceed with an excavation represents the first instance since the reported "discovery" at the Kamloops residential school. In fact, among more than twenty other residential schools where anomalies were detected through ground-penetrating radar, no excavations were conducted to verify the presence of children's remains. This underscores a quick need for excavations near other residential schools to uncover the truth surrounding these sites.

An intriguing aspect of the story relates to potential international involvement in response to the Pine Creek request for assistance upon the detection of *anomalies* in November 2022. Minister Marc Miller then signed an agreement in February 2023, allocating $2 million dollars to the International Commission on Missing Persons (ICMP) in the Netherlands to help identify and repatriate any human remains found by Indigenous communities.[163]

This organization, created on the initiative of President Bill Clinton and based in The Hague, specializes in identifying and repatriating human remains through collaboration with governments, civil society, and other entities, particularly in cases of human rights abuses, disasters, and other causes. The Minister asserted that, due to Canada's historical involvement in creating and funding the residential school system, its conflict of interest and status as a "perpetrator" of "genocide" necessitates bringing in an independent organization with relevant expertise. According to internal government documents, the Indigenous communities were seeking a unified strategy for addressing unmarked graves, and the ICMP was seen as a trustworthy partner in this regard.[164]

With the help of Indigenous communities, the ICMP would be expected to conduct a campaign in Canada to explore options for identification and repatriation of missing children using its state-of-the-art forensic

---

[163] Stephanie Taylor, "Ottawa to pay international organization $2M to advise Indigenous communities on unmarked graves," Canadian Press, February 7, 2023.

[164] Ibid.

archaeological and anthropological techniques and assessing interest in DNA matching and other approaches. It would then outline for the government a work plan, maintain regular communication, and provide written status updates.

The accord specifies that the Indigenous communities are not required to employ the services of the ICMP. Interested communities can choose this option and help in sharing "their experiences, thoughts and views to shape the work ahead." In order to ensure respectful proceedings, local Indigenous facilitators would lead every step of the way. A draft report was expected to be supplied by May 15, 2023, and the final report could be published without Ottawa's approval.[165]

The Chief of the Pine Creek Nation welcomed help from the international organization and was pleased the federal government took an important step "to get to the truth."[166]

But that was not the position of Kimberly Murray, appointed special interlocutor for missing children and unmarked burials at residential schools in June 2022. Murray's view was that the agreement "lacks transparency and places the commission under the influence of government bureaucrats." The government, she claimed, didn't consult Indigenous national organizations: "They didn't have any input on the contract."[167]

In March 2023, the Executive Director of the ICMP, Kathryne Bomberger, offered to involve Aboriginals directly in the excavations and try to convince Indigenous leaders that its organization is independent of the government. She also hired Sheila North, a Winnipeg journalist who is Cree and former Grand Chief of Manitoba, to facilitate community

---

[165] Crown-Indigenous Relations and Northern Affairs News Release, February 17, 2023.

[166] Taylor, "Ottawa to pay," loc. cit.

[167] Brett Forester, "Interlocutor on unmarked graves 'very concerned' by feds' $2M deal with international organization," *CBC News*, February 9, 2023.

engagement sessions.[168] However, Bomberger realized that it "is a hugely political issue in every single area I've ever worked."[169]

In late May, the National Aboriginal Advisory Committee on Missing Children from Residential Schools declined to collaborate with the International Commission due to lack of confidence in the organization, even though it has experience in Kosovo, Bosnia-Herzegovina, Montenegro, and Macedonia, among other locations with unidentified remains.

The reason given for this refusal was that in Canada, the project was too important and sensitive to be entrusted to a non-Aboriginal organization that had not already worked with residential school "survivors" before.[170] Kimberly Murray and Indigenous leaders did not want any outside involvement in excavation, just an "Indigenous-led investigation."[171]

Despite the initial deadline for the ICMP's final report in May 2023, this was extended to June, and as of August, the current status of the matter remains uncertain. Consequently, it's possible that the ICMP might not participate in any forensic excavation in Canada. The cautious stance adopted by Indigenous leaders raises questions about their confidence in the existence of remains in the ground.

Conclusion

It is all indeed an incredible story. It is extraordinary not simply in the alleged discovery of children's remains at the Kamloops residential school — but now at more than twenty other residential schools that has led to a spiral of false claims endorsed by the Canadian government and made

---

[168] Fraser Needham, "Missing persons organization to present Indigenous communities with options: director-general," *APTN National News*, February 24, 2023.

[169] Brett Forester, "International Commission looks to ease fears over unmarked graves contract," *CBC News*, March 15, 2023.

[170] Cosmin Dzsurdzsa, "Indigenous graves panel refuses to work with Hague-based missing persons org," May 30, 2023.

[171] Forester, "International Commission," loc. cit.

known everywhere by the world's media. The widespread coverage have led the Canadian public to believe in the credibility of these supposed findings, which are not findings at all.[172] This sentiment was even mirrored in the House of Commons in Ottawa on June 21, 2023, when Members of Parliament unanimously agreed "to observe a moment of silence to commemorate National Indigenous Peoples Day and mark the discovery of the remains of 215 children at a former residential school in Kamloops."[173]

It's important to note that as of the present time — two years after the announcement — no remains have been discovered either in Kamloops or at any other residential school where search efforts have been conducted. A crime requires full investigation by the police, physical evidence, verifiable documentation and, of course, excavation of the burial sites to ascertain both the identity of the bodies and the cause of death. The government and the RCMP have implemented a very surprising policy for what could be the biggest crime in Canadian history: to leave the decision to investigate to Aboriginal communities which could be construed as having a vested interest in not investigating.

In the absence of excavation thus far, the basis for these narratives rests primarily on rumours, the recollections of elderly individuals, and GPR-derived "ground disturbances." All of the accompanying emotionally charged stories, surely driven in part by political and financial motives, have taken precedence over the earnest pursuit of truth. In the absence of concrete evidence, these accounts must be regarded as more a product of imagination than reality.

This chapter was originally published as "In Kamloops Not One Body Has Been Found" in The Dorchester Review *online (January 11, 2022), a post that by November 2023 had received over 288,000 hits all over the world. An updated version appeared in the print edition,* The Dorchester Review, *Vol. 12 No. 1 (Spring/Summer 2022), pp. 27-36. The author has revised and updated his work for publication in this volume.*

---

[172] Tom Flanagan and Brian Giesbrecht, "The False Narrative of Residential School Burials," *The Dorchester Review* online, March 1, 2022.

[173] "National Indigenous Peoples Day," House of Commons, Hansard, No. 218, June 21, 2023.

Chapter Two

Graves in the Apple Orchard: Contextualizing and Questioning the Claims about Burials at the Kamloops Indian Residential School

Anonymous WordPress blog post

"Oral histories recall children as young as six years old woken [sic] in the night to dig holes for burials in the apple orchard." — Dr. Sarah Beaulieu

The following is a brief history of the apple orchard where Dr. Beaulieu's 2021 GPR survey identified 200 "probable burials." Using historical photographs and archival documents, several phases in the orchard's past are illustrated and discussed. This work is intended to contextualize Dr. Beaulieu's findings and to provide a reasoned basis for questioning her claims.

The apple orchard is located about 500 feet southeast of the former Kamloops Indian Residential School. It sits near a prehistoric housepit village, atop an extensive shell midden and ancient refuse pits. The area is considered archaeologically significant and has been the subject of assessments, test holes, and excavations from 1983 to 2004.

Much of how the site appears today is due to 130 years of intense agricultural activity and infrastructure projects.

During the late 19th and early 20th centuries, the Kamloops Residential School produced much of its own food in surrounding fields and orchards. Vegetables and other crops were grown in the school garden – 7 acres of fenced land along the South Thompson River.

In 1917 it was necessary to install extensive irrigation works to ensure the viability of crops. To transport water from a new pump house to the fields, students were made to dig hundreds of feet of ditches and, where the ground was not favourable, wooden flumes and stave pipes were installed. On reaching the top of the school garden, water was diverted to irrigation ditches as required.

With construction of a new school building in the mid-to-late 1920s came installation of a sewage disposal plant. The plant consisted of a septic tank and two underground disposal beds. The east bed was 0.35 acres in size and distributed wastewater through 2,000 lineal feet of land tile buried 3.5 feet below grade.[174] Following the site contours, the east bed extended under much of what would become the upper garden and orchard.

By 1928, after nearly 40 years of cultivation and irrigation, the school garden had become deeply furrowed in contrast to surrounding farmland. Countless irrigation ditches were dug and filled in, their locations lost to time.

By 1935, the original septic tank and sewage disposal beds were chronically clogged. As a temporary solution, the beds were bypassed and raw sewage was dumped, via open ditch, into a low-lying marshy area south of the school garden. This created very unsanitary conditions as large amounts of effluent collected, breeding flies and causing stench.[175]

A more permanent sewage solution was found in 1938-39 with the installation of a larger septic tank and bypass pipe that sent wastewater to the garden and orchard for irrigation. Septic sludge was diverted via pipe and flume to a 40 x 60 x 3 feet deep sludge drying basin located in the northwest corner of the orchard (Webb 1938 & 1939). It appears that this method of sewage disposal remained in operation for the next two decades.

Between 1930 and 1948, an apple orchard of at least 77 trees was planted over much of the school garden. The garden and orchard were also expanded northward up a slight incline and overtop part of the old 1920s septic field.

By 1954, much of the site was in a state of decline. While the upper orchard and a garden plot to the southeast remained in use, most of the lower orchard was derelict scrub land, nearly devoid of trees.

---

[174] E.H. Tredcroft, Report re Construction of Sewage Disposal Plant at The Kamloops Industrial School. Department of the Interior, Dominion Water Power and Reclamation Service, Canada, 1926.

[175] W.C. Warren, Report on Suggested Repairs and Improvements to Sewage Disposal System, Kamloops Industrial School, Kamloops Agency. Dominion Water & Power Bureau, Vancouver, B.C., 1937.

During this time, rumours of a graveyard circulated amongst students. "There was [sic] rumours of a graveyard but nobody seemed to know where it was – we didn't even know if it was true. And there was a big orchard there and we used to make up stories about the graveyard being in the orchard," said Emma Baker, who attended KIRS from grade 9 to 12 approximately between 1950 and 1955. "Dig a hole, somebody's missing, dig a hole, somebody's missing," said Chief Michael LeBourdais, recounting a story told by his uncle, a KIRS student in the 1950s.

By 1957, sewage wastewater had been flowing to the orchard and garden for nearly twenty years. It was time for a safer and higher capacity solution to waste management.

From 1957 to 1958, more than 30% (100,000 square feet) of the orchard was excavated for a sewage lagoon – a pond for the settlement and breakdown of septic waste. A large sewer main was trenched through the orchard from the northwest, bypassing the 1920s and 30s sewage systems.[176]

It is worth noting that this work took place after the orchard was allegedly being used to conceal burials. No graves were discovered.

From 1957 to 1959, a new Indian Day School (classroom block) was constructed south of the old residential school, just above the orchard and garden.[177] Foundations were dug deep into the site. No graves were discovered.

During the 1960s, as in the preceding decade, rumours of a graveyard circulated amongst students: "We're going to go steal apples, and then one night, one of the guys says no, we shouldn't. That's where they're burying people," said Chief Harvey McLeod, who attended KIRS from 1966 to 1968.

---

[176] V.G. Ulrich, Completion Report re Kamloops Indian Residential School Sewage Lagoon, Kamloops Agency. Department of Citizenship and Immigration, Indian Affairs Branch, Vancouver, B.C., 1958.

[177] G.P. Nicholas, "Archaeological Investigations at Eerb–77: Summary of The 2002 Field Season," *Archaeological Research Reports* 7. Department of Archaeology, Secwepemc Cultural Education Society-Simon Fraser University Program, Kamloops, B.C., 2004.

By 1974, the orchard and garden were largely disused. With few trees remaining, the area was highly visible to nearby school buildings.

It is unclear when the alleged burials are supposed to have ceased. In 1970, land surrounding the school was reverted back to the Kamloops Band and the school finally closed in 1978.[178]

By 1998, the former apple orchard and garden had become part of the Secwepemc Museum and Heritage Park. Archaeologists from Simon Fraser University were on hand to monitor construction of park facilities, including a concession, washrooms, and various underground utilities. A back-hoe trench 4 feet wide x 5 feet deep and 260 feet long was dug through the orchard for a water line. At least one ancient pit feature, containing animal bones, shells and other artefacts was located about 2 feet below grade.[179] No graves were discovered.

In 2002, the Simon Fraser University Archaeology Field School undertook a significant excavation in the orchard. 15 shovel test pits were dug, followed by an excavation of about 20 feet wide x 50 feet long and 6 feet deep. An additional area of approximately 7 feet square by 5 feet deep was excavated to the southwest. Amongst other features, a very large shell midden was found throughout the dig area.[180] No graves were discovered.

Macabre stories of a juvenile tooth found in the apple orchard originate from this 2002 dig. A possible human tooth was indeed discovered amongst assorted animal remains in the southwest excavation.[181] However, the SFU archaeology department has since stated that the tooth is not human.[182]

---

[178] Ibid. (and ditto)

[179] G.P. Nicholas, "Archaeological Investigations at Eerb–77: A Deep Floodplain Site on the South Thompson River, Kamloops BC," Archaeological Research Reports 3 (1999). Department of Archaeology, Secwepemc Cultural Education Society-Simon Fraser University Program, Kamloops, B.C.

[180] G.P. Nicholas, Archaeological Investigations at Eerb–77: Summary of The 2002 Field Season. Archaeological Research Reports 7 (2004). Department of Archaeology, Secwepemc Cultural Education Society-Simon Fraser University Program, Kamloops, B.C.

[181] Ibid.

[182] Frances Widdowson, "Billy Remembers," The American Conservative. February 15, 2022.

Again in 2004, the Simon Fraser University Archaeology Field School conducted a dig in the orchard. Seven pits, 7 feet square and up to 10 feet deep were dug near the 2002 excavation.[183] No graves were discovered.

From 2005 to 2021, relatively little changed in the orchard. Aerial images reveal assorted park furniture and historical reconstructions coming and going, but no significant alterations to the land.

Since the rumours of a graveyard began, more than 30% of the orchard has been excavated. Archaeologists have been active on site since the 1980s, conducting excavations and monitoring construction work. Deep trenches have been cut straight across the orchard and a sewage lagoon was excavated from the entire southwestern quadrant. No graves have ever been discovered.

When Dr. Beaulieu used GPR to scan the orchard in May of 2021, she was scanning a site heavily disturbed by centuries of human activity. Nevertheless, Beaulieu confidently claimed that 215 "probable burials" had been discovered.

In July 2021, Dr. Beaulieu admitted that 15 "probable burials" were actually "archaeological impact assessments, as well as construction." Evidently, well documented site work was not accounted for in her initial survey.

Several of the remaining 200 "probable burials" overlap with a utilities trench dug in 1998, as can be seen in drone photography captured after the GPR survey. Still other "probable burials" follow the route of old roads or correlate suggestively with the pattern of previous plantings, furrows, and underground sewage disposal beds.

As of June 2023, Dr. Beaulieu has not released a detailed report of her findings and no "probable burials" have been confirmed through excavation.

"200 anomalies remain as targets of interest. These targets of interest are 'probable burials' as they demonstrate multiple GPR characteristics of

---

[183] G.P. Nicholas, SFU-SCES Kamloops Archaeology Field School. Biennial Report 2003/2004. Department of Archaeology, Simon Fraser University, Burnaby, B.C., 2004.

burials. Only forensic investigation (excavation) will be able to conclusively determine this." – Dr. Sarah Beaulieu

Given that the apple orchard is deeply textured by centuries of human activity, how can it be said that Dr. Beaulieu's targets are more "probably" graves than probably other features of human activity?

With more than 30% of the orchard already excavated, is it probable that a staggering 200 burials were missed?

"GPR is not necessary to know that children went missing in the Indian residential school contexts. The fact – the knowing – has been recognized by Indigenous communities for generations. Remote sensing, such as GPR, merely provides some spatial specificity to this truth." – Dr. Sarah Beaulieu

Sources

Nicholas, G.P. (1999) Archaeological Investigations at Eerb–77: A Deep Floodplain Site on the South Thompson River, Kamloops, B.C. *Archaeological Research Reports 3*. Department of Archaeology, Secwepemc Cultural Education Society-Simon Fraser University Program, Kamloops, BC.

Nicholas, G.P. (2004) SFU-SCES Kamloops Archaeology Field School. *Biennial Report 2003/2004*. Department of Archaeology, Simon Fraser University, Burnaby, BC.

E.H. Tredcroft, Report Re Construction of Sewage Disposal Plant at The Kamloops Industrial School. Department of the Interior, Dominion Water Power and Reclamation Service, Canada, 1926.

Warren W.C. 1939 Completion of Sludge Drying Basin. Dominion Water and Power Bureau, Vancouver, BC. https://heritage.canadiana.ca/view/oocihm.lac_reel_c15090/729

Webb C.E. 1939 Memorandum re Operation of Sewage System at Kamloops Indian School. Dominion Water and Power Bureau, Department of Mines and Resources, Vancouver, BC. https://heritage.canadiana.ca/view/oocihm.lac_reel_c15090/698

2004 Kamloops IRS School Narrative (point form). Government of Canada.

Quotations

Chief Harvey McLeod: CBC News.
Chief Michael LeBourdais: The Fifth Estate.
Dr. Sarah Beaulieu: APTN News.
Emma Baker: CTV News.

Image Sources

1890s School Photographs: National Centre for Truth and Reconciliation Archives.

1917 & 1918 Site Survey & Irrigation As-Built Drawing: National Centre for Truth and Reconciliation Archives.

1918 Irrigation Photographs: National Centre for Truth and Reconciliation Archives.

1928, 1948, 1974, 1999 and 2004 Aerial Images: Kamloops Through the Years.

1954 Aerial Image: National Air Photo Library. Natural Resources Canada.

1966 Aerial Image: Digital Air Photos of BC. Government of British Columbia.

Image Showing Targets of Interest #1: The Globe and Mail.

Image Showing Targets of Interest #2: The Fifth Estate.

Image Showing Targets of Interest #3: The Canadian Mass Grave Hoax, YouTube.

Chapter Three

Digging for the Truth about Canada's Residential School Graves

Hymie Rubenstein

"To me, mass graves indicate genocide. It's much more than cultural genocide. It's actually genocide. Indian children were killed. Indian children went missing. All of that truth will be revealed" — Eleanore Sunchild, Cree lawyer and member of the Thunderbird First Nation.[184]

"We had concentration camps here ... in Canada, in Saskatchewan—they were called Indian Residential Schools...We are seeing the result of the genocide Canada committed here. We will not stop until we find all of our children." — Chief Bobby Cameron of the Federation of Sovereign Indigenous First Nations in Saskatchewan.[185]

"If we say everything is a genocide, then nothing is a genocide." — Irwin Cotler, chair of the Raoul Wallenberg Centre for Human Rights and former Minister of Justice and Attorney General of Canada.[186]

On May 27, 2021, the Tk'emlúps te Secwépemc Indigenous band of Kamloops, British Columbia, issued a press statement of seismic implications, literally and figuratively.[187] A ground-penetrating radar survey of the area surrounding the city's former Indian Residential School (IRS), the band claimed, had located the "remains of 215 children who were students" of the school. Despite making explosive claims about "missing children" and "undocumented deaths," the band was also careful to add that, "At this time we have more questions than answers." Such a

---

[184] Jason Warick, "'It's time Canada started listening to survivors': Cree lawyer says B.C. discovery more evidence of genocide," CBC News, June 1, 2021.

[185] Tanya Talaga, "A call to Canadians: Help us find every burial site. Bring every lost Indigenous child home. Prove that you are who you claim to be," *Globe and Mail*, June 25, 2021.

[186] Evan Dyer, "What does it mean to call Canada's treatment of Indigenous women a 'genocide'?" CBC News, June 5, 2019.

[187] Tk'emlúps te Secwépemc, "For Immediate Release," May 27, 2021.

note of caution didn't stop the media, politicians and nearly everyone else from acting as if they had more answers than questions.

The Kamloops discovery became Canada's George Floyd moment. Almost instantly there were angry vigils, public displays of grief and shame, solidarity speeches and promises to revolutionize society as we know it. Flags on government buildings were lowered to half-mast on Canada Day, turning what was once a day of national celebration into one of national mourning and recrimination. The flags remained at half-staff for over five months. Statues of former Canadian heroes were defaced, destroyed or removed, alongside more demands to rename streets and public schools.[188] There were calls for yet another apology by the Roman Catholic Church.[189] Some Catholics even claimed to have lost their faith over the announcement,[190] as over 70 Christian churches of various denominations were vandalized or burned down both on and off Indigenous reserves.[191]

The furor attending the Kamloops discovery accelerated as subsequent findings were announced in other provinces, with the number of purportedly identified graves now exceeding 2,600.[192] Frequently heard among the many public demonstrations and outcries at these announcements was that they amounted to proof of a heretofore hidden Holocaust perpetrated by Canada against its Indigenous population.[193] The Kamloops school was alleged to have been a concentration camp and the now-revealed burials evidence of horrific crimes.[194]

---

[188] Tyler Dawson, "Remove, rename and cancel: A cross-country look at fallout from discovery of the Kamloops graves," *National Post*, June 11, 2021.

[189] Tom Yun, "Catholic community leaders call on Pope Francis to apologize for residential schools," CTV News, June 8, 2021.

[190] Bernadette Hardaker, "Amid shameful residential-school revelations, I cannot remain a Catholic," *Globe and Mail*, July 5, 2021.

[191] Cosmin Dzsurdzsa, "UPDATE: A map of the 71 churches that have been vandalized or burned since the residential schools announcement," True North News, January 16, 2023.

[192] "Canadian Indian residential school gravesites," Wikipedia, last revision June 29, 2023.

[193] Jorge Barrera, "Ottawa's move to block statistical reports on residential schools 'modern-day colonialism,' says survivors what makes it real,' says Holocaust scholar in response to judge's comments," CBC News, May 27, 2020.

[194] Tanya Talaga, "A call to Canadians," *Globe and Mail*, June 25, 2021.

Indigenous activist Robert Jago was particularly raw in his claims, writing in the National Post that, "It is not possible to look at the unmarked graves of 215 children that were uncovered on the grounds of the former Kamloops Residential School and deny the reality of Canada's attempt at the genocide of Indigenous peoples. That this was a crime against humanity, and that the residential schools were created with malign intent is as true a fact as gravity or the sun-rise." According to Jago, questioning the validity of his genocide allegations should be considered equivalent to "Holocaust denial" and punished as hate speech, a charge still being made.[195]

But we must be sure of our facts when making sweeping – especially inflammatory or condemnatory – statements. Innocent until proven guilty remains the presumption in this country, regardless of what many see as ongoing colonialism and white supremacy.

Such claims are not mere rhetorical flourishes. Many legal experts have since asserted that the Kamloops discovery and all other investigations into unmarked residential school burial grounds across the country should be treated as actual, live crime scenes. Following what she termed the "discovery of the bodies of 215 children," Beverly Jacobs, acting dean and law professor at the University of Windsor, demanded that any church or government in Canada involved with the residential school system be immediately charged with genocide by the International Criminal Court.[196]

Similarly, David Butt, a Toronto criminal lawyer writing in the *Globe and Mail,* claimed "The discovery of thousands of unmarked graves of Indigenous children on the sites of former residential schools...looks and smells like criminal activity, and so these events cry out for serious and sustained professional investigation — and, where warranted, vigorous prosecution."[197]

---

[195] Robert Jago, "Why accepting reality of residential school harms is necessary," *National Post*, June 5, 2021.

[196] Beverly Jacobs, "Indigenous lawyer: Investigate discovery of 215 children's graves in Kamloops as a crime against humanity," The Conversation, June 7, 2021.

[197] David Butt, "What would a criminal-justice response to the grim residential-school discoveries look like?" *Globe and Mail*, July 12, 2021.

Curiously, none of these claims of criminality were accompanied by cries for police assistance or any effort to exhume even a single grave to verify their physical credibility.

Just the Facts

Serious concern over these ongoing findings is certainly warranted. The discovery of any potential graves should be handled with the utmost attention, particularly so in the present case given Canada's fraught history with Indigenous people. But if we are to treat this country's involvement with residential schools as a criminal matter, then surely we ought to heed the fundamental rules inherent to our justice system and all police investigations. Anything less would diminish the significance of the situation and undermine the opportunity for justice to be done as well as seen to be done.

First, we must approach the matter with an open, unprejudiced mind. We must never take anything for granted. We must avoid a rush to judgment. We must check and double check the veracity of all claims. And above all, we must be sure of our facts when making sweeping – especially inflammatory or condemnatory – statements. Innocent until proven guilty remains the presumption in this country, regardless of what many see as ongoing colonialism and white supremacy.

Despite all the allegations of criminality, public discussion of residential schools in Canada – particularly that portion of the conversation led by legal experts — appears to have ignored all these crucial precepts of our justice system. Rather, a set of unproven and contentious claims has apparently been accepted as fact. According to a Maru Public Opinion survey of online panellists, 55 percent of Canadians polled agreed that "given the context of the residential school era, what occurred was an act of genocide as opposed to an act of good intentions that had bad outcomes." An astounding 81 percent said they agreed the International Criminal Court should investigate.[198]

That most Canadians accept a horrifying accusation of genocide based on evidence that even the initial provider admits raises "more questions than answers" suggests emotion bordering on hysterical vigilantism has gotten far ahead of the facts in this matter. If we are prepared to treat this as a criminal matter, then we should go where the facts lead us. So, what do we really know about those graves in Kamloops and elsewhere?

Mass vs. Unmarked Graves

The first claim requiring a fact check is that the Kamloops findings constitute a "mass grave," as Cree lawyer Eleanore Sunchild is quoted at the top of this story. For clarification, this term signifies that multiple bodies have been found in one large grave, pit or trench. Such terminology has been used repeatedly in describing the findings in Kamloops, including in influential newspapers such as the *Toronto Star*, *Washington Post* and *New York Times*.[199] It is categorically not true. "This is not a mass grave," Tk'emlúps te Secwépemc band chief Rosanne Casimir explained at a subsequent press conference on June 4, 2021.[200] Rather, it is a collection of unmarked individual graves. (While the *Toronto Star* and *Washington Post* corrected their articles, the *New York Times* has not.) The distinction between a mass grave and unmarked graves is enormous. A grave can be unmarked for any number of reasons, including events that occurred long after interment, as we shall soon see. Creating a mass grave, however, is always a deliberate act. At its most benign, a mass grave might be necessitated by public authorities dealing with a mass-casualty event, such

---

[198] John Wright, "Residential Schools and a Mass Grave: Profound Impact, Shifted Views, Genocide Label, and Call for an International Criminal Court Investigation," Maru Public Opinion Press Release, June 10, 2021.

[199] Mass impact from discovery of graves, Jenna Cocullo, *Toronto Star*, May 31, 2021; Amanda Coletta, "Remains of 215 Indigenous children discovered at former Canadian residential school site," *Washington Post*, May 28, 2021; Ian Austen, 'Horrible History': Mass Grave of Indigenous Children Reported in Canada," *New York Times*, May 28, 2021.

[200] "Kamloops discovery 'not a mass grave,' says Tkemlúps te Secwépemc Chief," True North Wire, June 4, 2021.

as a tsunami, fire, or pestilence, when there isn't time or resources to bury everyone individually before the bodies themselves become a public health hazard.

At other times, the reason behind a mass grave is far more sinister. As Candice Malcolm explained in a *True North* commentary, "Mass graves are a hallmark of genocide. They conjure images of pure evil ... Hitler, Stalin, Mao and Pol Pot. These were truly evil leaders who used mass graves to cover their atrocities and crimes against humanity." More recently, mass graves featured prominently in the Rwanda genocide and in areas of the Middle East briefly controlled by ISIS; the predominant image in these cases is of blindfolded victims lined up along the edge of a huge pit and falling in after being murdered. As Malcolm notes, "The use of the term mass graves [when speaking of Indian Residential Schools] is wrong, and it is reckless."[201] Quite so.

Given Malcolm's sensible words, it is incomprehensible that Chief Casimir would deliberately and falsely recant her June 4, 2021 declaration with a formal resolution at the 2021 annual general assembly of the Assembly of First Nations by sponsoring an "emergency resolution" that, "the mass grave discovered at the former Kamloops Indian Residential School reveals Crown conduct reflecting a pattern of genocide against Indigenous Peoples."[202]

---

[201] Candice Malcolm, "Six things the media got wrong about the graves found near Residential Schools," *True North*, July 12, 2021. Cf. C.P. Champion, "From Katyn to Kamloops," *Dorchester Review* online, June 17, 2021: clearly at the time Champion believed initial reports of "the location by radar scanning of the remains of an estimated 215 children," which he called "another grim image and reminder that much of the experience of native people in Canadian history has been tragic." He also insisted on the marked distinction between deaths by disease at IRS and the mass murder of Jews in the Holocaust or the Soviet murder of Polish officers dumped in mass graves found by the Germans at Katyn.

[202] AFN Draft Emergency Resolution 01/2021, "Demanding Justice and Accountability for the Missing and Unidentified Children of Residential Schools," Moved by Kukpi7 Rosanne Casimir, Tk'emlúps te Secwépemc, B.C. and seconded by Kukpi7 Judy Wilson, Neskonlith, B.C., AFN Annual General Assembly, July 6-8, 2021.

ASSEMBLY OF FIRST NATIONS 2021 AGA RESOLUTIONS UPDATE REPORT December 2021

01/ 2021 Demanding Justice and Accountability for the Missing and Unidentified

Children of Residential Schools

Mover: Kukpi7 Rosanne Casimir, Tk'emlúps te Secwépemc, B.C.

Seconder: Kukpi7 Judy Wilson, Neskonlith, B.C.

THEREFORE BE IT RESOLVED that the Chiefs-in-Assembly:

1. Stand in solidarity with the Tk'emlúps te Secwépemc and all survivors of the Residential School System and their families and assert that the mass grave discovered at the former Kamloops Indian Residential School reveals Crown conduct reflecting a pattern of genocide against Indigenous Peoples that must be thoroughly examined and considered in terms of Canada's potential breaches of international humanitarian and human rights law.

2. Fully support United Nations Resolution 60/ 147: "UN Basic Principles and Guidelines on the Right to a Remedy and Reparation for Victims of Gross Violations of International Human Rights Law and Serious Violations of International Humanitarian Law," and assert that there is serious evidence that Canada and the churches have violated international human rights and humanitarian law through the hiding, damaging, interfering with and destroying of mass graves and the concealment of records and archival material about the schools with an intent to delay or hide identification of the sites.

Unmarked but Not Unexpected

Another definitional issue involves claims or assumptions that these graves have been "discovered." Despite the fact the Kamloops and subsequent announcements caught many Canadians unawares, most of these grave sites cannot be considered discoveries as the word is properly defined. Some may have been abandoned or neglected, while others have continued to operate to the present day, with some graves going unmarked for various reasons. But even when unmarked or having fallen into disuse, they were almost always part of local knowledge.

The same holds true for the identification of 182 unmarked graves by a ground-penetrating radar survey near the former Kootenay Residential School close to Cranbrook, B.C. about a month after the Kamloops announcement. In response to media alarm about the event, Sophie Pierre, the former chief of the St. Mary's Band, noted patiently to all who would listen that "There's no discovery, we knew it was there, it's a graveyard. The fact there are graves inside a graveyard shouldn't be a surprise to anyone."[203]

In most cases it was the ravages of time rather than overt racism or any other nefarious reason that caused them to become unmarked.

The St. Eugene Mission school in Kootenay was established by Oblate missionaries who settled there in the early 19th century. As in many other places, a church and hospital were eventually built and the original cemetery became the graveyard for the entire local Catholic community. But this was no guarantee of permanency. As Chief Joe Pierre of the ʔaq'am, a neighbouring band in Cranbrook, explained, "Graves were traditionally marked with wooden crosses and this practice continues to this day in many Indigenous communities across Canada. Wooden crosses can deteriorate over time due to erosion or fire which can result in an

---

[203] Adam MacVicar, "'We knew it was there': Former B.C. chief says unmarked graves near Cranbrook need more context," Global News, July 1, 2021.

unmarked grave. These factors, among others, make it extremely difficult to establish whether these unmarked graves contain the remains of children who attended the St. Eugene Residential School."[204] The fact that wood rots is a natural occurrence, not a sign of malign intent.

Following sensational media claims regarding the Cowessess First Nation's "discovery of 751 unmarked graves" around the Marieval Residential School in Saskatchewan,[205] band member Irene Andreas on various Facebook pages, such as CTV Saskatoon, offered this explanation of what transpired over the years:

> Dear Folks,
>
> Our leaders today are addicted to media sensationalism. I can see how the Marieval graveyard news is causing a lot of heartbreak and emotional breakdowns. Please listen to your elderly folks as well.
>
> We respected the Church. We respected the dead. We buried our dead with a proper funeral. Then we allowed them to Rest In Peace...
>
> To assume that foul play took place would be premature and unsupported. There is no "discovery" of graves. All your elders have knowledge of every grave. The Band office has records from the Bishop's office, the Church board and from Cemetery workers who were in charge of digging graves and burials.
>
> The Band office received a list of over 750 registered burials from the Bishop's office. Information is being put out there that doesn't recognize these facts.

---

[204] "ʔaq 'am Statement on Discovery of Unmarked Graves," For Release, June 30, 2021.

[205] Brooke Taylor, "Cowessess First Nation says 751 unmarked graves found near former Sask. residential school," CTV News, June 24, 2021.

So please, people, do not make up stories about residential school children being put in unmarked graves. No such thing ever happened.[206]

Who Rests Here?

Many commentators have further rashly assumed that every true grave uncovered on the grounds of a residential school represents the death of an attending student.[207] While this might seem likely, even logical, there is ample evidence suggesting it is not always the case. Regarding the St. Eugene Mission school in Kootenay, it is believed that the cemetery also contains the remains of the members of five neighbouring bands. As Sophie Pierre explains, "to just assume that every unmarked grave inside a graveyard is already tied to a residential school, we've got to be a little bit more respectful of our people who are buried in our graveyards."[208]

According to Jon Z. Lerat, a Cowessess band councillor, neither do all the graves at Saskatchewan's Marieval site contain the remains of Indigenous schoolchildren, as it too was used as a cemetery by the local municipality. After the announcement of the 751 unmarked graves, Lerat told the *Globe and Mail,* "We did have a family of non-Indigenous people show up today and notified us that some of those unmarked graves had their families in them."[209]

It should be remembered that residential schools were often part of a small and self-contained religious community. And in such cases, everyone within the community would likely be interred in the same graveyard. According to research by archaeologist Dr. Scott Hamilton of Lakehead

---

[206] Mark Bonokowski, "Hypocrite Trudeau adds a weak 'mea culpa' to his list," *Toronto Sun,* October 19, 2021.

[207] David MacDonald, "Canada's hypocrisy: Recognizing genocide except its own against Indigenous peoples," The Conversation, June 4, 2021.

[208] Adam MacVicar, "'We knew it was there'" Global News, July 1, 2021.

[209] Canadian Press, "Cowessess First Nation places solar lights to illuminate 751 unmarked graves at former residential school site," *Globe and Mail,* June 26, 2021.

University prepared for the Truth and Reconciliation Commission, "The cemetery at the Roman Catholic St. Mary's Mission [near Mission, B.C.], was intended originally for priests and nuns from the mission as well as students from the residential school. Three Oblate bishops were buried there along with settlers, their descendants, and residential students."[210]

That students were given the same treatment in death as bishops speaks of respect, not neglect.

What Lies Here?

The absence of any exhumation is said to reflect the belief that Indigenous burying grounds are considered sacred places, and therefore only Indigenous people should be involved in reserve mortuary issues despite all funding for such efforts coming from Canada's taxpayers.

But sacredness also applies to the cemeteries of other ethnic and racial groups along with the need to account for public spending, so this assertion smacks of special privilege.

Moreover, given that allegations of murder, even genocide, occurring at the Kamloops IRS have been bandied about for decades, it is passing strange why the band would resist a forensic examination of the alleged graves.

Conversely, if these were fresh burials based on firsthand witness accounts, is there any doubt that the band would have immediately demanded the RCMP carry out a thorough examination, the alleged sacredness of the area be damned?

Precisely this demand is now occurring in Winnipeg with Indigenous family members, leaders, activists, and media loudly demanding for months that a detailed search be carried out of the four-acre Winnipeg Prairie Green private landfill where the bodies of Morgan Harris, 39, and Marcedes Myran, 26, two missing Indigenous women, are suspected of having been recently buried. Both are presumed to be victims of the same

---

[210] Scott Hamilton, "Where Are the Children Buried?" National Centre for Truth and Reconciliation, NCTR.com, uploaded April 2021, p. 22.

attacker.[211] Such a search would take three years and cost as much as $184 million. (The effort would also present substantial risks for potential searchers given the hazardous materials buried in that location.)

By way of contrast, why have Kamloops band officials and residents not demanded even a minimally invasive investigation technique like "core sampling" at the presumptive burial site to quickly, safely, respectfully, and conclusively determine the contents of a single inconclusive radar hit?

Could the answer be that Kamloops officials fear that these GPR-detected soil disturbances don't represent the presence of any human remains?

Elementary logic alone suggests that it is reasonable to hypothesize that Kamloops band officials are reluctant to dig up the abandoned apple orchard beside the long-shuttered school where these children are said to be buried because they suspect no bodies — "missing" or not — will be found. Three excavations already undertaken — the Shubenacadie IRS, the Battleford Industrial School, and the Camsell Hospital site — have either produced negative results, confirmed that the bodies found were properly buried IRS students, or predated the IRS system.

Seen from the perspective of the Kamloops band, it might be far more prudent to keep this an enduring mystery rather than risk being exposed as supporting what some have called the great Canadian burial hoax.

What the Historical Record Reveals

To address the contents of the putative gravesites requires the transfer of attention from official mainstream-sanctioned unknowns to the growing body of unofficial but thoroughly documented evidence gathered since June 2021. None of this contrarian data, carefully collected, compiled, and published by impartial investigators with no financial or other stake in

---

211 Sarah Petz, "Chiefs, families push for search for remains at Winnipeg landfill that could take years, cost up to $184M" CBC News, May 12, 2023; Nathan Liewicki, "Forensic expert believes remains of missing women can be found at landfill near Winnipeg" CBC News, December 7, 2022.

keeping the story of thousands of "missing children" alive supports the legacy media and political narratives.

Data for the dozens of IRSs with students listed as missing was painstakingly collected by intrepid researcher Nina Green.[212] They prove that nearly all 51 students missing from the Kamloops IRS were buried in named cemeteries on their home reserves. Accordingly, few could have been buried in some "secret cemetery" in a former apple orchard, leaving the identity and fate of the others a mystery.

Green communicated all these data long ago to the relevant parties: the media, provincial and federal politicians, Indigenous leaders and activists, and academics focusing on Aboriginal issues. Only a couple bothered to acknowledge receipt of this critical material.

So, who or what is buried in the apple orchard?

"Who" could be people who died before the school opened in 1890, since no missing children were listed for the following period. It is surely conceivable that some of these pre-1890 corpses may have been murder victims, but there is no authenticated case of a homicide at the Kamloops IRS during its entire 88-year history. Not one.

As for the accusation that murdered children were buried in the apple orchard in the dead of night, once more elementary logic — as opposed to Indigenous folktales — says that this was inconceivable. The school is not in some remote part of the province; it has always employed band members; the apple orchard is located within eyesight just across the Thompson River from the city of Kamloops; and the school always saw a daily stream of visiting parents and dignitaries, tradespeople, school inspectors, and other parties. How could 215 children have been secretly buried with the whole of Kamloops and the entire Kamloops Band turning a blind eye?

"What" is undoubtedly the likely determiner. It suggests that the remains of dead animals, neatly-spaced apple tree stumps, and debris from various construction projects, including the laying of sewage tiles in the late 1930s

---

[212] "Death Records," Indian Residential Schools Records online, https://indianresidentialschoolrecords.com

in the exact place that newly-placed burial markers now appear, are what was revealed by the GPR probe.[213]

There is other indirect evidence as well. No named Indigenous relatives on the Kamloops reserve — or elsewhere in Canada — are frantically looking for a named but missing IRS child. This is because all students required signed applications to attend the IRS schools and were minutely followed in Quarterly Reports from entry to exit. Without such records, the schools could not receive operating funds from the Department of Indian Affairs.

Thousands more "missing children" could easily be found where their final resting place is bureaucratically buried, namely in carefully preserved school, church, and government records. This would only happen if the relevant parties —Indigenous activists, band leaders, and family members — showed any interest in doing so.

So far, these parties prefer to support fruitless GPR studies that have not turned up a single "missing" body, evidence they are pursuing a far different agenda, one rooted in the mantra "At this time we have more questions than answers."

Canada's Other Unmarked Graves

Unmarked graves are much more common in this country than most Canadians apparently assume. It is impossible to know how many people of all races and ethnicities who died a century or more ago did not have their final resting place marked in any permanent way, but the number is no doubt substantial.

Consider Kamloops' Pioneer Cemetery. This graveyard contains the remains of the early, mostly white, residents of the town dating from 1876 to 1901. Despite its significance, it has long since fallen into disrepair. Local historian Ken Favrholdt writes of the long struggle to maintain this plot of land: "Subscriptions were taken for the upkeep of the cemetery, but

---

[213] "Graves in the Apple Orchard," anonymous WordPress blog, undated. See chapter with the same title in this volume.

over the years it became overgrown, derelict and vandalized. Headstones were toppled...The area became used as a baseball park in 1949."[214]

While not every old cemetery will suffer the indignity of becoming a sports field, there are hundreds, perhaps thousands, of similar pioneer cemeteries throughout rural Canada that have been similarly neglected. Paupers' cemeteries, in which individual graves are not marked, can also be found across the country.[215] And GPR surveys of the areas around former federal penitentiaries and jails would likely reveal many more unmarked or forgotten graves of inmates as well.[216]

Then there is the heartbreaking story of the British Home Children, some 100,000 offspring of destitute parents sent to Canada between 1869 and 1948 to work as indentured servants for farm families in rural areas.[217] Many, perhaps most, were sent to Canada without their parents' consent and lived in often terrible conditions, sometimes including physical or sexual abuse.[218] Their last humiliation was to be buried in unmarked plots.[219] Many of these have only recently and privately been commemorated.[220]

---

[214] Ken Favrholdt, "Kamloops History: The cemeteries of Kamloops and Tk'emlups," *Kamloops This Week,* November 17, 2020.

[215] Steve Arstad, "The lost graves of Penticton's Lakeview Cemetery," *Penticton News*, November 11, 2016.

[216] Neetu Garcha, "In New Westminster, there's a 'forgotten' cemetery where rest the souls of some 'evil' inmates," Global News, June 21, 2018; Adam Mayers, "No secret where bodies are buried," *Toronto Star*, October 8, 2007.

[217] "Home Children, 1869-1932," Library and Archives Canada.

[218] Mark Gollom, "'It's like they never existed': Toronto monument will honour mistreated British Home Children," CBC News, October 1, 2017.

[219] Cynthia Reason, "British Home Children monument unveiled at Toronto's Park Lawn Cemetery," *Etobicoke Guardian*, October 2, 2017; updated May 5, 2023.

[220] "Canadians not interested in 'home children' apology: Minister," Toronto Star, November 16, 2009.

Even worse is the fate of tens of thousands of unknown,[221] unmarked or poorly maintained graves containing the remains of Canadian soldiers of multiple races and ethnicities who lost their lives in two world wars,[222] and today lie anonymous and alone in Canada and around the world despite having paid the ultimate price for their country.[223]

Finally, it must also be acknowledged that permanently marking graves is not a traditional Indigenous practice. Pre-contact funerary practices among Aboriginals in what is now Canada typically involved interring the dead with their personal belongings to ensure a safe passage into the spirit world. Depending on the group, this could involve drying and embalming the remains, burying bodies in a sitting position, marking them with red ochre, and placing the remains in middens, earthen mounds, stone cairns, or above ground on platforms or in trees.[224]

Today, most of these traditional burial sites are unknown and, if newly rediscovered, would have to be regarded as unmarked graves. When Indigenous people voluntarily converted to Christianity in the early colonial period, they adopted European burial habits, which emphasize maintaining recognition and protection of the site, while retaining many of their traditional beliefs about the hereafter.

Recognizing the multiple realities of unmarked graves throughout Canada does not mean we should ignore or downplay the significance of finding unmarked graves around former IRSs. All graves should matter. But the vast number of unmarked non-Indigenous graves across this country suggests caution should be exercised before declaring the discovery of unmarked graves near residential schools to be conclusive evidence of

---

221 Canadian Centre for the Great War, "The Lost: Canadian Soldiers Missing in the First World War," Vimy Foundation, February 17, 2017.

222 Canadian Press, "Tens of thousands of veterans buried in unmarked graves," CTV News, November 8, 2011.

223 Lee Berthiaume, "Graves of 45,000 veterans in disrepair due to funding shortfall," Canadian Press, July 17, 2017.

224 Kathryn McKay, "Recycling the Soul: Death and the Continuity of Life in Coast Salish Burial Practices," Master's Thesis, University of Victoria, 1999; "Tree Burials at Tsaxis," *Northwest Coast Archeology* online, January 24, 2010.

systemic racism or criminality – much less that a campaign of genocide was underway.

The Rules for Identifying Genocide

For Canadians who believe in the inherent fairness and goodness of their country, no accusation arising from the Kamloops discovery is as painful as the allegation of genocide. It is the worst crime any country or people can commit. Lately, however, it has been thrown around with the frequency of a schoolyard insult. But words should mean something, and the meaning of genocide is very specific.

The universally accepted means for determining the existence of genocide comes from the United Nations 1948 Convention on the Prevention and Punishment of the Crime of Genocide.[225] It set a rigorous standard with clear definitions. Article 2 states that genocide means any of the following acts committed with *intent* to destroy, in whole or in part, a national, ethnical, racial or religious group: killing members of the group; causing serious bodily or mental harm to members of the group; deliberately inflicting on the group conditions of life calculated to bring about its physical destruction in whole or in part; imposing measures intended to prevent births within the group; or forcibly transferring children of the group to another group.

Though the issue of "forcible transfers" is dealt with below it is important to clearly recognize here the salience of "intent." According to the UN Convention's formal post-1948 commentary, "To constitute genocide, there must be a proven intent on the part of perpetrators to physically destroy a national, ethnical, racial or religious group. Cultural destruction does not suffice."[226]

---

[225] Convention on the Prevention and Punishment of the Crime of Genocide, Dec. 9 1948, S. Exec. Doc. O, 81-1 (1949), 78 U.N.T.S. 277

[226] Genocide Convention Fact Sheet, Website of the Office on Genocide Prevention and the Responsibility to Protect, United Nations.

It is because of the specificity concerning intent and cultural destruction that Canada's Truth and Reconciliation Commission's Final Report, issued in 2015, could not declare the residential school experience a genocide. Instead, it employed the inflammatory but slippery concept of "cultural genocide," a phrase with no accepted legal standing. Despite this, many commentators have chosen to drop the adjective "cultural" and claim the residential school system was genocidal regardless.

But it is impossible to compare the experience of Canada's residential schools students with the well-documented genocides perpetrated against other people such as the European Jews, the Tutsi of Rwanda, or the Armenians of the Ottoman (Turkish) Empire.[227] Recall that the Turks brought about the deaths of approximately one million Armenians between 1915 and 1917, while in Rwanda between 500,000 and 800,000 Tutsi were slaughtered, often with machetes, in the astonishingly short period of less than 100 days beginning on April 7, 1994.

Confected academic efforts to liken Canada's experience to these horrific examples of rampant slaughter and bloodshed do great harm to the fundamental meaning of genocide,[228] as former federal Justice Minister Irwin Cotler, cited at the beginning of this chapter, has warned. Consider also that there has not been a single verified murder of a child at any Indian Residential School throughout the system's long history.

Given the importance of intent in identifying a genocide, it is also necessary to contemplate the broader sweep of Canadian policy towards its Indigenous peoples. Had the federal government truly formed an intent to wipe out Canada's Aboriginal population, such a terrible thing would have been relatively simple to implement. Yet the government often acted with the best interests of the native population in mind, even if the outcomes were not always ideal.

Consider, for example, that Sir John A. Macdonald, as prime minister, quadrupled Ottawa's native budget to deal with the crippling Western

---

[227] "Rwanda genocide: 100 days of slaughter," BBC News, April 4, 2019; "The Armenian genocide (1915-16): An Overview," *Holocaust Encyclopedia*, United States Holocaust Memorial Museum website.

[228] Andrew Woolford, "Genocide definition always shifting," Winnipeg Free Press, June 12, 2019.

famine in the early 1880s.[229] This event was caused by the collapse of the Prairie bison herds, an outcome over which Canada had no control; nonetheless, Macdonald mustered substantial government resources to meet the challenge. If his critics today claim he did too little,[230] they cannot argue that he did nothing. Consider also that Ottawa successfully vaccinated almost the entire native community against smallpox at great expense and effort, virtually wiping out this highly contagious killer among a people with no natural immunity to the disease.[231] If the federal government had truly wanted to rid Canada of its Indigenous people, it would not have fed or vaccinated them.

The Limitations of Ground-Penetrating Radar

The recent application of GPR to the search for unmarked graves has lent a scientific imprimatur to what was once a matter of oral and archival history. No doubt this has played a significant role in boosting the credibility of current claims made regarding criminality at residential schools. Yet we must be careful to avoid a false sense of precision based on this technology's appearance.

It is important to understand that GPR can only determine the presence of disturbed soil. It can't identify bodies, let alone count them, determine their age at death or answer the question of whether the bodies were "dumped" or given a proper burial. As Kisha Supernant of the Department of Anthropology at the University of Alberta explained to the *National Post*, "When a grave is dug, there is a grave shaft dug and the body is placed in the grave, sometimes in a coffin, as in the Christian burial

---

[229] Greg Piasetzki, "Sir John A. Macdonald Saved More Native Lives Than Any Other Prime Minister," C2C Journal, November 27, 2020.

[230] James Daschuk, *Clearing the Plains: Disease, Politics of Starvation, and the Loss of Aboriginal Life* (University of Regina Press, 2013).

[231] Peter Shawn Taylor and Greg Piasetzki, "The 19th-century Indigenous policy success story we've forgotten," *National Post*, Mar 28, 2019; William B. Spaulding, "Smallpox in Canada," *Canadian Encyclopedia*.

context. What the ground-penetrating radar can see is where that pit itself was dug, because the soil actually changes when you dig a grave."[232]

That is all it can do. As Supernant notes, the technology "doesn't actually see the bodies. It's not like an X-ray." Moreover, the technology cannot even discern organic matter, human or otherwise. News of this technological limitation likely comes as a surprise to the many legal experts, such as the University of Windsor's Jacobs, who rashly claimed "bodies" had been found.

A proper appreciation of ground-penetrating radar's actual abilities has led experts to clarify initial allegations made to and by the media. What was first reported as the "remains" of 215 children in Kamloops was later revised downward to 200 "probable burials" or "targets of interest" according to Sarah Beaulieu, the University of the Fraser Valley professor and ground-penetrating radar specialist who initially conducted the survey. Beaulieu cautioned about "multiple signatures that present like burials," but "we do need to say that they are probable, until one excavates."[233]

Beaulieu's investigation has so far covered two acres, or about one percent of the total 160-acre grounds of the Kamloops Residential School over a period of four days.[234] The remaining area will clearly take much longer to fully survey. Excavation of any individual suspected graves and the forensic analysis of the results could take several years.

A Lengthy and Time-Consuming Process Awaits

It should now be clear that many of the questions posed by the finding of residential school graves have not yet been answered. Uncovering the truth will be a time-consuming process. And as that unfolds, all parties involved

---

[232] Tyler Dawson, "How ground-penetrating radar is used to uncover unmarked graves," *National Post*, May 31, 2021.

[233] Michael Potestio, "Number of probable graves near former residential school pegged at 200," *Kamloops This Week*, July 16, 2021.

[234] Kendra Mangione, "Still 65 hectares to be surveyed at Kamloops residential school before total number of unmarked graves is known," CTV News, July 15, 2021.

must be expected to abide by the basic rules of justice to ensure that a comprehensive, independent, scientific, and unbiased investigation can be conducted. But there are reasons to worry that this may not be allowed to occur.

Consider criticism of the RCMP's involvement in the Kamloops discovery made by Murray Sinclair, the former chair of the Truth and Reconciliation Commission.[235] Sinclair claims the officers' habit of interviewing survey participants was "intimidating." According to the CBC, Sinclair said the Mounties should "not be pursuing those who are revealing information," such as researchers. Yet such inquiries are necessary to properly separate factual truth from speculation, exaggeration, or error (like the use of "mass graves").

Former Assembly of First Nations National Chief Perry Bellegarde has similarly argued that, "this [looking into the burials]... is spiritual work. It has to be done properly."[236] Bellegarde has not defined what he means by "done properly," although high-profile *Globe and Mail* columnist Tanya Talaga offers a clue. Talaga, a vocal proponent of the idea that the operation of residential schools was genocidal, recently argued that "The federal government or any colonial entity cannot be put in charge of how this recovery process is going to look ... Government bureaucrats can be nowhere near this."[237]

Declaring police, government, and other trusted fact-finding institutions off-limits from any investigation into the residential school burial issue is highly problematic. The principles of natural justice suggest that victims can never be allowed to control any criminal investigation, regardless of how much sympathy they may engender. All Canadians deserve to participate in the search for truth, particular given the serious allegations of genocide and other misdeeds made against our whole country.

---

[235] "RCMP investigating former residential school site in Kamloops, B.C.," CBC News, June 03, 2021.

[236] Kristy Kirkup, "Kamloops residential school has woken up world to 'genocide' in Canada, Bellegarde says," *Globe and Mail*, June 20, 2021.

[237] Tanya Talaga, "Indigenous peoples must lead the effort to recover residential school children," *Globe and Mail*, July 29, 2021.

And until we know more, commentators should abjure volatile language such as "genocide" and cease trivializing terms like "the Holocaust." With Canada's reputation as a law-abiding and peaceable country now in question, it is imperative that no limitations be placed on who can participate in this investigation, what questions they can ask, and where they can go for answers. We are all party to this case.

What We Do Know

As we await the outcome of a full, proper, and no doubt time-consuming investigation, Canadians should take the time to better educate themselves about what we *do* know about the history of Canada's residential schools. Much of that comes from the work of the Truth and Reconciliation Commission and other verifiable aspects of Canada's historical record.

To reach a fuller understanding of the meaning and significance of the unmarked graves – something all Canadians no doubt desire – will require a thorough forensic investigation of the gravesites and likely take many years. Significantly, this important process may be further delayed or even rendered impossible because the cemeteries have been declared sacred ground by some Indigenous leaders and elders,[238] a slippery claim given that there is little or nothing that is not today considered sacred by Indigenous people, including all life forms. If everything in the world is sacred, the word becomes meaningless.

As we wait for this uncertain process to unfold, there is still a lot we *do* know about the residential school system and its unmarked graves that can offer valuable context to the current debate. Despite frustrating gaps, enough information exists to clarify several crucial and contentious issues of public debate. Of special relevance in this search is the paper prepared for the TRC on unmarked graves by the already mentioned Dr. Scott Hamilton. His report is notable for its nuanced approach to the subject and ample use of statistics.[239]

---

[238] Guy Quenneville, "First Nations invite public to witness weekend search for unmarked graves at Sask. residential school site," CBC News, July 16, 2021.

[239] Hamilton, "Where Are the Children Buried?" loc. cit.

Canada's larger historical record also contains a wide array of archival evidence, in academic journals and original federal government source material, that can provide a fuller understanding of this difficult issue. The question of how and why Indigenous residential school children died, and how their deaths were reported and treated, is inextricably linked to the broader question of attendance. How many students were taught at residential schools and under what circumstances? The answers to these questions, in turn, are critical to unravelling the most contentious question of all: what was the core intention behind the residential school program itself?

The Accusations

One of the most frequently repeated criticisms of Canada's residential school system is that nearly all Aboriginal children attended such a school. In a 2010 speech to the United Nations, for example, former TRC chair Murray Sinclair asserted that, "For roughly seven generations nearly every Indigenous child in Canada was sent to a residential school."[240] Further, it is often claimed that many or all these students were there against their will. As part of its coverage of the graves issue, the *National Post* printed a Reuters report stating that, "For 165 years and as recently as 1996, the schools forcibly separated Indigenous children from their families, subjecting them to malnourishment and physical and sexual abuse."[241]

The notion that "nearly every" native child was taken from their parents and sent to a residential school where they experienced numerous horrors has become the accepted backstory to the residential school graves debate and plays a foundational role in current accusations of genocide. Given that "forcibly transferring children of the [persecuted] group to another group" is a recognized form of genocide under the Genocide Convention, a comprehensive and intentional plan to *permanently* remove all native

---

[240] "For the child taken, for the parent left behind," Speech by Chairperson, the Honourable Justice Murray Sinclair, Truth and Reconciliation Commission of Canada, 9th Session of the United Nations Permanent Forum on Indigenous Issues, United Nations, New York, April 27, 2010.

[241] "Statues of Queen Victoria, Queen Elizabeth II toppled in Canada," Reuters, July 2, 2021.

children from their parents and place them in boarding schools might approach this definition. But did such a thing occur?

A bit of history is in order. Residential or boarding schools for native children in Canada date back to 17th century New France (what later became Quebec). The opening of the Mohawk Industrial School in Brantford, Ontario in 1831 by the Anglican Church of Canada is sometimes considered the origin of the Canadian Aboriginal boarding schooling system; at the time of Confederation in 1867, there were 51 schools for natives in Canada, most of which were operated and paid for by churches. In 1883 the federal government agreed to fund three religious residential schools in Western Canada — a policy considered by some scholars to mark the beginning of Canada's formal government-run residential school system.

Regardless of the start date, it is important to note that these schools were initially created at the express request of Indigenous leaders who wished to secure a formal English-language education for their people. In fact, a federal requirement to provide education was a key component of the numbered treaties covering Western and Northern Canada. The following excerpt from Treaty 3, concluded in 1873, is typical: "Her Majesty agrees to maintain schools for instruction in such reserves hereby made as to her Government of Her Dominion of Canada may seem advisable whenever the Indians of the reserve shall desire it."

During his 1881 tour of Western Canada, Governor-General John Douglas Sutherland Campbell, the Marquess of Lorne, met with Indigenous chiefs who made repeated requests for better education. Dakota Chief Standing Buffalo asked, "Please give me a Church on my Reserve for I want to live like the white people." Cree Chief John Smith had a similar plea: "I want a teacher to learn the English language and to teach it to my children."[242]

The federal government responded to these demands with an educational system delivered by religious groups that provided basic reading and writing skills and had as its overarching goal the assimilation of Indigenous children into Western society. However objectionable we may

---

[242] J.R. Miller, *Shingwauk's Vision: A History of Native Residential Schools* (University of Toronto Press, 1996,).

find such an integrationist policy today, children were only sent to residential boarding schools when it was impractical to provide a local, on-reserve day school. As Scott Hamilton's report on unmarked graves acknowledges, "In many isolated communities with insufficient numbers to justify a day school, there was no alternative to enrolment in a residential school."[243]

Residential Schools Versus Day Schools

The TRC presented Canadians with the rough, unsourced estimate that 150,000 Indigenous students attended residential schools throughout the system's lifetime. This number now dominates public discourse. And while it is clear conditions in some residential schools were difficult, with many students reporting physical or sexual abuse to the TRC, it is equally clear that *many more* students attended day schools than residential schools, where allegations of such treatment are far rarer.

According to equally rough federal government estimates,[244] approximately 200,000 Indigenous students attended day schools after 1920, a figure that exceeds that of residential school students. United Church researcher John Siebert,[245] who spent six years digging into the church's archival records and government reports, offered a bit more precision. Siebert calculated that between 1890 and 1965 an average of 7,100 students attended residential schools annually, while 11,400 were educated at reserve-based day schools. This amounts to a 38/62 percent split. These figures are bolstered by data on the number of schools themselves. For example, in 1924 the Methodist Church, prior to merging with the Presbyterian Church to become the United Church, reported operating 11 residential schools and 39 day schools.[246]

---

[243] Hamilton, pp. 8-9.

[244] "Federal Indian Day School settlement claims process now open," News release, Crown-Indigenous Relations and Northern Affairs Canada, January 13, 2020.

[245] Richard Foot, "Researcher defends residential schools," *National Post*, March 17, 2001.

[246] "List of Indian residential schools in Canada," *Wikipedia*, last modified June 2, 2023.

Although they do not provide a comprehensive total figure, annual reports from the Department of Indian Affairs offer important evidence on the relative significance of day schools and residential schools on a yearly basis as federal government policy towards native education evolved. Up to 1920, most native students were enrolled in day schools.[247] Out of total enrolment of 12,196 in 1920, over 60 percent (7,477) were in day schools and the remainder (4,719) in residential or industrial boarding schools. (See page 15 of the source document.)

Over the next decade, the relative importance of residential schools grew, peaking in 1934.[248] Even in that year, however, only 46 percent of all Indigenous students were enrolled in a residential school; 53 percent were in day schools and one percent at provincial public schools. (also on p. 15.) Thus, even at its apex, the residential school system never housed most native students. By 1950 this tide had ebbed and 60 percent of all students were in day schools, with only 39 percent in residential schools and one percent in provincial public schools.[249]

Despite a frustrating lack of comprehensive school enrollment figures covering the entire period of federally-provided Indigenous education, it is obvious that residential schools always constituted a minority – and sometimes a small minority – of Aboriginal schoolchildren. And while the federal government has also apologized for and compensated former students of day schools, it is impossible to argue these numerically-dominant day schools constituted "forcible removal" or any type of "genocide," given that the students lived with their parents while in school.

[247] Annual Report, 1921. Dominion of Canada Department of Indian Affairs Annual Report for the Year Ended March 31, 1920, Library and Archives Canada, p. 126.

[248] Annual Report, 1934, pp. 81, 128. In 1934, 8,596 of the 23,573 school-age status Indian children, or 36.47%, were enrolled in residential schools.

[249] Annual Report, 1951, p. 17.

How Compulsory Was Compulsory Education?

It has also become common for commentators to claim that residential schools were akin to concentration camps.[250] This is a horrific charge that, if true, would bolster claims of genocide.

If not, it is a vicious calumny. Like genocide, the term concentration camp entails many negative connotations, including varying forms and degrees of neglect and/or deliberate abuse such as malnourishment or forced labour.[251]

Of course, the first requirement of any concentration camp is forcible confinement. Yet during the first several decades of native education, attendance at both day and residential schools was entirely voluntary and extremely modest. Sir John A. Macdonald, Canada's first prime minister, strongly opposed compulsory education for Indigenous people, even though children in Ontario had been required to attend public school through Grade 6 since 1871.[252] (In fact, some native bands during this time, such as the Mississaugas of the Credit River, imposed compulsory education requirements on their own membership.[253]

In 1920, 29 years after Macdonald's death, an amendment to the Indian Act gave the federal government the authority to send school-aged Indigenous children to either a day or residential school. As Volume Four of the TRC observes, "the 1920 amendment did not make residential schooling

---

[250] Richard Kool, "Is this Canada's Holocaust moment?" Victoria Times-Colonist, June 12, 2021; J.J. McCullough, "Canada is putting Indian residential schools at the center of its identity. Here's how it could change us," *Washington Post*, July 6, 2021.

[251] "Concentration Camps 1933-39," *Holocaust Encyclopedia*, United States Holocaust Memorial Museum website.

[252] Mark Woloshen, Ruth Sandwell, "Compulsory schooling in Ontario: 1871," *Snapshots of 19th Century Canada*, The Critical Thinking Cooperative and Ministry of Education, British Columbia, 2002, , p. 87.

[253] Annual Report, 1899, p. 50.

compulsory for all First Nations children." It only required they attend some form of schooling.[254]

A comparison of the 1920 and 1925 annual reports from the federal Department of Indian Affairs and federal census figures is instructive as to the effect compulsory education had on enrolment and attendance.

In 1920, as discussed above, Indigenous school enrolment was 12,196. This constituted 72 percent of the entire native population aged six to 15, as per the most recent census.

By 1925, when compulsory education was firmly established, the school-age native population had grown to 20,242 and school enrolment was 14,222, for a total enrolment rate of 70 percent — less than it had been in 1920.[255] Similar figures hold for later years. A careful review of the data reveals that the requirement of compulsory education had no visible impact on enrolment rates. This suggests parents held far more sway over whether their children went to school or not than is commonly accepted.

Federal statistics also reveal that actual day-to-day attendance was only a fraction of the total number of enrolled students, further undermining claims that compulsory attendance laws had any impact on showing up for class. In the 1920 school year, the final term prior to the imposition of compulsory education, in-class attendance across all schools was 7,629 out of 12,196 enrolled, for an attendance rate of approximately 62 percent. Further, the nationwide drop-out rate between Grades 1 and 2 was 64 percent. Of the 65 children attending the now notorious Kamloops Indian Residential School in 1920, 24 were in Grade 1 and just 10 were in Grade 2.

By 1925, the attendance rate had improved slightly to 69 percent. But the national drop-out rate was still greater than 50 percent. Actual attendance in Grade 1 was 6,251; in Grade 2 it was just 2,707. The evidence thus shows most students spent only a year or two in school. In 1955, 35 years

---

[254] Annual Report, 1921. Cf. Sharon Helen Venne, Indian Acts and Amendments 1868-1975, An Indexed Collection, (University of Saskatchewan Native Law Centre, 1981), p. 247, cited by Nina Green, "Two-Thirds Did Not Attend," *The Dorchester Review*, Vol. 12, No. 2, Autumn-Winter 2022, pp. 73-74, n. 18.

[255] Annual report, 1925.

after the imposition of compulsory attendance, the drop-out rate across the country between Grade 1 and Grade 2 was still nearly 50 percent.[256] (Although in that year Ottawa noted with some pride that it employed 63 "status Indians" as teachers in native schools.)

It can also be stated with reasonable confidence that quite a few native children had no schooling at all, belying claims of compulsory education. Academic research into attendance in native schools in B.C. cites a 1961 survey of British Columbia reserves that found one-third of natives aged 45 or older had never attended a formal school.[257] Researcher Siebert similarly calculated that between 1900 and 1950, 15 percent to 20 percent of natives nationwide did not attend any school.

This is not to deny that some children *were* forced to attend a residential school, many of which were located far from their homes.

A 2011 RCMP report on the force's involvement in residential schools shows the police service did play a role in apprehending runaways and enforcing attendance in the face of parental opposition, but this appears to have been a very minor one based on the few anecdotes provided.[258] Further, by the 1940s most of the children required to attend a residential school were there for social welfare reasons, such as the death or incapacity of a parent. They had nowhere else to go.

It is somewhat disappointing that despite six years of investigation and a $72 million budget, the TRC was not able to provide updated and comprehensive figures on the total number and percentage of students attending residential schools beyond its rough 150,000 estimate and yearly statistics gleaned from the Department of Indian Affairs' annual reports.

The complete story on native school attendance is still to be told. Douglas Farrow, a professor of theology and ethics at McGill University, has argued in the U.S. journal *First Things* that the commission chose to interpret its

---

[256] DIA Annual Reports.

[257] James Redford, "Attendance at Indian Residential Schools in British Columbia, 1890-1920," B.C. Studies, No. 44: Winter 1979/80.

[258] "The Role of the RCMP during the Indian Residential School System," Ottawa: RCMP, 2011.

main task as collecting the stories of former attendees rather than gathering hard, verifiable numbers. "It was not tasked with a full analysis of the historical record," Farrow writes.[259]

Yet the TRC's official mandate was "to reveal to Canadians the complex truth about the history and the ongoing legacy of the church-run residential schools, in a manner that fully documents the individual and collective harms perpetrated against Aboriginal peoples."[260]

The TRC's lack of comparative and contextual data came under criticism in 2015 when it released its final report. But perhaps with such a tendentious mandate, it is not surprising that the TRC would not look too hard for factual data that might undercut its narrative of harm.[261]

Home for the Holidays

With compulsory education only sporadically and weakly enforced, it is incorrect to paint residential schools as prisons or concentration camps. Most students went home on weekends if the schools were near their reserves; and at Christmas and over the summer break if they were not. For much of the time that Saskatchewan's Marieval School operated, for example, it was customary "for Indian parents of children attending ... to visit the school at any time but more especially on Sunday and take their children from the school to their homes or camps and eat a meal with them, sometimes staying with them several hours."[262]

The 1920 legislative amendments that imposed compulsory attendance also provided that the federal government would pay for the transportation costs of each student to return home for summer vacation.

---

[259] Douglas Farrow, "The History of Canada's Residential Schools," *First Things*, July 10, 2021.

[260] Honouring the Truth, Reconciling for the Future Summary of the Final Report of the Truth and Reconciliation Commission of Canada, 2015, p. 23.

[261] Hymie Rubenstein and Rodney Clifton, "Truth and Reconciliation report tells a 'skewed and partial story' of residential schools," *National Post*, June 22, 2015.

[262] Shuana Niessen, *Shattering the Silence: The Hidden History of Indian Residential Schools in Saskatchewan* (Faculty of Education, University of Regina, 2017), p. 73

By the 1950s, the federal government and churches began to scale back their participation in residential schools for reasons of cost and effectiveness. After this policy shift, some Aboriginal parents began to lobby vigorously to keep their children in these schools. A 1995 academic paper in the journal *Historical Studies in Education* includes testimony from a former Saskatchewan-based school superintendent about the situation in residential schools in the 1960s.[263] "We were inundated with applications," the unnamed superintendent explained. "That was one of the times of the year I dreaded the most ... when we had to go through these applications and turn down any number of people who had applied to put their children into residential school."

To quell demand for residential school spaces, the authors note, Ottawa resorted to denying family allowance cheques to native parents who insisted on enrolling their children in residential schools.

For all the complaints associated with residential schools – and they were legion and well-known among native communities by the 1960s – some parents still wanted their children to attend because they felt it was the best way for them to learn English and thus become integrated into a wider world of opportunity. In 1962, Stoney Nation Chief George Labelle hired a lawyer to petition the United Church to ask Ottawa to reverse the planned closure of nearby Morley Residential School. "It will be a great tragedy if this famous United Church mission school is closed. The Indians are only asking for a halfway chance to educate their children," the lawyer's letter read. The plea worked, at least for a while. The school survived until 1969.[264]

The TRC's Final Report contains the stories of many former students who attended unwillingly or had bad or painful experiences, facts which deserve to be acknowledged today despite lack of corroborating evidence. However, these outcomes were not universal. There are numerous other examples of parents who freely sent their children to these schools, just as

---

[263] Vic Satzewich and Linda Mahood, "Indian agents and the residential school system in Canada, 1946-1970," *Historical Studies in Education*, Spring 1995, 7 (1), pp. 45-69.

[264] Patricia Treble and Jane O'Hara, "Residential Church School Scandal," *Canadian Encyclopedia* online, March 17, 2003.

they freely accepted Western trade goods and religion, including Christian burial practices.

Many students and employees have offered recollections of their time at a residential school that contradict the accepted narrative.[265] Prime Minister Stephen Harper's 2008 apology for residential schools also recognized that "some former students have spoken positively about their experiences at residential schools," while acknowledging that many did not.[266] The archival record also supplies thousands of photos of residential school life, including a 1962 CBC documentary about the residential school in Kamloops that depicts many apparently healthy, animated, neatly dressed, and well-fed children.[267]

None of this evidence is meant to deny or diminish the stories of pain and hardship told by many former residential school students. But the complete story behind the residential schools and their graves is much more complicated than the narrative of concentration camps and genocide being presented today. Most native children did not go to residential schools. And most of those who did were not there by force. In fact, some students were there at the express demands of their parents, who were prepared to fight to keep the schools open.

A Disease's Terrible Toll

Setting aside the issue of how many Indigenous children attended residential schools, and why, it is clear that the Canadian government was generally unable to protect their health when they were attending school as wards of the state. While residential schools were supposed to teach Indigenous children English, arithmetic, farming, simple trades, and

---

[265] Robert MacBain, "Letters to Senator Beyak, uncensored," C2C Journal, April 16, 2018.

[266] "Prime Minister Harper offers full apology on behalf of Canadians for the Indian Residential Schools system," Press Release, Office of the Prime Minister, June 11, 2008.

[267] George Robertson, Arla Saare, John Seale, Gerry O'Connor, and Norman Rosen, "'The Eyes of Children' — life at a residential school," documentary filmed at Kamloops Indian Residential School, CBC Vancouver, aired on December 25, 1962. Posted on YouTube by the Frontier Centre for Public Policy, June 9, 2021.

domestic activities, and immerse them in Western cultural habits, it did not always grant them access to Western levels of health care. In his paper for the TRC, archaeologist Scott Hamilton estimated 3,200 students died over a 140-year period while registered at residential schools.[268] Subsequent research has since increased this total to 4,100. Some of these deceased children likely ended up in residential school graves now considered to be unmarked. The death of any child is obviously a tragedy, but before assigning blame for such an event, we need to better understand how they died.

Following the announcements of the unmarked graves, it became common for critics to propose many gruesome and grotesque reasons for the associated deaths. Former TRC chair Sinclair (also a retired Liberal Senator) told *The Guardian* newspaper he had heard "stories from survivors who witnessed children being put to death, particularly infants born in the schools who had been fathered by a priest. Many survivors told us that they witnessed those children, those infants, being either buried alive or killed – and sometimes being thrown into furnaces."[269] There is no credible evidence to support such horrific allegations of murder, and no mention of such events in the TRC's many publications.

In contrast, numerous credible sources point to the high susceptibility of Indigenous people to virulent diseases – in particular tuberculosis (TB) – as the overwhelming reason for deaths in residential schools. Much of this evidence comes from the work of Dr. Peter Bryce, the Department of Indian Affairs' chief medical officer at the turn of the 20th century. Bryce dedicated his career to improving the health of native Canadians and has lately been recognized as an early crusader or whistleblower for publicizing the system's flaws.[270] A large part of his reputation rests on a pamphlet he self-published in 1922 demanding improvements to the

---

[268] Hamilton, p. 42.

[269] Leyland Cecco, "Canada must reveal 'undiscovered truths' of residential schools to heal," *The Guardian*, June 27, 2021.

[270] Crystal Fraser, Tricia Logan, and Neil Orford, "A doctor's century-old warning on residential schools can help find justice for Canada's crimes," *Globe and Mail*, July 17, 2021; Lloyd W. Robertson, "How to Cool Canada's Overheated Statue Removal Business," *C2C Journal*, July 17, 2021.

conditions in residential schools, calling the policy of the day "a national crime."

Bryce surveyed dozens of residential schools in the early 1900s for the federal government and his report observes that, "of a total of 1,537 pupils reported upon nearly 25 per cent are dead, of one school with an absolutely accurate statement, 69 per cent of ex-pupils are dead, and that everywhere the almost invariable cause of death given is tuberculosis."[271] Similarly, Hamilton wrote, "It is clear that communicable diseases were a primary cause of poor health and death for many Aboriginal people during the 19th and early 20th Centuries…Tuberculosis was the prevalent cause of death."[272] In fact, TB was the leading cause of *all* Indigenous deaths beginning in the last third of the 19th century, exacerbated by devastating hardships and starvation, including the end of the bison hunt.[273]

And despite the vague horror stories Sinclair related to *The Guardian*, the TRC's final report also states categorically that, "Thousands of Aboriginal children died in residential schools. They were killed by relentless waves of epidemics – tuberculosis and a host of other infectious diseases – that swept repeatedly through the institutions." Nina Green's research, however, shows that the Report has confused the death of registered IRS students with their place of death and burial, which was mainly on their home reserves.

The toll extracted by TB in residential schools should properly be lamented. But it does not prove malevolence on the part of the federal government. As already mentioned, the Canadian government was not indifferent to the health conditions of the Indigenous population. In the 1880s, for example, it implemented a highly successful smallpox vaccination campaign in Indigenous communities that virtually wiped out

---

[271] "Historical Voices on Indian Residential Schools – Dr. Peter Henderson Bryce," FNESC/FNSA English First Peoples 10, 11, and 12, BLM 5, Teacher Resource Guide, p. 281.

[272] Hamilton, p. 3.

[273] J.W Daschuk, Paul Hackett, and Scott MacNeil, "Treaties and Tuberculosis: First NationsPeople in late 19th-Century Western Canada, a Political and Economic Transformation," *Canadian Bulletin of Medical History* 2006 23:2, pp. 307-330.

this deadly scourge.[274] TB, unfortunately, did not have an effective treatment during this time. And while it devastated native communities, TB also killed untold millions of people around the world – the rich, famous, and powerful among them – throughout the 1800s and early 1900s.

Hamilton did not excuse the poor results at residential schools, but he suggested caution must be exercised when assigning blame:

> While the appalling death rates within the Residential Schools to the middle of the 20th Century far exceeded that among non-Aboriginal Canadians, it must be considered in the context of health care and medical knowledge in early Canada. Many of the early residential schools were established within the first 50 years of Canadian Confederation, at a time of rapid economic development and large-scale immigration into regions with large Aboriginal populations. The more frequent contact resulted in rapid spread of disease to Indigenous populations with limited resistance to infectious disease.[275]

It is also important to note that even today in Canada the rate of TB infections among Indigenous people is 40 times higher than in the rest of society.[276] If Canadians are embarrassed by their predecessors' failures to deliver health care to Indigenous populations, what should they think about their own generation's efforts?

Comparing Tragedies

TB was not the only devastating disease to wreak havoc on residential schools. The Spanish flu epidemic, which killed between 50 million and

---

[274] Peter Shawn Taylor and Greg Piasetzki, "The 19th-century Indigenous policy success story we've forgotten," *National Post*, March 28, 2019.

[275] Hamilton, p. 4.

[276] Radha Jetty, "Tuberculosis among First Nations, Inuit and Métis children and youth in Canada: Beyond medical management," *Paediatrics & Child Health*, Vol. 26, No. 2, April-May 2021, pp. e78–e81.

100 million worldwide, had a similar impact on Canada's native student population.[277] According to Hamilton:

> Several of the schools were overwhelmed by the 1918-19 [Spanish] influenza pandemic. In 1918 all but two of the children and all staff contracted influenza at the Fort St. James, British Columbia, school and surrounding community. In the end seventy-eight people, including students, died. Initially, Father Joseph Allard, who served as the school principal, conducted funeral services at the mission cemetery. But, as he wrote in his diary, 'The others were brought in two or three at a time, but I could not go to the graveyard with all of them. In fact, several bodies were piled up in an empty cabin because there was no grave ready. A large common grave was dug for them.'[278]

These were tragic and frightening circumstances, to be sure. But were the conditions any worse than what was faced by non-Indigenous Canadians during the same pandemic? Consider this vivid account from the Canadian Centre for the Great War:

> Canada's size and lack of a centralised medical system made it particularly difficult to deal with the virus…and in isolated areas communities went for months without seeing a doctor under normal circumstances…While living in a rural area could limit medical help, life in cities during the flu epidemic was even more dangerous. Hospitals across Canada had more patients than they could handle, and informal treatment centres had to be set up for the cities' poorest. Undertakers did not have enough room to store the bodies of those who had died, and in many cases flu victims were buried in unmarked or mass graves. Walk deep enough into an old city graveyard in Canada and you will likely find unnamed flu victims.[279]

[277] Lynne Cohen, "The Spanish Flu Versus Covid-19," *C2C Journal*, September 26, 2020.

[278] Hamilton, p. 11.

[279] "Forgotten Casualties: Canada's Spanish Influenza Epidemic," Canadian Centre for the Great War, Vimy Foundation, 2017.

However poor health outcomes for native children may have been during the early 20th century, their situation was clearly not unique. The rest of society also experienced uncontrollable viral outbreaks, social despair, and unmarked graves during this time. But as treatment protocols improved, so did survival rates in residential schools. Following the Second World War, Hamilton wrote:

> The annual number of reported deaths declined to less than 15 per year…This likely reflects more effective public health measures coupled with use of antibiotics, and improvement in school operations. Given the severity of tuberculosis-related illness within the schools, the 1950s availability of drug-based treatment coupled with widespread inoculation was particularly important for the declining death rates. This is notable as it coincides with the time of the maximum number of schools and student enrollments.[280]

It is also necessary to consider whether a native child was better off living on a reserve than attending residential school. "The pattern of illness and death within the schools likely mimics that apparent on the Reserves," wrote Hamilton.[281] His report, leaning heavily on Bryce's work, describes a cycle of disease in which infants and children were infected at home on reserves and sent to residential schools, presumably for treatment in the infirmary, where they infected other children. In turn, those children were "sent home when too ill to remain at school, or because of being a danger to the other scholars, and have conveyed the disease to houses previously free," states his report. Bryce concluded likewise: "In no instance was a child awaiting admission to school found free from tuberculosis; hence it was plain that infection was got in the home [reserve]."[282] It was a vicious circle.

Considering the alleged gravesite discoveries in Kamloops and elsewhere, it is impossible to say if the students who may be buried there would have

---

[280] Hamilton, p. 11.

[281] Ibid., p. 10.

[282] P.H. Bryce, "The Story of a National Crime: Being an Appeal for Justice to the Indians of Canada" (Ottawa: James Hope & Sons, 1922).

survived had they stayed home. Bryce's work points out that the death rate from all causes on reserves was often double or triple the rate for the rest of Canadian society. As such, life was often even more perilous on the reserve than it was at a residential school; in fact the role played by the school environment remains a contentious issue in the academic literature.[283] One intergenerational study has concluded that, "children whose mother attended residential school fare better along health dimensions and yet worse along educational dimensions," suggesting mixed results from attending a boarding school away from home.[284]

Buried Far from Home?

Likely the most shocking aspect of residential school graves for many Canadians is that some students who died while attending school were buried on site rather than being returned to their families. Modern sensibilities may well regard this as evidence of institutional inhumanity. Yet local interment was normal practice across many government-funded institutions such as hospitals, mental institutions, poor houses and jails in earlier times, as it was along rail or canal construction sites as well.[285]

With budgets perpetually strained in the early 1900s – and given the lack of refrigeration and rapid transport – it was often impractical to send the bodies back home if the deceased child's reserve was far from the school. Instead, local churches took on the responsibility to bury the local indigent dead, as Hamilton's report explains.[286] Local burial was also a public health necessity during epidemics to prevent further contagion.

[283] P. Wilk, A. Maltby, and M. Cooke, "Residential schools and the effects on Indigenous health and well-being in Canada: a scoping review," *Public Health Review* 38, 8 (2017).

[284] Donna Feir, "The Intergenerational Effect of Forcible Assimilation Policy on Education," Department of Economics Discussion Paper DDP1501, University of Victoria, B.C., March 2015.

[285] Cynthia Simpson, "The treatment of Halifax's poor house dead during the nineteenth and twentieth centuries," Master's thesis, (Halifax: Saint Mary's University, 2011).

[286] Hamilton, p. 23.

That said, local burial was the exception, not the rule. Numerous archival records reveal that students who died at a residential school, such as the one in Kamloops, were returned to their parents via school truck or school car. Generally this occurred after an official inquiry was held to determine the cause of death. Responses to a death at school varied as circumstances changed. As Hamilton pointed out, "Some students died at the schools, while other seriously ill children were returned home, or admitted to hospitals or sanatoria where some may have later died. Some of the deceased were returned to their families for burial, but most others were likely buried in cemeteries on school grounds, or in nearby church, reserve or municipal cemeteries."[287]

One case described in Hamilton's report seems particularly insightful since it also reveals the laxity with which compulsory attendance was enforced in the 1920s:

> Clara Tizya, who grew up in Rampart House near Old Crow in northwestern Yukon, recalled 'in the early 1920's a girl had died at Carcross Indian Residential School and when they sent the body back, there were many rumours about the children receiving bad treatment and this scared the parents or gave them an excuse for not sending their children to school. And so, for the next 25 years, no children were sent out to the Carcross Indian Residential School.'[288]

The death recalled in this anecdote was obviously a tragedy. And it is suggestive of how bad conditions could be at some schools. But it also points to the ability of Indigenous parents to determine how, where and even whether their children were educated despite allegedly dictatorial government regulations.

---

[287] Ibid., p. 5.

[288] Ibid., p. 25.

The Way Forward

A rigorous search for facts regarding residential schools is not meant to minimize the suffering that occurred there. The health outcomes for native children were often terrible and the many deaths of former students furnish ample, heart-rending evidence of this. But it is necessary to recognize context as well as outcome. Mass death by infectious disease was not unique to Indigenous Canadians during this time. Nor does it appear conditions at residential schools were worse than the alternative – life in crowded homes on a reserve. In fact, it seems TB was generally introduced into the schools *from* the reserves. And when better treatments became readily available, they were provided to students at residential schools with salutary results.

Further, ample evidence emphasizes that only a minority of native students ever attended a residential school, that the federal government's policy of compulsory education spanned only part of the residential schools' era and, even when operative, was often feebly enforced. Actual attendance rates were far lower than official enrolment figures, and a drop-out rate of 50 percent between Grades 1 and 2 would surely be considered scandalous in Canada today. As such, it is impossible to sustain an argument that residential schools functioned as "concentration camps" or that the government's intent was the "genocidal" removal of all Indigenous children from their parents.

The pursuit of truth and reconciliation must rest on a firm factual basis.

A two-part version of this chapter was published online by C2C Journal *on August 7 and August 25, 2021, and contains additional material discovered since that date and files from Greg Piasetzki.*

Chapter 4

Mass Graves and other Fake Atrocities on the Blue Quills Indian Reserve

Hymie Rubenstein and Pim Wiebel

Lurid tales of murder carried out against students by employees at Canada's Indian Residential Schools (IRSs) have been circulating for years now, even though none has ever been formally investigated, much less proven.[289] Still, the stories keep proliferating and getting more gruesome based on "Indigenous knowings" told by paid elders and knowledge keepers the further removed they are from their occurrence.[290]

This is not to imply the absence of cases of residential school staff members using excessive force to discipline students or in other ways betraying the trust placed in them for the care of the children. It would be astonishing if such things had never occurred in a school system that employed many thousands of workers spanning a period of more than 100 years, not the least because harsh punishment and sexual exploitation were common in non-Indigenous boarding schools during the same era. Nevertheless, invoking unfounded allegations of homicide to bolster the outrageously fraudulent claim of residential school genocide is not only painfully misguided, but wickedly wrong.[291]

Tales Told by the Media, Indigenous Activists, and Experts

Among the latest of the macabre tales is one concerning students at the former Blue Quills IRS on the Saddle Lake Indian Reserve in Alberta 170

---

[289] Nick Boisvert, "Why criminal charges for deaths at residential schools would be unprecedented — and enormously complex," CBC News, June 27, 2021.

[290] "Ways of Knowing," Office of Indigenous Initiatives, Queen's University online; "Guidelines for Respectful Engagement with Knowledge Keepers & Elders," Indigenous education, Brandon University online.

[291] Cynthia Stirbys and Amelia McComber, "Indian Residential Schools: Acts of genocide, deceit and control by church and state," The Conversation, June 15, 2021.

kilometres northeast of Edmonton. The students are said to have been purposely infected with tuberculosis by feeding them tainted milk, a claim recently uttered by Leah Redcrow, executive director of the Reserve's Acimowin Opaspiw Society (AOS), an organization funded by Library and Archives Canada, whose mission includes searching for any unmarked burial sites of deceased Blue Quills IRS students.

According to Redcrow, in a Jan. 24, 2023 *CBC* news item titled Tainted milk led to deaths of Alberta residential school children,[292] based on an AOS report, "We feel that these children [at Blue Quills] were being deliberately infected with tuberculosis," a horrendous accusation we have easily and thoroughly debunked.[293]

But this leaves unanswered the larger question of the alleged murder by other means of Blue Quills IRS students.

The story of these allegations begins in 2004 when the community discovered what it believed to be a mass grave. "The mass grave had numerous children-sized skeletons wrapped in white cloth. This could possibly be from when there was an outbreak of typhoid fever in the school," according to Saddle Lake band council member Jason Whiskeyjack.[294]

The report says ground-penetrating radar (GPR) in October 2022 was used at the site at the Sacred Heart Cemetery, a graveyard on the Saddle Lake Indian Reserve where Blue Quills students who were from Saddle Lake were buried:

"They're not ground anomalies, these were people," Redcrow said. "These were people's family members."[295]

---

[292] Stephen Cook, "Tainted milk led to deaths of Alberta residential school children, group says," CBC News, January 24, 2023.

[293] Hymie Rubenstein, "Murder by milk, and other fantasies," The Western Standard, March 15, 2023.

[294] Paige Parsons, "Human remains found near Alberta residential school site likely children, First Nation says," CBC News, May 17, 2022.

[295] Cook, "Tainted Milk," loc. cit.

"It was one of the most horrific residential schools in Canada," said Eric J. Large, lead AOS investigator. "The amount of missing children is extensive... The institution was strife with violence, illness, starvation, abuse and death."[296]

"It can be safely stated that in our community of 12,000 people, each family has had four to five children who went missing from this institution," he continued.

On May 17, 2022, the Saddle Lake Cree Indian Reserve also revealed that "new archival work has helped explain numerous discoveries of human remains that it now believes are the unmarked graves of residential school students."[297]

The discoveries of partial human remains were accidentally made during ground excavations for new burials in the community's cemetery located near the former Blue Quills residential school site.

While community members who discovered the remains allegedly didn't understand the implications of their discovery and therefore reburied them, a team tasked with investigating burial sites connected to the school now believes community gravediggers have been uncovering the shallow, unmarked graves of children between the ages of four and 10 who attended the school.

"There were children-sized skeleton remains that were excavated. None of these skeleton remains were in caskets," Whiskeyjack said at a news conference.

In 2021, Saddle Lake Cree formed the *Acimowin Opaspiw Society* (AOS) to investigate possible burial sites, among other activities. Lead investigator and residential school survivor Eric Large and his team are said to have began compiling witness statements from community members who had discovered bodies, spoke to people who had missing family members, and reviewed archival records about the school.

---

[296] Jake Cardinal, "212 Confirmed Graves Of Children At Saddle Lake Cree Nation Residential School," Alberta Native News, June 1, 2022.

[297] Parsons, "Human remains," loc. cit.

According to Large, Catholic Church records obtained by investigators show that 212 students between the ages of 6 and 11 died at the school — "school children who never came home" and "whose remains are still unaccounted for" — between 1898 and 1931.

The number vastly outstrips federal records, which accounted for about 25 student deaths, he said.

The investigative team has previously said it believes there are even more children missing than the 212 they claim have been accounted for in church records. It also said that "in the past, many families were afraid or unable to speak out when a child never returned home from school. ... When all of these children went missing, there was nothing that anybody could do," Large said.

Then on January 24, 2023, AOS announced it had uncovered "physical and documented evidence of a genocide" based on details of its preliminary report into "missing children and unmarked burials" at the former site of the original Blue Quills Residential School.[298]

"The investigation's theory regarding the missing children of the Saddle Lake site, is that they are buried in undocumented mass graves," the report states. "One of the undocumented mass graves was located by accidental excavation, in 2004, at Sacred Heart cemetery. The mass graves will require a second excavation, and repatriation of remains followed by the identification by the coroner once DNA is collected from living descendants."

The report includes allegations that a "disciplinarian" who worked there from 1935 to 1942 was seen killing children. "The investigation has received disclosures from intergenerational survivors, whose parents witnessed homicides at the Saint Paul site," the undisclosed report states.

That staff member is accused of pushing boys down the stairs, killing them. "[He] would then threaten to kill the boys that witnessed if they said anything," it also claims.

---

[298] Sean Amato, "'Evidence of a genocide' found during search of Alta. residential school: First Nation investigators," CTV News, January 25, 2023.

While there is much work yet to be done, Redcrow said the alleged release of the AOS's 44-page preliminary report – a document not found on its Website though the site claims it will be released "soon" -- was important to provide survivors and families with what has been learned so far.[299]

How credible are any of these many assertions?

Ground Penetrating Radar Results Are Not Conclusive, Especially When Kept Secret

Although GPR can detect sub-ground disturbances and is particularly useful in determining sub-surface irregularities in known graveyards containing unmarked burial plots, it cannot confirm the presence of graves or human remains. Indeed, its intrinsic limitations were announced soon after a press release on May, 27 2021 that read:

"It is with a heavy heart that Tk'emlúps te Secwépemc Kukpi7 (Kamloops band) [Chief] Rosanne Casimir confirms an unthinkable loss that was spoken about but never documented by the Kamloops Indian Residential School. This past weekend, with the help of a ground penetrating radar specialist, the stark truth of the preliminary findings came to light – the confirmation of the remains of 215 children who were students of the Kamloops Indian Residential School."[300]

At the time, Chief Casimir said the results were released quickly after an early report from the scene by the technician doing the work, and that a full report would be released in June, a promise never kept.

In a live news conference sponsored by the band on July 15, the GPR technical specialist, Sarah Beaulieu, who performed the search just days before the preliminary results were made public, clarified this press release by not only reducing the number of "probable gravesites" from 215 to 200, taking into account previous excavation work that had been done in the area that could have influenced the results, but stressed her findings can't

---

[299] Acimowin Opaspiw Society website.

[300] For Immediate Release, Tk'emlúps te Secwépemc Kukpi7 (Kamloops Indian Band), May 27, 2021.

115

be confirmed unless excavations are done at the scene: "Which is why we need to pull back a little bit and say that they are 'probable burials,' they are 'targets of interest,' for sure."[301]

Racelle Kooy, a spokesperson for the Tk'emlúps te Secwépemc, said a full copy of Dr. Beaulieu's report would not be released to the public and media, but that "the core of the findings are contained in the release and Dr. Beaulieu gave an extensive presentation today."

Nothing could be further from the truth, partly seen from the fact that not even a redacted copy of her report has been released to date — just as none of the reports of identical searches all across Canada have ever been released for public and professional scrutiny.

More important still, there is credible evidence the 15 "probable burials" removed from the list, and likely all the rest of the ground disturbances at the abandoned apple orchard at Kamloops, are likely the result of historic excavations related to the installation of sewer and water infrastructure.[302]

All these assertions about the Kamloops "discovery" apply equally to Blue Quills.

Quelle Surprise! Cemeteries Contain Buried Remains Sometimes Interred en masse

It would be amazing indeed if graves were not found if a decision was made to excavate all the unmarked soil anomalies at Sacred Heart cemetery, if only because graveyards are supposed to contain bodies of the dead. It is unlikely, however, that the graves would be mass burials containing the remains of groups of Blue Quills students. A review of the death dates of the Blue Quills students listed in the National Centre for Truth and Reconciliation Memorial Register discussed below shows that

---

[301] Jana G. Pruden and Mike Hager, "Anthropologist explains how she concluded 200 children were buried at the Kamloops Residential School," *Globe and Mail*, July 15, 2021.

[302] "Graves in the Apple Orchard," WordPress website at https://gravesintheorchard.wordpress.com/

there were no instances in which more than one death occurred over a short period of time.[303]

Although it is unlikely that deceased Blue Quills students were buried in mass graves, such a finding would not represent an anomaly in either Canada or elsewhere. Mass burials were common around the world during epidemics because the risk of contagion and the lack of resources for customary funerals often necessitated quick and unceremonious interment:

"Undertakers [during the Spanish flu pandemic in 1918-19] did not have enough room to store the bodies of those who had died, and in many cases flu victims were buried in unmarked or mass graves. Walk deep enough into an old city graveyard in Canada and you will likely find unnamed flu victims."[304]

"During its peak, undertakers and gravediggers could not keep up with the work as hearses and coffins fell into short supply. In some places, funerals were limited to 15 minute gatherings; in others, bodies were buried in mass graves without ceremony."[305]

"The mass grave [at Burlington Heights, near Hamilton] is known as the 'cholera field' where the deceased were simply dumped, then covered in lime. Not only were there no coffins, but bodies in this location were buried without markers to identify them or as a sign of remembrance. Obviously, the use of the segregated pit saved time, space and prevented contamination... there is another burial location at the cemetery [in Hamilton] for Spanish flu pandemic victims...Not much is known about

---

[303] "106 death records found for students claimed to be 'missing' from 26 alberta indian residential schools as per national centre for truth and reconciliation lists," Indian Residentials Schools Records website.

[304] "Forgotten Casualties: Canada's Spanish Influenza Epidemic," Vimy Foundation website, May 26, 2017.

[305] Ibid.

those victims either, although there was an attempt at using ground penetrating radar with inconclusive results several years ago."[306]

How Many Blue Quills IRS Students Died?

Another false allegation concerning mortality at the Blue Quills Residential School is cited in a May, 2022 CBC article: "...Catholic Church records obtained by investigators show that 212 students died at the [original Blue Quills] school between 1898 and 1931."

The assertion of 212 deaths is a gross exaggeration. As noted in the same CBC article, Catherine Warholik of the Diocese of St. Paul stated that the records provided to the investigative team were for the entire parish, not specifically for the residential school. Nearly all cemeteries where residential school students were buried, including cemeteries like Sacred Heart, were reserve cemeteries serving the entire community. Since a minority of children attended residential school, most of the children buried in Sacred Heart Cemetery would not have had any association with the Blue Quills Residential School. They would have included pre-school age children, students attending the Saddle Lake Indian Day School, children who never attended school at all (some one-third of band school-age children), and former Blue Quills students who died after leaving the school. (Enrollment at Blue Quills was 45 in 1915 and peaked at about 200 in the 1960s.)

Moreover, enrollment numbers were always far less than half of the school-age population of the Saddle Lake band. Enrollments included students from other bands who would have been buried in cemeteries on their home reserves.

It is also often asserted that the students who died at residential schools are "missing." The students who died while enrolled at Blue Quills Residential School are not missing. The National Centre for Truth and Reconciliation (NCTR) Memorial Register lists 27 students who died at the

---

[306] Mark McNeil, "The mystery of Hamilton's cholera burial grounds: Should ground-penetrating radar be used at 1800s mass burial sites?" September 27, 2021.

school over its 99-year existence. All these students, two with no names, died before the end of the Second World War. Although no other information is given, an independent researcher has found the death certificates of 19 of them. In reviewing the certificates, it was found that 22 of the names on the NCTR list of 26 names belong to children who were Blue Quills students at the time of their death. Moreover, one was a 34-year-old male "widower," another was a 29-year-old "married woman," and one was an infant under the age of one. One student is listed twice.[307]

The death certificates provide the name of the deceased, the names of the parents, the date and cause of death, and the place of burial. They also include information such as the name of the physician who attended the student and the name of the coroner. All certificates are signed by the informant, or, in many cases, a parent or other close relative. The cause of death was always disease, most often tuberculosis. Nearly all the children died in hospital or at home, not in the school's infirmary. All were buried at Sacred Heart cemetery or at cemeteries on their home reserves.

There is no credible evidence of student deaths at the Blue Quills IRS beyond the 19 for whom death certificates have been found.

Was There Widespread Abuse of Children at the Blue Quills IRS?

As mentioned above, the CTV article published online in January 2023 cites another spurious allegation of heinous wrongdoing at Blue Quills taken from the AOS, namely, "allegations that a 'disciplinarian' who worked there from 1935 to 1942 was seen killing children…That staff member is accused of pushing boys down the stairs, killing them…. [T]he accused died in 1968."

The comprehensive NCTR archives for the Blue Quills IRS contain no mention of any conviction for physical or sexual abuse at the school. Neither the NCTR archives, nor the TRC reports, refer to an allegation of boys being pushed down a flight of stairs by a staff member. Surely the

---

[307] "106 death records found," loc. cit.

boys' parents or close relatives would have learned of the alleged homicides and inquired as to why the children had not returned home. It is unimaginable that having been told of the deaths, that they would not have sought answers. The fictitious nature of the story is further supported by the death certificates for children who died at Blue Quills during the years the accused staff member was employed at the school showing that four were boys, and that they all died of tuberculosis or other diseases.

This Blue Quills "Indigenous knowing," like others such as the tale of murders by priests at the Kamloops IRS and young children being forced to dig the graves in an apple orchard in the middle of the night, is another instance of a crude allegation thrown out without evidence or verification, and with the express goal of denigrating this boarding school. Like many fantastical claims invented to discredit a person or institution, the lurid tales of homicide at residential schools are based on murky rumours, at best. Often, they are simply outright fabrications. No matter how far-fetched, the allegations are difficult to disprove simply because they are unfalsifiable, based as they are on myths rather than facts. Accordingly, they have become part and parcel of a widely accepted residential school mythology, a mythology that pictures the schools as institutions of abject abuse, murder, and genocide.

The executive director of the Acimowin Opaspiw Society, Leah Redcrow, makes another astounding claim in the same CTV article where she states: "I myself didn't know that my grandfather had 10 siblings die in this school."

This would mean that nearly half the 22 deceased students at Blue Quills were members of the same family. It should be noted that no family name on the NCTR memorial list appears more than three times. Almost all surnames, including Red Crow, appear only once.

Creating false narratives to buttress the charge of residential school genocide does not advance the essential "truth" part of the truth and reconciliation equation. Rather, it serves as a theatrical distraction from a focus on finding solutions to the real problems Indigenous people face today. The current government's policy of unbounded spending on "Indigenous Priorities," purportedly to alleviate the impacts of colonization and residential schools, only deepens Aboriginal people's sense of dependence and victimization. The consequences are evident — growing gaps in life expectancy, poverty, education outcomes, incarceration, and mortality from drug overdoses. A fundamental question must be asked: Can the current regime in which over 600 scattered, "sovereign First Nations" and more than 3,000 reserves exist under the apartheid construct of the Indian Act and sustained for the most part by external government resources, be expected to offer a better future for Indigenous people? An honest consideration of that question would most definitely point to the need for sweeping reforms — reforms that the government and Aboriginal leadership, vested as they are in self-serving interests, would be sure to resist.

Conclusion: From Shock Journalism and Sloppy Research to Rational Contemplation and Factual Evidence

The May 17, 2022 CBC non-breaking news story — "Discovery of human remains near residential school site likely children, say investigators" — would have earned global headlines had it appeared at the same time in 2021. Now, even with the additional evidence presented above, many readers will simply sigh or roll their eyes, not because of any sense of genocide fatigue, but because more people are recognizing that the whole IRS student burial issue has been exaggerated beyond belief by the following parties: lazy, shock journalism reporters, including those employed by the CBC; rent-seeking Indigenous leaders; 4-Ps (power, privilege, prestige, and prosperity) addicted Indigenous advisors, consultants, and lawyers also seeking their share of the rent; "woke" humanities and social science academics; and compliant politicians using virtue signaling rather than concrete policies to solve the myriad of Aboriginal adversities and pathologies.

More particularly, should anyone be surprised that:

- Dead bodies are found in known and named community cemeteries;

- There are countless unmarked graves in graveyards around the country whose wooden markers and cheap wooden coffins used by the poor disintegrated long ago;

- The remains of children of all ages can be found buried in graveyards;

- Mass graves were routinely dug during times of plague to quickly bury infected bodies;

- Mass graves almost never contained coffins;

- There was a very high death rate 140 years ago among Indigenous children on the reserves and in the residential schools given their higher susceptibility than European children to imported diseases during the pre-vaccination era;

- Even today, there is a higher death rate among Indigenous children than non-Indigenous ones: "For most people in Canada, the risk of developing active TB is very low. However, the rates of active TB are higher among Indigenous peoples in Canada. The rate of TB in Inuit Nunangat is more than 300 times higher than in the Canadian-born, non-Indigenous population. The rate of TB among First Nations living on reserve is over 40 times higher than the Canadian-born non-Indigenous population";

- Most IRS children did not die at their schools but were sent to a nearby hospital for treatment or to their home reserves when they became very ill; if they died at home, they were buried in their reserve cemetery;

- If they died at a hospital, they were also sent home when this was practical;

- There is no mention of or question about how many skeletons have been unearthed in the community cemetery: any minimally competent reporter would have asked, "How many bodies are we talking about?" If they were wrapped in cloth, the bones would be held intact; if not, there are skulls and spines making it easy to determine how many were buried;

- Many or most of these skeletons may not even be those of children; they could be women who typically have smaller frames, possibly akin to that of a strapping ten-year-old boy;

- Stories of Blue Quills IRS being a school full of murder and other horrors need to explain why, as the NCTR has written, "When the federal government announced that it would be closing the school in 1970, Saddle Lake First Nation members occupied the school in protest. Their occupation ended with an agreement that saw Blue Quills become Canada's first residence and school controlled by First Nations people";

- A band official would speciously claim that "... in the past, many families were afraid or unable to speak out when a child never returned home. ... When all of these children went missing, there was nothing that anybody could do," deliberately ignoring that Indigenous people regularly complained to school officials and others when they were dissatisfied with conditions at the schools their children attended, that they sometimes kept their children home when unhappy with some feature of school life, and that when they complained, miscreant staff members were regularly dismissed;

- The OAS claim that the mass grave it says is made up of students from the Sacred Heart Residential School was the result of "a massive outbreak of typhoid fever that caused the entire student population to perish, and that those in the mass grave are most likely those children" has no evidentiary support. The school had a student population of 45 when it opened, and it reached around 200 by the 1970s. There is no record of the entire student population perishing from typhoid or any other disease in any given year or over any short period of time. Conversely, there was a major outbreak of typhoid at the University of Alberta in 1910 and one in central Alberta in 1944 with many deaths. It is unthinkable that if every IRS student at Blue Quills died of typhoid, this had been carefully covered up;

- The comment by Eric Large that "It can be safely stated that in our community of 12,000 people, each family has had four to five children who went missing from this institution," was never questioned by a curious media person. If the average family size was 10 people, that computes to 1,200 families losing an average of 4.5 children which translates into 5,400 missing children without even a whisper being heard or a report being written, a ludicrous assumption if there ever was one;

- No attempt was made by band officials to search for the reserves' so-called missing children in the public archives where the fate of most of them would easily have been found at little or no expense to the tax-paying public;

- The nameless children allegedly found in this community cemetery along with the thousands reputedly discovered all across the country using the inconclusive technique called "ground penetrating radar" are being falsely and illogically conflated with the thousands of named students recorded as "missing" in the National Centre for Truth and Reconciliation Memorial Register;

- The families of these missing children have not come forward because they can't even name these children, the last of whom died in 1945 and couldn't themselves have been students when the original Saddle Lake school closed in 1931. The new Blue Quills IRS was then built outside the reserve near St. Paul where it operated until around 1990. Some of the deceased students could have died while enrolled there and not returned to the Saddle Lake Reserve due to inclement winter weather or because they were orphans or abandoned children;

- There is no evidence of identified family members searching for named missing or murdered children;

- The band was not even aware that there were any missing children because, if the evidence of skeletal remains in the community cemetery is true, they were buried right under their noses in that cemetery. How could such children be "missing" as opposed to forgotten? and,

- The GPR and other band reports detailing the results of these and other studies have never been released by the Kamloops, Blue Quills, or other bands so that their credibility can be assessed by impartial scholars and other experts including the police.

This new "discovery," even with its recent sensational embellishments, should be seen for what it is: a story based on unverified, even unverifiable, "Indigenous knowings" that would have been even more explosive than the Kamloops one, absent everything that has been learned over the past year slowly sinking into the consciousness of the general population since Canada's very own day that will live in infamy until exposed as a myth, namely, May 27, 2021.

Well-dressed, healthy-looking students at the Blue Quills Indian Residential School

An earlier version of this chapter was published as "Mass Graves & Other Fake Atrocities" at The Dorchester Review *online, May 2, 2023.*

Chapter Five

Billy Remembers: The Tk'emlúps te Secwépemc and Kamloops Indian Residential School Moral Panic

Frances Widdowson

In grainy footage of a protest during the 2006 film "Unrepentant," a bandana-clad man identified by the caption "William Combes, Kamloops Residential School (Catholic Church)" is being interviewed. William "Billy" Combes, who was then living a hard life on the streets of Vancouver's Downtown Eastside (he died in 2011), states the following: "They want evidence, as a seven-year-old child I witnessed myself the burial of a child and I didn't know what was happening at that time. I was with another student and I asked him 'What's happening here? I see them digging a hole in the orchard' and he said 'They're burying another one.'" Standing behind Combes is Kevin Annett, a controversial defrocked United Church Minister, who has been disseminating the stories of Combes and others about the residential schools for about 25 years.[308] One of these stories, recounted by Annett, even claimed that Queen Elizabeth II and Prince Philip took a group of students from the Kamloops Indian Residential School (KIRS) on a picnic, and then abducted them. Thorough fact-checking has shown that the Royals did not even travel to Kamloops in 1964.[309]

---

[308] Terry Glavin, "Truth and Native Abuse: How one man's wild claims threaten success of Truth and Reconciliation" *The Tyee*, April 30, 2008.

[309] Reuters Fact Check, "Fact Check-Debunking claims about disappeared school children in 1964 in British Columbia, Canada," Reuters, March 24, 2021; Annet Preethi Furtado, "False: Queen Elizabeth and Prince Philip were convicted of the 1964 disappearance of ten students from Kamloops Indian Residential School in Canada," *Logically*, June 29, 2022.

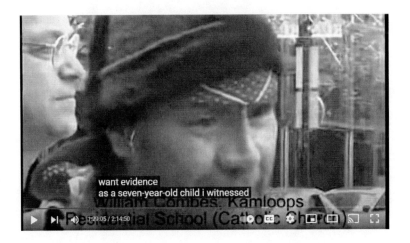

While the Queen Elizabeth "children abduction" story probably would be regarded with scepticism by most, many similar improbable accounts of "murders" and "missing children" are being repeated by Tk'emlúps te Secwépemc "Knowledge Keepers" and are now accepted as "truth." "Knowledge Keepers," after all, cannot be questioned because to do so would be perceived as "disrespectful." This raises questions about the extent to which the "oral tellings" of the "Knowledge Keepers," which have been provided as evidence for the existence of "secret burials" at KIRS, have been influenced by the lurid stories circulating over the past 25 years. These stories were given additional momentum in May 2021 and are now firmly ensconced within the Canadian consciousness.[310]

Upon closer examination, the circulation of these stories has some similarities with the moral panic started by the book *Michelle Remembers* that was published in 1980. The case involved Michelle Smith, who, after engaging in "recovered memory therapy," made sweeping claims about the satanic ritual abuse that Smith claimed to have endured. The book presented itself as being factual, but scrutiny of its contents did not

---

[310] Staff, "Claims of mass grave at Tk'emlups go back years," *Kamloops This Week*, May 28, 2021; Mary Katherine Keown, "Kamloops discovery 'a devastating reminder' of residential school tragedy, Sudbury's mayor says," *Sudbury Star*, June 1, 2021.

corroborate its claims.[311] This did not prevent it from instigating a social contagion, leading to a satanic abuse moral panic in the 1980s that resulted in over 12,000 unsubstantiated accusations being made.[312] Although the hysteria eventually subsided, this was not before a number of innocent people had their lives ruined.[313]

The satanic abuse moral panic was made possible by the implantation of false memories. Research in psychology has shown that it is easy to manufacture memories, especially in people who are emotionally disturbed.[314] The most famous example of this was the McMartin preschool trial in 1983.[315] In this case, the claims made about those accused of satanic abuse – Peggy McMartin and Ray Buckey – were eagerly and uncritically reported by the media.[316] Michelle Smith and others identifying as "survivors" of satanic abuse also met with the complainants, and were thought to have influenced their allegations against McMartin and Buckey. Furthermore, interview techniques using leading questions dramatically increased the incidence of remembered sexual abuse.[317] Pressure was used to obtain disclosures, since interviews rewarded testimonies about abuse and discouraged denials. Similar cases of mass

---

[311] Jeffrey S. Victor, *Satanic Panic: The Creation of a Contemporary Legend* (Chicago: Open Court, 1993).

[312] S. Hughes, "American Monsters: Tabloid Media and the Satanic Panic, 1970–2000." *Journal of American Studies* 51, No. 3 (2017): 691–719.

[313] Rael Jean Isaac, "The Last Victim," *National Review*, August 23, 2018.

[314] "Speaking of Psychology," Episode 91 – "How Memory Can Be Manipulated," with Elizabeth Loftus, PhD., recorded at the 2018 American Psychological Association convention in San Francisco. Transcript posted online, APA website apa.org, October 2019.

[315] Michael Snedeker and Debbie Nathan, *Satan's Silence: Ritual Abuse and the Making of a Modern American Witch Hunt.* New York: Authors Choice Press, 2001.

[316] David Shaw, "Where Was Skepticism in Media? Pack journalism and hysteria marked early coverage of the McMartin case," *Los Angeles Times*, January 19, 1990.

[317] Nadja Schreiber, Lisa D. Bellah, Yolanda Martinez, Kristin A. McLaurin, Renata Strok, Sena Garven and James M. Wood "Suggestive interviewing in the McMartin Preschool and Kelly Michaels daycare abuse cases: A case study," *Social Influence*, 1:1 (2006), pp. 16-47.

hysteria, in fact, have appeared periodically throughout history, from the Salem Witch Trials to the Hammersmith Ghost Hysteria.[318]

The current accusations of "Knowledge Keepers" about "secret burials" at KIRS take on a similar flavour. Furthermore, it is important to point out that these allegations have resulted in the extraction of numerous forms of compensation from governments, incentivizing Indigenous organizations to enthusiastically promote them. Although it is widely recognized that the residential schools caused a great deal of harm, and serious injustices were committed against many members of the Indigenous population, pretending to believe things that are highly unlikely to be true will do nothing to address the serious problems that we are facing. If we are to accept that reconciliation cannot occur without truth, wild accusations must be examined critically. In order to develop evidence-based policy, we need to enter into honest discussions to find out what actually happened at KIRS.

Constructing the Narrative of "215 Murdered Children"

On October 18, 2021, Justin Trudeau, the Prime Minister of Canada, travelled to Kamloops to meet with the Tk'emlúps te Secwépemc (formerly the Kamloops Indian Band) with an "Orange Shirt Day" pin firmly and visibly fastened to his lapel. The meeting was a strange sight, as the Prime Minister was being chastised openly by his hosts while sitting a few feet away from them, for failing to attend their Truth and Reconciliation Day ceremony a few weeks before. Then, the day after the meeting, a full page "Petition to Prime Minister Justin Trudeau from the Tk'emlúps te Secwépemc Family Heads" was published in *The Globe and Mail* and reported in the *National Post*.[319] The open letter stated that "In May of 2021, evidence of a horrific act of genocide was laid bare to the world, with the confirmation of at least 215 unmarked graves of little ones who attended the Kamloops Indian Residential School." The Petition demanded that "real acts of reconciliation" take place, which included funds for DNA

---

[318] Khalid Elhassan, "12 of History's Most Baffling Mass Hysteria Outbreaks," History Collection online, November 28, 2017.

[319] "B.C. First Nation gives Trudeau 'seven real acts' he can do to prove commitment to reconciliation," Canadian Press, October 19, 2021.

analysis, a permanent memorial, "supportive infrastructure in this sacred area," guaranteed revenues for services, a recognition of Indigenous rights and title, and "reconciliation progress" reporting.

The meeting and petition came about as the result of a long sequence of events that began with a press release announcing the "confirmation of the remains of 215 children who were students of the Kamloops Indian Residential School."[320] This announcement resulted in sensationalist media coverage that often referred to the discovery of a "mass grave." *The New York Times*, for example, stated in its article "'Horrible History: Mass Grave of Indigenous Children Reported in Canada" that "[a]n Indigenous community says it has found evidence that 215 children were buried on the grounds of a British Columbia school, one of the many in Canada set up to forcibly assimilate them." The story stated that the remains "included those of children as young as 3."[321]

And it was not just the media that have made these claims; there was an outpouring of grief and recriminations in universities. At my (now former) employer,[322] Mount Royal University, President Tim Rahilly stated that, "[t]he discovery of 215 innocent children found buried in unmarked graves at the site of a former residential school in Kamloops is nothing short of devastating. My heart goes out to everyone in our campus community feeling the impact of this discovery and the intergenerational trauma of residential schools."[323] Rahilly recommended that we look at the statement of Dr. Linda Manyguns (who had not yet started using lower case letters in her name to express her opposition to oppression).[324] Manyguns offered her "condolences and support to the Tk'emlúps te Secwépemc First Nations upon the discovery of the remains of 215 children, buried at the

---

[320] Tkemlúps te Secwépemc (Kamloops Indian Band), "For Immediate Release," Office of the Chief, Kamloops, May 27, 2021.

[321] Ian Austen, "'Horrible History': Mass Grave of Indigenous Children Reported in Canada," *New York Times*, May 28, 2021.

[322] "Fired Mount Royal University professor says she plans to appeal," CTV News, January 5, 2022.

[323] Tim Rahilly, "Statements on the remains of Indigenous children found," Mount Royal University, June 10, 2021.

[324] Linda Manyguns, "lower case as Indigenous 'eventing' support resistance," Mount Royal University, August 30, 2021.

site of the former Kamloops Indian Residential School," asserting that "[w]e must face the horror" that this elicited and "commit to finding the others who went missing." We were told that these assertions were "[r]espectfully supported by Dr. Elizabeth Evans, PhD, interim provost and vice-president, Academic and the Provost's Council, including MRU's vice-provosts and deans."

The president of my faculty association, Lee Easton, also weighed in on the matter.[325] He stated that he "was horrified by the discovery of the bodies of 215 children at Kamloops Residential School," and that "as President of the MRFA, I want to express my support and solidarity with our Indigenous colleagues, who are reeling from yet more evidence of the residential school system and its genocidal intent." One of these Indigenous colleagues, Gabrielle Lindstrom, a former Indigenous studies professor at MRU (and now an Educational Development Consultant in "Indigenous Ways of Knowing" at the University of Calgary), even maintained (on Twitter) that "215 little ones" had been "murdered" at KIRS.[326]

Dr. Gabrielle Lindstrom (Weasel Head)
@gabbylindstrom

After crying about the 215 little ones who were murdered in that residential school, I called my mom, a residential school survivor, to remind me that love, kindness & compassion cant be killed. the spirits of those who didn't make it inspire me to heal & to always choose love

6:31 PM · May 28, 2021 · Twitter Web App

10 Retweets **79** Likes

---

[325] Lee Easton, "215 Indigenous Children Found at Kamloops Residential School," undated 2021 post.

[326] Taylor Institute, University of Calgary website.

This statement was supported by numerous MRU professors. One colleague even argued a month later that "the murders of 'hundreds' (thousands?) of Indigenous children in Canada's catholic residential schools" justified the burning of churches (Taylor Institute Website).

Tim Haney
@HaneySociology

The Catholic Church isn't making reparations and hasn't apologized for the murders of **hundreds** (thousands?) of indigenous children in Canada's catholic residential schools. Yeah, people are p*ssed. I get it and don't blame them.

vice.com/en/article/y3d... via @vice

vice.com
More Churches Up in Flames in Canada as Outrage Against Catholic Church Gr...
The incidents occur amid ongoing reports of more than 1,000 unmarked graves of Indigenous children found at former residential schools, with the latest site ...

3:31 PM · Jul 1, 2021 · Twitter Web App

Because such statements were widely supported across the country, with almost no critical analysis, one could be forgiven for thinking that the claims about the "bodies of 215 children" had been substantiated. This is not the case.

What will be shown below is that there is no evidence to support the existence of remains at KIRS, not to mention the extraordinary claim of "215 murders." In a similar manner to the "Satanic panic" that began in the

1980s following the publication of the book *Michelle Remembers*,[327] the recollections of Billy Combes and others, after being widely disseminated, are likely to have been absorbed into the memories of Tk'emlúps te Secwépemc "Knowledge Keepers" and the wider public consciousness. This has been facilitated by Indigenous organizations intent on increasing compensation from the government, as well as "woke" academics and journalists who assume that the Indigenous "genocide survivor" identity must be accepted without question.

What is the Basis for the "Knowings" about the "215 Unmarked Graves"?

In the May 27, 2021 press release, Chief Rosanne Casimir stated that "[w]e had a knowing in our community that we were able to verify," and that "[t]o our knowledge, these missing children are undocumented deaths" with some being "as young as three years old." It turned out, however, that there was no "verification." Instead, a July 15, 2021 presentation by Dr. Sarah Beaulieu, the academic who had undertaken the survey of the area, stated that burials had not been confirmed but were "targets of interest" that had been identified with Ground Penetrating Radar (GPR).[328] During her presentation, Beaulieu cautioned that definitive statements about specific numbers, or even conclusions about the existence of any burials, could not be made until excavations were undertaken.

Dr. Beaulieu's presentation was supplemented by another press release from the Tk'emlúps te Secwépemc.[329] This noted that the survey was undertaken for three reasons: the oral histories of "Knowledge Keepers" had recollected "children as young as 6 years old being woken in the night to dig holes for burials in the apple orchard'"; "a juvenile rib bone" had surfaced nearby; and "[a] juvenile tooth was excavated from a shovel test pit during an impact assessment conducted by Simon Fraser University's

---

[327] Lawrence Pazder and Michelle Smith, *Michelle Remembers*, St. Martin's Press, 1980.

[328] "More investigations need to be done at site of former Kamloops B.C. residential school site," Global News, July 15 2021.

[329] For Immediate Release, Tkemlúps te Secwépemc (Kamloops Indian Band), July 15, 2021.

archaeology department." It was maintained that while "a juvenile tooth is not an indicator of loss of life," the other discovery of the "juvenile rib bone" meant that "this possibility should not be discounted."

Media coverage has noted that the existence of the juvenile rib bone and the tooth was confirmed by Dr. Beaulieu, and this had "helped investigators figure out where exactly to search."[330] With respect to the rib bone, it was claimed to have been found by a tourist in the early 2000s.[331] The tourist evidently provided the band with the bone, which was then "identified as human." Other accounts maintain that the bone was "found beneath the apple orchard" and "in the soil during another dig."[332] As the source for the information about the rib bone was Dr. Beaulieu, I tried to contact her by email several times in October 2021. My emails were not answered.

This silence about the "juvenile rib bone" is troubling. Generally, if a human bone is found, one does not just hand it over to an Indigenous group. Finding human remains is a serious matter, and this would have to be investigated by the police so as to determine the identity of the deceased person and if foul play had occurred. Therefore, questions need to be answered as to whether or not the bone has been determined to be human. If so, did the Tk'emlúps te Secwépemc involve the police in investigating this matter, and what were the results of the investigation?

Although the Simon Fraser University archaeology department's response to an inquiry on July 27, 2021 did not provide any information about the rib bone, except to say that they believed that a "community member" had found it, they did shed some light on the claim about the tooth. It was noted that this was identified as a *possible* human tooth in another dig by Dr. George Nicholas, but the tooth had now been determined as not human

---

[330] Castanet Staff, "Child's bone led to Kamloops residential school graves," *Alaska Highway News*, July 15, 2021.

[331] Christopher Foulds, "Excavation of probable burial sites at Tk'emlups yet to be undertaken," *Kamloops This Week*, September 17, 2021.

[332] Paula Newton "Thousands of children from Canadian schools for Indigenous communities may be buried in unmarked graves, officials say," KTVZ Channel 21 News, reposting from CNN, July 16, 2021; Amy Judd & Richard Zussman, "More unmarked graves likely to be discovered at former Kamloops, B.C., residential school: report," Global News, July 14, 2021.

(evidently Dr. Beaulieu was not aware of this when she gave her presentation). In response to attempts to get additional information about the tooth, the following reply was provided on July 28, 2021 by an archaeology department member: "I have been strongly advised by the TteS legal team not to respond to any queries from the public regarding the search for unmarked graves in Kamloops." It was also asserted that this request had been extended to include the entire archaeology department. Although it is impossible to know what has prompted the department of a public university to make such statements, this is possibly due to the federal government's *Tri-Council Policy Statement: Ethical Conduct for Research Involving Humans (TCPS2)*.[333] In its chapter on "Research Involving the First Nations, Inuit and Métis Peoples of Canada," there is encouragement of "respectful relationships" and "the "ongoing efforts of Indigenous peoples to preserve and manage their collective knowledge and information generated from their communities."

This close relationship between SFU and the Tk'emlúps te Secwépemc requires scrutiny.[334] The Tk'emlúps te Secwépemc partnered with Simon Fraser University's Department of Archaeology from 1991-2005. This partnership excavated all over the reserve for development purposes, including an area that overlapped with Dr. Beaulieu's GPR work. This is why, when Beaulieu belatedly learned about the project after May 27, she had to revise her estimate of 215 initial "targets of interest" down to 200. This revised number was relayed during her July 15 oral presentation.[335] This revision is important because it shows that the SFU Department of Archaeology did not consider 15 "targets of interest" identified by Beaulieu as being "probable burials," and so it is possible that the other 200 are similarly questionable.

[333] Tri-Council Policy Statement, "Ethical Conduct for Research Involving Humans," TCPS2 2018 ,Canadian Institutes of Health Research Natural Sciences and Engineering Research Council of Canada, Social Sciences and Humanities Research Council (Ottawa: Her Majesty the Queen in Right of Canada, 2019).

[334] George Nicholas and Nola Markey, "Secwepemc Cultural Education Society/Simon Fraser University (SCES-SFU) Indigenous Archaeology Program," in C. Smith, ed., *Encyclopedia of Global Archaeology*, Springer-Verlag Berlin Heidelberg, 2013.

[335] "More investigations need to be done at site of former Kamloops B.C. residential school site," Global News, July 15, 2021.

The possibility of the politicization of the SFU archaeology department is disturbing. Simon Fraser University is a public institution, and its ability to discuss research findings should not be controlled by the Tk'emlúps te Secwépemc or any other private entity. It also raises questions about whether the archaeological research undertaken about Indigenous "unmarked graves" has been compromised by a particular agenda. To what extent are the claims of Dr. Beaulieu and the other archaeologists working for Indigenous organizations, about their "confidence" in the probability of finding unmarked graves, valid? To make this determination, it is necessary to examine the degree of certainty provided by GPR.

What is the Degree of Certainty Provided by GPR?

On July 15, 2021, the Tk'emlúps te Secwépemc hosted a public presentation and media event to present the findings of the Beaulieu GPR survey.[336] The event exuded a politically charged atmosphere with many territorial land acknowledgements, prayers, and references to the ancestors. Chief Casimir spoke of the need to find the "truth" about the "missing children…whose remains were placed in unmarked graves." She explained that "we are not here for retaliation; we are here for truth telling" so as to "bring peace to those missing children, families, and communities." This would require "[following] the science," while "pay[ing] heed to what oral tellings survivors share with us." Casimir also pointed out that this would take a great deal of time and resources, and that "cultural and wellness supports" were available to help audience members deal with this "historic dark chapter" and the intergenerational trauma that it had created.

Beaulieu had been selected to do the survey because of her professional interactions with Dr. Eldon Yellowhorn, a SFU Indigenous studies professor and past president of the Canadian Archaeological Association. She gave her presentation on the report she had written about her use of GPR in what used to be the apple orchard at KIRS. Beaulieu explained that GPR was able to determine "subsurface anomalies," many of which were now "targets of interest." She noted that oral histories had "guided" the use

---

[336] "More unmarked graves likely to be found at former Kamloops residential school: report," Global News, on YoutTube, July 15, 2021.

of GPR; claims about children being awakened in the middle of the night to dig clandestine graves, it was implied, were true, and GPR provided the "special spatial specificity to this truth." While it was cautioned that the existence of remains could not be confirmed without excavation, a number of factors, in her view, made this a likely conclusion. Beaulieu pointed to the tooth and rib bone, "depressions in the orchard that correlate with the subsurface anomalies," the "east-west configuration of the subsurface anomalies" that were consistent with "typical Christian burial traditions," and, most importantly, the oral histories of the "Knowledge Keepers," as evidence of clandestine children's graves.

During her presentation, Dr. Beaulieu showed three slides of examples of the information that GPR had revealed. These slides showed how the GPR image for a "probable burial" differed from the representation of metal object anomalies, rocks, and tree root systems. Essentially, with burials, one could see the edge of the vertical shafts where digging had occurred, and the dome on top of it caused by the soil disturbances. In her answer to a journalist from the *Toronto Star*, Beaulieu also stated that the "probable burial" anomalies were fairly shallow — between .7 and .8 metres below the surface — and this fitted with the "Knowledge Keepers'" accounts of burying children, and the fact that smaller bodies require less soil to be dug up. There was no discussion of how a clandestine grave might differ from holes that were dug for other purposes. She also did not mention how an image for a burial that was 50-70 years old (the "oral tellings" had stated that KIRS burials had occurred in the 1950s and 1960s) would differ from ones that were more recent.

Dr. Beaulieu's presentation was followed by remarks from Dr. Lisa Hodgetts, the President of the Canadian Archaeological Association, and Dr. Kisha Supernant, an archaeologist from the University of Alberta. Hodgetts, referring to herself as a "settler," stated that she was grateful to the Tk'emlúps te Secwépemc for allowing her to "bear witness" to the "pain and trauma" that was being suffered by "intergenerational survivors." She encouraged all Canadians to hold governments and the churches accountable for the "thousands and thousands of missing children," asserting that funding should be provided to Indigenous groups to "chart their own path and own pace" for further collaborative and respectful work to "find missing children."

Dr. Supernant, the chair of the Association's Working Group on Unmarked Graves and Director of the Institute of Prairie and Indigenous Archaeology, stressed the need to work collaboratively and respectfully with Indigenous communities. Supernant commended Beaulieu's work, confirmed that there were a "number of highly probable burials," and referred to the "knowledge held in communities by knowledge keepers." Again, the need for more resources to undertake this work was stressed.

These presentations by archaeologists were followed by comments from RoseAnne Archibald, the Grand Chief of the Assembly of First Nations, and statements from three former KIRS students and "Knowledge Keepers" — Evelyn Camille, Leona Thomas, and Mona Jules. Although all talked about the destruction of culture and self-esteem caused by the schools, only Camille discussed the "missing children." Camille asserted that many children died from trying to cross the river and freezing to death when they were trying to make their way back home. She believed that many children had been "murdered," but that the "remains should be left undisturbed." Instead of excavating, Camille recommended "say[ing] prayers for the remains that are found" as this would "guide them home to finish their journey."

Grand Chief Archibald, after hearing these remarks, maintained that the Tk'emlúps te Secwépemc case had enabled the world to learn "how 215 innocent children died and were buried in unmarked graves," and that this "crime against humanity" constituted "genocide." She completely ignored the caution expressed by Beaulieu and the other archaeologists and argued that "this ground penetrating technology is revealing evidence, undisputable [sic] proof, that crimes were committed." On the basis of these "probable burials," Archibald argued that the "crimes have to be investigated" and "the criminals must be held to account." In "looking for ways to heal the trauma," Archibald recommended that Canadians call politicians to demand "reparations," "justice," and "action." Similar comments were made by Don Worme, the legal counsel for the Tk'emlúps te Secwépemc. According to Worme, "I think what we can say firstly that it is undeniable that those are graves. There is no question that there have been children gone missing. Our knowledge keepers from this community have told us so. We believe them."

These comments by Worme and Archibald show an astounding disregard for Beaulieu's tentativeness — that remains cannot be established until excavations are completed. Even worse, it appears that excavations will never be done because it is to be a "community driven process," and many argue that the "bodies" should not be disturbed. This raises questions about why people who actually think that "murders," "genocide," and "atrocities" occurred would not demand that forensic examinations be undertaken. If "the criminals must be held to account," as Archibald asserts, isn't the first step in this process to determine whether or not the "probable burials" actually contain the remains of Indigenous children? Or is the intent to convict people of "murder" on the basis of the "oral tellings" of the "Knowledge Keepers"?

Time and time again one sees assertions that GPR is being used to "confirm" the existence of children's remains. Even archaeologists make comments that "[t]he first part is the oral history from the survivors, and… archeology using ground penetrating radar can provide the scientific part of the story to show that 'yes, there are unmarked graves here.'"[337] So far, no information has been forthcoming about the fact that the burials in question would be over 50 years old, when it is recognized that there are "limitations of detecting graves for extended postmortem intervals."

It is maintained, in fact, that "[f]inding hidden bodies, believed to have been murdered and buried, is problematic, expensive in terms of human resource and currently has low success rates for law enforcement agencies." It is pointed out that "there is a general reduction in geophysical anomaly amplitude with increase in time since burial, so the sooner geophysical surveys can be undertaken the greater the chance of discovery." This means that it will be more difficult to see the indications of graves the longer bodies have been in the ground. Detection will be particularly difficult if bodies are buried without a covering; clandestine burials with unwrapped bodies are difficult to detect after ten years have elapsed.

---

337 Derek Cornet, "Archaeologist believes ground penetrating radar can show true reality of residential schools," *Prince Albert Now*, June 1, 2021.

It also is irresponsible not to point out that burials, even if they are "probable," do not necessarily involve human remains. In the literature on excavations being undertaken on the basis of GPR, there are many instances of the investigations finding other materials that are buried. In the case of the search for three boys who went missing in 1966 from South Australia, for example, a "subsurface anomaly that was consistent with the size, shape and depth of a burial that could have contained three small children" was found, but this turned out to be animal bones and garbage. Therefore, it seems unlikely that Dr. Beaulieu would be able to make specific claims about "probable burials" involving the 215 (and then 200) "targets of interest" after a period of 50-70 years had elapsed. And, as there has been a refusal to release her report, there is no way for the findings to be scrutinized by objective observers.

The "Tellings" of the "Knowledge Keepers"

As was mentioned above, the Tk'emlúps te Secwépemc press release of July 15, 2021 stated that "Knowledge Keepers" recall "children as young as 6 years old being woken in the night to dig holes for burials in the apple orchard." But who are these "Knowledge Keepers" and how reliable are their recollections? Do the recollections concern hearsay, or are they eyewitness accounts? To what extent have they been influenced by the stories that have been circulating for years in testimonies like those found in the film "Unrepentant"? Even the use of the description "Knowledge Keeper" should be disputed, as knowledge claims must be constantly challenged on the basis of the evidence available. What does it mean to say that knowledge is "kept"?

Chief Casimir has never identified the "Knowledge Keepers," nor has she specified what was said in their oral histories beyond what was asserted in the July 15 press release. It is possible that the names of the "Knowledge Keepers" are in Dr. Beaulieu's written report, but Chief Casimir has refused to release it. Four women are identified as "Knowledge Keepers" or "Knowledge Carriers" on the Qwelmínte Secwepemc website —

141

Colleen Seymour, Jeanette Jules, Mona Jules, and Rhona Bowe.[338] It also appears that some of these "Knowledge Carriers" are closely related, and they could have influenced the accounts of one another. This would impact their reliability.

In looking at the oral histories about secret burials at KIRS, the first eyewitness account of burials is claimed, by Kevin Annett, to have been made in 1998 (a search for earlier testimonies has found no reference to murders or secret burials). Annett asserts that Jessie (sometimes spelled Jesse) Jules made these allegations when he spoke at a United Nations-affiliated IHRAAM Tribunal held on June 12-14, 1998, which was organized "to investigate genocide in Canadian Indian schools." According to Kevin Annett, even though Jules feared that he would be punished by his home reserve if he "mentioned the dead kids," he told the tribunal that

> fellow Kamloops students were starved to death in underground chambers at the school and forced to sleep with children dying of tuberculosis after they tried running away. He
> named Catholic priests like Brother Murphy who sodomized kids with cattle prods and beat a boy named Arnold to death with a club. Jessie saw another priest push a young girl named
> Patricia out a window to her death. He even drew us a map of where he buried children at night at the order of the priests.[339]

In addition to having the first account of "buried children" at KIRS attributed to him, Jules is significant because of an alleged connection to Billy Combes (the footage of him in "Unrepentant" is the first recorded testimony of secret burials at KIRS). On page 95 of his book *Fallen: The Story of the Vancouver Four* (2017), Annett claims that Combes wrote a poem stating that his friend "Jessie" witnessed a secret burial with him. Combes is also quoted by Annett in the 2010 version of *Hidden From History: The Canadian Genocide* as stating the following: "A friend of mine and I were out scavenging for food, since they never fed us regular. We saw Brother Murphy dragging this bag towards a hole near the orchard.

---

338 "2020 Summer Speakers," Sexqétqcltcn 2020, Qwclmíntc Sccwépemc.

339 Kevin Annett, "Murder by Decree: Mass Graves of Children in Canada – Documented Evidence," WordPress blog post, April 25, 2013. Cf. *Dialogue* Magazine, Vol. 34, No. 4 (Summer 2021).

He turned it over and a small body fell into the hole, and he started throwing the dirt in."[340] Combes also claimed, in Annett's account, to have witnessed Brother Murphy killing a child by throwing her off a balcony, as well as him burying a child in the apple orchard with another priest.

As the clearly fictional claim regarding Queen Elizabeth abducting children indicates, however, one needs to be sceptical about the accounts Annett relays. The stories Annett attributes to Combes, in fact, are not even mentioned by him in his interview with *The Globe and Mail* in 2007.[341] It is also not known if these stories had any direct influence over the KIRS "Knowledge Keepers." But questions must be raised about how much the circulation of these grisly tales over social media and other forums has influenced the memories of those who attended KIRS. There is only one early account – in the book *Behind Closed Doors*,[342] which was published in 2000 – that has appeared independently of Annett's claims. In this book, Eddy Jules, presumably related to Jessie/Jesse Jules, was interviewed. His recollection implied that there was something untoward at KIRS, but this was hearsay and did not mention the apple orchard. In an account written up in the book on page 63, Eddy Jules states the following:

> [w]hen I was in Senior B I used to hear about girls getting pregnant down the other end of the building. They'd get pregnant, but they would never have kids, you know. And the thing was, they'd bring somebody in from over town who'd do an abortion, I guess. We used to hear it. It used to be really scary, hearing them open up the incinerator after what was going on. They'd open up the incinerator in the big boiler, and we would hear this big clang, and we'd know they would be getting rid of the evidence…it was a very, very scary thing. We'd wonder how many kids got thrown into that incinerator. We'd hear a clang and then they cranked the fire up…I think most of the kids realized what was going on, but there was nothing we could do. We couldn't say anything because

---

[340] Kevin D. Annett, Not "abuse" but mass murder! A Memorandum on Genocidal Crimes at the Catholic Kamloops 'Indian Residential School,'" Republic of Kanata online, May 30, 2021.

[341] Bill Curry and Karen Howlett, "Sexual abuse at heart of pain," *Globe and Mail*, April 25, 2007.

[342] A.S. Jack, *Behind Closed Doors: Stories from the Kamloops Indian Residential School* (Penticton: Secwepemc Cultural Education Society and Theytus Books Ltd., 2006).

no one would believe us. All of us that were going to school would hear the clang, and we would say, 'Oh, that's probably so and so's friend, and they gave her an abortion.'[343]

This hearsay changed substantially when Eddy Jules was interviewed by Morgan Hampton 20 years later on September 30, 2021. Unlike the account in *Behind Closed Doors,* Jules now claims to be an eyewitness to an event where he went into the medical room and saw "blood all over the floor." According to Eddy Jules:

> The door was ajar and there was this young girl laying there and this old non-native guy with glasses was holding something in his hands, and all the blood was on the floor. The girl, I never saw her after that day, and I realized what he was holding was a little baby that he just aborted, and it probably belonged to one of the men that worked there. He used a coat hanger, so I think that while he was pulling the baby out, he killed this young girl and she disappeared.[344]

Eddy Jules then claims to have seen the janitor throwing a fetus into the furnace. With respect to the secret burials, Hampton notes that Jules and other attendees had alluded to them for years, even though this was not mentioned in *Behind Closed Doors.* Eddy Jules now asserts that he was 11 years old when he saw a light in the apple orchard in the middle of the night. He also recounts that a student with a cleft palate was going to have an operation, but "years later we found that he was murdered, killed, because he pissed some guy off at the Residential School that didn't like the way he sounded."

Apart from the interconnected testimonies of Billy Combes and Jessie/ Jesse Jules, as well as this recently changed memory of Eddy Jules, there are no eyewitness accounts related to murders or burials. Dr. Ronald Ignace (who is related to Mona Jules), for example, said absolutely nothing about burials in his lengthy account of KIRS in *Behind Closed Doors.* On June 5, 2021, in a *Toronto Star* interview, however, Ignace claimed to

---

[343] Ibid., p. 63.

[344] Morgan Hampton, "Surviving the residential system: a KIRS story," *Merritt Herald*, September 30, 2021.

know all about them.[345] He recounted that, when he was a student at KIRS in the 1950s and 1960s, he had heard stories "for years" about students who were directed by staff to "dig some holes" in the middle of the night so that apple trees could be planted, and it was wondered why these plantings never occurred. Although Ignace had no first-hand knowledge of burials, Chief Casimir's announcement of Beaulieu's GPR results led him to assume that remains must have been found in the apple orchard. This caused Ignace, when he visited the surveyed site, to go up to one of the 200/215 stakes and make an offering of tobacco and say a prayer. Observing these stakes led him to conclude the following: "It's heartbreaking to see all of our people surreptitiously buried in the dark of night in shallow graves." According to Ignace, "[i]t's mind-boggling how they could ... do something as evil as that."

Mona Jules, Ron Ignace's aunt, also did not mention any secret burials in *Behind Closed Doors* (although she was interviewed anonymously, identification can be determined when she talks about the death of her sister, Nellie, at KIRS). On July 15, 2021, however, Mona Jules made the following remark: "In doing my research about the residential school and the death of those children, back in the 1500s, the Pope had ordered the death of children that were gathered up and put in those schools, if they were not Catholic, to kill them. That was a cold, terrible command, coming from someone in a high position."[346] Mona Jules had forgotten the title of the document from which she obtained this information, but maintained that it had the words "field study" in it. She then went on to state that "after hearing about those children, children being found along the orchards and other places, I often wondered what would have happened if I hadn't been able to say my night prayers in my language, would my life have been snuffed out because I wasn't Catholic?' Mona Jules is identified as one of Tk'emlúps te Secwépemc "Knowledge Keepers."

---

345 Douglas Quan, "'It tore our humanity apart': What life was really like at the Kamloops residential school," *Toronto Star*, June 5, 2021.

346 "Survivor of Kamloops B.C. Residential School says she remembers crying out for her parents," Global News, July 15 2021.

Another former student, Mary Percival, also now claims that she heard about the burials.[347] While Percival didn't mention burials during her testimony at the TRC hearings in 2013,[348] her recollection in 2021 was that students were told to stay away from the apple orchard because it was claimed "that children who died after running away from the school were buried there." In spite of this, Percival asserts that she often picked apples and played in the orchard. But if the apple orchard was levelled in 1962 or 1963 to build the new dormitory/hostel (now the Band Administration building), as Celia Haig-Brown says it was in *Resistance and Renewal*, then how could Percival, who only arrived at KIRS in 1962, have spent time playing in the orchard with other children and eating apples?

Even more of these kinds of stories have emerged with the airing of *The Fifth Estate* episode "The Reckoning: Secrets unearthed by Tk'emlúps te Secwépemc" on January 13, 2022.[349] In this program, nine Indigenous people connected to KIRS are interviewed – Harvey McLeod, Norman Retasket, Diena Jules, Jennifer Yvonne Camille, Michael LeBourdais, Audrey Baptiste, Ted Gottfriedson, Rosanne Casimir, and Manny Jules – and it is claimed that the residential school "was a place of horror for the children forced to live here." Only two eyewitness accounts are provided. Audrey Baptiste states that she saw four boys hanging in a barn, and that one of them never showed up for class the next day. Jennifer Yvonne Camille mentions seeing a coat hanger and blood in the furnace room. All the references to burials concern hearing stories about holes being dug, unnamed people going missing, and being warned not to go near the apple orchard. Although this program supposedly prides itself on "in-depth investigations," no critical questions are asked. The tone and interview style indicates that all stories should be believed.

The most surprising circumstance is that a CBC online article associated with *The Fifth Estate* episode uncritically recounts the allegation about a

---

[347] Wawmeesh Hamilton, "Kamloops residential school survivor says aunt may have been buried at the former school," CBC News, August 18, 2021.

[348] "Kamloops Hearing. Sharing Panel 115," National Centre for Truth and Reconciliation, May 29, 2013.

[349] "The Reckoning: Secrets Unearthed by Tk'emlúps te Secwépemc," *The Fifth Estate*, Season 47, Episode 10, aired January 13, 2022.

baby being thrown into a furnace.[350] According to Harvey McLeod, he was approached by a man who claimed to have done this after hearing about the "discovery of the suspected unmarked graves." According to McLeod, this man confessed that "he was given a box to put in [the furnace]. He didn't know what it was and then he was going to put it in there, and a baby fell out." Even more strange is the fact, noted in the piece, that "[f]ormer TRC chair Murray Sinclair issued a statement on June 1, 2021, on his facebook, after the discovery at the Kamloops Indian Residential School. He says that survivors shared stories about the furnace to the TRC." According to Sinclair, "[s]ome of the survivors talked about infants who were born to young girls at the residential schools who had been fathered by priests, having those infants taken away from them and deliberately killed, sometimes by being thrown into furnaces, they told us."

None of these stories, however, were ever published in the TRC reports. If the TRC thought that these events had occurred, surely judges like Sinclair would have thought it necessary to bring it to the attention of law enforcement. The omission seems to indicate that the stories were not seen as being credible at the time, as they smacked of the improbable claims being disseminated by Kevin Annett. It is shocking that what were once considered to be lurid tales attributed to a conspiracy theorist are now being credulously retold by Canada's publicly funded broadcaster.

Inadvertently, a major inconsistency is revealed in "The Reckoning," which should make everyone take pause. This is that it is now claimed that the search for the unmarked graves did not occur because of the recollections of the "Knowledge Keepers," or from finding "a juvenile rib bone" and "juvenile tooth," as was stated in the July 15 Tk'emlúps te Secwépemc press release. Instead, it was museum administrator Diena Jules who was the "driving force" behind the effort to find the unmarked graves. She initiated the search because the band received some grant money in 2019 to upgrade the community's Heritage Park. Because Covid-19 meant that some of the money could not be spent, Jules suggested that the band should use the funds to "look for the kids" because she wanted, for her own comfort, "to confirm where they are."

---

[350] Lynette Fortune, Linda Guerriero and Gillian Findlay, "Down in the Apple Orchard," CBC News, January 13, 2022.

The fact that the story has changed so much in only a few months is another indication of the questionable nature of this narrative. If the "truth" is really desired, what is needed is actual investigative journalism. All of these claims must be fact-checked and scrutinized alongside other forms of evidence.

Other circumstances that cast doubt on these testimonies are that there were three Indigenous teachers on staff at KIRS during the 1950s and 1960s — Joe Stanley Michel (now deceased), Benjamin Paul, and Mabel Caron (still living in Kamloops). These three Indigenous staff members are featured in the 1962 CBC documentary, "The Eyes of Children" (now considered, without explanation, to be a "propaganda film" by The Fifth Estate). Joe Stanley Michel was the first graduate (register #589) from the high school, which was established in 1950, and returned to KIRS to teach there from 1953-1967. He lived with his wife, Anna Susan Soulle (also a KIRS graduate, register #666) and their young family in a teacherage next door to the school building. Michel and Soulle were also interviewed in Celia Haig-Brown's *Resistance and Renewal* (1988), and did not mention burials.[351] Would all of these Indigenous people have kept silent about these alleged clandestine graves?

"The Eyes of Children" also offers a stark contrast to the macabre tales being told. Instead, one is shown footage of children enthusiastically crowding around one of the priests, playing sports, enjoying Christmas activities, and being taught dancing by a nun. The same three Indigenous teachers — Michel, Paul and Caron — can be observed giving classes and providing training in a machine shop. And while one can be taken aback by the dated style, the piousness of some scenes, and perhaps argue that the footage was edited or sanitized to exaggerate the happiness of the children, it is hard to believe that the children in this documentary would have been murdered or their babies thrown into a furnace.

The questionable nature of the evidence for assuming that there are 215 or 200 secret burials in an apple orchard – a likely non-existent juvenile rib bone, a report of GPR that will not be released and cannot even be discussed by the SFU archaeology department, and the highly questionable

351 Celia Haig-Brown, *Resistance and Renewal: Surviving the Indian Residential School*. Arsenal Pulp Press, 1988.

memories of people who have been made aware of the stories being circulated in various forums - makes one wonder why this narrative has gained so much currency in universities and media outlets across the country. With respect to Indigenous leaders, this can be explained by what I have called "neotribal rentierism,"[352] where compensation is extracted for wrongs that have been committed in the past. This rent-seeking has been assisted by "woke" non-Indigenous academics who assume that, to combat oppression, they must "shut up and listen" and unquestionably accept the Indigenous "genocide survivor" identity.

Neotribal Rentierism and Reified Postmodernism

In *The Globe and Mail* on October 25, 2021, it is stated that "two human-rights-tribunal orders that would result in billions of dollars in compensation for Indigenous children" will be "closely watched" in the context of "the Liberal government's commitment to reconciliation." There is reference to a "legal battle" taking place, and that this is occurring while "the issue of reconciliation with Indigenous peoples has come into greater focus for the country with the revelations of unmarked burial sites of former residential school students." And as was seen in the Tk'emlúps te Secwépemc's open letter, referred to at the beginning of this piece, this is just one area of funding that can be demanded on the basis of the "unmarked burial sites." It is part of wider rent-seeking efforts that rely upon characterizing Canada as a perpetrator of genocide.

The problem of trying to get to the truth of the "secret burials" is made worse by the fact that archaeologists are becoming increasingly concerned about their relationships with Indigenous organizations. We are told that the three hundred million dollars that has now been released to "search" for these "secret burials" must be "community led," requiring that they conform to the political demands of Indigenous organizations. This was seen in the connection between the Tk'emlúps te Secwépemc and the SFU archaeology department discussed earlier. Because of some undetermined connection, presumably due to a constraint from a funding arrangement or

---

352 Rodney A. Clifton and Mark DeWolf, *From Truth Comes Reconciliation: Assessing the Truth and Reconciliation Commission Report*, Winnipeg: Frontier Centre for Public Policy, 2021.

the desire to develop "respectful relationships," the Department of Archaeology at SFU has decided that it should not publicly discuss the findings about the unmarked graves.

These constraints on academic discussion do not just pertain to the discipline of archaeology. They are linked to wider developments in the academy, which concern how universities have been captured by what Helen Pluckrose and James Lindsay call "reified postmodernism" (known colloquially as "woke-ism").[353] According to Pluckrose and Lindsay, postmodernism was originally a relativist framework that focused on subjectivity in opposition to objectivity so as to contest the Enlightenment's promotion of science, reason, and the pursuit of a universal truth. Its ability to disarm the academy, however, meant that postmodernism gradually became "reified," leading to the aggressive demands that identities perceived to be oppressed be "made real."

In the case of the "Knowledge Keepers' tellings" and other testimonies about the "215 secret burials" in the apple orchard at KIRS, the identity that must be "made real" is the notion of being an Indigenous residential school (genocide) "survivor"; this is why there were so many uncritically accepted references to "mass graves," "denialism," and "murdered" children in universities across the country. If one questions the claim that the residential schools were genocidal, or argues that they provided educational benefits to students, it is asserted by one's colleagues that this is tantamount to being a Holocaust denier. Some scholars, including Milena Radzikowska, professor of Information Design at Mount Royal University, have explicitly said so.[354]

---

[353] Helen Pluckrose and James Lindsay, *Cynical Theories: How Activist Scholarship Made Everything about Race, Gender, and Identity—and Why This Harms Everybody* Pitchstone Publishing (Aug. 25 2020)

[354] Cf. Twitter, @DrRadzikowska, 11:12 am September 18, 2020.

Dr. Milena Radzikowska
@DrRadzikowska

Denying the genocide of Indigenous Peoples is the same as denying the Holocaust.

11:12 AM · Sep 18, 2020 · Twitter for iPhone

2 Retweets   **11** Likes

And just as teaching that the Holocaust did not occur would likely result in dismissal for academic incompetence, some professors claim that one should be fired for challenging the residential schools [genocide] "survivor" identity.[355] The university's widespread promotion of "decolonization" and "reconciliation" is now morphing into demands for affirmative acknowledgments from professors, as some Indigenous students, faculty, and staff claim that being exposed to dissenting positions creates a "culture of fear", and challenging the "genocide" narrative "conveys a tolerance for violent and lethal behaviour."[356]

While these kinds of intellectual constraints around the discussions of cases like KIRS are destructive for academic freedom and open inquiry, a more disturbing consequence is the impact that this is having on Indigenous peoples themselves. The acceptance of these lurid and highly improbable stories is causing increasing anger and bitterness about the past, as well as an inability to communicate, when what is needed are honest conversations about how to solve the educational, health and housing problems facing Indigenous communities. As has been said many times, there can be no "reconciliation" without truth.

Because of the accusations of "genocide" that have emerged with the moral panic brought about by the circulation of stories about "secret burials," "murders," and "mass graves," the actual problems facing marginalized

---

[355] Frances Widdowson, "The Residential Schools and Unmarked Graves: Why is open inquiry perilous?" Paper presented to the July 10, 2021 event, "Can We Discuss Those Unmarked Graves?" sponsored by the Society for Academic Freedom Scholarship and the Frontier Centre for Public Policy, posted online September 2021.

[356] SAMRU (Students Association of Mount Royal University), For Immediate Release, "Representation Executive Council condemns comments mocking the unmarked graves of Indigenous children" July 13, 2021.

Indigenous people are not being addressed. We are, once again, heading down a path where funds will be dispersed to alleviate problems that are not caused by a lack of money. As Evelyn Camille pointed out in her statement at the July 15, 2021 public presentation about the Beaulieu report, the residential school settlement of billions of dollars is just perceived as "[throwing] a few silver coins" at Indigenous people instead of actually addressing their suffering.

Much Indigenous deprivation – low educational levels, poor health, and high rates of violent criminality, alcoholism, sexual abuse, and suicide - is due to being economically isolated and receiving substandard services, especially a poor quality education. None of this will be rectified by spending billions of dollars on the allegations about "unmarked graves." This only benefits a tiny elite of Indigenous and non-Indigenous rent seekers to the detriment of ordinary Indigenous people. Money will be paid out to lawyers and consultants in what Albert Howard and I have called the Aboriginal Industry,[357] and new grievances will ensure that funds are diverted to complex agreements and bureaucratic processes that benefit no one. Portraying the residential schools as "genocidal" is at best a distraction; at worst, it acts to disguise the serious educational challenges that face any nation-state trying to incorporate isolated and marginalized tribal cultures into a modern economy and society.

This chapter was originally published in The American Conservative *online, February 15, 2022.*

---

357 Frances Widdowson and Albert Howard, *Disrobing the Aboriginal Industry: The Deception Behind Indigenous Cultural Preservation* (Montreal and Kingston: McGill-Queen's University Press, 2008).

Chapter Six

A Media-Fuelled Social Panic Over Unmarked Graves

Jonathan Kay

"The discovery of unmarked graves at a former Residential School in [the province of British Columbia] and the countrywide awakening it set off have been chosen as Canada's news story of the year by editors in newsrooms across the country," reported the CBC last December.[358] It was an apt choice — though not necessarily for the reasons described by the author.

Canada's unmarked-graves story broke on May 27th, 2021, when the Tk'emlúps te Secwépemc First Nation reported the existence of ground-penetrating radar (GPR) data that indicated regularly spaced subterranean soil disturbances on the grounds of a former Indigenous Residential School that had operated in Kamloops, BC, between 1893 and 1978.[359] In addition, the First Nation's leaders asserted their belief that these soil disturbances corresponded to unmarked graves of Indigenous children who'd died while attending the school.

The story became an immediate sensation in the Canadian media; and remained so for months, even after the GPR expert on whom the First Nation relied, Sarah Beaulieu, carefully noted that the radar survey results didn't necessarily indicate the presence of graves — let alone graves that had been unmarked, graves of Indigenous people, or graves of children. Contrary to what many Canadians came to believe during that heady period, GPR survey results don't yield X-ray-style images that show bodies or coffins.[360] What it typically shows are disruptions in soil and

---

[358] Dirk Meissner, "Canadian Press names Kamloops unmarked graves discovery Canada's news story of the year," CBC News, Dec. 16, 2021.

[359] Courtney Dickson, "Remains of 215 children found buried at former B.C. residential school, First Nation says," CBC News, May 28, 2021.

[360] John J. Schultz, "Detecting Buried Remains Using Ground Penetrating Radar," Final Report Submitted to National Institute of Justice, Office of Justice Programs, U.S. Department of Justice, April 2012. Award No. 2008-DN-BX-K132.

sediment. Investigators then need to dig up the ground to determine what actually lies underneath.

But those details were swept aside during what, in retrospect, appears to have been a true nation-wide social panic. As other Indigenous groups announced that they'd be conducting their own GPR surveys, media figures confidently asserted that the original Canadian Residential School student death-toll estimate of 3,201 would soon double or even triple.[361] One op-ed writer went so far as to declare that "the discovery of the graves of the children in Kamloops may be Canada's Holocaust moment."[362] Dramatic, tear-drenched acts of public atonement unfolded everywhere, with many July 1 Canada Day celebrations being either cancelled or transformed into opportunities for morose self-laceration.

I was one of many Canadians who initially got swept up with all of this — in large part because it seemed as if everyone in the media was speaking with one voice, including journalists I'd known and respected for many years. Looking back on the coverage, I note that headline writers mostly skipped over the technical bits about soil dislocations and such, and went straight to "bodies" and "graves." And the stories often were interspersed with credulous recitations of dubious tales featuring live babies being thrown into furnaces or buried alive.[363]

The whole mission of Canada's church-run Residential School system was to assimilate Indigenous people into white Canadian society, usually against their will, while forcing children to leave their families and communities for months or even years at a time. No one disputes that many students were subject to cruel (and sometimes even predatory) treatment and substandard medical care. Certainly, the death rate for Indigenous children attending these schools was much higher than that for children in the general population. No, I never bought into the idea that there was any kind of mass-murder plot going on at these schools. But it hardly seemed

---

[361] "Number of Indian residential school student deaths may never be known: TRC," APTN National News, June 2, 2015.

[362] Richard Kool, "Is this Canada's Holocaust moment?" *Victoria Times-Colonist*, June 12, 2021.

[363] Mary Katherine Keown, "Kamloops discovery 'a devastating reminder' of residential school tragedy, Sudbury's mayor says," *Sudbury Star*, June 1, 2021.

far-fetched that some victims of mistreatment and neglect had been buried in unmarked graves—"off the books," so to speak—by malevolent white teachers, school administrators, and priests seeking to evade responsibility for their actions.

The other important aspect to mention is that—like most other Canadians, I'm guessing—I believed we were only a few days or weeks from seeing real physical evidence plucked from the earth. So it didn't much matter to me that early commentators were temporarily playing fast and loose with the distinction between GPR data and actual corpses.

Canadians were being told that the old orchard in Kamloops where the GPR data had been collected was a *crime scene*—a site of mass murder, and the final resting place of 215 child homicide victims. As I've reasoned elsewhere: If you told Canadians that, say, 215 murdered white children were buried somewhere in Toronto, or Ottawa, or Vancouver, there'd be investigators and police crawling all over the place, looking for remains that could be tested and identified.[364] And so I naturally assumed the same thing would soon be happening in Kamloops.

Many of the abuses identified at the Kamloops Residential School and others like it date to the early decades of the Cold War. This means that some of the perpetrators of these claimed child homicides—that is, the staff who worked at these schools—could still be alive. Perhaps their crimes might even be studied and solved by inspecting the bones of children buried alongside one another. Surely, no effort would be spared to pull evidence from the ground immediately, so that criminal cases could be prosecuted before the passage of time allowed the killers to escape accountability for their racist bloodbath.

But then the weeks and months passed in 2021. Spring turned to summer, then summer to fall, and fall to winter, and … nothing happened. It's now been 14 months since the original announcement was made about presumed graves in Kamloops, and no physical evidence has been unearthed. No graves. No corpses. No human remains. In fact, as far as I can tell, there doesn't even seem to be any systematic effort by police or

---

[364] Jonathan Kay, Quillette Podcast #186: "Frances Widdowson on the Questions Canadians Aren't Supposed to Ask About Unmarked Graves," April 13, 2022.

First Nations leaders to commence such investigations. Eventually, it began to strike the general public that this was a very odd way to treat a mass murder scene, even as pundits and politicians refused to change their early, apocalyptic tone.

Which brings us back to that CBC announcement in December, which informed us that "the discovery of unmarked graves" had been Canada's biggest news story of 2021. That very statement encoded the polite lie, which most Canadian journalists have been encouraged to repeat in one form or another, that some known number of "unmarked graves" had well and truly been "discovered." The truth was (and remains) that the number of confirmed graves remains at zero. No one, to my knowledge, has found any human remains—i.e., body parts or tissue from decaying corpses—either at Kamloops or any of the other former Residential Schools, through the use of GPR.

So yes, the story did arguably qualify as "Canada's news story of the year" —but not insofar as it was a story about graves. Rather, it turned out to be a story about the herd behaviour of Canada's intellectual class. Thousands of politicians, writers, broadcasters, and activists spent months crowd-sourcing the creation of a completely unsupported national narrative, and then failed to correct the record once their rush to judgment had run headlong into reality.

I've been in journalism for a quarter century, and have witnessed plenty of bizarre controversies within my trade. But I've never witnessed anything similar to this phenomenon. It's like one of those case-studies in mass hysteria and popular delusion that you read about in history books.

Some dissenting voices did begin popping up in 2022, however. In February, Frances Widdowson, then a liberal arts professor at Mount Royal University in Calgary, wrote an article for a conservative US publication explaining how far-fetched rumours and urban legends dating to the 1980s seem to have informed the most lurid claims concerning the Kamloops Residential School.[365] A small publication called *The Dorchester Review* published a scathing article by Quebec academic Jacques Rouillard,

[365] Frances Widdowson, "Billy remembers," The American Conservative, February 15, 2022. See chapter with the same title in this book.

entitled "In Kamloops, Not One Body Has Been Found."[366] And in May, most significantly, a large newspaper called *National Post* published a blockbuster exposé by a well-known columnist, Terry Glavin, going blow by blow through the scandalously botched media treatment that has fuelled the unmarked-graves story since it first broke in the spring of 2021.[367] As Glavin took pains to emphasize, the main reason the story was bungled was that journalists got it wrong, not that Indigenous leaders lied about what they believed.

Glavin's piece was a watershed, as it represented the first explicit acknowledgement from a mainstream Canadian news outlet that the original narrative we'd all been asked to parrot in 2021 was unsustainable. And predictably, Glavin paid a price for speaking up. When it was announced that he'd be interviewed about his story for a well-known Toronto-based podcast, the chair of Canada's national arts funding agency, Jesse Wente, publicly intervened in an apparent bid to prevent the interview from going forward. (The host responded to this extraordinary development by sheepishly assuring Wente that he'd assign the segment to another interviewer.)[368]

> I wish you'd reconsider.
>
> I'm not sure you're equipped to have this discussion, nor am I convinced your guest can have a good faith conversation on the matter.
>
> I wish you'd consider what harm reduction might look like in these situations from a media perspective. Is it this?
>
> — Jesse Wente (@jessewente) May 30, 2022

---

[366] Jacques Rouillard, "In Kamloops, Not One Body Has Been Found," *The Dorchester Review* online, January 11, 2022. Updated version in the print edition of *The Dorchester Review*, Vol. 12, No. 2, Spring-Summer 2022, pp. 27-36. See chapter with the same title in this volume.

[367] Terry Glavin, "The year of the graves: How the world's media got it wrong on residential school graves," *National Post*, May 26, 2021.

[368] @JesseBrown tweet, May 30, 2022 and Replying to @jessewente and @TerryGlavin, May 30, 2022. Jesse Wente at some point deleted his account.

As for Widdowson, her university fired her after she spoke out about unmarked-graves misinformation circulating in Canadian university circles.[369] And Prof. Rouillard's article in *The Dorchester Review* attracted condemnation from no less an official than the federal Minister of Crown-Indigenous Relations, Marc Miller, who on Twitter denounced any expressed scepticism of the pre-set graves narrative as "ghoulish" and "retraumatizing for survivors."[370] Shockingly, Miller also called the article "part of a pattern of denialism"—as if the author were on moral par with a Holocaust denier. (Miller didn't refer to the article by name, but the target of his rhetoric was abundantly clear.)[371] Given all this, it should not be surprising that at least one expert in this kind of site inspection (whose identity is known to Glavin,[372] though not to me) has chosen to publish his comprehensive critique anonymously.[373]

It bears emphasizing that no respectable academic or journalist is denying the fact that thousands of children died while attending Canada's Residential Schools (the last of which closed in the 1990s). The critiques summarized in the paragraphs above, rather, are limited to the specific claim that the final resting places of hundreds, or even thousands, of dead Indigenous children have been identified over the last 14 months using GPR.

Even the most reputable media outlets sometimes get stories wrong, of course, *Quillette* included. And for the most part, they will publish corrections and clarifications if a fact-checking critic presents evidence of a journalistic error. In particularly egregious cases, they might even retract an article entirely. But the unmarked-graves story is unusual—perhaps even unique—because the faulty coverage has been a systematic feature

369 CBC News, with files from Sarah Rieger, Hannah Kost and Jade Markus, "MRU fires professor who espoused benefits of residential schools and criticized BLM movement," January 4, 2022.

370 Marc Miller @MarcMillerVM tweets, January 27, 2022.

371 Ibid.

372 Terry Glavin, "Impatience grows among Tk'emlúps people for answers on graves," *National Post*, July 20, 2022.

373 "Graves in the Apple Orchard," https://gravesintheorchard.wordpress.com/ undated 2022 blog post. See chapter with the same title in this volume.

across the entire Canadian journalistic landscape since the day the story broke. It isn't limited to one publication, or even to one type of publication.

This herd-driven aspect of the social panic has yielded a perverse incentive structure among journalists, whereby no single media outlet had any interest in walking back its previously published misinformation, because each could evade criticism simply by pointing to the (equally erroneous) work of everyone else. Why take the gratuitous reputational hit that goes along with admitting one's own mistakes when all your competitors are staying mum?

That incentive structure explains why the treatment of dissidents such as Glavin has been so harsh: If even a few columnists break ranks, it makes it harder for everyone else (including politicians such as Justin Trudeau, who went all in on the unmarked-graves story from the get go) to evade criticism and accountability. This, I believe, is why institutional players such as Miller and Wente have attempted to smear Rouillard and Glavin, moves that seem aimed at intimidating other journalists into silence. After all, money could be at stake. It's worth noting that Wente leads a federal funding body that annually doles out $500 million to Canada's creative class.[374] For his part, Miller serves a government that subsidizes Canadian journalists to the tune of about $700 million every year.[375] Being branded as a "denier" by a government official might put your share of that money at risk.

All of what I'm discussing here, I realize, will seem very much tied up with Canada's parochial media scene, which is known to operate in an amateurish, herd-like manner even in the best of times. But when it comes to the unmarked-graves story, the most influential (and, I would argue, irresponsible) media player hasn't been a Canadian outlet at all, but rather the *New York Times*. The newspaper's articles on this subject have been

---

[374] Simon Brault, "We Need Art Now More Than Ever, but There Is No Art Without Artists: Blog post from the Director and CEO, Canada Council for the Arts, February 15, 2022.

[375] Jonathan Bradley, "Which media were included in Trudeau's $10 million top-up fund: Government subsidies for selected news organizations keep growing," Canadaland.com, December 1, 2021.

riddled with completely obvious errors since the day after the story first broke. None of these errors have been corrected, despite the passage of over a year since their original publication.

And to be clear: I am not talking here about errors of tone, emphasis, shades of meaning, or omission. I am speaking of flat-out Trump-Won-The-2020-Election-style false information—what some call "fake news."

Most spectacularly, on May 28th, 2021, it was the *Times* that told the world that the discovery of a "mass grave" had been "reported in Canada."[376] It's a claim that exists—again, to this day—in the headline sitting above an article written by veteran correspondent Ian Austen, in which the reporter relates that "an Indigenous community in British Columbia says it has found evidence of ... a mass grave." The truth is that no Indigenous community said any such thing. In fact, the leader of the First Nations community that Austen was referencing, Rosanne Casimir of Tk'emlúps te Secwépemc, explicitly told the media that there was no mass grave, and disavowed usage of the term.[377]

The New York Times

'Horrible History': Mass Grave of Indigenous Children Reported in Canada

An Indigenous community says it has found evidence that 215 children were buried on the grounds of a British Columbia school, one of the many in Canada set up to forcibly assimilate them.

By Ian Austen

Published May 28, 2021 Updated Oct. 5, 2021

---

[376] Ian Austen, "'Horrible History': Mass Grave of Indigenous Children Reported in Canada," *New York Times*, May 28, 2021.

[377] Tim Petruk, "Casimir says Tk'emlups find is series of unmarked graves, not a mass burial," *The Squamish Chief*, June 5, 2021.

The small handful of other outlets that printed some version of the *Times*'s incorrect mass-graves news included the *Toronto Star*,[378] which, to its credit, quickly corrected the mistake; and the *Washington Post*, which not only corrected the mistake, but included an editor's note at the top of the article, fully detailing the newspaper's original lapse. Meanwhile, despite having updated the article as recently as September 5, 2022, the *Times* still parades the original "mass graves" error in its headline.

This *Times'* purported bombshell—and the horrifying image it elicited, of corpses piled like timber as in some horrific scene out of Bosnia or Rwanda—predictably made international news, giving the world's dictators a chance to excoriate Canada while deflecting from their own human-rights atrocities.[379] This was *The New York Times*, after all, not some local rag. Shortly after the *Times* set the tone in this manner, Trudeau ordered Canada's flags to half mast (where they would remain, incredibly, for more than five months), and dramatically went down on one knee to place a teddy bear on the site of a former Residential School in Saskatchewan as cameras clicked.

Journalism is history's first draft, produced on deadline. And one might easily understand how errors got into that first *Times* article, especially given that initial reports of the Kamloops GPR findings were being published in *The Wall Street Journal* alongside claims that the data accorded with the lore of (unidentified) Indigenous "knowledge keepers."[380] It would have been a brave journalist who, amid such furious national garment-rending, pointed out that locally circulated memories about unmarked child graves do not amount to evidence on par with actual human bones and tissue unearthed from the ground, no matter the ethnicity of the knowledge-keeping community.

---

[378] Jenna Cocullo, "Mass impact from discovery of graves," *Toronto Star*, May 31, 2021. "Editor's note: This story was first published May 31. This version removes the term 'mass grave,' as that description was inaccurate."

[379] Hans Hanley, "China weaponizes discovery of graves at Canadian residential schools to avoid Xinjiang criticism," Digital Forensic Research Lab online, January 21, 2021.

[380] Kim Mackrael, "Canadian Graves of Indigenous Found With Help From Oral Histories," *Wall Street Journal*, July 15, 2021.

But the May 28 article wasn't an isolated mistake. Ten days later, the same *Times* reporter penned a follow-up report that, to this day, bears a sub-headline referring to "the discovery of the remains of hundreds of children."[381] Like Austen's first story, this one is flat out wrong. No "remains" have been discovered.

How Thousands of Indigenous Children Vanished in Canada

The discovery of the remains of hundreds of children at the sites of defunct schools in British Columbia and southern Saskatchewan has rekindled discussion of a sinister time in Canada's history.

 By Ian Austen

Published June 7, 2021 Updated March 28, 2022

The article text indicates that "the remains of more than 1,000 people, mostly children, have been discovered on the grounds of three former residential schools in two Canadian provinces since May," a statement that is also absolutely untrue; and that "the remains of 200 people, mostly children, were found in unmarked graves on the grounds of [a] former boarding school in British Columbia," which, again, is totally false. At one point, we are informed by Austen that, "In July, the Penelakut Tribe in British Columbia said it had uncovered about 160 undocumented and unmarked graves." As Glavin reports, that's not what the Penelakut Tribe said.[382]

Two weeks after that, Austen and a second Canadian-situated *Times* reporter, Dan Bilefsky, co-wrote a third article, this one published under

---

381 Ian Austen, "How Thousands of Indigenous Children Vanished in Canada," *New York Times*, June 7, 2021 updated March 8, 2022.

382 Glavin, "The year of the graves: How the world's media got it wrong on residential school graves," loc. cit.

the (again, absolutely false) headline, "Hundreds More Unmarked Graves Found at Former Residential School in Canada."[383]

The New York Times

Hundreds More Unmarked Graves Found at Former Residential School in Canada

An Indigenous group said the remains of as many as 751 people, mainly children, had been found in unmarked graves on the site of a former boarding school in Saskatchewan.

 By Ian Austen and Dan Bilefsky

Published June 24, 2021   Updated July 30, 2021

That article informs us that "the recent unearthing of remains in Canada has reverberated globally," a whopper that juxtaposes the entirely false claim that there'd been any kind of "unearthing" of human remains, alongside the completely accurate observation that the story has garnered international attention—largely thanks to the *Times*'s own erroneous reporting. With the Tk'emlúps community itself now agitating for clarity on what actually lies below the ground's surface,[384] it will be interesting to see how Austen and Bilefsky proceed with further articles—as the two journalists are now tasked with lecturing their Tk'emlúps interviewees about all those remains of deceased relatives that, according to these same reporters, were unearthed at least a year ago and are presumably now sitting in some mysteriously undisclosed location.

The sub-headline on that *Times* article informs us that "An Indigenous group said the remains of as many as 751 people, mainly children, had been found in unmarked graves on the site of a former boarding school in Saskatchewan." Unlike the other examples I've listed, this one at least has the *Times* journalists attributing their information to a third party. But even on this score, the article neglects to note that Canada's National Centre for Truth and Reconciliation identifies only nine children from the institution

---

383 Ian Austen and Dan Bilefsky, "Hundreds More Unmarked Graves Found at Former Residential School in Canada," *New York TImes*, June 24, 2021, updated July 30.

384 Glavin, "Impatience grows among Tk'emlúps people for answers on graves," loc. cit.

in question—Marieval Indian Residential School—who died during its entire century-long period of operation. It's a fact that casts rather a lot of doubt on the claim offered in the sensationalistic *Times* headline.

And yes, I realize that reporters typically don't write their own headlines. But these *Times* mistakes can't be blamed on any editor, because the errors go well beyond the display copy. The text of the co-authored June 24th article, for instance, (falsely) informs us that "the remains of 215 children were found in unmarked graves on the grounds of [a] former church-run school for Indigenous students in British Columbia." It's a sentence that contains both the unambiguously false statement that the "remains of 215 children" have been found, alongside the piggyback fiction that these remains were found in "unmarked graves."

The nature of the mistakes vary from one *Times* story to the next. But all of the stories are alike to such an extent that they grossly misrepresent the nature of the information that was announced in May 2021 and thereafter. As noted above, the novel findings presented by Indigenous groups didn't identify graves, bodies, or human remains, but rather soil dislocations that may or may not be associated with a human burial. And as GPR experts have been cautioning since the technology first began being used by police officers and archaeologists many years ago,[385] such dislocations can be traced to everything from old irrigation ditches to backhoe trenches. The area where the Kamloops GPR data was recorded has been put to multiple agricultural uses over the decades, which means that anyone looking for graves in the area is at risk of encountering all manner of false positives.

And even if any of these dislocations do turn out to indicate the presence of graves, classifying them as "unmarked" may not be straightforward. As has been widely noted, an old grave that bears no markings in 2022 wasn't necessarily "unmarked" at the time it was used for burial, since rapidly degrading wooden crosses were commonly employed as markers until well into the 20th century.

A further complication is that many of the cemeteries located on or near Residential School properties were used by religiously observant Indigenous and non-Indigenous communities alike. Cadmus Delorme,

---

[385] Schultz, op. cit.

Chief of the Cowessess First Nation in Saskatchewan, where Trudeau staged his maudlin teddy-bear photo-op, for instance, told the media flatly, "This is a Roman Catholic grave site. It's not a Residential School grave site."[386]

It's entirely possible that unmarked, previously unknown graves may one day be definitively identified at Kamloops and other former Residential School campuses; and that such graves will then be found to contain the remains of Residential-School students. But neither Austen nor Bilefsky nor anyone else has yet produced information to support the claim that this evidence has already been collected. And when I asked the *Times* to explain how their reporters had arrived at such plainly speculative conclusions, all I got by way of answer was a statement from a corporate staffer that read: "We are confident in the accuracy of our reporting. All of our articles have made it clear that the gravesite findings are based on the analysis of ground penetrating radar and these findings are supported by expert corroboration."[387]

Ian Austen isn't a stranger to me. I've met him, and we've occasionally conversed over social media and email about stories of mutual interest. He's a skilled and dedicated journalist whose work I've read appreciatively for many years. That's one reason I'm singling him out when there are so many other journalistic offenders I could name: It says a lot about the depth of the social panic surrounding the unmarked-graves story that even a reporter of Austen's stature was impelled to abandon the high standards he brings to his other work.

I refuse to believe that anyone at the *Times* set out to tell lies. It seems more likely that they instinctively believed, on some gut level, that the GPR data signalled the existence of child murder victims. They treated it as a revealed moral truth, and so imagined themselves duty bound to use their *Times* platform to spread the story globally, advocate for Indigenous rights, and educate Canadians about a dark historical legacy. Numerous other journalists did exactly the same thing, and, in so doing, got swept up

---

[386] Jorge Barrera, "Catholic register, survivors offer clues to who may be buried in cemetery next to Marieval residential school," CBC News, July 20, 2021.

[387] Email to the author.

by the collective fervour. But now that the story hasn't gone the way their guts told them it would, they (very understandably) are embarrassed at the prospect of admitting their mistakes.

In truth, it probably doesn't matter much if the *Times* ever gets around to correcting its mistakes, because it's not as if Canadians haven't noticed the glaring absence of physical evidence to back up the breathless claims they first heard in mid-2021. Many feel duped by the unmarked-graves story, especially given the way it was held up, both inside and outside Canada, as a pretext to trash their country. Over the last 14 months, it hasn't just been the *Times*, but the journalistic trade as a whole, that's squandered a good deal of the trust and affection held by readers and viewers.

However, it may prove to be Indigenous people themselves who lose the most from this whole sad episode. Given how much terrible treatment was meted out to First Nations, Inuit, and Métis communities over the course of Canadian history, there is surely no shortage of *real* evidence of past atrocities waiting to be found by researchers. It seems inevitable that some day in the future, actual bodies will be brought to the surface—genuine, uncontestable evidence of a real historical atrocity that formerly had been unknown or obscure. If, in that authentic moment of discovery, journalists and politicians suddenly find that it's become impossible to arouse the interest and sympathies of a jaded, untrusting Canadian public, let's not pretend that we won't know the reason why.

This chapter was originally published in Quillette *online, July 22, 2022.*

Chapter Seven

Canada's Descent into Collective Guilt: How the Media Used Soil Disturbances to Make an Entire Country Hate Themselves

James Pew

In May of 2021 a devastating Canadian story made headlines. The Chief of the Tk'emlups band in Kamloops, B.C. announced that 215 unmarked graves were found using ground-penetrating radar on the site of a former residential school.

Canada's legacy media made the shocking announcement: "Grief, sorrow after discovery of 215 bodies, unmarked graves at former B.C. residential school site" (Global News). South of the border on the same day the *Washington Post*'s headline read: "Officials Discover Remains of 215 Indigenous Children at Former Canadian Residential School Site."

The *Washington Post*, along with many major news outlets, didn't sugar coat anything. Whereas Global News exercised some restraint by referring to the discovery of 215 "bodies" in unmarked graves, the *Washington Post* said what many Canadians were thinking: that 215 "Indigenous Children" had been discovered. Or had they?

The Canadian residential school system was a network of boarding schools for First Nations children. The last government-funded residential school closed in 1996. It is claimed that many Indigenous children who attended them never returned home.

Commonly considered one of the darkest chapters in Canadian history, recognition of the harms caused to "survivors" of residential schools has been an essential element of Canada's Truth and Reconciliation commitments to Indigenous Canadians.

As the news cycle around the discovery of the alleged 215 unmarked graves in Kamloops evolved, the language the media used evolved. It wasn't long before the scene was being described as an "unmarked mass grave."[388] A stark and dramatic image indeed.

I will always remember the sadness and shock expressed by so many fellow Canadians in the weeks that followed, but things got worse, and confusingly bizarre on June 24 with another bombshell. The *National Post* headline read, "'Like a crime scene': 751 unmarked graves reported found at former Saskatchewan residential school."[389]

Many people on social media, some of whom already believed the country was systemically racist, used the sensational headlines as an opportunity to declare it undeniable proof of Canada's murderous genocidal history. Others said it demonstrates the evil white supremacist colonial underpinnings of the nation, while others were sorrowful and apologetic, insisting the tragic events reinforced the importance of the Truth and Reconciliation work ahead of us.

Around this time I began hearing the first rumblings of "Cancel Canada Day." The national day of celebration, formerly Dominion Day, expected to happen on July 1, was shaping up to be ... awkward to say the least.

On June 30th, one day before Canada Day (six days after the last "discovery"), another 182 soil disturbances/unmarked graves were discovered by the St. Mary's First Nation (a member of the Ktunaxa Nation) at the site near the former St. Eugene's Mission Residential School. Less than two weeks after that, Chief Joan Brown of the Penelakut First Nation announced that at least 160 unmarked graves were located on the grounds of the former Kuper Island Indian Industrial school, off Vancouver Island.

Canada Day came and went with muted fanfare, many Canadians choosing quiet personal reflection over celebration. Some wore orange shirts to events instead of red. The fact that we were in the middle of the Covid-19 global pandemic with limited options for group gatherings added to the

[388] Joan Bryden, "Commons holds special debate on remains of 215 children found at residential school," The Canadian Press, CTV News, June 1, 2021.

[389] Christopher Nardi, "'Like a crime scene': 751 unmarked graves reported found at former Saskatchewan residential school," *National Post*, June 24, 2021.

sadness and outrage over unmarked graves fuelled by North American legacy media.

But seemingly everyone, from legacy media to the regular folks on social media, either missed or glossed over a number of facts relating to the nature and locations of the unmarked graves. Automatically claiming genocidal guilt, instead of seeking clarity of facts and context, seems to be the way we operate when it comes to Canadian Indigenous issues.

In July 2021, Prime Minister Justin Trudeau reassured Canadians that "the government will continue to tell the truth and work in partnership with First Nations to fight systemic racism with real, concrete actions."

Bob Chamberlin, former vice-president of the Union of B.C. Indian Chiefs, said the following about future discoveries not yet made:

> What we're going to find is ... a very large number of unmarked graves across this country, which are going to speak very loudly about the path that this country set out to destroy children, family, culture, language, traditions and remove us from our land which everyone is enjoying today, except First Nations.

So they know of the existence and general locations of unmarked undocumented graves? They do seem to be "discovering" them fairly rapidly. What is going on?

If you read only the headlines of the legacy media's coverage, both in Canada and south of the border, which if we're being honest is the extent of what many do, you can't help but form a clear impression of the horribleness of the "shocking" and "traumatic" discoveries. Reading a little deeper past the headlines, the message is that these discoveries are tragic confirmations of the terrible stories Indigenous people have been telling for years.

There is some truth in all of this reporting. Problems with the Canadian Residential School system were well known before any unmarked soil disturbances were discovered. However, through omission and manipulation of facts, the legacy media was complicit in the misrepresentation of these discoveries in order to feed the lucrative, woke,

169

anti-West grievance economy, including Canada's corrupt Aboriginal Industry.[390]

Everything today is viewed through the cynical lens of radical critical theory. Critical theory has been called Americanized postmodernism; I like to call the current iteration critical wokeism. It asserts that the relatively peaceful and pluralistic first-world societies of the West are actually oppressive regimes upholding the white patriarchal power structure left over from colonialism, and serving the interests of public enemy number one: White men.

Like the authoritarian Diversity and Equity administrators of universities, legacy media accept this ahistorical meta-narrative as truth. The casual claim is that Canada is a systemically racist and white supremacist country built on colonialism and genocide. Many now consider it an act of violence to argue that there is more to Canada's history than oppression. However, while Canada is not perfectly free from racial discrimination, the charge of systemic racism is not backed up with convincing data and is more likely to be the product of deranged and unfounded assumptions that, although they make compelling headlines, are really just ways media companies and activists cash in on woke-ness. In my essay Re-Evaluating Canada's (Un)Truth and Reconciliation Commission, I offer an argument for why claims of genocide and cultural genocide are not consistent with the facts.[391]

Hate Inc., a book published in 2021 by veteran American journalist Matt Taibbi,[392] does an amazing job of explaining the business models of legacy media, their methods of story generation, and the hidden pressures that narrow the range of allowable discourse (a central theme of Noam Chomsky's and Edward Herman's classic *Manufacturing Consent*).[393]

---

390 I have written about this elsewhere in "The Corruption Of Canada's Indigenous Victim Industry," Woke Watch Canada Newsletter, Substack, February 17, 2022.

391 Re-Evaluating Canada's (Un)Truth and Reconciliation Commission, Woke Watch Canada Newsletter, Substack, February 17, 2022.

392 Matt Taibbi, *Hate Inc.: Why Today's Media Makes Us Despise One Another* (OR Books / Counterpoint Press, 2019).

393 Edward S. Herman and Noam Chomsky, *Manufacturing Consent: The Political Economy of the Mass Media* (Pantheon, 1988).

There will always be some version of a grand narrative that we assume (in varying degrees) to be true. But the one we are currently suffering is a shallow and wildly unfair indictment of the West and the people in it. Legacy media are powerful arbiters of this nonsense. Their success, Taibbi explains, is dependent on getting everyone outraged, at each other and the West in general.

"Hatred is the partner of ignorance, and we in the media have become experts at selling both," wrote Matt Taibbi.

Non-legacy media do not suffer from the same discourse-narrowing pressure to conform to false narratives. Candice Malcolm's journalism, published by Canadian independent media organization True North, regarding the unmarked graves of former residential schools, serves as a case in point.

In July of 2021 she posted an article to the Truth North website titled "Six Things The Media Got Wrong About The Graves Found Near Residential Schools." As the title of her piece states, the graves were found "near" former residential schools, not "at" former residential schools, as the legacy media reported.[394]

"When it comes to the coverage of graves identified near residential schools in three First Nations communities, the legacy media in Canada has done a tremendous disservice to all Canadians – especially First Nations...They have created a moral panic, and continue to fan the flames of racial division ... This panic came to a breaking point over the weekend, when prominent statues were knocked over and at least 25 churches in Western Canada were either vandalized or completely burnt down," wrote Malcolm.

Prime Minister Justin Trudeau said the anger Canadians feel towards the federal government and Catholic Church is "real and it is fully understandable given the shameful history we have all become more aware of."[395] In the first couple months after the initial discovery of unmarked

[394] Candice Malcolm, "Six things the media got wrong about the graves found near Residential Schools," True North, July 12, 2021.

[395] Quinton Amundson, "Church fires, vandalism condemned," *The Catholic Register*, July 6, 2021.

graves near former residential schools, dozens of churches were burned to the ground or vandalized across the country – eight of which occurred in First Nations territories.

In speaking about the vandalism inflicted on the African Evangelical Church in Calgary, Alberta, premier Jason Kenney said, "These folks came to Canada with the hope that they could practise their faith peacefully. Some of them are traumatized by such attacks. This is where hatred based on collective guilt for historic injustices leads us. Let's seek unity, respect and reconciliation instead."[396]

A July 4, 2021 article in *The Guardian* chronicled St Anne's church, the "spiritual home to the Upper Similkameen Indian Band," the fourth church on Indigenous lands recently destroyed by arson.

As reported in *The Guardian*, "The church meant so much to all of us, especially our ancestors," Carrie Allison, an elder who helped maintain the church, said in a statement. "When your hurt turns to rage it is not healthy for you or your community."[397]

Candice Malcolm explained the facts around what exactly had been found near former residential schools. At this time no excavation had actually been done. The existence of graves is suspected because of the results of ground-penetrating radar scans, which can locate the presence of the characteristics of a grave, but not whether the site is occupied by human remains, including child remains.

Even if graves do exist on these sites, the ground-penetrating radar "confirms" the presence only of multiple single graves, not as some media reported "mass graves," an image widely associated with genocide. When you are trying to evoke rage, powerful allusions of genocide are a great way to do it.

A common Indigenous practice was, and still is, the use of wooden grave markings. Over time these grave markings disintegrate and disappear.

---

[396] Twitter, @jkenney, July 1, 2021.

[397] Leland Cecco, "Burned churches stir deep Indigenous ambivalence over faith of forefathers," *The Guardian*, July 4, 2021.

Could this explain the prevalence of both unmarked and undocumented graves? Record keeping in the past was not up to today's standards. Could perhaps the use of biodegradable grave markings have contributed to the "disappearance" of old cemeteries now re-appearing as unmarked grave sites?

This conclusion is reinforced by reports from members of communities where graves were discovered, who have informed the media that they do not believe all graves contain children and that most likely a mix of people from the community (along with some residential children possibly?) are the occupants of the graves.

As Malcolm wrote in her True North story, "Tucked away at the very end of a *Globe and Mail* report on the findings at the Cowessess reserve in Saskatchewan, it said this:

> It appears that not all of the graves contain children's bodies, Lerat (who is one of the band leaders) said. He said the area was also used as a burial site by the rural municipality. ... "We did have a family of non-Indigenous people show up today and notified us that some of those unmarked graves had their families in them – their loved ones," Lerat said. ... "So what we have here is an abandoned community cemetery, where people of different backgrounds were buried."[398]

"That's quite a leap from the original storyline that these graves belong to children who had died at a residential school," Malcolm wrote.

Malcolm's True North piece, and her continued journalism, stand in stark contrast to the Canadian legacy media. It is clear, in my view, that for whatever reason, the majority of Canadian legacy media promotes a dangerous narrative unfairly painting Canada and its citizens (especially white straight conservative Christian types) as systemically racist, upholding a primarily white male power structure that oppresses women,

---

[398] Jana G. Pruden, Kristy Kirkup, Mike Hager, and Carrie Tait, "Cowessess First Nation discovers hundreds of unmarked graves at former residential school site," *Globe and Mail*, June 23, 2021.

BIPOC, and those who identity as LGBTQ.[399] It's a depressing and uninspired narrative indeed, and one that holds little congruence with the truth.

Few seem to care about the actual facts surrounding the unmarked graves. The opportunity to perform virtue through self-loathing is too tempting for many to resist, so there is a morbid eagerness to accept the claim that the Canadian government and Catholic Church committed genocide against Indigenous people.

Even if every one of the thousands of graves they find turn out to be children from residential schools, the fact will remain that legacy media rushed to condemn the Canadian government and Catholic Church for an assumed genocide — well before a proper investigation was possible.

Is it wrong to think that Canadians deserve better? Stories that shock and outrage make great breaking news, get on-going repetitive coverage, and solidify the narratives that become the new "normal" from which all further action, media amplification and criticism proceeds. But these media narratives do not agree with basic reality.

Thankfully we have a group of Canadian researchers diligently seeking truth regarding residential schools and Indigenous issues in general. Take a look at Hymie Rubenstein's substack - The Real Indian Residential School Newsletter.[400]

My personal feelings regarding Canada's treatment of Indigenous peoples can best be described as sadness, regret at human failings, and that empty feeling that accompanies the knowledge injustice has been committed. If I may state the obvious; it is easy to blame people from the past for what is so clearly seen as wrong today. That being said, I do believe there have been injustices both past and present and whether intentional or not, the people of Canada sometimes do fail each other. No one is blameless.

---

[399] "Gender Nonconformity Is A Straight White Person's Ticket To Woke Acceptance," Woke Watch Canada, Substack, November 10, 2021.

[400] Hymie Rubenstein, The REAL Indigenous Issues Newsletter, on Substack.

You can say these things, recognize that oppression and violence has been omnipresent throughout history, feel a sense of historical injustice, a need for present day truth and reconciliation, *and* reject woke notions of present-day systemic/structural racism perpetuated by the invisible hand of white supremacy.

Like many Canadians I feel sadness regarding aspects of our national legacy, but do I personally feel guilt? No. Guilt is for those who commit crimes and hurt others. My "whiteness" doesn't automatically make me adjacent to the crimes of other white people. I have a guilt-free conscience because I try to practise kindness. I'm not so sure the "White Fragility" woke crowd can honestly make this claim.

Originally published on James Pew's Substack, The Turn, *as "Canada's Descent Into Collective Guilt," March 27, 2022.*

Chapter Eight

The Banality of Genocide, Made in Canada

Michael Melanson

On October 27, 2022, Member of Parliament Leah Gazan (Winnipeg Centre-NDP) presented a snap motion in the House of Commons to have the Indian Residential Schools (IRS) officially recognized as a genocide according to Article II of the United Nations Convention for the Prevention and Punishment for the Crime of Genocide.[401] The motion was passed, apparently unanimously, with no debate, in less than a minute.

This was not a reputable day for the House.

Aside from the fact that the House of Commons assigned criminal guilt where no court has upheld or even heard a case against Canada for the worst of all crimes, the UN Convention is no longer the guiding jurisprudence. On July 1, 2002 the Rome Statute, of which Canada is also a signatory, became the internationally recognized framework for adjudicating genocide.[402] The Rome Statute established a "statute of limitations" on genocide in which no prosecution for that crime could occur for acts committed prior to the date when the statute came unto effect for a signatory state.[403]

Either everyone sitting in the Commons that day was unaware of the Rome Statute or they assented to a quixotic pantomime. If the UN Convention had effectively been superseded, then finding Canada guilty of genocide under those terms carried no legal consequences. On the other hand, for Members of Parliament to oppose the motion could have come across as politically damaging. Sitting in Opposition, it might be considered incumbent on the Conservative Party of Canada to offer some challenge to the motion. Given the remarkable speed with which the motion passed,

---

[401] "MPs back motion calling on government to recognize residential school program as genocide," CBC News, October 27, 2022.

[402] Rome Statute of the International Criminal Court.

[403] *Ibid*; Article 24.1.

perhaps there was prior agreement to pass the motion if the UN Convention was mentioned instead of the Rome Statute. Passing the motion as Gazan presented it was simply symbolic.

Even by the effectively defunct terms of the UN Convention, the motion was a dubious feat of chicanery. Article II stipulates that there must be intent in order to consider any act or acts as genocidal. Genocide cannot be a crime of neglect and under both the UN Convention and the Rome Statute, the legal task of proving genocide amounts to proving mass murder in the first degree.

Like the necessarily equivocal claim of cultural genocide, the October 27 motion reduced genocide to rhetorical ordnance. Even so, the condemnation of Canada as a genocidal enterprise is dangerous because of how civilly corrosive the accusation is when reckoned in historic terms. For one thing, it means that, through the 139 years of the Indian Residential School system, Canada committed the world's longest-running genocide prior to any of the other five genocides officially recognized by the HoC. Unkind critics could claim, and have claimed, that Canada's example informed Hitler's genocide of the Jews. (In fact it is to the Armenian genocide that Hitler is believed to have referred when he said, with regard to killing civilians in Nazi-occupied Poland, "Who remembers the Armenian massacres?"[404])

The last residential school closed in 1998, so unlike the genocide of Armenians, the event is not so distant as to make prosecution impracticable. If Canada is "the godfather of genocide" in the modern era, what justice is due? If Canada is extrajudicially found guilty of genocide, is our sentencing and punishment also placed outside of the courts?

In the hope of forestalling the possibility of further vigilante retribution, let's examine the extraordinary claim that Canada is in breach of all five clauses of Article II of the UN Convention, of which no state or party has previously been found guilty. The following is the actual wording of the UN Convention:

---

[404] Joachim Fest, *Plotting Hitler's Death: The Story of German Resistance* (New York: Metropolitan Books, 1997), p. 5.

In the present Convention, genocide means any of the following acts committed with intent to destroy, in whole or in part, a national, ethnical, racial or religious group, as such:

(a) Killing members of the group;

(b) Causing serious bodily or mental harm to members of the group;

(c) Deliberately inflicting on the group conditions of life calculated to bring about its physical destruction in whole or in part;

(d) Imposing measures intended to prevent births within the group;

(e) Forcibly transferring children of the group to another group.

The ersatz prosecution fails on the point of proving intent because it is next to impossible to show the genocidal intent in educating a people. Educating someone presupposes their continued existence. In the entirety of IRS history no more than one-third of eligible students attended at any one time and the ratio was often less in any given year. Where is the intent to destroy in a programme that targets far less than the majority?

Even more confounding for the prosecution with regard to establishing intent is the fact that after 1980, many of the few schools that remained open were run by Indian bands themselves, such as the Lebret (Qu'Appelle) Residential School, which was administered by the band from 1973 until its closing in 1998.[405] Are these band councils complicit in genocide or was there some point in time when the schools ceased being genocidal? Did band councils have to revise the daily operations of the schools so the schools would no longer be lethal? When Cross Lake's residential school burned down, the band asked for it to be rebuilt. That's like Jewish inmates asking that Sobibor be rebuilt after it was destroyed in a prisoner revolt.

As we will see, the claim of a genocide by residential schools strains credulity at every turn.

---

[405] National Centre for Truth and Reconciliation.

It has been argued that genocidal intent can be proven in a callous remark, attributed to Duncan Campbell Scott, that the purpose of the schools was "to kill the Indian in the child." That quotation is now known to be apocryphal. But even if it were a real quotation, the idea it expresses draws a distinction between killing the *Indian* in the child and harming the child itself. Whatever the phrase "killing the Indian" meant — and presumably it meant overcoming the barriers to managing life in a modern society — it is clearly not advocating the physical death of the child.

Killing Members of the Group

Concluding in 2015, the Truth and Reconciliation Commission (TRC) found no credible evidence of a single homicide committed against any students by any staff throughout the entire history of the IRS.

There were some student-on-student homicides resulting from arson. But a genocide that doesn't involve killing defies the concept of genocide.

The absence of murder has been answered with the notion of "cultural genocide." Academics such as Andrew Woolford and Sean Carleton have argued that destroying Indigenous culture amounts to destroying a group in part and that the destruction of culture can lead to a loss of life through profound loss of identity and social cohesion.[406] This argument implies that suicides can be attributed to the loss of culture and construed as genocide

Woolford points out that the principal author of the UN Convention on genocide, Rafael Lemkin, initially included the deprivation of culture as a genocidal act. Be that as it may, in the end the UN Convention *omitted* the destruction of culture in the final draft. The problem with deeming destruction of culture as genocidal is that, given the fluid nature of culture and the human tendency to adopt cultural aspects from other groups, for the purpose of assigning criminal liability it would be impossible to distinguish when loss of culture was voluntary or involuntary. If some aspects of a culture were seen as being worthy of adoption, such as

---

[406] Andrew Woolford and Sean Carleton, "Ignore debaters and denialists, Canada's treatment of Indigenous peoples fits the definition of genocide," *The Conversation*, October 25, 2021.

learning to speak English, becoming or seeking to remain a Christian, or learning how to play the piano, can it ever be sufficiently clear when the acquisition of new culture is a harm?

Woolford's argument depends upon seeing culture as static and believing that humans are of limited cultural capacity. It means positing that humans can belong to only one culture, the one they were born into, and that the culture learned at school displaced the culture they had prior to attending.

But the reality of human culture is that it is profoundly syncretic: humans have always adopted and integrated aspects of culture from other peoples. The growth and Christianization of the Roman Empire, the evolution of popular music, and the development of the English language since *Beowulf* are a few examples that come readily to mind.

The implication of Woolford's argument is that Indigenous people lack the same agency as other peoples in adopting cultural aspects from other peoples and that the modern world is inherently inimical to their existence as Indigenous people. Integral to that line of reasoning is a prescriptive view that Indigenous people should, as much as possible, remain identifiable as Indigenous people by retaining and maintaining their pre-Contact culture.

The practical effect of this intersection between the Noble Savage stereotype and social determinism is that Indigenous people should always look inward and insulate themselves from the outside world. Activist scholars tend to overlook that colonialism has also brought the invaluable boon of cosmopolitanism, which everywhere has been the social precursor to civil rights.

"The movement back to nature proves itself against nature a thousand times over, because development is a part of nature and turning back is against nature," remarked Victor Klemperer in his famous diaries.[407] The exemption of Indigenous people from human development for the sake of being more like traditional people verges on exclusion. Apart from that, it ignores the lived reality of Indigenous people since the 16th century: First

---

[407] Victor Klemperer, *I Will Bear Witness: 1933-1941* (Modern Library Paperback Edition, 1999) p. 292.

Nations were very quick to adopt European clothing, weapons, shelter, and other technologies voluntarily as soon as they could.. The first Indigenous people to meet Jacques Cartier eagerly traded the clothes off their back for the trinkets the French offered.

The TRC determined that the residential schools were a cultural genocide, which is juridically meaningless but which allowed the commission to *obliquely* accuse Canada of genocide. While the accusation of cultural genocide relieved the TRC of meeting the difficult legal tests of proving genocide, it also glossed over some troubling implications. For one, most of the residential schools were denominational and attendance at a particular school was generally determined by which denomination the family followed. This means that prior to enrolling their children in an IRS, the parents or grandparents had *already* adopted the Christian faith. The parents could therefore be said to have "participated" in the destruction of their childrens' culture before their children attended an IRS. Again, that would suggest that the parents and grandparents were themselves devoid of agency and could not really have embraced Christianity while believing in God and wanting to learn more about Him.

The claim of cultural genocide also relies on the presumption that all children who attended an IRS came from families that were practising their traditional culture. The reality is that almost no family would have just been traditional. Rifles, motors, and radios, for instance, would already have been found in many Indigenous households. Again, this is because it is an ordinary part of human behaviour to adopt cultures and technologies to better fulfil human needs.

To further illustrate this point: consider the presence of a radio or television in a home on an Indian reserve. The devices bring outside culture into the home. Who is responsible for bringing that radio or TV into the household? Who turns it on? Who decides what channel it will be tuned to? The criminality of cultural genocide cannot be found — because it is impossible to determine who is liable for exposing children to cable television. Who takes the blame for *Bugs Bunny*?

The assertion that the schools were cultural genocide remains nevertheless a popular complaint. However, it rests on a popular myth about the schools: that they generally sought to suppress and eradicate Indigenous culture.

There are claims that students were punished if caught speaking their native languages. That may have been the case in some instances but for many schools, there were no such prohibitions and day-to-day functioning of the schools would have been impractical given how often children spoke mostly their respective languages. If a child didn't speak any English, how could they be told to do anything if some level of translation or interpretation wasn't available? Cree syllabics were created by dedicated missionaries at the schools. Many of the schools had Indigenous names. And there is growing evidence of children speaking and singing in their native languages at school events.

But supposing the schools did actively seek to suppress the expression of Indigenous culture, how could the schools prevent that culture from being expressed when the students weren't in attendance? What cultural interdiction could a school exert in the privacy of a family home when the child was back for weekends and holidays? Were the schools so effective in drumming culture out of their students that students, returning to the reserve or moving to the city after graduation, did not or could not reacquire their traditional culture at will?

The claim that members of the group were killed at Indian Residential Schools has recently been animated by the supposed discovery of unmarked graves at former school sites across Canada. Beginning with the sensational announcement on May 27, 2021, that unmarked graves had been "discovered" by ground penetrating radar (GPR) in an old apple orchard at the Kamloops Indian Residential School, Canadians were soon beset with repeated and ongoing stories of unmarked graves being discovered all over Canada, ostensibly by GPR.[408] An unmarked grave suggests a wrongful death. For those who wished to accuse Canada of unqualified genocide, here finally was what seemed like irrefutable evidence: the remains of children's bodies had been "found."

Except that they haven't been. Of the very few excavations that have occurred at any of these sites, no remains have been found. Neither are

---

[408] "Remains of 215 children found buried at former B.C. residential school, First Nation says," CBC News, May 28, 2021.

there corresponding reports of children who went missing from the schools.

Adding considerable confusion to the situation, bona fide cemeteries have been scanned with GPR with predictable results. Finding an unmarked grave in an abandoned cemetery is easily explained by the deterioration of wooden markers over time; there is nothing to suggest that these graves were not initially marked. Short of thorough archival research and exhumation, it is impossible to determine that these are the graves of former students, much less that those students were killed at the schools.

It remains a major point of contention how there could be so many suspicious deaths or burials when the TRC itself published no credible evidence of staff-on-student homicide.

MP Leah Gazan's genocide motion capitalized on the sensationalism of the Kamloops announcement as much as it did on the willingness to condemn Canada and the reluctance to demand due process. Given the scale and horror of the accusation, criminal investigation has been conspicuously lacking.

Causing Serious Bodily or Mental Harm to Members of the Group

Since there was no debate in the House of Commons over Gazan's motion, it was left unexplained what acts that occurred in the schools are considered to be "serious bodily or mental harm." Is it the strapping of students? Corporal punishment was generally common practice in all schools in this period. Is it taking away someone's favourite shirt? School uniforms were a standard policy at the IRS, and sometimes replaced worn or lice-infested clothing. There are some lurid claims, including the use of a homemade electric chair, but these have yet to be proven as anything more than apocrypha or confabulation. Harsh as the treatment of students may have been in some instances, such acts by themselves do not prove genocide where there is no intent to destroy people.

"Deliberate ... physical destruction in whole or in part"

The Convention mentions "Deliberately inflicting on the group conditions of life calculated to bring about its physical destruction in whole or in part." This is usually said to have happened in the way residential school administrators handled students with infectious diseases. But it would have to be shown that schools routinely placed infected children with other students in order to infect those other students and thereby cause death. In fact, records show clearly that schools sought to isolate infected students as much as conditions allowed, or send them to hospital. Given that proving intent is critical to proving genocide, any attempt to improve conditions or engage medical professionals indicates benevolent intent.

Scale and system matters, too, in prosecuting genocide. To prove the schools are in breach of this clause, it would need to be shown that most schools deliberately inflicted deadly conditions. This would therefore mean that it would need to be shown what directives were issued to the schools to do so, and who issued those directives.

Preventing Births

The Convention refers to "Imposing measures intended to prevent births within the group." This would include forced sterilization. What IRS sterilized its students? Considering that many of the schools were run by Catholic organizations, it strains credulity to believe a faith known for promoting fertility and opposing contraception would contradict one of their main tenets and conduct forced sterilizations of Indigenous children. Bear in mind that residential schools were often located on reserves; how likely is it that a sterilized girl wouldn't have mentioned her experience to a parent? Yet there is no proof of such an occurrence.

Again, this is another damning accusation in the blogosphere and the media environment that was unquestioningly accepted without debate in the House of Commons. No evidence was presented that anything like this happened at the schools and none was demanded.

Forcibly transferring children of the group to another group

The clause most frequently cited by proponents of the genocide narrative is "Forcibly transferring children of the group to another group." It was drafted by the UN in response to the Nazi practice of abducting children of so-called "Aryan" appearance (blonde-haired and blue-eyed) in the Eastern countries they occupied and sending them to live with ethnic German families back home. Thousands of Polish and Ukrainian children are believed to have been permanently removed from their natural families and homes in this way to increase the Aryan population.

Consequently this clause presupposes that the transfer must be intended to be permanent. There is also a presumption of racial similarity between groups. But permanent transfer was never the intention of the IRS because, as at any school, graduation was expected and students were free to return to their homes thereafter. As well, throughout the school year students were often allowed to go home for weekends, Christmas holidays, and summer breaks.

Finally, in the short history of genocide prosecution, no party has ever been found guilty of breaching this clause. That would make it another first for Canada — and another scurrilous allegation that defies reason.

It is often argued that assimilation was a type of permanent transfer between groups since a student's culture was stolen and a "white" culture instilled in its place. But assimilation and genocide are opposing processes. Genocide requires dehumanizing the target group whereas, presumably, making someone more like you humanizes that person to you. Assimilating someone presupposes they will continue to live among your people. It suggests that Government policy was actually designed to fit more Indigenous people to be able to live and prosper among other Canadians in cities, towns, and rural communities.

To make the case that assimilation is genocide, it would have to be shown that the minds of the day understood assimilation to be fatal and intended for Indigenous people to lose their lives. But the converse is true: policymakers of the day considered assimilation to be *progressive* because it gave Indigenous children the means to partake of the work, wealth, and other benefits of Canadian society. Leaving children to suffer penury and starvation on reserves was regarded as morally wrong, and education was part of the solution.

The irony of someone like Leah Gazan or former Senator Murray Sinclair arguing that assimilation is genocidal is that they can only make these arguments public now because they are assimilated to a high degree. Some have argued that the IRS had a policy of "forced" assimilation, whereas for individuals such as Sinclair assimilation was voluntary. However, if the professional success of Murray Sinclair exemplifies the opportunities achieved by assimilation, it is difficult to argue there was *lethal* intent behind compelling assimilation. *Genocidaires* do not anticipate a net benefit for their victims.

The case for and against assimilation isn't helped by a general failure to distinguish between civic and cultural assimilation. Becoming a jurist, senator or parliamentarian are examples of civic assimilation, as is learning to speak at least one of Canada's official languages, getting a Social Insurance Number, and opening a bank account.

If expectations of cultural assimilation once existed, they have since been permanently relegated to the dustbin of history since Canada officially adopted multiculturalism. Everyone is free to define their own culture so long as it doesn't violate any laws. Multiculturalism reflects Canada's confidence in itself, that our state and society can welcome the world's peoples and find common cause here. Our national creed of multiculturalism is, however, antithetical to the notion of preserving traditional Indigenous culture. The historic reality is, of course, that the Indigenous peoples of Canada were themselves informally practising multiculturalism since the first European settlements, adopting new technologies and customs as they saw fit for the next two hundred years before Confederation, including requesting and helping to build schools for themselves.

But if Canada is the archetypal genocidal state, will the peoples of the world come to shun us? If Canada is attacked, who will defend us, especially if we are, by our own confession,[409] committing what advocates like to call an ongoing genocide?[410]

The sad and sordid truth of it all is that almost no one takes the claim of a Canadian genocide seriously. The dance of injudicious conceit and supine deference has reduced genocide to a banality, an accusation for which no prosecution can be expected.

Canada, it seems, has brought into the world the concept of a non-criminal, uncorroborated genocide. This is an innovation the world can do without.

Canada has dumbed down genocide, making it into an everyday occurrence, a daily media and online slur, well on its way to eliciting no particular response or reaction.

To those states where genocide is or has been plotted and committed, Canada now serves as the convenient "what about" riposte. Once a country that stormed the beaches of Normandy and liberated the Netherlands, were we just wrestling with our erstwhile doppelgängers, if not our protégés? We have willingly squandered any moral authority we had to condemn another state of genocide.

For the record, there have been some citizens who have tried to take the accusation of genocide seriously and seek justice in court.

On June 3, 2021, a week after news broke of alleged children's remains being "found" at Kamloops Indian Residential School, a team of lawyers filed a complaint against Canada with the International Criminal Court.[411] Speaking at the inaugural "National Gathering for Unmarked Graves" held in Edmonton in September 2022, a former ICC president and judge, Dr. Chile Eboe-Osiji, informed the audience that: "There is no pathway to the International Criminal Court for the situation of the historical Indian

---

[409] "Trudeau says deaths and disappearances of Indigenous women and girls amounts to 'genocide'," CBC News (Jume 4, 2019).

[410] "A Legal Analysis of Genocide: Supplementary Report of the National Inquiry for Missing and Murdered Indigenous Women and Girls" (2019).

[411] Miller, Brendan Myers, "*Coalition of Canadian Lawyers Demand International Criminal Court To Investigate Discovery of 215 Sead Indigenous Children In Kamloops, B.C.*," Foster LLP (2021).

residential school system in Canada."[412]

Undaunted by that rebuff, special interlocutor Kimberly Murray at the fourth National Gathering for Unmarked Graves in June 2023 called for the criminalization of "residential school denialism," a neologism that belies a species of Holocaust envy.[413]

Then-federal Justice Minister David Lametti has said he is open to "all possibilities to fighting residential school denialism," which adds an ominous tone as I write this. "An iron broom for iron times" as the saying went — in the days of the regime whose crimes necessitated the creation of laws against genocide.

Even Adolf Eichmann had his day in court. As the passing of Gazan's genocide motion shows, Canada's crimes against Indigenous people are so profound as to warrant dispensing with such legal norms as the presumption of innocence, due process, and showing the accused the evidence against them. Our guilt is so obvious as to merit conviction without trial, so self-evident that parliamentarians were justified in their usurpation of the role of the judiciary.

If residential school denialism can be punished like Holocaust denial, should Canadian genocidaires be punished like Nazis? Or should they be convicted without trial as Canada has been. Upon whom would the task of punishment fall? If no one, then anyone? Perhaps vigilante justice will stop at burning churches and reducing Canada Day to a collective exercise in *Schadenfreude*. After all, Canada has already severely punished Canada, both psychologically and financially. But what punishment is due to the criminals who not only committed history's longest-running genocide but are also *currently* waging "ongoing" genocide against Indigenous people? Convicted as we are, even if anyone resolved to appeal our conviction, they could soon find themselves arrested on charges of criminal "denialism."

---

412 Melanson, Michael & Green, Nina, *"Canada's 'Genocide'- Case Closed?"* The Dorchester Review online, October 27, 2022.

413 "Unmarked graves report lays out challenges — including fighting denialism," *Toronto Star*, June 16, 2023.

The genocide narrative is toxic to Canadian civil society. If a guilty party is seen as the most evil of all, then the worst of all punishments can be sought. In which case, being paid back in anything less than our own coin should be considered a mercy.

Originally published online as "Genocide for Dummies," by the Frontier Centre for Public Policy, November 4, 2022.

Chapter Nine

We Had a "Knowing": The False Narrative of IRS Burials

Tom Flanagan and Brian Giesbrecht

On May 27 and July 15, 2021, press releases from Chief Rosanne Casimir of the Tk'emlúps te Secwépemc First Nation (Kamloops Indian band) in British Columbia announced that the "remains of 215 children," "some as young as three years old," had been found, and that this had come about because "we had a knowing in our community that we were able to verify," and that the search had been based on Knowledge Keepers' oral histories.[414]

The Kamloops press releases were quickly followed by similar announcements at Marieval, Saskatchewan,[415] then Cranbrook,[416] and later Williams Lake, both in British Columbia. Since then, a number of articles and videos have suggested that these claims are a massive fraud or giant hoax. The truth is even more disturbing. They are not simply a fraud or hoax. Many of the people accusing residentials schools, and Catholic clergy in particular, of murdering thousands of Indigenous children in horrible ways and secretly disposing of their bodies — with the help of six-year-old conscripts — actually believe their bizarre claims. What is going on?

Residential schools took centre stage after Barbara Frum's 1990 CBC interview with Phil Fontaine, in which the then Manitoba Regional Chief of the Assembly of First Nations unexpectedly made allegations of widespread sexual abuse at the residential school he had attended as a child: "In my grade three class ... if there were 20 boys, every single one of them ... would have experienced what I experienced. They would have

---

[414] Tkemlúps te Secwépemc, Press releases, May 27 and July 15, 2021.

[415] Jorge Barrera, "Catholic register, survivors offer clues to who may be buried in cemetery next to Marieval residential school," CBC News, July 20, 2021.

[416] Adam MacVicar, "'We knew it was there': Former B.C. chief says unmarked graves near Cranbrook need more context," Global News, July 1, 2021.

experienced some aspect of sexual abuse."[417] Although Fontaine did not elaborate, the scale of what he described suggested widespread student-on-student abuse.

Since that interview, preposterous stories have taken hold and become deeply-rooted in First Nations communities — stories of murders and clandestine burials on a large scale, of babies thrown into furnaces, of children imprisoned in underground chambers and cisterns, hanged in barns, and shocked in electric chairs,[418] with the result that $321 million dollars of federal government funding has been committed to searching for unmarked graves all over the country, and helping survivors heal from their trauma.[419]

There is no documentary evidence to support these stories. There is no record, for example, of a single student being murdered at a residential school —never mind thousands — in the 113-year history of residential schools. Nor — and this is key — are there any records of Indigenous parents claiming that their children went to residential schools "never to be seen again," as claimed by Truth and Reconciliation Commissioner Marie Wilson.[420]

This has not stopped Indigenous leaders from proclaiming these conspiracy theories as fact, nor has it stopped the media and general public from believing them. In 2021 there were vigils across the country for the 215 children supposedly buried in secret by Catholic priests and brothers in the apple orchard at the former Kamloops Indian Residential School, despite the fact that the RCMP and the BC Coroner declined to investigate, suggesting they did not give credence to the claims. To make matters worse, the original story of 215 burials in the apple orchard at Kamloops was amplified in a CBC Fifth Estate program, "The Reckoning: Secrets

---

[417] "Phil Fontaine's 1990 account of physical and sexual abuse at residential school," Interview with Barbara Frum, CBC Archives.

[418] Jorge Barrera, "The horrors of St. Anne's," CBC News, March 29, 2018.

[419] Tom Cardoso, "Ottawa commits $321-million to search for residential school graves, help survivors," *Globe and Mail*, August 10, 2021.

[420] Nancy Knickerbocker, "The Gladys We Never Knew," *The Tyee*, July 4, 2015.

Unearthed by Tk'emlúps te Secwépemc,"[421] to include stories of sexual abuse, children who mysteriously disappeared, the lifeless bodies of four boys hanging in a barn, abortions, and babies thrown into the school furnace.[422]

At a press conference on January 25 at Williams Lake in the Cariboo region of British Columbia, Chief Willie Sellars ventured further into the realm of the fantastic. Not only did he allege that the priests and nuns at St Joseph's Indian Residential School had committed almost every heinous act that could be imagined — murder, torture, gang rape, lashing and starvation of children, and the usual "priest throws baby into incinerator" trope — but according to Chief Sellars there was an effort at all levels to hide the evidence of these horrendous crimes: "[There is] clear evidence that religious entities, the federal government and the RCMP have knowingly participated in the destruction of records, and the cover-up of criminal allegations."[423] Although not a single police report, newspaper account, or any other historical record supports these allegations of murder and secret burials, distinguished Indigenous leaders, including TRC Commissioners Murray Sinclair, Wilton Littlechild, and Marie Wilson, as well as former Kamloops chief Manny Jules and Dr. Ron Ignace,[424] appear to believe tales of six-year-olds secretly burying bodies late at night. Meanwhile politicians and journalists hold their tongues, and offer no pushback against stories that are clearly fictional.

In the light of this widespread public acceptance, similar claims of murdered and secretly buried Indigenous children can be expected from other First Nations flush with cash enabling them to pursue these frantic searches for thousands of "missing children" they honestly believe were

---

[421] "Kamloops residential school survivors recall students going missing, digging of graves in orchard," from CBC, The Fifth Estate, available on Youtube.

[422] Lynette Fortune, Linda Guerriero and Gillian Findlay, "Down in the Apple Orchard," CBC News, January 13, 2022.

[423] Angie Mindus, Monica Lamb-Yorski, Ruth Lloyd, "'93 is our number': Williams Lake First Nation releases findings in residential school probe," *Tofino-Ucluelet Westerly News*, January 25, 2022.

[424] Douglas Quan, "'It tore our humanity apart': What life was really like at the Kamloops residential school," *Toronto Star*, June 5, 2021.

killed in hideous ways and secretly buried at residential schools all across the country.[425]

It is worth noting that prior to the interview with Phil Fontaine in 1990, one would have had to look very hard to find anything even resembling these claims. It was only after the Fontaine interview that stories of residential school atrocities gained ground, even though they were contradicted by the explicit evidence of some contemporary Indigenous leaders.

Former Dene Chief Cece Hodgson-McCauley, whose weekly newspaper column, Northern Notes, ran for thirty years, was the most outspoken. In a column in 2018, she wrote: "We all heard of horrible lies created by some individuals in order to receive as much money as they could."[426] In her final column she said, "I always tell you the truth."

In his autobiography, *Breaking Trail*, Senator Len Marchand, the first status Indian to be appointed to the federal cabinet, recounted his experience at Kamloops Indian Residential School, which he attended by his own choice for a year. Marchand praised the quality of teaching there and said he knew of no abuse: "The reader might be expecting me to tell a few horror stories about physical and sexual abuse at the residential school. But I know of no incidences [sic] at KIRS."[427]

Chief Clarence Jules, a respected three-term chief of the Kamloops band, also attended Kamloops Indian Residential School. In *Our Chiefs and Elders*, published in 1992, he complained that he had been strapped for speaking his own language at the school, but thought it was "probably the best system we had around at that time."[428] He said nothing about murder

---

[425] Bryan Eneas and Michelle Song, "Survivor has advice for officials probing possible graves at former residential school: 'Keep digging,'" CBC News, February 20, 2022.

[426] Josh Campbell, "Residential school column in News/North draws criticism from N.W.T. elders," CBC News, January 16, 2018.

[427] Len Marchand and Matt Hughes, *Breaking Trail*, (Caitlin Press: Prince George, 2000), pp. 18-19, 15-16.

[428] David A. Neel, *Our Chiefs and Elders: Words and Photographs of Native Leaders* (Vancouver: UBC Press, 1992).

and mayhem, nothing about secret burials or any of the other fantastic claims now being made.

However his son, Manny Jules, who attended KIRS as a day student from 1959 to 1967,[429] and was briefly chief of staff to Phil Fontaine,[430] when asked in a June 1, 2021, interview on CBC's "The Current" whether he had heard stories of secretly buried children, said: "Everyone did. I heard them, you know, from my parents and I heard them from other residential school survivors. You know, you just know that this is the situation right across the country."[431]

This is hard to believe since, prior to Chief Casimir's press release a few days earlier, Manny Jules had never publicly mentioned secret burials, or reported them to the RCMP during his own tenure as chief. Nor did he ever search for the burials he claimed he knew about from his parents, despite the fact that he participated in an archaeological excavation program on the Kamloops Reserve led by Dr. George Nicholas of Simon Fraser University.[432] In a 2013 report, Dr. Nicholas wrote: "There was, however, a degree of First Nations participation in some of these projects. In fact, former Kamloops Chief Manny Jules met his wife, Linda, while they were both working on an archaeological project."[433]

Many other successful Indigenous people attended KIRS, including John Jules, another of Chief Clarence Jules' sons, who became an archaeologist and was a "traditional knowledge keeper."[434] Another successful student

---

[429] Padraig Moran, Kate Cornick, and Julie Crysler, "Discovery of Kamloops remains confirmed what they suspected. Now action must match words, says survivor," CBC Radio, June 1, 2021.

[430] Paul Barnsley, "Jules resigns as AFN chief of staff," Aboriginal Multi-Media Society (AMMSA.com), *Raven's Eye*, 7:9, January 30, 2004.

[431] Transcript, Matt Galloway, "The Current," Tuesday June 1, 2021, CBC Radio, June 1, 2021.

[432] George Nicholas, "Why heritage isn't just about things," Tedx Yellowknife, Tłįchǫ Research and Training Institute seminar, on YouTube, December 7, 2015. (Dr. Nicholas is Professor of Archaeology at Simon Fraser University, developed and directed SFU's Indigenous Archeology Program on the Kamloops Indian Reserve from 1991 to 2005.)

[433] Nicholas, George, "Archaeology as a Transformative Practice in Secwepemc Territory," Archaeology Department, Simon Fraser University, 2013 (draft).

[434] John Jules, Obituary, *Vancouver Sun*, October 19, 2010.

was Joe Stanley Michel, the first graduate of the Kamloops Indian Residential School, who returned to teach at the school from 1952 to 1967 and resided with his wife and children in a teacherage on the school grounds.[435]

Not one of the many distinguished Indigenous individuals who spent their formative years at a residential school said anything publicly about students who disappeared, or were murdered, or hung in a barn, or thrown into furnaces, nor did they report such allegations to the RCMP. So where did all of these stories about residential school atrocities come from?

It seems the concern about residential schools generated by the Fontaine interview was manipulated and spurred forward by the conspiracy theories of Kevin Annett, a defrocked United Church minister and self-styled "gut-level anarchist"[436] with an ambition to "change the world fundamentally" and "make a revolution."[437]

Annett has made it his life's work, after his dismissal by the United Church due to his very obvious problems,[438] to disseminate gruesome allegations about residential schools, particularly the Kamloops one. On May 30, 2021, only a few days after Chief Casimir's press release, Annett claimed on one of his websites that the school was "an especially notorious Special Treatment center designed to inflict particularly cruel and severe punishment, experimentation and torture on native children." He claimed his "investigators" had interviewed thirty-nine former KIRS students who reported tales of torture, rape, imprisonment, forced sterilization, deadly

[435] George Robertson, Arla Saare, John Seale, Gerry O'Connor, and Norman Rosen, "'The Eyes of Children'— life at a residential school," film documentary filmed at Kamloops Indian Residential School, CBC Vancouver, aired on December 25, 1962. Posted on YouTube by the Frontier Centre for Public Policy, June 9, 2021.

[436] Kevin A, "Unrepentant Radicals: Kevin Annett and Larry Gambone in Conversation," YouTube, Posted October 19, 2016.

[437] InfiniLor, "Who Is Kevin Annett?" YouTube, filmed June 24, 2013 in Nanaimo; posted June 27, 2013.

[438] Pacific Mountain Regional Council of the United Church of Canada, "Kevin Annett: Truth, for Reconciliation," June 27, 2021.

government experiments, ritual Satanic cult killings, child trafficking, secret burials, and general mayhem.[439]

Since the mid-1990s, Annett, the self-described "founding citizen of the Republic of Kanata," has made a career of promulgating these stories in a steady stream of books, interviews, websites, videos, public events, and even sham human rights tribunals.[440] In 2017, in *Fallen: The Story of the Vancouver Four*, he publicized the delusions of sad, alcoholic Indigenous men he befriended on Vancouver's skid row,[441] including William Combes, who died in 2011. Combes was reputedly the author of two stories widely circulated by Annett: the claim of burials in the apple orchard at the former Kamloops Residential School, and the claim that Queen Elizabeth kidnapped ten children from the school while on a picnic at Deadman's Creek in 1964. This bizarre tale has circulated on the internet for a decade, even though the Queen did not visit Western Canada in 1964.[442]

In 2006 Annett filmed the documentary "Unrepentant," which shows grainy footage of the apple orchard at the Kamloops school, with a voice-over by William Combes describing a burial he witnessed there.[443] This implies that the Kamloops Band gave Annett permission to shoot video footage in the apple orchard on the Kamloops reserve in 2006, thus linking Annett and the Kamloops Band to the tale of secret burials in the apple orchard fifteen years prior to Chief Casimir's announcement in a press release on May 27, 2021, of the discovery of "the remains of 215 children, ... some as young as three years old."[444] Why did the Kamloops Band not report these alleged burials to the RCMP in 2006? Or later, in 2008, when

---

439 Kevin D. Annett, Not "abuse" but mass murder! A Memorandum on Genocidal Crimes at the Catholic Kamloops 'Indian Residential School,'" Republic of Kanata online, May 30, 2021.

440 RationalWiki, "International Tribunal into Crimes of Church and State."

441 Kevin D. Annett, *Fallen: The Story of the Vancouver Four*, CreateSpace Independent Publishing Platform, 2017.

442 Reuters Fact Check, "Fact Check-Debunking claims about disappeared school children in 1964 in British Columbia, Canada," Reuters, March 24, 2021.

443 Tana ka, "Unrepentant: Kevin Annett and Canada's Genocide," YouTube, February 8, 2018.

444 Tk̓emlúps te Secwépemc, "Remains of Children of Kamloops Residential School Discovered," Press Release, May 27, 2021.

the alleged burials were again brought to the notice of the Kamloops Band in an article in *Kamloops This Week*?[445]

After filming "Unrepentant," Annett attempted to bring it to the attention of First Nations, the federal government, Canadian churches and the United Nations,[446] via demonstrations about the "Canadian Holocaust [sic] against Onkwehon:weh children,"[447] fake tribunals,[448] and a promotional tour which included screenings in Ottawa,[449] Victoria,[450] and the Mohawk First Nation reserve at Brantford.[451]

In September 2010, four years after the release of Unrepentant with its footage of the apple orchard on the Kamloops reserve, Annett published *Hidden No Longer*, containing an appendix listing "Mass Graves at former Indian Residential Schools and Hospitals across Canada," including one in the orchard at Kamloops and another in an orchard at the former Mohawk Institute at Brantford, now the Woodland Cultural Centre:

> Brantford : Mohawk Institute, Anglican church (1850-1969), building intact. Series of graves in orchard behind school building, under rows of trees.

[445] Staff, "Claims of mass grave at Tk'emlups go back years,"Kamloops This Week, May 28, 2021.

[446] Steve Bonspiel, "Digging up the past: Residential School Tribunal uses pressure tactics to locate mass graves," *The Nation* online archives, April 25, 2008.

[447] Unsigned, "Ending the whitewash of genocide in Canada," *Tekawennake News*, April 8 2009.

[448] Louis Baudoin-Laarman, "Mass graves at Canadian residential school: false story, unrelated photo," Agence France-Presse AFP Fact Check, November 1, 2019.

[449] "Ending the whitewash," loc. cit.

[450] Michael D. Reid, "Focus on school abuse fallout," *Victoria Times Colonist*, June 8, 2007.

[451] Andrea Lucille Catapano, "The Rising of the Ongwehònwe: Sovereignty, Identity, and Representation on the Six Nations Reserve," Ph.D thesis, Stony Brook University, December 2007, p. 214.

Kamloops : Catholic school (1890-1978). Buildings intact. Mass grave south of school, adjacent to and amidst orchard. Numerous burials witnessed there.[452]

In April 2011, encouraged by Annett's claim in *Hidden No Longer* that he knew exactly where bodies were buried at the former Mohawk Institute in Brantford, the Mohawk Nation of Ouse/Grand River invited Annett to lead a search for unmarked graves. According to Annett's account in a long blog post entitled "Murder By Decree," interviews with former students, ground-penetrating radar searches, and excavation took place that fall.[453] But when Annett tried to pass off animal bones as those of dismembered four-year old children at an Occupy Toronto protest in November 2011,[454] he was exposed as a fraud and publicly denounced by the Mohawk First Nation.[455]

What of the alleged burials in the orchard at the Mohawk Institute? Archaeological excavation took place in the summer of 2017,[456] and according to a follow-up story in the *Two Row Times* on June 2, 2021, Annett's claim of burials, as well as the claims of former students that babies were buried there, were definitively disproved, while Annett himself had "lost the confidence of the Mohawks."[457]

Among the recurring community stories involving the Mohawk Institute are the accounts of former students who claimed there were babies buried beneath the apple trees in the school's orchard. As part of the Woodland

---

[452] Kevin D. Annett, *Hidden No Longer: Genocide in Canada, Past and Present*, an "updated new edition of *Hidden from History: The Canadian Holocaust* (3rd ed.), published by The International Tribunal into Crimes of Church and State and The Friends and Relatives of the Disappeared," self-published, September, 2010.

[453] Kevin Annett, "Murder by Decree: Mass Graves of Children in Canada – Documented Evidence," WordPress blog post, April 25, 2013.

[454] SupportLocalScene, "Kevin Annett at Occupy Toronto" YouTube, posted November 29, 2011.

[455] Kanyen'keháka Ronyáhten, "Kevin Annett ITCCS and Mohawk Elders," YouTube, posted May 29, 2012.

[456] Jim Windle, "Mush Hole Archeology Revealing Much," *Two Row Times*, August 9, 2017, pp. 2, 15.

[457] Jim Windle and Nahnda Garlow, "Kamloops discovery reopens concerns about former Mohawk Institute," *Two Rows Times*, June 2, 2021, p. 4.

Cultural Centre's revitalization and Mohawk Institute Memorial Park plans, those apple trees were removed and an archeological investigation was done of the area which did not uncover any human remains.[458]

Oddly, Two Row Times brushed off the fact that allegations of secret burials by former students had been definitively disproved with the offhand comment that "thankfully" no human remains were found.

Despite these setbacks, the Mohawk Nation continues to believe stories about secretly buried children, and plans further searches for which ample funding is available: the Ontario provincial government has allocated a total of $20 million to finance searches for unmarked graves at residential schools throughout the province.[459]

Kevin Annett continues to propagate his increasingly bizarre allegations, including his claims involving Satanic cults. In "Billy Remembers," Frances Widdowson compares Annett's claims to the emotional hysteria surrounding supposed Satanic sexual abuse recounted in the book *Michelle Remembers*,[460] and the "daycare abuse cases" of the 1980s and early 1990s, which resulted in "over 12,000 unsubstantiated accusations."[461]

Annett linked residential schools to Satanic rituals immediately after the Kamloops announcement on May 27, 2021. Moreover he claimed in a recent video that the Vatican plans to have him assassinated on a date which is significant to a Satanic sect:

> This is Kevin Annett, Eagle Strong Voice. It's January the 8th, 2022. The Vatican assassination bureau known as Santi Alleganza [sic] or the so-called Holy Alliance has essentially put out a contract on me that I will die on or before February 21st, 22nd(?)

[458] Ibid.

[459] Don Mitchell, "Ground search at former Mohawk Institute in Brantford, Ont. set to begin," Global News, November 8, 2021.

[460] Lawrence Pazder and Michelle Smith, *Michelle Remembers*, St. Martin's Press, 1980.

[461] Nadja Schreiber, Lisa D. Bellah, Yolanda Martinez, Kristin A. McLaurin, Renata Strok, Sena Garven & James M. Wood, "Suggestive interviewing in the McMartin Preschool and Kelly Michaels daycare abuse cases: A case study," *Social Influence*, 1:1 (2006), pp. 16-47, cited by Frances Widdowson, "Billy Remembers," *The American Conservative*, July 15, 2022.

which is a high point in the Ninth Circle Satanic sect official ritual network operating out of Rome. We have that as solid proof.[462]

Annett's decades-long crusade and the steadily increasing stream of stories of atrocities by former students of residential schools have wrought considerable damage to Christianity in Canada. More than a dozen churches have been destroyed by arson,[463] while many others have been vandalized.[464] These crimes were widely attributed by the media and Canadian government officials to "understandable" anger at the discovery of thousands of graves of residential school children, though Prime Minister Trudeau later said violence was "unacceptable."[465] No perpetrators have been identified or brought to justice.

This anti-Christian sentiment has been largely directed against the Catholic Church and the Catholic religious orders which operated and staffed many residential schools. Although Catholic-run institutions comprised only 43% of all Indian residential schools in Canada,[466] Catholic residential schools are featured in most of the media coverage of these alleged atrocities. It is almost always a priest who is said to have thrown babies into a furnace, not a Protestant minister or pastor, and it seems always to be a priest or brother who orders six-year-olds to secretly bury the children he has murdered.

Sometimes these claims involving alleged Catholic perpetrators defy the known facts of the case. Secret Path, Gord Downie's graphic novel about the death in 1966 of Chanie Wenjack, is now widely taught to Canadian

---

[462] Lauren Southern, "The Insane Origins of the "Mass Graves" Story," YouTube, posted January 31, 2022.

[463] Cosmin Dzsurdzsa, "A map of the 71 churches that have been vandalized or burned since the residential schools announcement," True North Centre online, updated January 16, 2023.

[464] Jason Herring, "Calgary police investigate after at least 11 Catholic churches vandalized with orange and red paint," *Calgary Herald*, July 1, 2021.

[465] Rachel Gilmore, "'Unacceptable and wrong': Trudeau says vandalizing churches can hurt those seeking 'solace'" Global News, July 2, 2021; Brian Lilley, "Trudeau explains away arson attacks on churches," *Toronto Sun*, July 5, 2021.

[466] Clifton, Rodney A. and Mark DeWolf, *From Truth Comes Reconciliation* (Winnipeg: Frontier Centre For Public Policy, 2021), p. 34.

children.[467] In it, the villains are a priest and nuns, despite the fact that Chanie Wenjack was from a Protestant family and attended public school in Kenora while boarding at the Cecilia Jeffery Residence, a Presbyterian hostel that had earlier been a residential school.[468] In fact, there is no evidence that Wenjack ever met a priest or a nun in his entire life.[469] Why this emphasis on Catholic villains? It is hard to know,[470] but the anti-Catholic rhetoric is troubling.

It is also troubling that money and active encouragement from federal and provincial governments are driving this unrealistic narrative. As noted earlier, the federal government has given First Nations communities $321 million dollars to search for "missing children" who simply aren't there. But government spending has spiralled even more seriously out of control. The federal government recently announced that $40 billion dollars will be spent on the Indigenous child welfare issue.[471] As Professor Tom Flanagan explains, that profligate spending was only possible given the current frenzy surrounding "unmarked graves."[472]

There is no obvious solution to a problem that results in a steady stream of press releases and media coverage as Indigenous communities use federal money to search for bodies that have never been shown to exist. The attitude of the current Liberal government is only making a bad problem worse. Crown-Indigenous Relations Minister Marc Miller's recent announcement that he believes all of these claims without reservation —

---

[467] Gord Downie and Jeff Lemire, *Secret Path*, New York: Simon & Schuster, 2016.

[468] Robert MacBain, "The sad truth about Chanie Wenjack," *C2C Journal* (online only), October 2, 2017.

[469] Brian Giesbrecht, "Teaching the Residential School Story," Frontier Centre for Public Policy blog post, November 2, 2017.

[470] Kevin P. Anderson, *Not Quite Us: Anti-Catholic Thought in English Canada Since 1900* (Montreal and Kingston: McGill-Queen's University Press, 2019); Philip Jenkins, *The New Anti-Catholicism: The Last Acceptable Prejudice*. Oxford: Oxford University Press, 2004.

[471] Ryan Tumilty, "Government announces $40-billion settlement over Indigenous child-welfare system," *National Post*, January 4, 2022.

[472] Tom Flanagan, "The Road to Reparations: A $40 Billion Settlement for Indigenous Child Welfare," Fraser Institute Bulletin (Vancouver: Fraser Institute 2022).

no matter how preposterous — is truly alarming.[473] More alarming still is his denunciation of anyone who questions the claims. He has even hinted at making such questioning illegal hate speech.

Whatever the current government does or does not do, the strong belief within the Indigenous community that Canada has acted murderously towards them in the past and is continuing to commit genocide against them and their culture in the present will poison relations for years to come, and make it very unlikely that Indigenous young people will have happy and successful lives. How can they, if they believe that they are living in a racist country that has systematically killed their ancestors, and despises them? Even when the current government departs, it will be very difficult for any new government to change this deeply entrenched belief. In fact, if a new regime takes charge and reduces the remarkable flow of money to Indigenous issues and communities that has occurred since 2015, the country can only expect bad things to happen from people who are convinced that they are the permanent victims of an evil system.

None of this is to suggest that the people who reside in First Nations communities do not have many legitimate grievances, or that many people were not harmed in residential schools. The concerns are real, the harm is real, and both must be addressed. However, believing stories that are not true does none of that.

One thing has become clear. Where excavation has taken place after GPR searches,[474] nothing has been found — no human remains, no graves. The list of former residential schools and Indian hospitals where excavation has yielded nothing and stories of burials have been proved untrue includes the former Mohawk Institute at Brantford, the former Shubenacadie Indian Residential School in Nova Scotia,[475] the Charles Camsell Hospital in

---

[473] Kristy Kirkup, "Crown-Indigenous Relations Minister Marc Miller concerned about 'concerted' efforts to deny experience of residential schools," *Globe and Mail*, January 28, 2022.

[474] The burials at Marieval and Cranbrook have not been excavated, but it has been established that the soil disturbances found by GPR in both places are in known community cemeteries. Cf. Adam MacVicar, "'We knew it was there': Former B.C. chief says unmarked graves near Cranbrook need more context," Global News, July 1, 2021.

[475] Frances Willick, "No evidence found of unmarked graves related to Shubenacadie Residential School," CBC News, August 4, 2021.

Edmonton,[476] and the Kuper Island Indian Residential School in British Columbia.[477] It thus appears that stories told by former students of their experiences at residential schools are not "knowings" or the "oral histories of Knowledge Keepers," as Chief Casimir would have it. "We've always known," was the refrain often heard.[478] They are merely stories told by human beings whose memories, like the memories of all other human beings, are fallible and frail.

What is needed is concrete evidence that the burials at Kamloops and Williams Lake actually do exist, something which can only be accomplished through excavation. In the CBC Fifth Estate program mentioned earlier, former chief Manny Jules stated that the spokespersons for the families in the Kamloops Band have now all agreed that excavation should take place.[479] Since the Kamloops site has been more than once declared a crime scene by Chief Rosanne Casimir and by former AFN Chief RoseAnne Archibald, to preserve trust on all sides this excavation should be done under RCMP supervision by expert archaeologists with no connection to the Kamloops Band.

This chapter originally appeared as "The False Narrative of Residential School Burials" in The Dorchester Review *online, March 1, 2022.*

---

[476] Stephen Cook, "No remains uncovered at former Camsell Hospital site: 21 spots flagged by ground-penetrating radar only turned up debris," CBC News, October 22, 2021.

[477] "B.C. First Nation says more than 160 unmarked graves found," CBC News, July 12, 2021.

[478] Denise Wong, "'We've always known': Kuper Island residential school survivor not surprised by discovery of remains," CityNews Everywhere, Vancouver, July 13, 2021. Patrick White, "What a long-forgotten B.C. RCMP task force uncovered about residential school abuses," The Globe and Mail, September 13, 2021.

[479] "Kamloops residential school survivors recall students going missing, digging of graves in orchard," from CBC, The Fifth Estate, loc. cit., January 2022, cited in "One Year Later Still No Evidence of Unmarked Graves" Frontier Centre for Public Policy (fcpp.org).

Chapter Ten

Neither Truth Nor Reconciliation

D. Barry Kirkham KC

Review of *From Truth Comes Reconciliation: Assessing the Truth and Reconciliation Commission Report*. Rodney Clifton and Mark DeWolf, eds. Frontier Centre for Public Policy, 2021. 343 pages.

The Truth and Reconciliation Commission (TRC) published its multi-volume Report in 2015.[480] These documents purport to be the definitive history of Indian Residential Schools (IRS) in Canada.[481] Certainly, it has been treated as if it were. Virtually all commentary from the media, government, and universities has accepted it as gospel.

The Report was denunciatory in the extreme in respect to residential schools. It has been profoundly influential. For example, the vandalizing and removal of statues of Sir John A. Macdonald can be traced to the fact that IRS were initiated under his government. The people who seek to cancel Sir John ignore the fact that Canada was committed in various treaties to provide Aboriginals with an education, and IRS were the only means to fulfil that obligation in respect to small reserves without the population to justify a day school.

They also ignore the fact that Macdonald did *not* make attendance mandatory. Egerton Ryerson, a famous educator, has also been cancelled due to his support in the middle of the 19th century for government sponsored education facilities to teach agrarian techniques to Aboriginals,

---

[480] Truth and Reconciliation Commission of Canada, Final Report (McGill-Queen's University Press, 2015).

[481] Residential schools were often referred to in the early days as industrial or boarding schools. Industrial schools focussed on teaching students a trade, such as carpentry. Boarding schools attempted to teach agrarian techniques. The TRC does not distinguish between the experiences of students at different types of residential schools.

despite the fact he had nothing to do with the IRS system commenced in Canada in 1883, as two historians pointed out in *The Dorchester Review*.[482]

Senator Lynn Beyak, who stated that while the residential schools did considerable harm, they also did some good — something that the TRC Report itself argues in its Part 1 and Part 2 "History" volumes — was removed from the Senate's Aboriginal Peoples Committee and from the Conservative Party caucus for suggesting that IRS were anything other than an unmitigated evil and that her correspondents should be allowed to say so and have their views published.

Internationally, Canada's reputation has been stained. The United Nations has called Canada onto the carpet, though the International Criminal Court has refused to hear any case for "genocide." Still dictatorships such as Russia and China have been delighted to deflect criticisms of their own human rights violations by pointing to the TRC's denunciations of Canada's schools for Indigenous children. The absurd accusation of "mass graves" could never have gained traction but for the TRC's having created a climate where such an outrageous claim could seem plausible.

The TRC performed a valuable public service in taking extensive testimony concerning the history of residential schools. It provided the opportunity for Aboriginals who had suffered greatly from abuses perpetrated at the schools to tell their story. The Report is comprehensive, to say the least, in summarizing all things that went wrong. It is not my purpose to address the 94 recommendations or "Calls to Action" made by the Report, nor to advocate a favourable view of IRS.[483] Rather my purpose is to address the question of whether the TRC Report is a reliable history.

In *From Truth Comes Reconciliation: Assessing the Truth and Reconciliation Commission Report*, authors Rodney Clifton and Mark DeWolf — both of whom were students and/or staff at residential schools — demonstrate that the TRC Report is not a fair and balanced history.

---

[482] See "Assault on Decency," by Robert Stagg and Patrice Dutil, *The Dorchester Review*, Vol. 11, No. 1, Spring/Summer 2021, pp. 64-69, and online, "The Imbecile Attack on Egerton Ryerson," August 12, 2021.

[483] Pdf. available online https://nctr.ca/records/reports/

Their work is supported by eight other contributors of chapters: Joseph Quesnel, Frances Widdowson, Gerry Bowler, Hymie Rubenstein, Brian Giesbrecht, Masha V. Krylova, Lea Meadows, and Marshall Draper, who worked with Clifton and DeWolf on the project over several years.

The authors acknowledge that there is much truth in the TRC Report, but point out that its bias and incendiary claims "display a contempt for truth that helps to make a reader suspicious of anything else the Commission asserts," as Gerry Bowler, professor of history at the University of Manitoba and a senior fellow at the Frontier Centre for Public Policy, writes on p. 132 of the book.[484]

The contributors make it clear that their objective is not to denounce the TRC but to provide a good faith critique and restore balance to the legacy of the schools. There is much of importance in Cliton and DeWolf's fine corrective to what is fast becoming the received and indeed authorized version of Canadian residential schools history.

Genesis

Professor J. R. Miller has written elsewhere a comprehensive review, *Residential Schools and Reconciliation,* of how Canada came to confront their unhappy legacy.[485] The federal government announced in 1969 that it intended to phase out residential schools. By the 1980s the various churches that had run them commenced a reassessment of their work, recognizing they had failed in many respects. Numerous apologies were issued.

The Royal Commission on Aboriginal Peoples (RCAP) sat between 1992 and 1996. Its lengthy report dealt with most aspects of Canadian treatment

---

[484] Clifton and DeWolf, p. 132.

[485] J.R. Miller, *Residential Schools and Reconciliation* (University of Toronto Press, 2017.) Cf. Idem, *Shingwauk's Vision: A History of Native Residential Schools* (University of Toronto Press, 1996). Miller reviewed Joseph Boyden's novel *Orenda*, "Of Orenda and Clerical Scapegoats," *The Dorchester Review,* Vol. 4, No. 1, Spring-Summer 2014, pp. 11-13.

of Aboriginals.[486] It heard much testimony concerning terrible experiences some native children had experienced at the schools. In its report it recommended a further inquiry. One consequence of the RCAP was the creation of the Aboriginal Healing Centre. Funded with $600,000,000 of public money, the Centre worked on the process of healing "survivors" of the schools. In the period 2003-2012 it published several books on the history of IRS, which were made available throughout Canada free of charge.

In the 1990s revelations of abuse at residential schools began to surface. Some criminal convictions were obtained against perpetrators of sexual and nonsexual assaults. A torrent of civil litigation followed. By 1999 thousands of legal actions had been commenced. Widdowson quotes a figure of over 5,500 from Miller, whereas she herself reports 11,000. (p. 99). Class action lawyers became very active importuning natives to sign on to various lawsuits. Eventually all parties managed to negotiate the Indian Residential Schools Settlement Agreement, 2005 ("IRSSA").

Every Indigenous student who attended a residential school was entitled to a payment of $10,000 plus $3,000 for each year of attendance, for merely being an IRS student (the "common experience" payment). If a student alleged abuse the student would receive substantial additional compensation (the "Independent Assessment Process"). This process invited former students to file a claim listing all complaints of abuse. Compensation was awarded on a points system. The more complaints, the higher the compensation. The claims were not investigated with much scrutiny (Clifton-DeWolf, p. 46). Many former students received awards of over $100,000 and some awards were as high as $450,000.[487]

One of the terms of the IRSSA was that Canada would establish a commission to conduct a full investigation. The primary mandate of such a commission was to provide a complete historical record. The establishment of the TRC was the fulfilment of that commitment.

[486] Report of the Royal Commission on Aboriginal Peoples (Ottawa: Queen's Printer, 1996).

[487] Clifton-DeWolf, p. 37; Widdowson in Clifton-DeWolf, p. 102; Miller, *Residential Schools,* chapter 6.

South Africa

There have been several Truth and Reconciliation Commissions established throughout the world in the 21st century. They have drawn their inspiration from South Africa. Both the Canadian and South African commissions were charged with the momentous task of determining the true history of events where there would inevitably be much disagreement and varying interpretations. However, there are profound differences in the approaches of the two commissions.

The story of the South African TRC is told by its vice-chair, Alex Boraine, in *A Country Unmasked* (Oxford, 2000).[488]

The first major difference was in the selection of the members of the Commission. President Nelson Mandela refused to appoint the commissioners until a rigorous process was followed.[489] An independent committee was formed which sought out potential members. It held public hearings. After vetting 299 potential commissioners, it submitted 25 names to Mandela. Mandela appointed 17 commissioners, choosing from a broad range of experiences, so as to ensure the Commission represented a full range of society. In South Africa, the commission was not packed with adherents of the African National Congress (ANC).

The IRSSA stipulated that "consideration shall be given to at least one of the three commissioners being an Aboriginal." Appointments were made by Order-in-Council. The chief commissioner, Justice Murray Sinclair, is a Métis.[490] The other two commissioners were Chief Wilton Littlechild and Dr. Marie Wilson, who is married to an Aboriginal. All three are distinguished Canadians but there was no attempt to appoint anyone who might have a view that IRS were anything other than an unmitigated evil. The TRC report commences with a mission statement from each of the three commissioners. Chairman Sinclair leaves no doubt where he stands.

---

[488] Alex Boraine, in *A Country Unmasked* (Oxford University Press Southern Africa, 2000).

[489] Ibid., p. 71.

[490] "The Honourable Justice Murray Sinclair, LL.B., DU, DCL, LL.D. (Hons)," Métis Museum, Gabriel Dumont Institute of Native Studies and Applied Research, Saskatoon.

He denounces IRS in the harshest possible terms and attributes virtually every single problem experienced by Canadian Aboriginals to IRS.

The second major difference between the two TRCs is that the South African commission was mandated to discover the full truth as to violations of human rights, no matter who committed them. While this was a contentious point at the commencement of the process, Mandela wanted a truthful history from the Commission. The Commission insisted that it hear evidence about human rights violations committed by members of the ANC. For example, the Commission spent nine days of hearings investigating the reign of terror perpetrated by Mandela's wife, Winnie, and her United Football Club, during the time Mandela was incarcerated.[491] The commission also insisted on investigating the covert operations of the Kwazulu-Natal. There was a clear commitment to producing a reliable history in the belief that only such a history could produce a basis for reconciliation.

Of course, South Africa had the gift of leadership from the man who was and is the very embodiment of truth and reconciliation. Nelson Mandela inspired not just South Africa but the entire world.

Boraine summarizes the purpose of the Commission this way:

> What a truth commission can do, and what the South African Commission certainly attempted to do, is to seek not only knowledge, acknowledgement, and accountability, but also restoration. One of the primary motivations for and objectives of the Commission was to bring about a measure of healing to a very deeply divided society in which many citizens have been severely hurt. The search for reconciliation and restoration is in my view an integral part of coming to terms with the present ... We come to terms with the past not to point a finger or to engage in a witch hunt but to bring about accountability and to try and restore a community which for scores of years has been broken.[492]

---

[491] Fred Bridgland, *Truth, Lies and Alibis: A Winnie Mandela Story* (NB Publishers, 2018); Ken Menon, *All Black Lives Matter: Bondage, Violence, Subjugation* (AuthorHouse UK, 2023).

[492] Boraine, p. 295.

The South Africa Commission sought testimony from the violated and the violators. It was uniquely bestowed with the power to grant amnesty to violators who agreed to confess to the full truth of their sins.

There has been almost no criticism of the South African TRC's factual findings as to what occurred during *Apartheid*. Consistent with its mandate and balanced group of commissioners, it produced a fair and balanced history of a despicable regime which practiced not only *Apartheid*, but tyranny, torture, and even murder in pursuit of its goals.

In contrast, the Canadian TRC's was given a biased mandate: "to reveal to Canadians the complex truth and the ongoing legacy of the church-run residential schools, in a manner that fully documents the individual and collective harms perpetuated against Aboriginal peoples," writes Hymie Rubenstein in *From Truth Comes Reconciliation* (p. 161), a retired professor of anthropology at the University of Manitoba who blogs about Indigenous matters.[493]

Given this biassed mandate, Bowler asks the question, "Is this a case of Lewis Carroll's 'Sentence First-Verdict Afterwards?'"[494]

While the TRC rigorously pursued the task of fully documenting "all individual and collective harms perpetrated against Aboriginal peoples," it failed to give a balanced picture of "the complex truth."

The Process

The TRC held hearings throughout Canada over three years. The purpose was to hear the stories of anyone who wanted to appear. Aboriginals with favourable and unfavourable experiences told their stories, as did former employees at the schools. There was no power of subpoena. Nor was there cross-examination. Witnesses could tell their stories either in public or private. Over 6,000 witnesses appeared. In many cases a hostile environment existed which deterred any person with a favourable story

[493] Rubenstein, "The REAL Indigenous Report."

[494] Clifton-DeWolf, p. 122.

from appearing. The environment encouraged former students to provide the most lurid accounts, and in some cases to change their story from a previously favourable version, Widdowson writes (p. 108).

Brian Giesbrecht, a former Manitoba superior court judge, concludes that some of the testimony would not withstand cross-examination. He comments that the TRC "showed a lack of concern with the truthfulness of the evidence."[495]

Volumes 1 to 4 of the TRC Report record the testimonies, some of which came from witnesses who had good things to say about their experiences. A serious problem arises with the Report's summary, contained in volumes 5 and 6, entitled *Legacy* and *Reconciliation,* as well as with the introduction to volume 1.

Murray Sinclair claimed that his Commission's report would provide Canadians with a permanent record in which all experiences, all perspectives would be "woven into the fabric of truth."[496]

However this book rigorously challenges the validity of Sinclair's self-congratulatory claim to have woven the "fabric of truth."

Certainly, the TRC had sufficient resources available to perform its task well. It spent $60,000,000 of public money over six years. The report totals 3,500 pages.

Yet Clifton and DeWolf's introduction concludes:

> Surprisingly — and more than a little disheartening — the Commission's *Summary* and *Legacy* volumes do not adequately or even-handedly summarize the material that is found in the other four volumes. Given the amount of media coverage these two volumes seem to have received, this is a grave concern.
>
> Another issue is that the number of negative generalizations stated in the *Summary* and *Legacy* volumes are not supported by

---

[495] Clifton-DeWolf, p. 173.

[496] "Many Threads are Woven Into the Fabric of Truth," *Calgary Herald,* August 5, 2010.

evidence presented in the other volumes. Testimony that is favourable to the IRS system, collected from school administrators, employees, and non-Indigenous IRS students, is provided in many volumes, but these testimonies and their significance are absent from the crucial *Summary* and *Legacy* volumes. Consequently, those two highly publicized volumes appear to be not much more than biased interpretations of the Commission's findings.

The TRC Report also makes a number of incendiary claims that go well beyond the actual evidence the Commission collected. Many of these claims appear designed to inflame readers' emotions rather than present well-reasoned and balanced information and arguments.[497]

The collection thereafter proceeds to fully document these criticisms. Professor J. R. Miller, the foremost expert on residential schools, and generally a supporter of the TRC, also commented on the harshness of vols. 5 and 6, compared to the testimony actually taken. Miller added, "The Final Report contained far too many errors, some of them serious."[498]

Genocide

The TRC Report commences with an interpretation of Canadian policy towards Aboriginals. The Report stakes its ground at the outset of vol. 1, with the conclusion that "The central goals of Canada's Aboriginal policy were to eliminate Aboriginal governments; ignore Aboriginal rights; terminate the Treaties; and through a process of assimilation, cause Aboriginal people to cease to exist as distinct legal, social, cultural, religious, and racial entities in Canada."

Not content to make this accusation, the TRC goes on to show its true animus:

---

[497] Clifton-DeWolf, xviii.

[498] TRC Reports, Review By J.R. Miller, April 10, 2016 in *BC Studies* No. 191, Autumn 2016, pp. 169-175.

Physical genocide is the mass killing of the members of a targeted group, and *biological genocide* is the destruction of the group's reproductive capacity. ... In its dealings with Aboriginal people, Canada did all these things." (Emphasis added)

The TRC claims that the IRS system was based on the assumption that Aboriginal peoples were "subhuman."

The allegation of physical genocide, defined as the intentional extermination of an identifiable group, likens Canadian Aboriginal policy to the Final Solution of the Nazis. One could not imagine a more serious charge. However it is a charge utterly devoid of factual foundation. As Richard Gwyn states in *Nation Maker,* the second volume of his biography of Sir John A. Macdonald:

> The defining difference [between Canadian and American policies on Aboriginals] is that Canada did not kill Indians; in the course of the 19th century some 400,000 American Indians were killed, principally by the U.S. Army in the West. [In Canada] the only deaths were the small number killed during the N.W. Rebellion.[499]

One would have expected the horrific allegation of physical genocide to be supported by some data, or facts, or something. But there is no attempt anywhere in the TRC Report to provide any support for this blood libel.

Then there is the charge of *biological genocide,* the charge that Canada destroyed the Aboriginals' reproductive capacity. It is another blood libel devoid of factual foundation. Indeed, the population of the Indigenous people in Canada at the commencement of IRS was fewer than 100,000. Today it is in the range of 1,600,000.[500]

The book under review concludes that allegations of genocide are "simply untrue and historically indefensible" and are "fabrications," noting that the TRC cites no evidence to support the charges. The genocide charge

---

[499] Richard Gwyn, *Nation Maker: Sir John A. Macdonald: His Life, Our Times* (Random House, 2011), p. 426.

[500] Bowler in Clifton-DeWolf, p. 130.

"displays a contempt for truth that helps to make a reader suspicious of anything else the Commission claims."[501]

Indeed much stronger language is justifiable. These two charges of genocide are reprehensible, and utterly incompatible with the search for truth. It is quite astonishing that the TRC has not been broadly denounced for these false charges. And yet on the contrary, the House of Commons on Oct. 27 passed an NDP-sponsored motion "calling on the federal government to recognize Canada's residential schools as genocide."[502] That such a motion should be unanimous is inexplicable. Such madness would normally be supported only by a handful of extremist MPs firmly in the grip of a post-colonial mindset.

Cultural Genocide

The TRC also charges Canada with the offence of "cultural genocide," which it defines as follows:

> *Cultural Genocide* is the destruction of those structures and practices that allow the group to continue as a group. States that engage in cultural genocide seek to destroy the political and social institutions of the targeted group. Land is seized, and populations are forcibly transferred and their movement is restricted. Languages are banned. Spiritual leaders are persecuted, spiritual practices are forbidden, and objects of spiritual value are confiscated and destroyed. And, most significantly to the issue at hand, families are disrupted to prevent the transmission of cultural values and identity from one generation to the next.

The charge of "cultural genocide" received some traction when it was repeated by the Chief Justice of Canada, Beverley McLachlin, relying on the TRC Report as her source of information.

---

[501] Ibid., pp. 130-32.

[502] "'Historic' motion to recognize residential schools as genocide backed unanimously by MPs," *National Post* / Canadian Press, October 28, 2022.

In doing so the Chief Justice breached a fundamental rule that sitting judges must not comment publicly on issues. Justice Tom Berger of the B.C. Supreme Court was previously strongly criticized by the Canadian Judicial Council for doing just that, and felt he had no choice but to resign. McLachlin, as *ex officio* chair of the Council, apparently felt herself immune from its strictures. The fact that such a charge could be believed and repeated by such an eminent person underscores how influential the TRC has been.

Bowler in the book under review refutes the cultural genocide claim as reaching "the territory of just plain fiction,"[503] and comments:

> Finding a reference to "cultural genocide" at the very beginning of this important Report probably forces readers to wonder why the government of Canada signed treaties, established reserves, published dictionaries in Indigenous languages, banned relatively few Indigenous traditions — such as the potlach — that actually hindered their economic progress, and never forbade Indigenous people from speaking their languages in residential schools or anywhere else."

Widdowson adds:

> ...the use of the word "genocide" in connection with culture is a rhetorical strategy designed to impede rational discussion of the residential schools. The term"'genocide" has historically been used to refer to the intentional extermination of an identifiable group of people. Adding the adjective "cultural" completely changes the meaning of the word by turning the inevitable and unstoppable processes associated with integration into a crime against humanity.[504]

Clifton and DeWolf remark in their Introduction:

> From a Commission charged with discerning and communicating the truth, this false statement is worrying and, even, incendiary.

---

[503] Clifton-DeWolf, p. 131.

[504] Ibid., p. 78.

Not only is there little evidence supporting this claim, but the
policies and actions of both missionaries and government officials
clearly contradict it.[505]

Unlike the TRC, Clifton and DeWolf quote actual testimony in support of
these statements. It also cites the obvious goal of Canada historically,
partly through IRS, to provide Indigenous children with the knowledge,
skills, and values needed to participate in Canadian society, which
certainly was laudable in the face of the collapse of their way of life — the
disappearance of the buffalo and the much-reduced fur trade.[506]

Having made these wrongful allegations concerning Canadian Aboriginal
policy, the TRC turns to its mandate of reviewing IRS. The pattern of
serious denunciations, often with little evidence in support, is continued.

Alleged Medical Experiments

The TRC claims that IRS students were repeatedly made the subject of
medical experiments and even compares those experiments with the ones
carried on by Nazi doctors in the concentration camps. As the Clifton-
DeWolf volume states, "This claim is so serious that we have spent a
considerable amount of time and effort examining it for relevant
information that the TRC has not identified."[507] The details of each of
these so-called "experiments" are then reviewed.

One was in fact a medically-supervised change in diet to increase the
intake of Vitamin D. Another was an attempt to deal with an outbreak of
dysentery, where doctors attempted to determine whether five-day or ten-
day treatments were most effective. The book mildly suggests that the
TRC's comparison to Nazi death camps "weakens the credibility of the
TRC Report." Much stronger language would appear to be in order.

---

[505] Ibid , xx

[506] Ibid., p. 81.

[507] Clifton-DeWolf, p. 49.

216

Forced Attendance?

Central to the TRC Report is the contention that Canada "forced" attendance on reluctant Aboriginals. In the words of Commissioner Wilson, "Aboriginal children were torn from their mothers' arms." On Apr. 10, 2010, which is to say at the beginning of the TRC's work, Sinclair took it upon himself to address the United Nations Permanent Forum on Indigenous Issues. He asserted:

> For roughly seven generations *nearly every Indigenous child in Canada was sent to a residential school.* They were *taken* from their families, tribes and communities, and *forced* to live in those institutions of assimilation.[508] (Emphasis added)

As to this foundational claim that Canada imposed IRS on reluctant Aboriginals and enforced attendance, three points are of critical importance. First, the Aboriginals themselves required, in the treaties signed with Canada, a *commitment from Canada* that it would provide their children with an education. For instance, Treaty 6 with the Plains and Wood Cree states:

> Her Majesty agrees to maintain schools for instruction in such reserves hereby made as to Her Government of the Dominion of Canada may seem advisable, whenever the Indians of the reserves shall desire it.[509]

Thus, by the 1870s Canada was *legally required to provide schooling* for Aboriginals. Day schools were built and staffed on reserves where the population was sufficient but many reserves were not large enough to justify a day school. Residential schools were the only means by which Canada could fulfill its treaty obligation.

Secondly, when Canada commenced the IRS system in 1883, attendance was *not* compulsory. It was only in 1920 that legislation was enacted which

---

[508] Green, "Two-Thirds Did Not Attend," loc. cit.

[509] Michelle Filice, "Treaty Six" *Canadian Encyclopedia.*

granted the government the power to make attendance compulsory, but that power was never exercised. The book observes at p. 55, "As historian J.R. Miller correctly points out, 'At no time in the history of residential schooling in Canada were parents compelled to send their children to residential schools.'"[510]

An article published by *The Dorchester Review* online, and afterwards in print, "They Were Not Forced," by Nina Green, Brian Giesbrecht and Tom Flanagan,[511] also demonstrates that prior to 1920 it was only at day schools that attendance was compulsory. The authors state, "If there was no day school on the reserve, the Department [of Indian Affairs] refused to commit children to [a residential school] located off the reserve *because it was not the Department's policy to separate children from their parents.*" (Emphasis added).

Green *et al.* point out that IRS were mostly "filled to capacity, and some had waiting lists." They note that "this is a far cry from Commissioner Marie Wilson's claim that status Indian children were ripped from their parents' arms."

The Assessment points out that several bands were anxious to have the schools and contributed to the cost of construction. Further, "As late as the 1940s and 1950s, when the federal government began to close residential schools, many tribes, bands and parents requested that they remain open," writes Rubenstein.[512]

Thirdly, and directly at odds with Sinclair's claim that "*nearly every* Indigenous child was sent to a residential school," a majority of the children who attended school went to *day* schools. About 30% of Aboriginal children did not attend *any* school. This is noted in the book under review and also in another online article in *The Dorchester Review*

---

[510] "Murray Sinclair's Fabrications," by James C. McCrae, *The Dorchester Review* online, August 3, 2022.

[511] Tom Flanagan, Nina Green, and Brian Giesbrecht, "They Were Not Forced," *The Dorchester Review* online, April 21, 2022; in print, *The Dorchester Review*, Spring/Summer 2023, Vol. 13, No. 1, pp. 49-56.

[512] Clifton-DeWolf, p. 154.

by Nina Green entitled, "Two-Thirds Did Not Attend."[513] Most students attending residential schools were able to return home regularly.

Furthermore, the average attendance of the one-third of Indigenous children who attended IRS was 4.5 years.

The statement made by Chairman Sinclair to the United Nations, as quoted above, is demonstrably an untruth. He could not have been unaware of it.

Positive Experiences

While the TRC announced it wanted to hear from school staff and other non-Native peoples, the oral record that the Commission collected was composed overwhelmingly of people self-identified as Survivors. A professional historian on the TRC staff said that the commissioners' actions "were not consistent with its claims to wish to include non-Aboriginal voices on the record." Indeed, her budget for the project on school staff was cut from $100,000 to $10,000 and she was told that the Commission would not transcribe the interviews she had conducted. Thus, very few former staff came forward to speak publicly, writes Lea Meadows, who herself graduated from and taught at a residential school.[514]

The TRC refers to positive testimony from staff, but in these terms: "Many staff members spent much of their time and energy attempting to humanize a harsh and destructive system." The book under review remarks that readers "can see how the TRC attempted to make positive evidence into something negative," lamenting that, "It is not surprising that the legacy of the IRS system has generally been regarded as wholly negative by the Canadian public."[515]

Rodney Clifton and Mark DeWolf also attended Residential Schools either as students or staff. Clifton's wife is Indigenous and is an IRS alumna.

---

[513] Nina Green, "Two Thirds Did Not Attend," *The Dorchester Review* online, July 13, 2022; afterwards in print, *The Dorchester Review*, Autumn/Winter 2022, Vol. 12, No. 2, pp. 68-74.

[514] Clifton-DeWolf, p. 257.

[515] Ibid., p. 57.

They speak with knowledge of positive experiences. Their book contains lengthy accounts of such experiences.

Tomson Highway, the Cree playwright, classical pianist, and Order of Canada recipient, said this about his experience at an IRS:

> All we hear is the negative stuff, nobody's interested in the positive, the joy in that (Indian Residential) school. Nine of the happiest years of my life I spent at that school. I learned your language, for God's sake. Have you learned my language? No, so who's the privileged one and who is underprivileged?
>
> You may have heard stories from 7,000 witnesses in the process that were negative. But what you haven't heard are the 7,000 reports that were positive stories. There are many very successful people today that went to those schools and have brilliant careers and are very functional people, very happy people like myself. I have a thriving international career, and it wouldn't have happened without that school.[516]

One can only wonder at the Orwellian process that led to the cancellation of Senator Lynn Beyak by Conservative colleagues, including leader Andrew Scheer, for stating that some Aboriginals had positive experiences. She was suspended and faced expulsion on two grounds: for permitting "offensive" letters submitted by Canadian citizens online to remain on her website; and secondly, for refusing to submit to "anti-racism" training.[517]

Root of All Problems?

Canada started to wind down IRS in the 1950s. Very few remained in the 1980s. Yet in 2015 the TRC Report asserted that:

---

[516] Tomson Highway, quoted by Rubenstein in ibid., p. 163.

[517] "Senate votes to suspend Lynn Beyak again despite her apology for posting offensive letters on website," *National Post*, February 27, 2020; "Facing push to expel, Lynn Beyak retires from the Senate," CTV News, January 25, 2021.

The closing of residential schools did not bring their story to an end. The legacy of the schools continues to this day. It is reflected in the significant educational, income, and health disparities that condemn many Aboriginal people to shorter, poorer, and more troubled lives. ... The disproportionate apprehension of Aboriginal children by child welfare agencies and the disproportionate imprisonment and victimization of Aboriginal people are all part of the legacy of the way Aboriginal children were treated in residential schools. Many students were permanently damaged by residential schools. Separated from their parents, they grew up knowing neither respect nor affection.[518]

The TRC Report went on to allege the damage to the "survivors ... profoundly affected their partners, their children, and their grandchildren, their extended family and their communities." Furthermore, the report says, "Students ... who were treated as prisoners in the schools sometimes graduated to real prison."

Thus, everything negative in the lives of Aboriginals since 1883 and continuing as of 2015 is attributed to IRS. The TRC does not attempt to justify this conclusion in light of the facts that only one-third ever attended, and then only for an average of 4.5 years. Taking twelve years as the limit for attendance at primary school, the average attendance of Aboriginal children who actually attended an IRS was therefore 37.5% of their potential school years. Of the total school years of all Aboriginal children, one-third of 37.5%, that is, 12.4% were spent at an IRS.

Clifton and DeWolf observe that, "Many Canadians would doubtless agree that they have seen poverty, marginalization, alcohol and drug abuse, and family breakdown in non-Indigenous communities where no one ever attended a residential school."[519] They properly note that the TRC's claims that all of the serious problems Indigenous people face today can be traced to the residential school experiences of their ancestors "looks tenuous at

---

[518] Clifton-DeWolf, p. 57.

[519] Ibid., p. 58.

best." J.R.Miller makes a similar observation in his book.[520] Again, these deserve much rounder condemnation.

Responsibility

Canada has accepted, both morally and legally, that it bears responsibility for the horrendous sexual abuses perpetrated on students of residential schools by pedophiles on staff (not necessarily by teachers, clergy, or religious) and, as the authors indicate, by older Indigenous students. Canada funded virtually the entirety of the billions of dollars paid out under the IRSSA: it paid $1.9 billion to fund the common experience payments and another $3 billion towards the Independent Assessment Process. It funded the work of the Aboriginal Healing Centre and the two commissions (RCAP and TRC), the collective cost of which was probably $2 billion. Canada tendered sincere apologies, starting with Prime Minister Harper on Jun. 11, 2008 in the House of Commons.

Clearly it was the churches who operated the schools which were more at fault than Canada for the abuses. In early settlements, prior to the IRSSA, the churches acknowledged responsibility for 60-70% of the blame. The United Church and Anglican Church each paid $25,000,000 towards the IRSSA. Catholic Church entities agreed to pay $29,000,000 in cash and over seven years to use best efforts to raise another $25,000,000. However, the Catholic entities paid only $10,200,000 in total and were released from any further obligation.[521]

Treatment of Children

The TRC Report provides no comparative treatment of what was happening to children elsewhere at the time. For example in citing the harsh discipline meted out, the Report does not acknowledge that corporal punishment was common in those days. English boarding schools, for

[520] Miller, pp. 230-33.

[521] Ibid., pp. 152-4.

example, routinely caned students in the belief it was building character. As Rubenstein summarizes the matter:

> ... The TRC Report fails to place the history of IRS into the broader context of how Canadian children were treated at the time. During the IRS period, thousands of children in Great Britain resided in harsh boarding schools, thousands more were forced to live in horrific workhouses, and thousands more — the "Home Children" — were sent to Canada in what was essentially a forced migration process ...

> Up until the 1960s, thousands of [non-Indigenous] Canadian children and teens languished in hospitals, sanatoria, orphanages, reform schools, homes for unwed mothers, and mental institutions. Virtually all of these children were treated in ways that would be considered inhumane, perhaps even criminal, by today's standards. Saying this is *not* to justify treating Indigenous children in an inhumane way, but simply to note that in the not-so-distant past, life was very difficult for many Canadian children.[522]

Reconciliation

In respect to the widely accepted narrative of IRS perpetrated by the TRC the book concludes: "This narrative is not only a distortion of what most of us would regard as truth: it is also a wrong-headed and quite possibly harmful attempt to explain the current state of Indigenous people in Canada today."

Whither reconciliation? Boraine's message concerning the objective of a truth and reconciliation commission, quoted above, is "not to point a finger or engage in a witch hunt." Similar thoughts are expressed in the foreword to Clifton and DeWolf's book, written by Leighton Grey:

> If there is to be restoration to friendly relations, or the making of one view or belief compatible with another, then we must first

---

[522] Clifton-DeWolf, p. 160.

abandon the post-modernist infatuation with the pretence of taking moral responsibility to make amends for the past. Reconciliation is not about laying blame or demanding that the other side take a knee. That is capitulation, not reconciliation. In order for there to be true reconciliation in the proper sense of the word, there must first be understanding, and a respect for a diversity of opinions and viewpoints about the legacy of IRS. Only through an examination of all sides of the question can we reach a true understanding of what occurred and why.[523]

By demonstrating that the TRC report contains egregious untruths, Clifton and DeWolf's book, *From Truth Comes Reconciliation*, makes a major contribution to reaching a more balanced understanding of residential schools. One can only hope that the volume, privately published by the Frontier Centre, gets a wide distribution, that more news reporters and op-ed writers will read it, and that a copy is sent to every Parliamentarian, legislator, Indigenous chief, and church authority across Canada.

This chapter was originally published as "Neither Truth Nor Reconciliation" in The Dorchester Review, *Vol. 12, No. 2, Autumn-Winter 2022, pp. 75-84.*

---

[523] Clifton and DeWolf, p. x.

Chapter Eleven

Asking for Evidence Now Counts as "Denialism"

Jonathan Kay

It's now been more than two years since Canada was convulsed by claims that 215 unmarked graves of Indigenous schoolchildren had been discovered on the grounds of a former residential school in Kamloops, British Columbia. No actual bodies or human remains were in evidence—just ground-penetrating radar data indicating regularly-spaced soil dislocations. But you wouldn't have known that from the breathless manner in which the story was reported at the time. A Global News headline announced the "Discovery of Human Remains at Kamloops Residential School Grounds."[524] Another, at the Toronto *Star,* declared, "The Remains of 215 Children Have Been Found."[525]

I was one of the many Canadians who believed these headlines. The racist abuses meted out by Canada's 19th- and 20th-century-era residential-school system, which had been created to "civilize" Indigenous people and strip them of their culture, have been widely discussed for decades. Given this dark history, it wasn't hard to believe that some of the priests and educators who ran these schools hadn't just been cruel and negligent (this much was already known), but also had committed acts of mass murder against defenceless children.

Without waiting for the hard evidence to be sprung from the earth, flags were lowered, July 1st Canada Day celebrations were cancelled, Justin Trudeau took a knee for the cameras, and the whole nation went into an utterly unprecedented collective period of self-flagellation. Before the summer was over, Trudeau pledged more than $300 million in new funding

---

[524] "Discovery of human remains at Kamloops Residential School grounds," *Global News*, May 28, 2021.

[525] Douglas Quan and Omar Mosleh, "The remains of 215 children have been found. Now, Indigenous leaders say, Canada must help find the rest of the unmarked graves," *Toronto Star*, May 28, 2021.

for Indigenous communities,[526] so they could complete the grim task of scouring the earth for child corpses. The Canadian Press later called it the story of the year.[527]

Twenty-four months later, much has changed. During this entire period, not a single unmarked grave, body, or set of remains is known to have been found at Kamloops, nor at any of the other First Nations communities that conducted similar ground-penetrating radar surveys.

This doesn't mean that graves and bodies won't be found at some indeterminate point in the future. But given that the originally announced radar data would have indicated to Indigenous groups and forensic investigators exactly where any suspected human remains would be lying, the passage of two years without the reported unearthing of physical evidence can only be described as a strikingly odd development.

As I noted in a recent article for *The Critic*, a British magazine,[528] and at *Quillette*,[529] this is a subject that many polite Canadians are scared to talk about. In 2021, the assumed discovery of those 215 unmarked graves took on the quality of a sacred national narrative. Pointing out the holes in that narrative that have since developed, as I am doing here, feels like secular sacrilege.

Moreover, there's a considerable amount of political capital at stake. During the 2021 federal election campaign, Trudeau campaigned on a promise to make amends for the murderous horrors inflicted upon Indigenous Canadians by his forebears. And Indigenous leaders, quite understandably, were happy to take the Prime Minister's money as he did so. Journalists assured their readers, listeners, and viewers that the presumed graves offered further proof that Canada was a "genocide state,"

---

[526] "Ottawa pledges $320 million to search for residential school graves and support survivors," Canadian Press, August 10, 2021.

[527] Dirk Meissner, "Canadian Press names Kamloops unmarked graves discovery Canada's news story of the year," CBC News, December 16, 2021.

[528] Jonathan Kay, "Canada's grave errors," *The Critic*, April 2023.

[529] Idem, "A Media-Fueled Social Panic Over Unmarked Graves," *Quillette*, July 22, 2022. See the chapter with the same title in this book.

thereby sparking all manner of new charitable initiatives, hashtags, and T-shirt campaigns.[530] After all this, few public figures have any incentive to admit that perhaps we all might have waited for the facts before setting about the garment-rending with such gusto.

Only one large Canadian media outlet, the *National Post*, has dared publish a full and frank analysis by Terry Glavin of how everyone got the unmarked-graves story wrong.[531] Other outlets have either ignored the story's denouement altogether, or have gone further by denouncing revisionism as a symptom of bigotry. At the *Star*, for instance, an activist guest op-ed writer opined that asking authorities to produce physical evidence in regard to the claimed graves is tantamount to "a racist rant bordering on genocide denial."[532]

Yet even as they publicly hew to the orthodox line on the unmarked-graves story, Canadian reporters and editors are now adding language that signals the growing uncertainty about what actually lies beneath the ground. The aforementioned Global News, a large multimedia brand, offers an informative case study. In 2021, a Global headline alluded (incorrectly) to the "discovery of human remains." In a story published a year later, it was a "finding of unmarked graves."[533] Then last month, on the second anniversary, the editors retreated to the more lawyerly formulation, "*Suspected* unmarked graves" (my emphasis).[534] Elsewhere in its 2023

---

[530] Idem, "Canada Called Itself a Genocide State. Iran was Listening," *Quillette*, September 23, 2022.

[531] Terry Glavin, "The year of the graves: How the world's media got it wrong on residential school graves," *National Post*, May 26, 2022.

[532] K.J. McCusker, "Genocide deniers ask: Where are the bodies of the residential schoolchildren?" *Toronto Star*, January 28, 2022.

[533] Dirk Meissner, "How the finding of unmarked graves in Kamloops triggered a year of reckoning," Canadian Press, May 18, 2022.

[534] Christa Dao," Repercussions of suspected unmarked graves two years later," Global News, May 27, 2023.

reports, Global has referred to "potential unmarked graves,"[535] and "plausible unmarked graves."[536]

Like most Canadian media outlets, Global hasn't gone back to correct its earlier reports on the subject, let alone offered any kind of candid explanation for why it is doing so. And so the unmarked-graves story now exists in an odd limbo state—having gradually become more dubious with every passing month, but not so dubious that it has been formally debunked.

Even some foreign media sites have failed to correct their reporting. On May 28, 2021, a *New York Times* reporter named Ian Austen told readers that a "mass grave" containing Indigenous children had been "reported in Canada."[537] In fact, not only had no "mass grave" been found, but no Indigenous community had made such a claim. The leader of the First Nations community being referenced explicitly told the media there was no mass grave, and disavowed usage of the term.[538]

It's been two years since the *Times* ran this claim, with no correction forthcoming. Nor has the *Times* corrected an equally bungled 2021 follow-up report by the same author, the sub-headline on which referred to "the discovery of the remains of hundreds of children."[539] No "remains" had been discovered, either then or now.

The desire to protect the unmarked-graves narrative remains especially strong among Canada's ruling Liberals, whose Minister of Crown-Indigenous Relations has taken the rather extraordinary step (for a liberal democracy, at least) of instructing reporters not to report heretical facts. In

[535] "Potential unmarked graves found at Port Alberni residential school," Global News, February 21, 2023.

[536] "171 plausible unmarked graves located at former residential school in Kenora, Ont.," Global News, January 18, 2023.

[537] Ian Austen, "'Horrible History': Mass Grave of Indigenous Children Reported in Canada," *New York Times*, May 28, 2021.

[538] Tim Petruk, "Casimir says Tk'emlups find is series of unmarked graves, not a mass burial," *The Squamish Chief*, June 5, 2021.

[539] Ian Austen, "How Thousands of Indigenous Children Vanished in Canada," *New York Times*, June 7, 2021.

early 2022, when a few writers, notably in a small history publication called *The Dorchester Review*, began saying out loud how odd it was that no bodies had yet been discovered in Kamloops,[540] the minister, one Marc Miller, denounced these Canadians as being "part of a pattern of denialism and distortion that has coloured the discourse on Residential Schools in Canada. They are harmful because they attempt to deny survivors and their families the truth."[541]

Miller's suggestion here is that "the truth" of the graves' existence should be taken as a matter of faith by those of pure (political) heart, regardless of what evidence happens to be available. By adding in the word "denialism," Miller plainly seeks to compare those of impure heart to Holocaust deniers.

And yet, last month, Miller himself felt compelled to hedge awkwardly when tweeting on the two-year anniversary of the unmarked-graves story—excoriating those who make "sickening attempts" to "deny" history, while also referencing the "finding of over 200 *suspected* unmarked graves" (my emphasis).[542] The s-word betrays Miller's hypocrisy: If acknowledging that those 200-plus graves in Kamloops might not actually exist qualifies someone as a "sickening" genocide denier, then Miller seems to belong on the list.

Later on in his thread, Miller seems to suggest that the truth of the graves' existence is beside the point anyway, because the very act of discussing the issue "remain[s] traumatic for the community, survivors and their families."

And so writers should resist the temptation to dispute the credulous 2021 consensus, Miller tells us. Instead, he instructs journalists to assume the role of monks tasked with "reflection and contemplation of the work that remains to ensure Indigenous Peoples heal."

---

[540] Jacques Rouillard, "In Kamloops, Not One Body Has Been Found," *The Dorchester Review* online, January 11, 2022.

[541] Marc Miller on Twitter, January 27, 2022.

[542] Marc Miller on Twitter, May 27, 2023.

Miller's sanctimonious demands don't carry the force of law, thankfully. But it isn't hard to imagine that changing. In a report released on June 16, 2023, Kimberly Murray, the independent special interlocutor appointed by Trudeau to investigate the issue of unmarked graves, exhorted politicians to give "urgent consideration" to "civil and criminal [legal] sanctions" against residential-school "denialism."[543] It's an idea that had already been promoted by an MP named Leah Gazan.[544] And Canada's then Justice Minister, David Lametti, said he was open to the proposal.[545]

Like Miller, Murray seems to regard claims of unmarked graves at Kamloops and elsewhere as morally unfalsifiable, since they are "Survivors' truths." She repeatedly suggests that the mere act of requesting physical evidence is, itself, evidence of denialism. On this point, Murray approvingly quotes the chief of a First Nation in western Canada who

> subtly addresses denialism by stating that "[w]hether or not unmarked graves are found, there is enough documented oral and archival evidence to say that these burials do or did exist." The community acknowledges that the voices of Survivors, who have first-hand accounts of what happened in Indian Residential Schools, should be prioritized over anything else.

The question of what Murray wants banned under the category of "denialism" isn't clear, however. On page 104 of her report, she references (1) statements, such as those contained in this article, that scrutinize specific claims being made about suspected graves on specific Indigenous reserves; (2) broader statements that cast doubt on the existence of unmarked graves at any residential school; and (3) even more generalized statements, which serve to "defend the Indian Residential Schools System [and] deny that children suffered physical, sexual, psychological, cultural, and spiritual abuses." All of these are described by Murray as detestable utterances. But it isn't clear which, if any, Murray wants to criminalize.

543 "Sacred Responsibility: Searching for the Missing Children and Unmarked Burials," Interim Report, Independent Special Interlocutor, June 16, 2023.

544 Olivia Stefanovich, "NDP MP calls for hate speech law to combat residential school 'denialism'," CBC News, February 18, 2023.

545 Stephanie Taylor, "Canada needs legal tools to fight residential school denialism, report says," Canadian Press, June 16, 2023.

At other points in her report, Murray goes further, suggesting that the deniers' ranks encompass anyone who does not pledge his or her belief that residential schools were instruments of literal genocide. "Failing to acknowledge the deliberate genocidal harm inflicted on Indigenous children becomes a barrier to reconciliation and reinforces a culture of denialism in the Canadian population," she writes. This would suggest that people could be "deniers" without saying or writing anything at all, if they had not heeded Murray's exhortation that "each of us must stand up and speak out" in the manner she prescribes.

In the long run, however, this kind of semantic analysis likely won't matter much, since any legal effort to censor "denialism" (however that word is defined) would almost certainly be struck down by courts as an infringement on free speech. Canadian constitutional principles permit laws that ban the wilful promotion of "hatred" against identifiable groups.[546] But no one can seriously argue that asking for evidence of unproven murder allegations, or offering dissenting theories about residential schools come close to meeting that standard.

And yet this isn't a spectacle that Canadians should ignore: The fact that public figures are even taking this kind of censorship proposal seriously speaks to just how desperate they are to avoid a critical reexamination of the country's 2021 unmarked-graves social panic. Trudeau and his ministers must know that the moment of reckoning can't be put off forever. My guess is that they're just hoping they won't be in office when it arrives.

This chapter was originally published in Quillette *online, June 20, 2023.*

---

[546] Supreme Court of Canada, *R. v. Keegstra*, [1990] 3 SCR 697 December 13, 1990 per Dickson, Robert George Brian; Wilson, Bertha; La Forest, Gérard V.; L'Heureux-Dubé, Claire; Sopinka, John; Gonthier, Charles Doherty; McLachlin, Beverley.

Chapter Twelve

Integration, Forced Assimilation, or Genocide?

Pim Wiebel

"I come to you, then, like so many missionaries before me who have proclaimed the name of Jesus among the native peoples of Canada — the Indians, Inuit and Metis — and have learned to love you and the spiritual and cultural treasures of your way of life. The missionaries...have shown respect for your patrimony, your languages and your customs. As I remarked on the occasion on my previous visit, the 'rebirth of your culture and traditions which you are experiencing today owes much to the pioneering and continuing efforts of missionaries.'" — Pope John Paul II, 1987

"It is necessary to remember how the policies of assimilation and enfranchisement, which also included the residential school system, were devastating for the people of these lands." "I apologized, I asked forgiveness for this work, which was genocide." — Pope Francis, 2022

How dissonant these statements from the two Popes during their respective visits to Canada: John Paul II's enlightened and hopeful remarks; Francis' uninformed and dark admonishments.

European contact and colonization did indeed contribute to profound changes to Indigenous cultural and social life. But the notion that the Department of Indian Affairs, churches, and schools collaborated to forcibly and genocidally assimilate the Indigenous people into a Euro-Canadian Christian identity does not hold up to scrutiny.

Missionaries from the various Christian denominations were by definition involved in proselytizing. Their methods, however, were neither forcible nor absolutist. There were no forced conversions or baptisms. The provision of material aid, such as treaty payments, was not made conditional on conversion to Christianity.

Nevertheless, in response to missionary teaching and preaching, the majority of Indigenous people adopted the Christian faith. The Department of Indian Affairs categorized the Indian population by religion in the censuses it published in its annual reports. In 1897, just under a fifth of the Indian population in the provinces, and nearly half in the Northwest Territories, were identified as adherents of an Aboriginal belief. (The term "pagan" was used at least until 1913,[547] when it was replaced with "Aboriginal beliefs."[548]) By 1940, 4 percent of the population was identified as holding Aboriginal beliefs, and by 1957, the last year in which Indian Affairs reported religious affiliation, the proportion fell to under 3 percent.

Indian Affairs encouraged and supported economic development on all reserves, regardless of whether or not the population was predominantly Christian. Some bands that had largely kept the Aboriginal beliefs made substantial economic progress. One example of this was the Obidgeweng Band in Ontario: They "are all pagans, [but] they are industrious and well-to-do."[549]

The residential schools are presented as the primary instrument of Canada's policy of "forced assimilation." The notion, firstly, that the vast majority of Indigenous children attended residential schools and that their impact, therefore, was all-encompassing, is unfounded. This idea was given impetus and wide currency by the former head of the Truth and Reconciliation Commission, Murray Sinclair, when he declared at the United Nations in 2010 that, "For roughly seven generations nearly every Indigenous child in Canada was sent to a residential school. They were taken from their families, tribes and communities, and forced to live in those institutions of assimilation."[550]

---

[547] Indian Affairs Annual Report, 1913, passim.

[548] Annual Report, 1914, tables. The term "pagan" appears a few times in the text of this and subsequent reports.

[549] Annual Report, 1890, p. 61.

[550] Truth and Reconciliation Commission of Canada, "For the child taken, for the parent left behind," 9th Session of the United Nations Permanent Forum on Indigenous Issues Speech by Chairperson, The Honourable Justice Murray Sinclair, April 27, 2010, p. 3.

The truth is that no more than one-third of school-age *status First Nation* children, and even a smaller proportion of the general population of *Indigenous* children, were ever enrolled in residential schools.[551] In many periods, particularly after the 1950s, the percentage of enrolment was far lower. The vast majority of children attended on-reserve day schools, or, in later periods, integrated provincial schools. But attendance at day schools was often irregular, and before the mid 20th century, as many as one-third of Indigenous children did not attend any school at all.

Residential schools primarily served reserves that did not have sufficient population to support a day school. Even today, dozens of remote reserves do not have high schools. Young people in those communities who want to finish their schooling are "forced" to leave their families to board in distant towns or cities.

In 1920, Indian Affairs attempted to bring the Indigenous population into compliance with general Canadian compulsory attendance laws through an amendment to the Indian Act. The amendment, however, did not require attendance at a residential school, but rather that, "Every Indian child between the ages of seven and fifteen years who is physically able shall attend such day, industrial or boarding school as may be designated by the Superintendent General. Provided, however, that such school shall be the nearest available school of the kind required."[552] It has been well documented that the Canadian compulsory school attendance laws were only loosely applied in the case of Indigenous children, and that forced attendance at the residential schools was rare, occurring primarily in cases of neglect or abuse in the home.[553]

Far from being instruments of cultural suppression, as Pope Francis asserted, the residential schools were committed to a process of integration of the Indigenous and "Canadian" cultures. The 1937 Indian Affairs Annual Report states, "An encouraging feature of the educational effort

---

[551] Nina Green, "Two-Thirds Did Not Attend Residential School," *The Dorchester Review* online, July 13, 2022.

[552] *Consolidation of Indian Legislation*, Volume II, 1868-1975, Department of Indian and Northern Affairs

[553] Nina Green, Brian Giesbrecht, Tom Flanagan, "They Were Not Forced," *The Dorchester Review* online, April 21, 2022.

during the year was discovered in the ... tendency and willingness of the Indians to recognize the value and distinctiveness of their arts and crafts. Consideration has been given to ways and means whereby the Indian population can be encouraged to conserve still further their ancient values and skills and thus contribute to the cultural life of the nation."[554]

The residential schools aided the survival of Indigenous traditions by incorporating traditional music, dance, and art into classes and school activities. The Indian Affairs reports and other sources are replete with examples of the residential schools' encouragement of Indigenous cultural expression:

- At the Cluny, Alberta, school in 1938, students dressed in beaded costumes danced to the rhythm of Indian drums and war songs to an audience of over 300.[555]
- In 1963, the school at Cardston hosted a troop of Blackfoot actors who showed a film on Blackfoot life in the early days, followed by a pageant depicting Blackfoot traditions and featuring a sundance.[556]
- A choir from the Portage La Prairie school sang in English and Cree at Expo '67 in Montreal.[557]
- In the 1950s, the Gordon's School in Saskatchewan established a powwow dance troupe that travelled extensively in Canada, the United States, and several European countries.[558]
- The Alberni school in British Columbia hired Victoria artist George Sinclair to teach classes. One of his students, Judith

---

[554] Annual Report, 1937, p. 254.

[555] Nina Green, *"'Our Dear Children': Sisters' Chronicles of Indian Residential School," The Dorchester Review* online, April 1, 2022.

[556] Ibid.

[557] *Canada's Residential Schools: The History, Part 2 1939 to 2000, Final Report of the Truth and Reconciliation Commission of Canada,* Volume 1, p. 479.

[558] Ibid., p. 479.

Morgan, became renowned throughout North America for her work depicting Indigenous themes.[559]

- In 1958, students at the Sir John Franklin School in Yellowknife were encouraged to develop skills in Inuit handicrafts. Many reached a high standard of work, and several did commissioned work on their own time.[560]

Although tensions between the residential schools and the parents and bands occasionally surfaced, in most periods the schools enjoyed strong support from First Nations. Several residential schools were established under Indigenous leadership. The Chief of the Kamloops band, Louis Clexlixqen, was a champion of education, and in 1890 he founded the Kamloops Residential School.[561] John Brant, son of the famous Mohawk Chief, Joseph Brant, established a school at Six Nations that was the predecessor of the Mohawk Industrial School.[562]

At a Catholic Indian League convention held in Hobbema, Alberta, in 1959, the 100 Indian leaders in attendance urged the creation of a central residential vocational school that would serve Indian children from throughout the province. The leaders further maintained that "Catholic parents have the duty and the right of educating and training their children in Catholic schools."[563] Hobbema, Alberta, renamed Maskwasis in 2014, is the very place where Pope Francis delivered his excoriation of residential schools in July, 2022.

The government began implementing a policy of closing residential schools in the late 1950s. The schools at that time struggled with long waiting lists as parents did not want their children placed in integrated schools, where, it was feared, they would be subjected to racism. A Saskatchewan Indian Agency Superintendent reported in the early 1960's

---

[559] Ibid., p. 482.

[560] *Ibid.*, p. 483.

[561] Duane Thomson, "Clexlixqen, Louis," *Dictionary of Canadian Biography*, vol. 14, University of Toronto/Université Laval, 1998.

[562] The Mohawk Institute, Indian Affairs, Report of the Superintendent General, 1930.

[563] "Indian League Urges Vocational Schools," *Indian Record*, Vol. XXII, No. 9, November 1959.

that, "We were inundated with applications ... That was one of the times of the year I dreaded the most ... when we had to go through these applications and turn down any number of people."[564]

An Indian Affairs plan to close the Marieval Residential School in Saskatchewan in 1971 met with vehement opposition from band members. The band cited three reasons it wanted the school to remain open: 1) their children would face certain discrimination in the provincial schools as had occurred elsewhere; 2) the residential schools met an essential need by providing a home and education for orphans and children from broken homes or from impoverished families who could not properly care for them; and 3) the children sent to foster homes were not receiving proper discipline or religious instruction as they (the elders) had received in the residential schools. One band spokesperson stated, "The Indian people passed a resolution asking that the school remain open and it should not be up to the department to say whether the school should be closed."[565]

As the residential schools were in most cases administered by churches, it is unsurprising that they were imbued with a Christian ethos. As most parents had converted to Christianity, at least nominally, the Christian character of the schools met with little objection, and as we have seen, often had the parents' strong support. Parents who were not Christian were encouraged, but not forced, to send their children to residential schools. "This band [at Qu'Appelle, Northwest Territories] continues to send a few children to the Regina and Qu'Appelle industrial schools, but the pagan element, which largely predominates, is still pronouncedly averse to parting with their children. There is reason to believe, however, that the spirit of opposition to the schools is diminishing, and that before long substantial progress will have been achieved in this respect," said the Indian Affairs annual report for 1900.[566] The schools held the view that Christian teachings would foster a better morality, as they saw it, but a confession of faith was not forced on the students. At the Muncey, Ontario, Industrial School, the Principal reported, "The moral conduct of the pupils

---

[564] Vic Satzewich and Linda Mahood, *Indian Agents and the Residential School System in Canada, 1946-1970*, Historical Studies in Education, (1995), pp. 61-62.

[565] "Chiefs Request School be Kept," *Regina Leader-Post*, November 19, 1971, p. 2.

[566] Annual Report, 1900, p. 295.

has been highly commendable, and about two-thirds of the number have made a profession of religion and have given many proofs of sincerity."[567]

It is alleged that residential schools were responsible for the loss of traditional languages. In fact, residential school students were far more likely to retain their traditional languages than Indigenous children who attended other types of schools.[568] This pattern continued into the next generation. Youths whose parents attended a residential school were twice as likely to be fluent in an Indigenous language as youths who had no family history of attendance.

Whereas residential schools typically restricted, or attempted to restrict, the use of native languages in settings such as the classroom, students had many opportunities for using them, for example on playgrounds and other places outside classes.[569] At the Cluny, Alberta, school, the national anthem was sung in Blackfoot or Cree, and church services were sometimes conducted in those languages.[570] Half the staff at Stringer Hall in Inuvik were Indigenous, and they spoke to the children in their native language.[571]

The churches and residential schools did not seek to eradicate traditional languages, as is often claimed. Clergy from the various denominations were instrumental in the development of native language syllabics. Students at the St. Anthony's Residential School, located on the Onion Lake Reserve in Saskatchewan, wrote in a local newspaper: "Father Principal comes to teach us the Cree Syllabics. We are very glad to learn this writing because it is our own language and we will be able to write to our parents and grandparents. Then they will be able to understand the

---

[567] Annual Report, 1888, p. 141.

[568] First Nations Information Governance Centre, *National Report of the First Nations Regional Health Survey Phase 3: Volume One*, (Ottawa: March 2018), pp. 164-165

[569] Rodney A. Clifton, *Some Other Truths About Indian Residential Schools*, C2C Journal, May 19, 2015.

[570] Green, *"'Our Dear Children.'"*

[571] Rodney A. Clifton, *My Life in Two Indian Residential Schools*, C2C Journal, September 5, 2022.

writing and to write letters to us when they wish. Our sincere thanks to Father for teaching us this writing."[572]

While the residential schools were instrumental in sustaining traditional languages and customs, they were at the same time aimed at integrating students into the Canadian society and economy. Immersion in English, and the teaching of agricultural and trades skills, were part of this process. Students were encouraged to join organizations such as 4-H clubs, and given tours to scientific points of interest in connection with their school studies. Group visits were made to industries to introduce students to the "world of work."[573]

Students were encouraged to attend schools that offered them the best career opportunities: "Quite a number of the more advanced pupils have gone from these schools [day schools on Walpole Island] to the Mount Elgin Institution at Muncey, to the Shingwauk and Wawanosh Industrial Institutions at Sault Ste. Marie, and to the public schools at Sarnia, in quest of education of a higher order than the day schools on the reserve afford. One of these youths, after completing a course at the Shingwauk institution entered Trinity College school [a prestigious private boarding school] at Port Hope, where he distinguished himself by carrying off some prizes..."[574]

In the 1912 Indian Affairs Annual Report, we read: "Many [students from the Mohawk Industrial Institute and the other Six Nations schools] have advanced to higher education, of such four are now attending the Caledonia High school, one is at the Hamilton Collegiate Institute, one at the Brantford Conservatory of Music, one is in third year at McMaster University, one graduated in medicine at Queen's University last spring, two are at Brantford Business College, three are in hospitals training for nurses, five are teachers on the reserve, one is clerk in the Indian office at

---

[572] Green, "'Our Dear Children.'"

[573] Annual Report, 1961, p. 22.

[574] Annual Report, 1888, p. 20.

Brantford, two have graduated as nurses from John Hopkins Hospital, Baltimore, and two from Greenwich Hospital ..."[575]

The residential school students who returned to the reserves after graduating were well prepared for success, particularly in agriculture: "Our school buildings, in most cases, compare favourably with white schools similarly situated and also in the work performed in the class-room and in the equipment provided. The course of study is that prescribed for the provincial, public and separate schools and is strictly followed. There is land for farming and gardening purposes provided at practically all the residential schools. The pupils are thus enabled to receive a general knowledge of agriculture which should be of great benefit to them after leaving school."

Support for the ex-pupils continued after graduation. "The granting of assistance to graduates has been continued. Upon leaving school a female ex-pupil may be given a sewing machine or household furniture. A male ex-pupil may be given a grant of cattle, horses, implements, harness or building material."[576] The Grouard, Alberta, school helped graduates establish a cooperative for the manufacture of beaded slippers and leather goods in which the students were to "share equally in the profits."[577] Indian Affairs education budgets included such line items for assistance to ex-pupils pursuing post-residential school studies as: "Maintenance and tuition of Indian pupils at colleges, institutions and white day schools $27,164."[578]

Indian Affairs reported the positive contributions ex-residential school pupils made to conditions in the reserves: "A gradual but steady improvement is observed in the Indian habitations and in their mode of living; this is largely attributable to the efforts of the ex-pupils, whose influence for good is a gratifying tribute to the educational policy of the

---

[575] Annual Report, 1912, p. 526.

[576] Annual Report, 1921.

[577] Annual Report, 1944, p. 15.

[578] Annual Report, 1934, p. 195.

department."[579] "The educational policy of the department has borne
fruit…The ex-pupils put into practice the teaching that industry and
perseverance is the secret of a successful livelihood. As a general rule their
operations have been tended with satisfactory results and have proved an
object lesson to the less progressive of their neighbours."[580]

Recent research on former students has shown the long-term benefits of a
residential school education. The 2008-2010 First Nations Regional Health
Survey found that 38 percent of adults who had attended a residential
school had less than a high school education, versus 40.5 percent of adults
who had not attended a residential school; 22.2 percent had a diploma from
a trade school, community college, or university, versus 17.9 percent of
those who had not attended; and 4.1 percent of the residential school group
had an undergraduate degree, versus 3.6 percent of the non-residential
school group.[581] A 2013 study by Professor Donna L. Feir of the University
of Victoria found that residential schooling was associated with
substantially greater likelihood of being employed in the labour market and
less future reliance on welfare income.[582]

These results are especially impressive because children from severely
disadvantaged backgrounds were given priority for enrolment in residential
schools.

It is claimed that the residential schools committed a form of "removal"
genocide by permanently separating children from their families and home
communities. The reality was that many of the students at residential
schools located near or on their home reserves went to be with their family
at the end of the school day. Most of the others spent holidays and long
summer breaks with their families. A 1920 amendment to the Indian Act
stipulated that "a regular summer vacation is provided for, and the

---

[579] Annual Report, 1915, p. 36.

[580] Annual Report, 1921, p.57.

[581] *First Nations Regional Health Survey*, First Nations Information Governance Centre, p. 205.

[582] Donna L. Feir, "The Long Term Effects of Forcible Assimilation Policy: The Case of Indian
Boarding Schools," *Canadian Journal of Economics* Vol. 49, No. 2, May 2016, pp. 429-866.
University of Victoria, November 2013, p. 435.

transportation expenses of the children are paid by the department."[583] When the students' residential school years were complete, they returned to their home communities or other places of their or their parents' choosing.

Many parents took a proactive interest in their children's school experiences. There are records of parents attending the schools' special events and programs.[584] Although it was difficult for parents who lived far away from the schools to visit their children, such visits did occur.[585] Some schools provided accommodation for the parents' overnight stays.[586]

Although Indian Affairs viewed some Indigenous customs as highly objectionable, with only a few exceptions that I note later, the government did not forcibly ban them. Polygamy, a custom followed in many tribes, was one such practice. It was common for Blackfoot men, for example, to have several wives, and some of the Chiefs had more than a dozen.[587] In some tribes, girls as young as ten were entered into polygamous marriages.[588]

Indian Affairs and the missionaries sought to limit the practice of plural marriage, not by compulsion, but through persuasion: "The inculcation in the minds of Indians of principles that will lead them, *from conscientious convictions, to abandon voluntarily* the habit of polygamy…is, I submit, the work of those who charge themselves with the responsibility of imparting instruction to them in the tenets of Christianity [emphasis added]."[589]

---

[583] Annual Report, 1920, p. 14.

[584] Green, *"'Our Dear Children.'"*

[585] Clifton, *"Some Other Truths."*

[586] Green, *"'Our Dear Children.'"*

[587] Sister Annette Potvin, *The Sun Dance Liturgy of the Blackfoot Indians*, Ottawa, Canada (1966), p.27

[588] Canada's Residential Schools: *The History, Part 1 Origins to 1939 The Final Report of the Truth and Reconciliation Commission of Canada* Volume 1, pp. 655-656

[589] Annual Report, 1884, p. 61.

Grave Error

Some "progressive" historians suggest that the suppression of polygamy among the Indigenous was an unjustified intrusion that was harmful to the tribes' social harmony. They dismiss contemporaneous accounts by persons who observed that polygamous arrangements were often accompanied by serious abuses and harms, and give unquestioned credence to the representations of others who suggested that the practice was innocuous and even positive. The judgment of history, however, is that polygamy has been, and remains, a hindrance to human progress. That is why the overwhelming majority of countries, including all Western democracies, have outlawed the practice. It has been settled long ago that plural marriage is born of the notion of an inherent inequality between women and men, and invariably causes great harm to society, and to women in particular.

Canada formally outlawed polygamy in 1890. The prohibition, however, was almost always unenforced in the case of the Indigenous. Only one Indigenous man, a member of the Kainai band in Alberta, was ever prosecuted for having plural wives (in 1899). Despite the adoption of the anti-polygamy law, Indian Affairs continued to maintain the position that polygamy should be ended gradually through persuasion: "To this [missionary] influence must also be attributed, to a large extent, the ... *ever-increasing willingness* to abandon the old-time custom of plural marriages ... [emphasis added]."[590]

Another practice that met with the strong disfavour of Indian Affairs was the buying and selling of wives. The practice was common among Chiefs and wealthier "commoners" in the West Coast tribes.[591] An Indian Affairs agent at Heshquiaht, on Vancouver Island, reported, "I found all well at the mission and was present at two marriages in church, this tribe having given up the heathen custom of buying their wives."[592] The practice was abandoned over time, not as a result of legal prohibition, but in large part

---

[590] Annual Report, 1896, p. 474.

[591] Eugene E. Ruyle, "Slavery, Surplus, and Stratification on the Northwest Coast: The Ethnoenergetics of an Incipient Stratification System," *Current Anthropology*, Vol. 14, No. 5 (December 1973), p. 612.

[592] Annual Report, 1885, p. 181.

243

as a result of missionary influences. (Indian Affairs' use of the term "heathen" was abandoned in the early 20th century.)

The damaging impacts of certain Indigenous mourning traditions were of grave concern to Indian Affairs. One such practice is illustrated in this account of what followed the deaths of two leaders of the Brokenhead Band in Manitoba in 1890: "[Brokenhead] met with a heavy loss this year, when two of their councilors [sic] died, John Raven and Wayashishsing; they were both good men, one a Christian, the other a pagan - their places will be hard to fill, as they were conscientious, sober and industrious men. Wayasbishsing, before he died, called his family and friends around him, and made his family promise him, in the presence of all, not to leave the house, and to continue to make improvements on his place and that they were only to mourn for him two days. This is a great advance for a pagan, and one which I hope will be followed; as heretofore, when one of the family died, they left the house, gave away all their property, cut up and scarified themselves, and did nothing sometimes for months, and then, as it were began life again some distance from their old home. This is one of the great drawbacks to the prosperity of the pagans, and I am glad to say that the family of Wayasbishsing faithfully carried out his wishes."[593]

This custom gradually died out in a voluntary manner along with polygamy and the selling of wives.

Government prohibitions on aspects of the sundance are often cited as examples of unjust and forced assimilation. Indian Affairs and the churches did in fact object strenuously to the torture ritual that was central to the ceremony, and that was an element of the initiation of young men into the status of "brave." It involved making cuts to the skin of the chest and legs, inserting sticks, attaching ropes to the sticks and tying them to a pole, and having the young man dance around the pole until the stick inserts were torn away.[594] This ritual was often preceded by penitential mutilations carried out on a number of other young men.[595]

---

[593] Annual Report, 1890, p. 107.

[594] Potvin, *Sun Dance Liturgy*, pp. 110-115.

[595] Ibid.

Over time, missionary teaching led to the voluntary abandonment of the torture test: "Consequent upon the increased educational facilities afforded, and the other civilizing influences under which the Indians of the North-West are being constantly brought, the *gradual abandonment* by many of their old heathen celebrations, such as the sun dance, was to be looked for, and those who still indulge in the latter ceremony now omit a feature in it which formed the most objectionable, but which with the Indians perhaps was the most important feature in the performance, namely the torture test [emphasis added]."[596]

In 1885, "The Indians [at the Sarcee Reserve in Alberta] held their usual 'sun dance'... but on account of the wet weather, and lack of candidates for the torture act, I do not think it was a success from an Indian point of view ..."[597] And, in 1886, "The usual sun dance was held in June [at the Assiniboine Agency], the interest taken in it is quickly dying out and they express themselves to the effect that "it is their last."[598]

A renowned and influential Blackfoot Chief, Crowfoot, played a prominent role in the decline of the sundance, and the torture element in particular: "When the renowned Head Chief of the Blackfeet, Chapo-Mex-i-co, Anglicé Crowfoot, objects to the continued celebration by his people of these heathenish ceremonies, we may surely be said to have heard their death knell. And their partial cessation furnishes an additional proof of the progress of civilization among the Indians of the North-West."[599] On one occasion, Chief Crowfoot lent his voice and aid to an Indian Affairs agent to stop the infliction of torture on a young man at a sundance.[600]

Sundance ceremonies typically lasted many days, and Indian Affairs officials were concerned that they interfered with farming schedules. An Indian agent at the Assiniboine Agency wrote, "I should be glad if they were disgusted as it is an unmitigated nuisance, always occurring at the

---

[596] Annual Report, 1888, p. 61.

[597] Annual Report, 1885, p. 173.

[598] Annual Report, 1886, p. 266.

[599] Annual Report, 1888, p. 62.

[600] Ibid., p. 70.

time they should be working at the crops."[601] Over time, many Bands made adjustments to the scheduling of the sundances to accommodate the farming needs: "Almost all the Indians attended their annual sun dance at Indian Head, but waited until seeding and fencing were completed before going, and returned to their work immediately upon the conclusion of the dance, an encouraging improvement upon their conduct last year"[602] And, "The Peigans did better in weeding their fields on account of their not having had any sun dance. It would *appear that they have given up* this annual feast, as they did not hold it this year [emphasis added]."[603]

Through an amendment to the Indian Act, the government in 1895 outlawed any celebration or dance of which the wounding or mutilation of the dead or living body of any human being or animal forms a part or is a feature." Indian Affairs adopted the following policy governing the implementation of the law:

> In the matter of sun-dancing and similar rites of a quasi-religious character, so long as these do not involve the depraving and ruinous features of torture, mutilation or the giving away of property [there was a particular concern about the disposal of property families had received from the government], the religious aspect in which they are regarded by the pagan Indians, who alone engage in them, cannot advisedly be disregarded, and in such instances *only methods of persuasion can be pursued* [emphasis added].[604]

Prohibitions on the sundance were generally ignored, and in 1951 the ban was struck from the Indian Act.[605]

Whether the ban on the torture rite was a progressive step, or an unjust intrusion into a cultural practice, is a debate that could be had. We know

---

[601] Annual Report, 1885, p. 173.

[602] Annual Report, 1887, p. 237.

[603] Ibid., p. 265.

[604] Annual Report, 1896, p. 474.

[605] Rene R. Gadacz, "Sundance," *Canadian Encyclopedia*, February 7, 2006.

which side of the issue the Chief of the Blackfoot Confederacy would have supported.

The potlatch was another cultural practice that was subjected to a degree of prohibition. The traditional potlatch of the West Coast tribes is described in the *Canadian Encyclopedia*: "Valuable goods, such as firearms, blankets, clothing, carved cedar boxes, canoes, food and prestige items, such as slaves and coppers, were accumulated by high-ranking individuals over time, sometimes years. These goods were later bestowed on invited guests as gifts by the host or even destroyed with great ceremony as a show of superior generosity, status and prestige over rivals."[606] Most of the slaves held by West Coast Chiefs and "nobles" had been captured in internecine wars. Slaves were kept as chattel, and sometimes they were executed at potlatches as a symbolic disposal of property.[607] Slavery, and the killing of slaves, continued well past the mid-19th century.[608]

The status of "Chief" was ascribed by birth, and potlatches served to validate and solidify the Chiefs' wealth and prestige.[609] The "commoners" participated in giving away property along with the Chiefs, but the Chiefs were soon re-enriched at the next potlatch, while the commoners remained poor.[610]

Potlatches continued well into the latter part of the 19th century, but their character had significantly evolved by that time: "The excitement of these and kindred gatherings is the chief attraction to Indians of the present day, though of course many attend to buy or sell canoes, horses, skins, & c. The great majority care nothing about the potlach [sic] itself..."[611] Some chiefs

---

[606] Idem, "Potlatch," *Canadian Encyclopedia*, February 7, 2006.

[607] John Douglas Belshaw, *Canadian History: Pre-Confederation, Slavery*, (October 2020).

[608] Conner White, *To Admonish or Abolish: The End of Indigenous Slavery in British Columbia, 1830-1890, BA Honours Thesis*, University of Victoria, 2023, p. 25.

[609] Eugene E. Ruyle, "Slavery, Surplus, and Stratification on the Northwest Coast: The Ethnoenergetics of an Incipient Stratification System," *Current Anthropology*, Vol. 14, No. 5 (Dec., 1973), p. 605.

[610] Ibid., p. 616.

[611] Annual Report, 1885, p. 179.

wished to continue the old style potlatches, but many disagreed. "Chief Lohar and his family have long expressed themselves anxious to do away with the potlach, and the object of this gathering was to pay their debts, ie., blankets and other articles lent them at former potlaches [sic]."[612]

The federal government banned the potlatch in 1884 via an amendment to the Indian Act. The ceremony was seen as wasteful of personal property, and as with the sun dance, there was worry that the multiple-day ceremonies interfered with farm work: "In Cowichan valley there has not been so much land cultivated this year as last owing, in a great measure, to the large [potlatch] gathering held at Comeakin village, at the time when the spring work ought to have been done. This gathering, which was estimated at about two thousand, continued for nearly a month..."[613]

The ban on the potlatch was lifted in 1951, but today it is practised mostly as a cultural festival with the distribution of small gifts.

One hopes that Pope Francis, in making his charge of genocide, in including in this charge the residential schools, was not in any way comparing the Indigenous experience in Canada with an atrocity on the scale of the Nazi holocaust. Some activists, Indigenous and non-Indigenous, do suggest such an equivalency. They allege that the residential schools practiced a physical genocide through purposeful neglect and abuse, and, in some cases, homicide. The evidence, however, shows that the very opposite was true, that the schools actively and compassionately promoted the physical well-being of the students:

- By mid-20th century, the residential schools essentially eliminated the scourge of tuberculosis that ravaged First Nations communities. This was accomplished through a program of

[612] Ibid.

[613] Ibid.

comprehensive vaccination.[614] The incidence of tuberculosis was always much lower in the schools than in the reserves.[615]

- Whereas residential school death rates were significantly higher than in the general Canadian school-age population in the early decades of school operations, by the mid-20th century they were virtually equal.[616]

- The residential schools began renovating and constructing buildings with proper ventilation early in the 20th century,[617] several years before the Toronto Public Schools built its first such school in 1914. The Toronto school has been falsely touted as the first of its kind in Canada.[618]

- The charge that the residential schools wantonly neglected the health of students by ignoring the presence of contagious diseases such as tuberculosis is absurd on its face, given that the staff lived in close proximity to the students and were well aware that diseases were spread through person-to-person contact.

- Many residential schools served as medical centres for surrounding communities; for example, for the prevention and treatment of trachoma in the Prairies in the 1930s.[619]

- Rural schools in Canada were described at a 1919 Dominion Council of Health meeting as "not fit to raise swine in," and as having inadequate heating and lacking playing areas.[620] From early

---

[614] Dr. Scott Hamilton, *Where are the Children buried?*, Dept. of Anthropology, Lakehead University, undated, p. 11.

[615] Truth and Reconciliation Commission of Canada, *Honouring the Truth, Reconciling for the Future, Summary of the Final Report of the Truth and Reconciliation Commission of Canada* (2015), Graph 5, p. 92; *Canada's Residential Schools: The History, Part 2 1939 to 2000, The Final Report of the Truth and Reconciliation Commission of Canada*, Volume 1, Table 36.1, p. 193.

[616] Truth and Reconciliation Commission of Canada, *Honouring the Truth, Reconciling for the Future, Summary of the Final Report of the Truth and Reconciliation Commission of Canada* (2015), Graph 4.

[617] Annual Report, 1911, p. 41.

[618] Melanie Zettler, "How Toronto's first open-air school responded to the tuberculosis crisis more than 100 years ago," Global News, September 30, 2020.

[619] Annual Report, 1932, p. 10.

[620] Christopher Rutty, PhD, and Sue C. Sullivan, *This is Public Health: A Canadian History*, p. 2.8

on, most residential schools provided indoor and outdoor facilities for sports and exercise. In 1898 the Kuper Island School in 1898 built a "new gymnasium…[which] proves to be a very useful addition to the school, for besides giving opportunity for athletic and calisthenic sport, it is supplied with a permanent stage which makes it of great value for receptions and entertainments."[621] At the Blood school, "Recreation three times a day after each meal, football, swimming, fishing, shooting with bows and arrows … Boys and girls each have their own playgrounds, and are always under the supervision of an attendant."[622]

- Throughout the residential school era, and particularly after the Second World War, residential school teams won numerous local, national and international championships in hockey, boxing, lacrosse, cross country skiing, and other sports. Although school administrators sometimes submitted complaints to Indian Affairs about the lack of funds to improve recreational facilities, the numerous sports successes could not have been achieved had the players not been well coached and had access to good sports facilities and equipment.

- Residential schools implemented the rigorous nutritional standards set by the Canadian government in the 1950s. The health benefits were long-lasting. Research has found that residential school students were taller and less obese as adults than would have been the case if they had attended other kinds of schools.[623] The residential schools attended to the nutritional needs of students in earlier periods as well. The 1925 Indian Affairs Annual Report states, "Milk herds are being tested [there was a concern broadly in Canada about diseases carried in milk] and the children's diet at these institutions carefully controlled. In the Prairie Provinces, travelling nurses visit Indian schools regularly to this end. The department is cooperating with the Canadian Junior Red Cross in the promotion of better health for Indian children." Indian Affairs

---

[621] Annual Report, 1898, p. 580.

[622] Annual Report, 1910, p. 726.

[623] Donna L. Feir, M. Christopher Auld, "Indian residential schools: Height and body mass post-1930," *Canadian Journal of Economics*, Vol. 54, No. 1, February 2021, pp. 126-163.

noted in its 1944 report that in outlying districts where the supply of vegetables was limited, the Department distributed 13 tons of vegetable biscuits fortified with vitamin B flour.

- The close association between poor nutrition and the incidence of disease is well known. Had residential school students been exposed to severe and chronic malnutrition, the schools would have experienced persistently high levels of disease and morbidity. The residential schools, however, experienced a precipitous decline in all-cause death rates,[624] and mortality from tuberculosis from the very early 1900s on.[625] There were periods in which residential schools struggled to provide a nutritious diet. But the schools were not alone in this. The general Canadian population had difficulty securing adequate nutrition in times of economic hardship. Malnutrition was so widespread in Newfoundland and Labrador during the Great Depression that it was considered to be a major factor in the uncontrolled spread of beriberi and tuberculosis.[626] Nearly half of Canadians enlisting for service in the Second World War were malnourished, and researchers have found that 60 percent of all Canadians were undernourished at that time.[627] A 1920 study found that 26 percent of students in the Toronto public schools were malnourished and in a "serious state of health."[628]

That residential school attendance was associated with so many favourable health outcomes is especially remarkable in light of the fact that the schools gave priority to the admission of orphans and children from severely disadvantaged or abusive backgrounds.

---

[624] Truth and Reconciliation Commission of Canada, *Honouring the Truth, Reconciling for the Future, Summary of the Final Report of the Truth and Reconciliation Commission of Canada* (2015), Graph 3, p. 91.

[625] *Honouring the Truth, Reconciling for the Future*, Graph 5, p. 92.

[626] Jenny Higgins, "Great Depression – Impacts on the Working Class," Heritage Newfoundland & Labrador online, 2007.

[627] Transcript: Ian Mosby: *Food in Canada During WWII*, TVOToday, May 13, 2015.

[628] Aleck Samuel Ostry, *Nutrition Policy in Canada, 1870-1939* (UBC Press, 2006), p. 23.

In summary, relations between Canada and the Indigenous people have always been, and remain, complex. They have featured processes of both cultural assimilation and cultural integration. Occasionally, they involved the suppression by law of elements of traditional customs. But in making sweeping assertions of forced assimilation and genocide, Pope Francis has distorted the history of Canada's relations with its Indigenous people in the eyes of the world. In doing so, he has committed a grave injustice against the Indigenous people and all Canadians.

This chapter originally appeared as "Integration, Forced Assimilation, or Genocide" on the Woke Watch Canada Newsletter *on Substack, January 3, 2023.*

Chapter Thirteen

Everybody's Favourite Dead White Male

Greg Piasetzki

For Canadians with an interest in honest history, Mark Antony's funeral oration of Julius Caesar set over 2,000 years ago seems truer than ever. Over the past several years many of our country's most significant past figures have been toppled from their plinths, erased from city maps and struck from public records in a paroxysm of historical cleansing. Among the victims: Sir John A. Macdonald, Egerton Ryerson, Edward Cornwallis, Sir Hector-Louis Langevin, Matthew Baillie Begbie, Samuel de Champlain, General Jeffrey Amherst…the list goes on and on.

Whatever good these dead white men may have done in their lives – particularly their significant roles in creating modern Canada – has today been "interred with their bones." Any single act or statement at odds with the purported values of contemporary Canada is sufficient to warrant their public condemnation followed by swift obliteration from our recognized past. The crucial test for many concerns an association, however remote or tangential, with Canada's fraught Indian Residential School system.[629]

Ryerson, for example, was long celebrated as the pioneer of free public schooling in English Canada.[630] Yet a brief he wrote in 1847 offering his thoughts on what a government-run school system for native Canadians might look like – four decades before such a thing came into being – is now considered evidence of his participation in the many failures of residential schools in the 20th century. And reason enough to remove his name from Ryerson University in Toronto.

Similarly, Langevin was a key figure in French/English relations during the period leading to Confederation and in the new Dominion's early years. As federal Minister of Public Works he was responsible for the construction of

---

[629] Hymie Rubenstein, "Digging for the Truth about Canada's Residential School Graves" *C2C Journal* online, August 7, 2021.

[630] Lynn McDonald, "The historical record vindicates Egerton Ryerson," *Financial Post*, Sep 9, 2021.

many residential schools, although not the underlying policy that animated them. Regardless, in 2017 Langevin was judged connected to the schools and his name quickly vaporized from one of Parliament Hill's most significant public buildings.[631]

Then there is Macdonald, once regarded as Canada's greatest statesman and founder of our country. Today, he is described in the darkest possible terms: a purveyor of genocide and plotter of assimilation. Again, the case against him typically centres on residential schools and their now-discredited policy of mandatory attendance. This despite the fact mandatory attendance was not introduced until 1920, 27 years after his death, and was ever only half-heartedly enforced.[632] Plus, Macdonald was a tireless and progressive supporter of Indigenous rights and wellbeing, as is amply documented by his historical record.[633] But none of that matters. A single deed or word is now reason enough for cancellation.

Amidst all the current laments over colonialism and white supremacy, however, there is one dead white male from the previous century whose reputational trajectory has moved in the opposite direction. As the memories of his many peers lie in disgrace and tatters, that of Dr. Peter Henderson Bryce, a senior public health official at the turn of the 20th century and heretofore a minor character in Canada's historical record, is rising triumphant.

A New Hero for Our Times

Bryce today is widely feted as a "hero" for his efforts to improve residential schools. In 1907, as chief medical officer of health for the Department of Indian Affairs, he investigated the dismal health conditions at these schools in western Canada and issued an official report that

---

[631] Peter Shawn Taylor, "The case for keeping 'Langevin Block,'" *Maclean's*, June 29, 2017.

[632] Nina Green, Tom Flanagan, and Brian Giesbrecht, "They Were Not Forced," *The Dorchester Review* online, April 21, 2022; in print, "They Were Not Forced: The Indian Act and Regulations Prior to 1920," *The Dorchester Review*, Spring/Summer 2023, Vol. 13, No. 1, pp. 49-56.

[633] Greg Piasetzki, "Sir John A. Macdonald Saved More Native Lives Than Any Other Prime Minister," *C2C Journal* online, November 27, 2020.

received considerable public and political attention.[634] Later, he tangled over further reforms with Duncan Campbell Scott, the imperious bureaucrat who ran Indian Affairs for several decades and is now widely regarded as a racist. Bryce was eventually sidelined in this struggle.

After retiring, however, he self-published the pamphlet *The Story of a National Crime: An Appeal for Justice to the Indians of Canada* in 1922 in an attempt to bring renewed attention to the matter. For this, Bryce is now celebrated as an early "whistleblower."[635] It is a renaissance that has been driven largely by Indigenous scholars and activists.

Cindy Blackstock, a much-quoted Indigenous professor at McGill University, recently co-wrote in the *Canadian Medical Association Journal* that Bryce "stands as a hallmark of...moral conviction and courage."[636] Blackstock, who is also the executive director of the First Nations Child and Family Caring Society of Canada and a key figure in litigation over the federal government's treatment of native children in the modern welfare system, presents herself as a relentless critic of Canadian Indigenous policy. Yet she appears to have adopted Bryce as something akin to a saviour figure.

Blackstock organized a well-publicized refurbishment of Bryce's grave site in Ottawa's Beechwood Cemetery in 2015 and says she leaves spiritual offerings when she visits.[637] She also claims to read aloud excerpts from recent court rulings at his graveside, presumably as a way of communing with his spirit. And a mailbox Blackstock installed beside Bryce's headstone has become a repository for fan mail from other present-day admirers. "Thank you for your courage and care," someone recently wrote

---

[634] P.H. Bryce, "Report on the Indian schools of Manitoba and the North-West Territories" (Ottawa: Government Printing Bureau, 1907).

[635] Idem, "The Story of a National Crime: An Appeal for Justice to the Indians of Canada" (Ottawa: James Hope & Sons, 1922).

[636] Travis Hay, Cindy Blackstock, Michael Kirlew, "Dr. Peter Bryce (1853–1932): whistleblower on residential schools," *Canadian Medical Association Journal*, March 2020, 192 (9) pp. E223-E224.

[637] Alistair Steele, "Dead reckoning: Canada's national cemetery is bringing truth about residential schools to light," CBC News, June 19, 2021.

to Bryce, who died in 1932. "You had great courage and spoke the truth," said another.[638]

A transcendental mailbox is not the only example of Bryce's new-found celebrity. Three scholars, two of whom are Indigenous, wrote a lengthy paean to Bryce in *The Globe and Mail* this past summer. "Bryce's work fell on refusing ears," they explained. "We should listen to him now."[639] Yet another Indigenous scholar, Pam Palmater of Ryerson University, well-known for her acerbic views of white Canada, is equally laudatory of Bryce in the academic journal *Aboriginal Policy Studies*. "In the early 1900s, Dr. Peter Bryce exposed the genocidal practices of government-sanctioned residential schools, where healthy Indigenous children were purposefully exposed to children infected with tuberculosis, spreading the disease through the school population," she wrote last year. (Her claims are untrue, but that seems beside the point.) The long-dead Bryce even makes regular appearances on social media; his picture was recently featured on CBC's Instagram feed with the caption, "He tried to raise the alarm about residential school conditions in the early 1900s."[640]

To cap off Bryce's remarkable rebirth, the historical organization Defining Moments Canada next year plans a national commemoration of Bryce's 1922 pamphlet, now hailed as "The Bryce Report," to mark its 100th anniversary. This slim 20-page volume, out of print for nearly a century, is available on Amazon for $24.50.

Bryce's reputation has thus achieved a level of veneration and respect no other white Anglo-Saxon Protestant male from Canada's distant past has reached in recent memory. That this elevation is almost entirely due to the efforts of Indigenous scholars and activists makes his ascent all the more remarkable. Such a curious state of affairs deserves a closer look. Can the facts of Bryce's life sustain his current level of adoration? Can anyone's?

---

[638] "Peter Bryce gets his own mailbox in advance of first National Day of Truth and Reconciliation," Beechwood Cemetery blog post, August 18, 2021.

[639] Crystal Fraser, Tricia Logan and Neil Orford, "A doctor's century-old warning on residential schools can help find justice for Canada's crimes," *Globe and Mail*, July 17, 2021.

[640] Pamela Palmater, "Genocide, Indian Policy, and Legislated Elimination of Indians in Canada" *Aboriginal Policy Studies*, Vol. 3 No. 3 (2014), pp. 27-54.

The Man and His Times

Bryce was born in 1853 into a prosperous Presbyterian family in Mount Pleasant, a small town west of Hamilton, Ontario. He attended the University of Toronto where, among other degrees, he acquired a Bachelor of Medicine. He received several medals for exceptional achievement and in 1880 opened a medical practice in Guelph, Ontario. Two years later, Bryce received a political patronage appointment as secretary of the Ontario Board of Health and was later appointed deputy registrar of vital statistics. As such, Bryce frequently found himself at the forefront of the burgeoning field of public health.

Through most of the 1800s, deadly diseases such as typhoid, cholera, smallpox, tuberculosis (TB), and diphtheria wreaked havoc on urban populations around the world. These health threats were for centuries widely assumed to be caused by "miasma," or bad air arising from decaying organic matter. Individuals were thought to be sickened by their environment rather than contact with infected individuals. Only after the pioneering work of scientists such as Louis Pasteur and Robert Koch was belief in miasma supplanted by germ theory, and the understanding that these diseases were spread by tiny particles of living matter through person-to-person contact.

As part of his provincial duties, Bryce was highly visible in promoting health-related measures, including the need for better municipal garbage, sewage, and water treatment. And he showed decisive leadership when necessary. In 1895 he sought to quell a typhoid outbreak by ordering the closure of all private wells in the southwest Ontario city of Brantford and the provision of free water to those affected.

Bryce was also an early advocate of statistics as a tool for improving public health and was involved in the collection and tabulation of data on causes of death and disease outbreaks. In 1900, thanks to his rising reputation, he became the first Canadian appointed as president of the American Public Health Association.

Judging by his many appearances in the contemporary press, Bryce was also a stereotypical Victorian gentleman with wide-ranging, if somewhat idiosyncratic, interests and a strong desire for public attention. In 1882 he gave a lecture on hypnotism at the Canadian Institute and noted the technique's particular effectiveness on "emotional persons and oftener in the female sex than in the male." In 1897, speaking to the Women's League about TB, he argued for the "total demolition" of infected houses. (We now know that many common disinfectants, including vinegar, effectively kill the tuberculosis bacterium, making demolition unnecessary.)

Bryce was particularly interested in the link between building design and disease, especially with respect to air flow and natural light. In *The Globe* in May 1898 he decried the layout of Toronto's public schools, declaring the "ventilation, lighting, heating, floor and air space allowed each pupil to be totally inadequate." Given recent experience with Covid-19, such opinions seem rather farsighted. As for his reasons, "The immediate effects of the foul air are to injure the nutrition of the child. The appetite and digestion are disordered, and every tissue and primarily the nervous system is affected," he explained to *Globe* readers, mustering more conviction than evidence. Despite his outsized reputation today, Bryce was very much a man of his times.

Dr. Bryce Goes to Ottawa

In 1904 Bryce received another patronage appointment, this time from the Liberal government of Sir Wilfrid Laurier, as chief medical officer for the federal departments of the Interior and Indian Affairs. Bryce had no particular expertise with native issues and his initial duties consisted primarily of compiling an annual statistical report based on input from departmental staff across the country. At a time when health care in Canada was entirely privately funded and delivered, Indian Affairs employed over 200 full- and part-time medical personnel serving Indigenous reserves and schools in fulfilment of federal treaty obligations.

In his first departmental report in 1905, Bryce was struck by the great variation in death rates between native and non-native Canadians, a situation that set his inquiring, data-focused mind to work. Among non-natives, the reported annual death rate was 15 per thousand, yet on some reserves in western Canada it exceeded 70 per thousand – or 7 percent of the entire Indigenous population every year. For the Mohawks of the Bay of Quinte in Ontario, however, the rate was a mere 7 per thousand – half the Canadian average. Clearly some reserves were experiencing terrible health outcomes, while others were not. What was going on?

To gain insight, Bryce compared the Six Nations Mohawks of the Grand River (death rate 18 per thousand) with the nearby Chippewas of Sarnia (52 per thousand). His conclusions, informed by the prevailing attitudes of his era and his own observations, strike a distinctly discordant note today:

"Perhaps there has been a greater admixture of white blood in the Six Nations...the real and essential difference is that the Chippewas have lived much by other work than farming available in Sarnia and on the river, while the lawlessness in the matter of liquor-selling, peculiar to the border, has helped to make the difference. It is primarily a difference in moral development, with its accompanying lagging behind in material advancement, both of which are chief factors in determining the health of any people."

Bryce's belief that inter-marriage (admixture) and assimilation into white society offered Indigenous people protection from disease and that the Chippewas' health problems were related to their "moral development" were commonly-held opinions among educated people of his time. Such positions today would obviously be met with outrage and charges of racism. In his report the following year, Bryce again returned to the theme of assimilation, noting the "invaluable admixture of white blood with its inherited qualities in improving the health of native communities."[641]

The TB Problem

Bryce's modern-day elevation by Indigenous scholars rests on setting aside his now-heretical views on native society and instead focusing on his work regarding health conditions in residential schools. While smallpox was

---

[641] Indian Affairs, Annual Report, 1906.

initially the greatest threat to Indigenous people during the colonial period, an effective federal inoculation campaign wiped out the disease throughout Canada's native communities by the turn of the 20th century.[642]

During Bryce's time, TB had become the predominant killer of Indigenous people. It is a slow-moving and insidious disease; over 90 percent of people infected with TB show no symptoms and are not contagious. Only once their immune system is weakened by another ailment such as a cold or the flu (with poverty a frequent accelerant) does the disease become active and highly contagious. An infected person gradually loses lung function and weight, wasting away over a period of up to a decade. Hence TB's historical name of "consumption."

In 1907, amid growing concerns about reported high rates of TB at residential schools, Indian Affairs ordered Bryce to conduct a tour of native boarding schools across western Canada and report on what he found. He visited 35 schools in three months. And while there are several flaws in his statistical methods, Bryce's observations delivered a devastating indictment of Canada's residential school system as it operated in 1907.

According to Bryce's data, of 31 students reported discharged from the File Hills residential school in Saskatchewan, "9 died at school" and another six died thereafter, for an observed mortality rate of nearly 50 percent. Overall, "of a total of 1,537 pupils reported upon, nearly 25 per cent are dead." What Bryce found was undeniably grim. As for the reason, "everywhere the almost invariable cause of death given is tuberculosis," he reported. Given that the health condition of most incoming students was recorded as "good," Bryce reasonably surmised that the schools themselves were a major factor in the disease's transmission. From his report:

"The defective sanitary condition of many schools, especially in the matter of ventilation have been the foci from which disease, especially tubercular, has spread, whether through direct infection from person to person, or indirectly through the infected dust of floors, school-rooms and dormitories."

---

[642] Peter Shawn Taylor and Greg Piasetzki, "The 19th-century Indigenous policy success story we've forgotten," *National Post*, Mar 28, 2019.

Bryce's 1907 official report emphasized three areas for improvement: enhanced ventilation and floor space standards, better medical screening of students prior to entry into school and mandatory "calisthenics" (or physical exercise) for all students to bolster their overall health.

The Government's Response

Bryce's report was prepared and delivered to his superiors by June 1907, just a month after his return. Bryce's reputation as a whistleblower partly rests on claims by his current supporters that this report was not formally released by his department due to its critical nature. According to the online entry on Bryce in the *Canadian Encyclopedia*, "The Department of Indian Affairs did not publish Bryce's report. It was leaked to journalists, however, prompting calls for reform from across the country."

This is inaccurate. As a memo found by the author in the national archives reveals, copies of Bryce's report were delivered to all Members of Parliament and Senators, as well as senior representatives of all churches involved in operation of native schools and, further, to the principal of every Indian boarding school in the country, with a request for comments.[643]

As for the political fallout, the report was debated in the House of Commons when the Conservative opposition grilled the government on Bryce's finding of "defective sanitary conditions" at the schools. "The matter is of course one of very grave importance. It has been taken up with the authorities who are in direct charge," Frank Oliver, the Minister of Indian Affairs, dutifully replied.[644] Bryce's report was also mentioned in many newspapers, including *The Globe* and *Toronto Star*. "The report is significant," declared the *Victoria Daily Colonist* on November 16, 1907 under the headline "Indian Schools Deal Out Death."

---

[643] Report by Dr. P.H. Bryce on his Tour of Inspection of Indian Schools in Manitoba, Saskatchewan and Alberta," Library and Archives Canada, RG10 Vol 4037, Microfilm reel C-10177, File 317021.

[644] House of Commons *Debates*, 10th Parliament, 4th Session, Vol. 1, column 623.

Beyond erroneous assertions that Bryce's report was never publicly released, the surrounding mythology further claims that Ottawa deliberately ignored it, as Blackstock has alleged in an op-ed in *Maclean's*.[645]

In truth, Bryce's 1907 report was handled as minister Oliver promised. Bryce's troubling findings played a key role in setting the agenda for negotiations the very next year between Ottawa and the various churches operating residential schools. This process culminated with the signing of a new federal funding arrangement in 1911 that tied significant increases in the budget for native schooling to new, tougher building standards for the church-run schools.

The new contract was notable for its specific ventilation and air space requirements, setting the minimum at 500 cubic feet per student in dormitories and 250 cubic feet per student in classrooms. It also directed that no student should be admitted into a residential school "until, where practicable, a physician has reported that a child is in good health." Finally, all teachers in residential schools were required to use the textbook *Callisthenics and Games* for "improving and strengthening the physical condition of the boys and girls."[646] The new 1911 standards are thus directly traceable to Bryce's three original observations. Despite what his many supporters may claim today, Bryce scored a policy hat trick.

The new standards had an immediate and salutary effect on school facilities. At Marieval Indian Residential School on the Cowessess 73 Reserve in Saskatchewan, lately in the news as a result of the purported discovery of over 700 unmarked graves on its grounds, enrollment was temporarily curtailed in order to comply with the government's new health rules. "According to the latest requirements of the department as to air space, our school will need to be enlarged to provide sufficient accommodation," the school reported in 1912.[647] A modern new wing was necessary to bring the school into compliance with regulations.

---

[645] Cindy Blackstock, "Screaming into silence," *Maclean's*, June 30, 2021.

[646] Indian Affairs, *Sessional Papers*, No. 27, January 14 , 1911, p. 439.

[647] *Annual Report*, 1912, p. 532.

To meet its obligations arising from the 1911 agreement, the federal government's budget for Indian education rose sharply from $321,988 in 1907 (see page 975) to $539,145 in 1911 (see page 443).[648] This seems a stunning show of support for the residential school system, particularly given the modest nature of most federal budgets in the early 1900s. Unfortunately, the First World War derailed the department's ambitious modernization plans and these increases soon disappeared. By 1922, however, Indian Affairs' budget for Indigenous education was once again on the rise, hitting a record $1,360,000. And by this time, Ottawa had built or remodelled nearly 30 residential schools to the new, healthier standards advocated by Bryce.

A Focus on Reserves

During the ongoing federal-church negotiations, Indian Affairs in 1909 asked Bryce to look more closely at the source and spread of TB among students at residential and day schools. It had been accepted by Bryce and many others that the schools themselves were significant transmitters of the disease. From his 1906 annual report for Indian Affairs (which again expresses opinions about Indigenous society that would be considered scandalous today):

> That the prevalence of tuberculosis amongst the bands is…due directly to infection introduced by one member of a family into a small, often crowded, house, and there, as dried sputum collects on filthy floors and walls, is spread from one to another so certainly and at times so rapidly that one consumptive has in a single winter infected all the members of a household as certainly and rapidly as if he had had small-pox.
>
> That from such houses infected children have been received into schools, notably the boarding and industrial schools, and in the school-room, but especially in the dormitories, frequently over-

---

[648] *Annual Report,* 1907, p. 975; cf. idem, *Annual Report,* 1911, p. 443.

crowded and ill-ventilated, have been the *agents of direct infection* (Emphasis added).[649]

In 1909 Bryce and colleague J.D. Lafferty, also a medical doctor, carried out examinations on 243 children at eight native schools in the Calgary area. Their report stated that TB was present in all ages of children they examined, with excessive mortality displayed in pupils between 5 and 10 years old.[650] Crucially, no child awaiting admission to school was found to be free from TB, leading Bryce and Lafferty to the conclusion "that the primary source of infection is in the home" and that "the tuberculized older person in the home is the essential source of the infection."

Bryce and Lafferty's assertion that family members on reserves, and not church-run, government-funded residential schools, were the true source of TB infections among Indigenous students was reinforced a decade later with the results of the first comprehensive Canadian TB screening study conducted in 1920.[651] This Saskatchewan study employed a newly-invented skin test that could reveal even the dormant stage of TB.

The study sampled a cross-section of the population and found that, even among pre-school non-Indigenous children, 44 percent had TB. Among children at residential and on-reserve day schools, the average infection rate was a stunning 92.5 percent. A further and equally surprising result was that the age group at greatest risk of mortality, on reserve and off, was infants under the age of 1. As these youngsters had obviously not yet attended any school, the findings strongly suggested the source of TB was in the home.

(It should be noted that even today Indigenous Canadians living in remote areas continue to suffer vastly excessive rates of TB. Among non-native

---

[649] *Annual Report*, 1906.

[650] Correspondence relating to Tuberculosis Among the Indians in the Various Agencies across Canada," 1908-1910, p. 253 (microfilm stamped p. 357453), cf, LAC RG10, Vol. 3957, Microfilm reel C-10166, No. 140754-1.

[651] A.B. Cook, R.G. Ferguson, J.F. Cairns, and R.H. Brighton, *Report to the Government of Saskatchewan by the Anti-Tuberculosis Commission* (Regina: King's Printer, 1922).

Canadians, the current rate is 0.6 per 100,000; among Indigenous Canadians it is 24, and specifically among Inuit 170.[652])

In the years following his 1909 study, Bryce used his annual reports for Indian Affairs to advocate for a shift in TB programs away from schools and towards reserves. He also continued to promote the idea that assimilation offered the best permanent solution to native health problems. In his 1912 report he again noted that reserves with the lowest rates of TB deaths were those that had integrated the customs of "white people and the unconscious assimilation of the ideas and practices of civilized communities."

Bryce's "Other" Recommendations

Bryce continued his regular work at Indian Affairs until 1914, when friction with his boss, the previously mentioned Duncan Campbell Scott, came to a head. According to Bryce's self-published pamphlet, the reason for this conflict was Scott's opposition to a set of additional recommendations Bryce had prepared on his own following his 1907 and 1909 reports and that he promoted internally in the department. As he would later explain in his post-retirement version of events, "The recommendations contained in the report were never published and the public knows nothing of them."

In the current narrative that casts Bryce as heroic whistleblower, Scott has become the moustache-twirling, reform-thwarting villain. Beyond his lengthy career in Indian Affairs, Scott was also an accomplished artist and public intellectual. He was a well-known writer of fiction, plays, and poetry, for which he is ranked among the famous "Poets of Confederation." He also served as president of the Royal Society of Canada and held honorary doctorates from Queen's University and the University of Toronto.

---

[652] Radha Jetty, "Tuberculosis among First Nations, Inuit and Métis children and youth in Canada: Beyond medical management," *Paediatrics & Child Health* 26:2, April-May 2021, pp. e78–e81.

Today Scott is chiefly remembered as a racist bureaucrat who believed the purpose of the residential school system was to "kill the Indian in the child." (While commonly attributed to him, this is actually a misquote.[653] Scott did, however, say many comparable things, including that the goal of residential schools was to "get rid of the Indian problem." What he appears to have meant was that he hoped natives would eventually become fully engaged participants in Canadian society.)

Bryce claims he made repeated remonstrances to Scott demanding that action be taken on his follow-up recommendations. In his own 1910 memo in reply, Scott laid out his objections to Bryce's plan, arguing they were "impractical" and would shift the focus of residential schools from education to "a sanitorium system." Co-author Lafferty also disagreed with Bryce. In March 1911, after Bryce felt he had been stonewalled by Scott, he went over his supervisor's head to plead his case with deputy superintendent Frank Pedley, the highest non-elected official in the department, as well as Pedley's boss Oliver, the federal Minister of Indian Affairs. From Bryce's letter to Oliver:

> It is now over 9 months...and I have not received a single communication with reference to carrying out the suggestions of our report. Am I wrong in assuming that the vanity of Mr. D. C. Scott, growing out of his success at manipulating the mental activities of Mr. Pedley, has led him to the fatal deception of supposing that his cleverness will be equal to that of Prospero in calming any storm that may blow up from a Tuberculosis Association or any where else, since he knows that should he fail he has through memoranda on file placed the responsibility on Mr. Pedley and yourself.[654]

---

[653] Andrew Stobo Sniderman, "The man wrongly attributed with uttering 'kill the Indian in the child,'" reviewing Mark Abley, *Conversations With A Dead Man: The Legacy Of Duncan Campbell Scott*, in *Maclean's*, November 8, 2013.

[654] Scott to Oliver, March 16, 1911, quoted in *The Story of a National Crime*, p. 6.

Setting aside the Shakespearean reference,[655] Bryce's letter clearly put Oliver in a difficult position. He could not accept Bryce's demands – which clearly imply incompetence on the part of one official and arrogance on another – without undermining his senior staff and the government's management structure. In many organizations, "going over someone's head" is a firing offence. In the end, no action was taken on Bryce's demands. Then in 1913 Pedley resigned amid a departmental scandal and Scott took over as deputy superintendent, where he would remain until 1932.

With his rival Scott now firmly in control of the department, Bryce found himself on the outside. From 1914 to 1921, Bryce remained on the payroll of Indian Affairs, but he no longer wrote the annual health report. It appears he did no work at all for the department. Whatever the reason for this unusual arrangement, Bryce received seven years' salary for no known effort. While he continued to work for the Department of the Interior, he was silent about residential schools throughout this time.

The Retired Whistleblower

In 1921 Bryce retired in a huff at age 68 after failing to get himself appointed deputy minister of the newly-created federal Department of Health. Clearly upset at how he had been treated, he returned to his concern about health conditions at residential schools. The result was *The Story of a National Crime*, now hailed as a significant historical document worthy of centenary celebration.

As his present-day supporters claim, its 20 pages amply detail Bryce's interest in native health and his opinion on the necessity for action, as well as listing his follow-up recommendations that were overruled by Scott. But anyone who takes the half-hour necessary to read the entire booklet cannot fail to notice that Bryce had other objectives beyond mere munificence.

[655] "There is no harm done," Prospero assures Miranda in *Tempest*, I.ii, but the reader knows it is far from being the whole truth.

Nearly a quarter of the document is consumed with Bryce's complaints about his severance package and what he perceives as shabby treatment by the bureaucracy. "I had a right to aspire...to the position of Deputy Minister of Health," he grouses. It is, to put it briefly, a self-serving rant. Even Blackstock in her *CMAJ* hagiography admits that "Bryce's words do betray a slight self-interest."

As historian John S. Milloy told the Royal Commission in 1996, and repeats in his 1999 book *A National Crime*, "Much of Bryce's 1922 narrative is the self-interested tale of his failed ambitions in the Department and of his unsuccessful attempt to secure the appointment as first deputy minister of the Department of Health."[656]

Of course, many whistleblowers have complicated and overlapping motivations. If we are to judge Bryce on his status as a significant source of information regarding government mismanagement or intransigence towards Indigenous issues, then what should really matter are the details, rather than his delivery method.

So here, in Bryce's own words from his 1922 pamphlet, are the recommendations he claims the government ignored to its shame:

1. *Greater school facilities* [for native students], since only 30 percent of the children of school age were in attendance;

2. That boarding schools with farms attached be established near the home reserves of the pupils;

3. That the government undertake the complete maintenance and control of the schools...and further it was recommended that *as the Indians grow in wealth and intelligence they should pay at least part of the cost from their own funds*;

4. That the school studies be those of the curricula of the Province in which the schools are situated;

---

[656] John S. Milloy, Testimony, pp. 125-128, Cf. Milloy, *A National Crime: The Canadian Government and the Residential School System 1879 to 1986* (University of Manitoba Press, 1999).

5. …That the department provide for the management of the schools, through a Board of Trustees, one appointed from each church…;

6. That Continuation schools be arranged for on the school farms…; and,

7. That the health interests of the pupils be guarded by a proper medical inspection and that the local physicians be encouraged through the provision at each school of fresh air methods in the care and treatment of cases of tuberculosis (emphasis added).

The list is at sharp odds with Bryce's current reputation among Indigenous activists as a truth-telling "hero." The first and second items would have required a tripling of the number of residential schools in Canada and the closure of most on-reserve day schools, where most native children received their education. Although this list does not say so explicitly, it implicitly suggests the imposition of compulsory education long before such a thing was actually established by Scott.

In downplaying the issue of compulsory education, Bryce deliberately or inadvertently manipulated his own legacy by omitting several contentious recommendations from his earlier list that caused him so much grief with Scott. One of these explicitly stated "compulsory schooling should be enforced for Native children" and another called for sweeping reduction in day school operations in favour of greater use of residential schools.

The inescapable conclusion is that Bryce was a strong and outspoken supporter of compulsory education for all Indigenous students and that he preferred residential schools over convenient on-reserve day schools. These are not popular opinions today.

Then there is the problematic third recommendation from the 1922 list, suggesting native families be made to pay for the privilege of sending their children to residential schools. Such a thing seems grotesquely humorous, given how Indigenous fans of Bryce such as Palmater routinely characterize the entire residential school system as "genocidal."

It is uncertain whether Bryce's recommendation that Ottawa assume complete control over the schools and relegate churches to an oversight role on a proposed national Board of Trustees would have been to the benefit of students. And while his expurgated list contains a few sensible suggestions, most are either unlikely to have made any noticeable difference or fall outside the competency of a chief medical officer.

Remember that Bryce had no authority or expertise in areas of funding, curriculum, or organizational structure. And, as Scott noted in his 1910 memo, implementing Bryce's ideas (including those omitted from the 1922 list) would have shifted the schools from educational institutions to health-care-focused operations under the guidance of the chief medical officer, namely Bryce. Beyond giving Bryce control of the entire school system, such a significant policy shift would have required legislative approval since it appeared to violate the federal government's treaty obligations. All of this likely explains Scott's refusal to accept Bryce's follow-up report, regardless of any personal animosity.

Then again, what if Scott *had* accepted and Ottawa implemented Bryce's recommendations? Indulging in a bit of counterfactual history, it seems inevitable that Bryce's reputation today would be experiencing a very different arc. Instead of a brave whistleblower, he would likely be remembered as a deluded bureaucrat who put himself in charge, tripled the number of residential schools, forced all Indigenous kids to attend, and then demanded that Indigenous parents pay for the privilege of sending their kids to school off-reserve.

Bryce would thus be regarded as a villain on par with Scott or Macdonald and an accomplice in, if not the architect of, the alleged federal policy of genocide. As such, Bryce would certainly not be receiving transcendental fan mail or the other accolades and attention currently directed his way. That he is widely regarded as a hero today seems the result of the very great stroke of luck that he was ignored in his time. There is considerable irony in recognizing how long-time foil Scott has become responsible for Bryce's beneficent reputation today.

A Hero for Our Time?

Like all interesting and consequential figures from the past, Bryce was a complicated individual. He was in some ways a pioneer of public health. As chief medical officer for Indian Affairs, Bryce used modern statistical methods to understand and tackle the serious problems of Indigenous health. His 1907 inspection tour revealed disturbing evidence of high mortality rates and poor sanitation practices at the schools and his report brought public attention to bear on the issue. His observations were implemented in full and with reasonable dispatch by the federal government, with positive results.

Two years later, Bryce's study of Calgary Indigenous students was equally revelatory and established that reserves were the ultimate source of TB infections. His attempts to bring greater attention to native health issues after retirement can be considered further to his credit. He clearly had a passion for Indigenous health at a time when few others did. For all this, Bryce deserves ample recognition.

But despite the adulation heaped upon him today, Bryce was very much a man of his times. Much of his published work betrays the common prejudices and errors of his era, including the superiority of white culture and the benefits of assimilating natives into white society; many of his compatriots have been discredited and cancelled for similar sins.

Further, the foundation of Bryce's reputation as a heroic whistleblower appears misplaced, particularly given the attention paid to his official 1907 report. As for his heralded follow-up recommendations, a close inspection reveals them to be deeply flawed and largely unworkable, and his motivations for revealing them largely self-indulgent. In fact, long-time nemesis Scott appears to have done Bryce's future reputation an enormous favour by refusing to accept them.

All of which brings us to the great mystery of Bryce's current elevation to secular sainthood. Contrary to how most of his contemporaries have been treated, Bryce has been excused all his faults so that his other achievements can be celebrated. But surely his many present-day promoters, including academics such as Blackstock and Palmater, have read his 1922 pamphlet and other works and are aware of how discordant and problematic his recommendations, opinions, and attitudes seem today.

So why have Bryce's advocates chosen to celebrate his accomplishments *in spite of* evidence of his many past mistakes, in sharp contrast to how nearly every other significant character from Canada's past has been treated in recent years? It is a singular puzzle. Perhaps Bryce's disparate treatment is meant to offer white Canadians expiation through a single righteous figure. Or maybe it is intended to counter criticism that the popular approach to Canadian history is unrelentingly negative.

Then again, it is possible the chance to invent a narrative of a brave whistleblower attempting to shine a light on the federal government's habitual disregard for Indigenous health proved so attractive it overwhelmed other concerns about veracity, consistency, or principle. Regardless, if an accommodation can be made for Bryce — if his evil can be "interred with his bones" so that his good may live on — then surely a similar effort can be made for his many cancelled peers as well.

By all means, Canadians should reflect on the complex and occasionally inspiring story of Dr. Peter Henderson Bryce and assign credit where due to his achievements and good intentions. But in doing so, we should be prepared to extend that same understanding and indulgence to the rest of Canada's now-darkened pantheon of historical figures — some of whom are far less compromised than Bryce. Canadians must learn to appreciate their history as it actually happened, regardless of whether that proves narratively or politically convenient.

This chapter originally appeared online in C2C Journal *as "Everybody's Favourite Dead White Male: The Mysterious Resurrection and Celebration of Dr. Peter Henderson Bryce," November 12, 2021.*

Chapter Fourteen

Were the Residential Schools Agents of Genocide?

Ian Gentles

For some years the view that Canada's Indian Residential Schools were tools of genocide has been gathering the momentum of a juggernaut. It all began when Phil Fontaine, the Grand Chief of the Assembly of First Nations, declared, on a coast-to-coast radio program, that he had suffered physical and sexual abuse at a residential school.[657] More and more people then came forward to testify that they too had been abused. The Royal Commission on Aboriginal Peoples of 1996 indicted the residential schools for the "horrors" committed under their watch, leading the Department of Indian and Northern Affairs to issue a statement to the effect that the residential schools were guilty of creating a "tragic legacy."[658] Then Beverley McLachlin, Chief Justice of the Supreme Court of Canada, weighed in with the pronouncement that what had originally been called assimilation was, in the language of the 21st century, "cultural genocide."[659] This was echoed in the summary volume published by the Truth and Reconciliation Commission, which alleged that for over a century the government's central aim was to "cause Aboriginal peoples to cease to exist ... which can best be described as 'cultural genocide.'"[660] By now that phrase had become commonplace. In the summer of 2022 Pope Francis lent his authority to the accusation that the schools in themselves

---

[657] CBC, The Journal, October 30, 1990. Rosemary Nagy and Robinder Kaur Sehdev, "Introduction: Residential Schools and Decolonization." *Canadian Journal of Law and Society*, vol. 27:1 (2012), p. 67. [Yet Fontaine later told the historian J.R. Miller that *"he had not attended a residential school"* [emphasis added], *Residential Schools and Reconciliation: Canada Confronts its History*. Toronto: University of Toronto Press, Toronto, 2017, p. 46, n. 10.

[658] Nagy and Sehdev, p. 67; Michael Seear, "The health and rights of Indigenous populations: *An Introduction to International Health*," 2nd edn. Toronto: Canadian Scholars' Press, 2007, p. 426.

[659] "Unity, diversity and cultural genocide: Chief Justice McLachlin's complete speech," *Globe and Mail*, May 28, 2015.

[660] TRC, *Honouring the Truth, Reconciling for the Future: Summary of the Final Report of the Truth and Reconciliation Commission of Canada* (Ottawa: Truth and Reconciliation Commission of Canada, 2015) p. 1.

were genocidal.[661] Finally, the Canadian House of Commons took only a few seconds to pass unanimously a resolution, without any qualification, that Canada's Residential Schools were "genocide." With the crushing weight of all these authorities combined, how could anyone question that Canada's Residential Schools were guilty of genocide against our First Nations People? So much weight has the accusation gathered that the Minister of Justice has recently declared his sympathy for Kim Murray's call for criminal prosecution of any who question the dominant narrative — Residential School "denialists" as they are now called. If enacted, such a law could result in the jailing of lawyers, judges, professors, and journalists, all of whom have dared to question that narrative, and continue to publish their views widely.[662]

Below I will do just that: scrutinize and question the justice of the genocide indictment.

First, some background. The Residential Schools were founded by the government of Sir John A. Macdonald in the late 19th century. The Indian population was in decline, partly because the fur trade — for many years mutually profitable to white traders and Indigenous trappers — was no longer economically viable. A second factor was the decline of the buffalo hunt. By mid-century the herds were thinning out, and in the spring of 1879, for reasons that have never been adequately explained, the buffalo did not return to the western plains. Many Indigenous people were now in desperate straits. Whereas their population had been around 200,000 when Europeans first began arriving in North America, in what is now Canada it shrank steadily for most of the 19th century, reaching its low point of 73,000 in 1883. Part of the government's program to rescue them from extinction was to establish day schools and boarding schools that would offer an education to fit Indigenous people to be productive citizens in a modern industrial society. The objective was unabashedly assimilationist. Because the pure hunting, trapping, and fishing way of life was evidently doomed, it was believed that a new way of life based on agriculture,

---

[661] "Pope says genocide took place at Canada's residential schools." *Ka'nhehsí:io Deer* · CBC News, July 30, 2022.

[662] For a broad selection of their many articles and other publications, see the website of the Indian Residential Schools Research Group, IRSRG.ca.

mining, or industry would offer a more promising future for the majority of the Indigenous people.[663] Dating from the last years of the 19th century, their population rose steadily until it has now reached over 1.8 million. That strong population growth is hardly evidence of genocide.[664]

The government of Sir John A. Macdonald, in power for much of the later 19th century, was far from unsympathetic to the needs of Indigenous people. In 1870, for example, responding to Louis Riel's demand for a province for the Métis and Indigenous peoples of the West, the Dominion government created Manitoba. Macdonald ensured that the new province got off to a good start by providing federal subsidies, setting aside land for the Métis, and giving Manitoba strong representation in the federal parliament.[665] Further evidence of Macdonald's sympathy was his government's granting the vote in 1885 to all male, property-owning status Indians — the same voting qualification that applied to other Canadians.[666]

Like so many other government projects, the Residential Schools were for a long time underfunded. The early buildings were for the most part cheaply constructed, badly heated, and poorly ventilated. In many schools the students shivered during cold winter nights, and transmitted infections in overcrowded classrooms. The food was substandard, and there never seemed to be enough of it.[667]

In these unhealthy and overcrowded institutions, it is alleged, the children were susceptible to every kind of illness. Contagious diseases — tuberculosis, influenza, pneumonia, smallpox, whooping cough, and

[663] Frances Widdowson, 'The political economy of truth and reconciliation', in Rodney A. Clifton and Mark Dewolf, *From Truth Comes Reconciliation: Assessing the Truth and Reconciliation Report.* Winnipeg: Frontier Centre for Public Policy, 2021, pp. 73-84. I have profited immensely from this and other writings by Frances Widdowson.

[664] "Indigenous peoples – 2021 Census promotional material," Statistics Canada, September 21, 2022.

[665] Tattrie, Jon and Andrew McIntosh. "Manitoba and Confederation," *The Canadian Encyclopedia,* 15 May 2020, *Historica Canada.* www.thecanadianencyclopedia.ca/en/article/manitoba-and-confederation.

[666] Leslie, John F. "Indigenous Suffrage". *The Canadian Encyclopedia,* 31 March 2016, *Historica Canada.* www.thecanadianencyclopedia.ca/en/article/Indigenous-suffrage.

[667] J.R. Miller, *Residential Schools and Reconciliation,* pp. 15, 53.

diphtheria among others — spread like wildfire. The students, we are told, took these diseases back to their reserves, causing great mortality among the First Nations people.

The reality is different. All Canadian children suffered very high mortality before the 20th century. From the early 1900s onward the Residential Schools were actually in the *forefront of the battle to reduce childhood mortality*, and pioneered measures that helped achieve that end.

The greatest killer everywhere in the 19th and early 20th centuries was tuberculosis. The Residential Schools were swarming with TB and other infections in the early 1900s. They mostly did not refuse admission to children suffering from contagious diseases, tuberculosis in particular. Had they denied them admission, they would have had virtually no students, since almost all First Nations children were bearers of the tubercule bacillus at some stage of development. It must be emphasized that overwhelmingly it was children from the reserves who brought tuberculosis into the schools, not the other way around. "In no instance was a child awaiting admission to school [in 1909] found free from tuberculosis; hence it was plain that *infection was got in the home primarily*," wrote Dr Peter Bryce [emphasis added]. He blamed this on the crowded and unsanitary conditions on the reserves.[668] As we shall see, TB was far deadlier on the reserves than it was in the schools.

Yet two years earlier Dr. Bryce, then Chief Medical Officer in the Department of Indian Affairs, had issued a scathing indictment of the residential schools for their deplorable sanitary conditions and abysmal ventilation which, he said, were contributing to the unchecked spread of TB. The Dominion government and the school administrators took his words to heart. They began significant increases in funding, and remodelled many schools to improve ventilation and personal hygiene. Over the following fifteen years, 30 residential schools were built or remodelled to the new healthier standards. The largest school, on the

---

[668] P.H. Bryce, *Report on the Indian Schools of Manitoba and the Northwest Territories*. Ottawa: Government Printing Bureau, 1907; Bryce, *Story of a National Crime* p. 5.

Kamloops reserve, also installed a large septic tank for sewage treatment purposes.[669]

At the beginning of term 1938 the Blue Quills School took the precaution of arranging lung X-rays for all its students at the local hospital, while "Dr. Davison came to the School to give the skin test to the newcomers. He said that the four girls at the hospital, being treated for T. B., will soon be able to come back to school."[670] Was this the practice at other schools? We don't know.

Steps were also taken to eliminate bovine tuberculosis from the herds that supplied milk to the schools. Medical inspectors were appointed for each province to visit the schools. A number of hospitals and sanatoria were built on the reserves. Dr. George Adami, Professor of Pathology at McGill University, who worked with Bryce in combating childhood TB, wrote to the Deputy Minister, "I can assure you my only motive is a great sympathy for these children, who are the wards of the government and cannot protect themselves from the ravages of this disease."[671] In 1933 Dr. George Ferguson launched an experimental trial with the new BCG [Bacillus-Calmette-Guérin] vaccine. To demonstrate his conviction that this would benefit, not harm, Indigenous people, Dr. Ferguson first vaccinated his own six children. His program at Fort Qu'Appelle, Saskatchewan was a remarkable success. There was an 80 percent reduction in active cases of TB among the school children who were vaccinated and *no deaths*.[672]

All these achievements were ultimately overshadowed by the introduction of streptomycin, a specific drug for the tubercle bacillus. This was the first of some ten drugs that were to have overwhelming effectiveness in treating

[669] E.H. Tredcroft, Report on the Construction of a Sewage Plant at Kamloops School 1924. National Archives Canada, Indian Affairs, RG 10 volume 6450, file 882-9, part 2. Microfilm or scanned pdf. copies of many such documents are held at various institutions, e.g. UBC and USask.

[670] Public Archives of Alberta, PR1971.0220/5767, *Moccasin Telegraph*, pp. 22, 24, 26, 31.

[671] *Bryce, Story of a National Crime*, p. 6.

[672] G. J. Wherrett, *Miracle of Empty Beds: History of Tuberculosis in Canada* (Toronto: University of Toronto Press, 1977), p. 109; NCTR, Report, vol. 1, *Origins to 1939*, p. 432.

tuberculosis. From 1944 onwards, among both First Nations people and the population at large the incidence of TB plummeted.[673]

Overall TB mortality among First Nations people fell by 92 percent in the 25 years between 1930 and 1955.[674] Research buried in volume 2 of the *History* published by the TRC tells us that from 1943 to 1953, the annual TB death rate for the First Nations population as a whole dropped from 626.6 to 100.0 per 100,000.[675] During the same period, the annual TB death rate in the residential schools went from about 230 to 20 deaths per 100,000. In other words, *TB mortality in the schools fell from 35 percent of First Nations TB mortality in 1943, to barely 20 percent of First Nations TB mortality by 1953.*[676] The progress made by the residential schools in conquering tuberculosis during that crucial decade is truly remarkable.

Yet to this day, the First Nations mortality rate remains much higher than among the rest of the Canadian population. Long after the last Residential School closed its doors for good, the rate of tuberculosis among First Nations people is a shocking forty times higher than among the rest of the country's population.[677]

As with tuberculosis, the Residential Schools can boast a favourable record in the great Spanish Influenza epidemic that struck the world in 1918-19. True, First Nations people were ravaged by the epidemic, which carried off the young (under age 20) more than any other age group.[678] First Nations

---

[673] Wherrett, p. 17.

[674] Ibid., p. 252.

[675] *Canada's Residential Schools: The History, Part 2 1939 to 2000 The Final Report of the Truth and Reconciliation Commission of Canada Volume 1.* Montreal and Kingston: McGill-Queen's University Press for the National Truth and Reconciliation Commission, 2015. p. 193, Table 36.1

[676] NTRC *History*, vol. 1 Part 2, 1939-2000, p. 191, graph 36.3. The NTRC has (perhaps deliberately) made it difficult to perform this comparison because it gives the figures for overall First Nations TB mortality in the form of a table, showing deaths per 100,000, while it gives the figures for Residential School mortality in the form of a graph as deaths per 1000. Because the latter are in the form of a graph, the figures are only approximate. Nevertheless, the vastly superior record of the residential schools is incontrovertible.

[677] Greg Piasetzki, "Everybody's favourite dead white male," *C2C Journal*, Nov. 12, 2021, reproduced under the same title as a chapter in this book.

[678] Mary-Ellen Kelm, 'British Columbia First Nations and the Influenza Pandemic of 1918-1919', *BC Studies*, no. 122 (1999), p. 37.

mortality was many times higher than in the general Canadian population. Yet, in the schools for which we have precise information the death rate was under 27 percent of the rate for all First Nations people, and this is reported in the TRC Report.[679] It is further proof that the Residential Schools were anything but the primary sources of infection.

Trachoma is not a disease that is heard much of these days, but in the early part of the last century, it was "a most serious health problem" because it could often end in blindness among children. At least one school (Blue Quills) kept a close watch on its students' eyesight. As reported in the *Moccasin Telegraph* in 1941, "On April 24th, Dr. Walls came to see how our eyes were. During class, we all went up and it was not long before all our eyes were examined. Dr. Walls was very pleased with the appearance of our eyes and we thank Sister Chouinard for the good care she has given us."[680]

A number of residential schools pioneered in the treatment of trachoma, with the result that the 1935 Report of the Department of Indian Affairs announced that "the number of acute cases in the schools has greatly diminished." By 1939 the incidence of trachoma among Residential School students was down 50 per cent. Sulfanilamide treatment, which began at the end of the 1930s, soon practically eliminated the disease.[681]

Throughout the 20th century, as they battled against the ravages of disease among their students, the leaders of the residential schools and their overseers in the Federal Government were motivated by a desire to help the children achieve a healthier, happier life. At the beginning of the century Hayter Reed, Deputy Superintendent of Indian Affairs, wrote that the objective of the government's policies was "gain in general health, in physical growth, in freedom from sickness and deaths and in school

---

[679] Canada's Residential Schools: The *History*, Part 1. Origins to 1939. Volume 1. Montreal and Kingston: McGill-Queen's University Press for the National Commission on Truth and Reconciliation Commission, p. 439. Total mortality in the schools at the time from all diseases was less than 27% of First Nation mortality from the Spanish Flu alone. (1,000 per 100,000 vs. 3,770 per 100,000). Ibid., pp. 436, 376, graph' 16.1.

[680] 'Gene Steinhauer – Grade IV.' *Moccasin Telegraph*, vol. 4, no. 4, 1941, p. 18. The "Moc Tel" was published between 1941 and 1990 by the HBC Northern Stores Division.

[681] Dominion of Canada, *Annual Report of the Department of Indian Affairs for the year Ended March 31 1935*. Ottawa: King's Printer; NCTR, *Report*, vol. 1. *Origins to 1939*, p. 448.

attainments." Dr. Lafferty, who with Dr. Peter Bryce had been appointed to examine the incidence of tuberculosis among children in select residential schools, echoed this sentiment: "all our regulations are designed to obtain healthy pupils."[682] A few decades later Dr. D.A. Stewart argued that the number one reason for stepping up the fight against TB in First Nations communities was because "we took and occupied his country, but especially because we brought him the disease."[683]

What about the allegation of substandard food and inadequate servings? It is true that some students complained that the meals were un-nutritious, inedible "mush," but others said they liked the food, especially the sweetened porridge.[684]

There is a baffling entry in the NTRC *History*, citing a meal menu at Gordon's Indian Residential school for May 1931 as an example of the poor and inadequate diet offered to the students. The authors seem utterly unaware that Canada was then in the depths of the Great Depression, when many Canadian families worried about where their next meal was coming from. The sample menu was: "breakfast — boiled eggs, rolled oats, sugar and milk, bread, butter, tea, cocoa; dinner [the mid-day meal] — soup, cold roast beef, vegetables, potatoes, bread, rice pudding; supper — beef stew (including vegetables?), bread, butter, jam, tea."[685] By what stretch of the imagination can this be called an insufficient diet? It is more than many Canadian families could afford.[686] Another piece of positive evidence comes from the student magazine, *St. Anthony's News*, Onion Lake, Lloydminster, Saskatchewan, in which Grade 7 student Clarence Quiney wrote, referring to a lunch of "soup, sandwiches, dessert and sweet cold

---

[682] Correspondence Relating to Tuberculosis among the Indians in the Various Agencies across Canada. Public Archives Canada, 1908-1910. RG10, Volume number: 3957, Microfilm reel number: C-10166, File number: 140754-1, pp. 257, 271.

[683] D.A. Stewart, *Canadian Medical Association Journal*, 1936, cited in NTRC *Report*, vol. 1, *Origins to 1939*, p. 433.

[684] *The Survivors Speak*, pp. 73, 77.

[685] *Canada's Residential Schools, The History, Part 1, Origins to 1939*. Montreal & Kingston: McGill-Queens University Press for the National Truth and Reconciliation Commission, 2016, p. 501.

[686] Barry Broadfoot, *Ten Lost Years: 1929-1939: Memories of Canadians Who Survived the Depression* (Garden City: Doubleday Canada, 1973).

juice," that "we are thankful to have such good dinners."[687] (The lad added that a supervisor "brought an owl which looked very funny" and they fed it "bits of our dinner – crumbs and crusts.")

Fortunately we now have objective findings that put this limited evidence in perspective. A study recently published in the *Canadian Journal of Economics* found that before 1950 children placed in residential schools were indeed often undernourished   thanks mainly to government underfunding. However, reforms instituted in the 1950s resulted in a dramatic improvement in the children's health. Depending on the region of the country, those born after 1930 experienced an increase in height of up to one inch, and a decrease in body mass index (BMI). Demographers have long considered it axiomatic that increased height is an infallible indicator of an increased standard of living. Not only did the students' height increase significantly, their attendance at residential school was also linked to lower obesity as an adult. They were also less likely to be underweight, and there was also a lower prevalence of diabetes. Contrast these improvements with the high mortality that prevailed in the early part of the twentieth century – two to three times the Canadian average. By the early 1950s mortality in the schools had fallen dramatically, to the point where it was similar to that of non-Indigenous Canadian children. It cannot have been lower on the reserves, where, as late as 1965 the vast majority had no electricity and lacked access to indoor toilets. Finally, the results for diabetes and self-assessed health provide further evidence that residential schooling *"had a positive impact on the physical health of those that attended."* [emphasis added].[688]

It is well known that breast-feeding has a positive influence on infant health. Donna Feir has found that the children of mothers who attended a residential school were six percent more likely to have been breast-fed than those whose mothers did not attend a residential school.[689] The findings of another study are more striking. Of the children with at least

---

[687] *St. Anthony's News,* vol. xii, no. 2, p. 19 (April 1963), Public Archives of Alberta, PR 1971.20/5253, reproduced at the "Indian Residential Schools Records" website.

[688] Donna L. Feir and M. Christopher Auld, "Indian residential schools: Height and body mass post-1930," *Canadian Journal of Economics,* vol. 54 (1), Feb. 2021, pp. 129, 134, 155, 158.

[689] Feir, "The long-term effects of forcible assimilation policy," op. cit.

one parent who attended a residential school, 61 percent were breast-fed; of children who had at least one grandparent who attended (but no parent) 60 percent were breast-fed. By contrast, only 44 percent of children, none of whose parents or grandparents attended, were breastfed.[690] Indigenous people with direct family experience of residential school were thus better-informed about neonatal nutrition, and made better neonatal nutritional choices, than those who lacked the experience.

Drug abuse is a scourge on many First Nations reserves, but here again the residential schools emerge with a superior record. Among First Nations adults who attended a residential school 73 percent claimed never to have used any other drug apart from cannabis, while only 61 percent of those who had not attended a residential school made this claim.[691]

What about binge drinking, another serious problem in First Nations communities? The most recent Survey (2015-17) found that adults who had attended a residential school were significantly less likely — by a margin of 42 percent to 32 percent — to binge drink than those who had not attended a residential school.[692]

All these results are especially striking when we recall that for most of the twentieth century the residential schools gave priority in admission to those from severely disadvantaged backgrounds – neglected, orphaned, or destitute status Indian children, or those suffering from poverty, violence, or drunkenness on the part of their parents.[693]

These authoritative studies show conclusively that the myth of the Residential Schools as agents of genocide should be consigned to the garbage can, where it has always belonged.

---

[690] *National Report of the First Nations Regional Health Survey Phase 3: Volume One*, (Ottawa: First Nations Information Governance Centre, 2018), p. 163.

[691] *First Nation Regional Health Survey, 2008-10*. Ottawa: First Nations Health Authority, 2012, p. 204.

[692] Figure 6.10, p. 160.

[693] Nina Green, Brian Giesbricht, Tom Flanagan, "They were not forced," *The Dorchester Review* online, April 21, 2022; James Redford, "Attendance at Indian Residential Schools in British Columbia, 1890-1920," *BC Studies*, no. 44 (winter, 1979-80), pp. 48-50; *The Survivors Speak*, p. 19.

What about the charge that by forbidding students to speak their native languages or practice their traditional spirituality, the residential schools were guilty of cultural genocide against the people of Canada's First Nations?

First of all it needs to be kept in mind that only a small minority of First-Nations children ever attended a residential school. Attendance peaked in the 1930s when it reached about one-third of all First Nations children who attended any school.[694] There were in addition many who did not attend any school, residential or other. From then on the percentage declined steadily. By 1968 it was down to 13 percent, and for the rest of the century it declined even faster.[695] Given their minority status it is hard to see how the residential schools can have been primarily responsible for the decline of Indigenous culture.

It is also interesting that "Indigenous parents and leaders commonly preferred residential schools over alternatives such as day schools and provincial public schools." Indigenous parents often feared that in the provincial public schools their children would be exposed to racist bullying on the part of white students.[696] Another consideration is the inability of many impoverished parents on the reserves to provide their children with the necessities of life. That is why "Indigenous parents strenuously objected when, after 1950, the federal Indian Affairs Department began transitioning away from residential schools, to enrolling more children in day schools and provincial public schools."[697] As late as the 1960s, "a Saskatchewan Indian Agency Superintendent reported, 'We were inundated with applications [for enrolment of children in the residential schools] ... That was one of the times of the year I dreaded the

694 "Residential Schools Overview," National Centre for Truth and Reconciliation, University of Manitoba, April 3, 2015.

695 Truth and Reconciliation Commission [TRC], *History*, part 2, 1939-2000, p. 10. See also Nina Green, 'Two-thirds did not attend.' *Dorchester Review*, vol. 12 (2), autumn/winter 2022, pp. 68-74.

696 TRC, *History*, part 2, pp. 74, 93.

697 Vic Satzewich and Linda Mahood,"Indian Agents and the Residential School System in Canada 1946 to 1970" *Historical Studies in Education*, vol. 7, no. 1 (spring 1995), pp. 45-69.

most ... when we had to go through these applications and turn down any number of people."[698]

It is abundantly clear that Indigenous parents exercised agency over the education of their children. To imply that they passively submitted to government orders to enrol their children is insulting. In fact, as a study of the BC schools notes, heads of families signed contracts with the schools to educate their children. While cases of involuntary enrollment undoubtedly occurred, "they were scattered and usually unauthorized."[699] Parents had firm expectations. Some wanted to see "all their people put on a level with their white neighbours." Others expected that their children would experience improved health at school. Others sent their children because the other parent had died, or their marriage had broken down. In two schools for which records have survived almost 50 percent of the students were orphans.[700] Other parents frankly recognized that their children would fare better in a residential school such as Shubenacadie than in a broken home. "But I could tell you that our lives outside the residential school was bad enough that she [my mother] felt ... that it was better for us to be there than with other family members, ... We were safer in her eyes to be there than at home."[701]

To some extent at least the Schools fulfilled these parental expectations. The students who attended enjoyed higher than average rates of graduation from high school, and higher than average rates of subsequent employment.[702]

What about the accusations of abuse, about which so much has been written? It is true that at least up until the 1960s the discipline in most schools was very strict. Corporal punishment, whether administered with a

---

[698] Ibid.

[699] James Redford, 'Attendance at Indian Residential Schools in British Columbia, 1890-1920', *BC Studies*, no. 44 (Winter 1979-80), p. 43.

[700] Redford, 'Attendance', pp. 43, 44-5, 48.

[701] TRC, *Report*, 5 vols. Ottawa, 2015. Vol. I, *The Survivors Speak*, p. 21.

[702] Donna L. Feir "The long-term effects of forcible assimilation policy: The case of Indian boarding schools," loc. cit., p. 435.

strap on the palm or posterior, or a wooden ruler on the knuckles, was common. It is often forgotten that corporal punishment was standard practice in Canadian schools until the 1960s and beyond. It had a greater emotional impact on Indigenous than on non-Indigenous children. Why? Because traditional child-rearing practices usually involved much less resort to corporal punishment than it did among the population of European descent. Nevertheless, the searing accounts of terrible brutality — up to and including murder — inflicted on countless thousands of Residential School students are highly exaggerated. The findings of the Indian Residential Schools Adjudication Secretariat are that "the vast majority of schools in most decades have five or fewer cases of [physical or sexual] abuse."[703] Those cases therefore can represent only a tiny percentage of the students who attended. By contrast, the rate of sexual abuse suffered by children among the general Aboriginal population was 25 to 50 percent In other words, the Residential Schools were a relatively abuse-free sanctuary for Aboriginal children.[704]

If the schools were indeed bent on genocide of whatever kind, how are we to explain the impressive array of both extra-curricular activities and skills training that most of them appear to have provided? The 1925 Report of the Department of Indian Affairs (DIA) offers us this glimpse into some of these skills and activities:

> The progress made at Indian day and residential schools in the Province of British Columbia has been particularly gratifying. In addition to the regular academic courses, special vocational courses have been successfully organized. These courses, for girls, consist of the treatment and spinning of locally grown wool and the knitting of woollen garments, Cowichan sweaters, and socks, dressmaking, fruit preserving, crochet work, and home management, and for boys, boat-building, auto mechanics, Indian arts and crafts, and elementary agriculture. The Koksilah, Inkameep, and Ste. Catherine schools have been outstandingly

---

[703] Ibid., p. 458.

[704] The study, published in 2009, covers the 20-year period from 1989 to 2009. Delphine Collin Vezina, Jacinthe Dion, Nico Trocmé, "Sexual Abuse in Canadian Aboriginal Communities: A Broad Review of Conflicting Evidence," *Pimatisiwin: A Journal of Aboriginal and Indigenous Community Health* 7(1) (Jan. 2009), p. 35.

successful in the organization of *these courses, all of which are based on the needs of the Indians on the adjoining reserves* [emphasis added]. The teacher in charge of the Inkameep Indian day school, has succeeded in the dramatization of a number of Indian legends. The presentation of these at the Banff Drama School created a great deal of interest amongst Indian educationists in Canada and the United States.[705]

Here is what the DIA Annual Report of 1961 had to say about such activities:

> Indian students are encouraged to participate with non-Indians in such extra-curricular activities as track and field contests, as well as meetings of Guides, Scouts, Cadets, and 4-H clubs. Indian pupils enjoy participating in music and drama festivals as well as contributing many excellent items for display in exhibitions of school work and of Indian craft. School bands are not uncommon, and several excellent groups of dancers are active among Indian students. To enrich their experience, tours are sometimes arranged to local historic or scientific points of interest in connection with their school studies, or to nearby industries or places of employment, to introduce older students to the "world of work" outside the reserve.[706]

What about the men and women who staffed the schools? It is now known that most of them were well qualified for their work. The DIA Annual Report in 1961 recorded that no fewer than 87 percent could boast professional training.[707] The NCTR interviewed none of these teaching professionals, but took the word of numerous former students who accused them of callousness, excessively severe discipline, sexual abuse, and general cruelty. Yet there are a surprising number of testimonies to happy experiences remembered by former students. Tomson Highway, Canada's

[705] Canada Department of Mines and Resources, *Report of Indian Affairs for the Fiscal Year ended March 31, 1941*, pp. 165-6.

[706] Canada Department of Citizenship and Immigration, *Report of Indian Affairs Branch for the Fiscal Year ended March 31, 1961*, p. 61.

[707] *Report of Indian Affairs Branch for the Fiscal Year ended March 31, 1961*, p. 58.

most distinguished First Nations author, has raved about how the Guy Hill Residential School near The Pas, Manitoba, launched him on a professional musical and literary career that would have been otherwise impossible. Run by the Oblate Fathers and Sisters of St Joseph, its building accommodating 200 students, was situated on the edge of an "emerald-watered lake." Its facilities — including gymnasia, playrooms, lounges, laundry rooms, kitchens, giant boiler room, [etc.] — constituted "a labyrinth, ... a kingdom of magic." At night, "with the crisp clean sheets, warm wool blankets and central heating I am in heaven."[708] Elsewhere he has declared, "Nine of the happiest years of my life I spent at that school ... There are many very successful people today that went to those schools and have brilliant careers and are very functional people, very happy people like myself. I have a thriving international career, and it wouldn't have happened without that school."[709]

The late Senator Len Marchand also reported a very positive experience at the Kamloops residential school. He entered it in 1949-50, at the age of fifteen. The classrooms he wrote, "were big, well-lit rooms, with desks as modern as any you could have found on the west side of Vancouver in 1949. And the teachers were just as good." Marchand enjoyed playing sports at the school — baseball, basketball and hockey. He took pleasure in the achievements of his fellow students, and wrote proudly about the school's Holstein cattle winning blue ribbons at the Armstrong Fair, and Sister Anne Mary's "superb" choir which "cleaned up at the annual local music festival." In conclusion he firmly declared, "I was never abused, and *I never heard of anyone else who was mistreated at the Kamloops school* [emphasis added]." About the priests, nuns and brothers he wrote, "they meant well by us, they genuinely cared about us, and they all did their duty by us as they saw fit."[710]

---

[708] Tomson Highway, *Permanent Astonishment: A Memoir*. Doubleday Canada, 2021, p. 110, 117, 142

[709] "Tomson Highway Has a Surprisingly Positive Take on Residential School," *Huffington Post*, December 15, 2015.

[710] Len Marchand and Matt Hughes, *Breaking Trail*. Prince George, B.C.: Caitlin Press, 2000, pp. 14, 15-16.

That is why it is no surprise that when alumni from Kamloops organized a reunion for former students in 1977, no fewer than 280 individuals including luminaries such as future Senator Len Marchand, former principal Bishop Fergus O'Grady, and others attended and signed the guest book.[711] And yet this is the school whose staff, 10 or 20 years earlier, are accused of having murdered and buried in unmarked graves 200 or 215 of the children under their care. If this accusation were true how could we explain the large turnout to the school reunion?

Another well-known First Nations writer, Richard Wagamese, wrote about his mother's experience at the Presbyterian-run Cecilia Jeffrey School outside Kenora, Ontario. "My mother has never spoken to me of abuse or any catastrophic experience at the school. She only speaks of learning valuable things that she went on to use in her everyday life, things that made her life more efficient, effective and empowered."[712]

Several other lesser-known students also testified to the National Truth and Reconciliation Commission about their positive experiences. Speaking of his two-and-a-half years at the Stirland Lake School in Ontario, Paul Johnup stated, "I learned things there ... I got to know people ... from other communities ... [Besides my academic course,] I learned carpentry, mechanical, electrical." Lillian Kennedy enjoyed being at the Fort Alexander School. "I think I learned lots from the nuns ... And I got along with everybody. I had lots of friends." Jennie Thomas recalled how a teacher at one of the B.C. schools encouraged her to read. Shirley Ida Moore had positive memories of a supervisor at the Norway House School named Mrs. Saunders who made chocolate Easter eggs for the students. Geraldine Shingoose had fond memories of the principal of the Lestock School, Father Desjarlais. "I really, really liked him ... He treated us good." His staff by contrast, fell short of the high standard he set. Jeanne Rioux found the Edmonton School to be a refuge from an unloving home. "I was happy to be there because it was less hurting and less anger." Martha Mingoose formed a group of four friends at the Cardston School.

---

[711] "Reunions," Indian Residential Schools Records website. The website contains much information about the Kamloops and other residential school reunions. The original guest book is in the possession of the NCTR.

[712] "The Good Side of the Residential School Story Is Valid Too." *Calgary Herald*, May 4, 2008.

"We always laughed, we always shared stories, we always talk[ed] Blackfoot ..." Alphonse McNeely at the Aklavik School said there were frequent school picnics where they "played all kinds of games on the lake, and ... just [had] fun." The Spanish boys' school had regular movies on Sunday nights. Saturday was the highlight of the week for the boys at the Presbyterian school in Kenora, Donald Copenace recalled, because a big box of comic books would be brought out for them to dive into. Mary Rose Julian valued what she learned at the Shubenacadie school. "I learned English. That was my objective for going there in the first place. ... and another thing I learned was I learned how to take care of kids." Moreover, she never experienced any physical abuse: "I was there a year and a half; a nun never laid a hand on me." Percy Tuesday, who attended the Kenora School, stood up for himself and won justice from the principal. He and his friend were keen guitarists who loved to jam together. One day one of the supervisors confiscated his guitar, apparently for no reason. "So I went, I went storming up to the principal's office, and I told him, 'this guy took my guitar, I want it back now.' And I was, I was mad. I had it back within ten minutes."[713]

Organized sports were a big feature at many schools. Gyms, skating rinks and playing fields were common facilities. A few schools, such as the Kamloops school had swimming pools — a rarity at most Canadian public schools during the 20th century. Some students said candidly that sports were the only thing they liked about the schools. Hockey was a favourite, and there were many organized teams. "Participation in athletics gave students a sense of accomplishment." "While she was at the Blue Quills school, Alice Quinney looked forward to sports days. "Track and field day was a day when your, your parents got invited to come and watch you perform in your track events." At the Beauval, Saskatchewan, School the new principal had a greater interest in sports than his predecessor. "We started having new skates, start having good, good socks. We starting [sic] having bought, [two sets of sweaters], Toronto Maple Leafs and the Montreal Canadiens. ... And Maple Leafs, we used them at home, and then when we go out and play out we have to be Canadiens. Eventually the principal bought the team facemasks, ... [and] all that stuff for us." "Orval

---

[713] *The Survivors Speak: A Report of the Truth and Reconciliation Commission of Canada* (2015), pp. 185-9.

Commanda recalled that sports played a positive role in his life at the Spanish, Ontario, boys' school." The School boasted a whole range of sports for every season: basketball and track and field, as well as pole vaulting, high jumping and shot put in the fall, hockey in the winter, and softball, baseball, lacrosse in the summer.[714]

Other students found satisfaction in the arts. "The Kamloops school dance troupe, run by Sister Leonita, became well known throughout British Columbia." Jean Margaret Brown recorded that "being in a dance troupe I was made to feel special. But the work that we did to be in that dance group was really, really harsh."[715] By the 1960s, Aboriginal artists, such as Henry Speck, an alumnus of Alert Bay, were being brought into some schools to give lessons in drawing. Others learned carving from the Joseph brothers.[716] The authors of *The Survivors Speak* acknowledge that, "Many students have positive memories of their experiences of residential schools and acknowledge the skills they acquired, the beneficial impacts of the recreational and sporting activities in which they engaged, and the friendships they made. Some students went ... [on to] develop distinguished careers."[717]

Visual corroboration of this favourable assessment is found in the over 20,000 photographs in the NCTR archive. For many of the photos the Commission unfortunately has made little effort to record the school or the date when the picture was taken — a considerable archival lacuna. The photographic archive could have been rendered much more useful had they taken the trouble to do this. Nevertheless, in picture after picture we see students, very often smiling, reasonably well-dressed, and showing no indication of being sick or malnourished. The thousands of pictures and the positive testimonies that reinforce the favourable impression conveyed by the written and printed sources are all but ignored in the final, "Summary" volume of the NTRC *Report*.

---

[714] Ibid., p. 191.

[715] *The Survivors Speak*, pp. 193-4.

[716] Ibid., pp. 194-5.

[717] Ibid., p. ix.

Buried in the archives are also a number of the school magazines written, edited, and published by the students themselves. Almost uniformly they present us with a picture of cheerful, humorous optimism, and the extensive extra-curricular activities that the students engaged in. The *Moccasin Telegraph*, which was published by students at the Blue Quills School in Alberta, included articles in Cree, among them the following sample entries:

"We were very happy to be back at school. —Emilia Bisson – Grade IV' (vol. 2, number 1, Sept. 1938. p. 9)

"In the girls' room, we have a new Radio this year which Father Balter bought for us. We enjoy it very much. We like best the dance music and the cow-boy songs. —Elizabeth Houle – Grade V.' (p. 9)

"On Sunday, Sept. 25th, we played foot-ball against the Indian men. The score was 3 to 2 in favor of us. In the afternoon, we played baseball with them and we won the game, 7 to 4. Father bought us a base-ball out-fit. — Elie Noel Grade V' (p. 10)

"The Fathers and Sisters are very good to us." —Mary Patenaude, Grade 3. (p. 15)

"On Father Balter's birthday we had a big picnic... When we got there, all the girls went in wading in the water. Then the boys started to play games... After the games, we took our dinner under the trees... Then we had more games and then it was time for supper... When the boys and Sisters were back, we had fire-works.... That was the nicest holiday we ever had." —Victoria Janvier – Grade V' (p. 17)

"The Fun We Had at Treaty Time"

"On the 19th of July, we had Sports Day at Saddle Lake. First, they played base-ball. The Saddle Lake Team played ball with Stry, Hamelin, St. Paul, Ashmont, and Spedden. While the men were playing, the Saddle Lake girls played soft ball with the Ashmont girls. ... Then came the children's races and the men's races also." —Elizabeth Wood – Grade VI Sr.' (p. 18)

Sledding

"This year, we go often sliding down hill and have lots of fun. We go everyday after dinner and at four o'clock till half past four. ... Father gave us thirty-six new sleds this year and we still have the sleds from last year too." —Caroline Cardinal – Grade V', (vol. 2, no. 2, Oct. – Nov. 1938, p. 8).

"Simon Collins, a grade-five student, was taught to play the organ. 'At first, I played only with one hand, but now I play with both hands ... I thank Father Bouchard for teaching me." (p. 19).

A Long Sleigh Ride

"In the afternoon [Jan. 18, 1940], fifteen of the big girls went for a sleigh ride. One of the Sisters and two boys came with us. It was a little cold, but we did not care.... We went as far as St. Brides, which is about eight miles from our School ... While coming home, we tipped over, but I am glad to say that no-one was hurt. Some were all covered with snow and many of us lost our rubbers. After this, ... it was quite dark already. ... We were all cold, but we surely enjoyed our trip even though we tipped." — Caroline Piche, Grade VI'. (Vol. 3, no. 3, Jan.-Feb. 1940, p. 3).

Hockey and Skating

"We had a very good season of skating and amusing ourselves on the ice. Our best hockey team played several games with outside teams. I think we lost more games than we won, but we had much pleasure just the same. Our rink was bigger and better this winter. When the ice is good it is a great pleasure to go out and skate at night. Last winter, we only had one light, but this past winter we had three." —Moses Cardinal Grade VII' (Ibid., p. 14)

The New Radio and Record Player in the Girls' Room

"When Father Pratt went to Edmonton in March, he bought a new radio and gramophone for the Girls' Recreation Room. The gramophone makes us happy when it plays cowboy songs and dances. —Mathilda Blackman Grade V" (vol. 4 no. 4, 1941, p. 8).

Hunting with Sling Shots

"On our holiday, April 30, the master let us go hunting. We made many sling-shots this spring and we have our names on them. ... There were four or five boys in each party, ... and we went away hunting. We started at half past one ... We had a very good time hunting and it made a pleasant holiday. We brought home some game, but some of the boys had already made fires, cooked their game and had eaten it." —David Martial – Grade VII." (Ibid., p. 24)

Other activities included a school choir, baseball and softball, and a hockey team that played frequently against other schools. The staff bought hockey equipment for the team out of their own pockets.[718]

There is also plenty of other archival evidence, apart from student magazines, that the schools promoted a variety of enriching activities from the late 19th century onward: baseball, football, pitching quoits, swimming, fishing, shooting with bows and arrows, skipping, and in winter, skating, hockey, curling, hockey games, gymnastics, and cadets. Hockey was taken particularly seriously, with the Residential School teams winning several championships. The schools also fostered cultural activities: reading (in school libraries), play productions, choirs, dancing. Some of these dance troupes and choirs travelled extensively — to the U.S., Mexico, and Europe as well as across Canada. The schools provided

---

[718] Public Archives of Alberta, PAA, PR1971.0220/5767; Archives of the Grey Nuns, Montreal. The school magazine *St Anthony's News*, of the Onion Lake School, Lloydminster, Saskatchewan contains similarly upbeat accounts of student activities for the years 1963-1966. PAA, PR 1971.020/5253.

extensive training in art and native handicrafts, and again, many prizes were won.[719]

In addition to unique first-hand student testimony, we also have the records of the nuns who taught at the Hobbema, Cluny, Cardston, Delmas, and Onion Lake Schools. They kept chronicles over a period of many years, documenting their work on a daily basis. From these chronicles we learn of the great love the nuns cherished for the students under their care. Since they lived in the schools full-time they were far more than teachers. They nursed students with longstanding illnesses such as tuberculosis. They dealt heroically with epidemics of measles, scarlet fever, whooping cough and influenza, doing their best to check the spread of these infections from the reserves into their schools. Rather than go home to their parents, sick children sometimes remained at school because there they would get better care.[720]

The sisters can also take credit for "many joyous occasions at the schools," including frequent picnics, outdoor excursions and sports activities. The sisters at Cluny held a banquet one year (1954) for their school hockey team, which won the trophy after competing with all the teams from the West and the North-West Territory.[721]

They also provided treats for the children, like trips to the movies, or the purchase of a record player at Cardston. At Cluny there was carol singing on Christmas Eve, and a special meal following the mass. In 1939 the students at Hobbema were taken to Edmonton to see the King and Queen during their visit to Canada. After graduation many students returned to be married in the school chapel. Others returned to the schools as employees. Sometimes students ran away on a whim, but they usually returned. In October 1939 nine girls ran away from Hobbema. Why? Because Sister Jean d'Avila had cut their hair, probably for hygienic reasons.[722]

---

[719] Department of Indian Affairs, Annual Reports 1896, p. 527; 1898, pp. 466, 471, 495, 569, 580; 1908, p. 648; 1910, pp. 476, 700; 1912, pp. 780, 855; TRC, *Report*, part 2, pp. 471, 478-9, 482-3.

[720] Nina Green, "'Our dear children': Sisters' Chronicles of Indian Residential Schools," *The Dorchester Review* online, April 1, 2022.

[721] Ibid.

[722] Ibid.

Parents frequently praised the Sisters for their achievements in educating their children. Indeed on some reserves, such as Cluny and Cardston, the parents actively opposed the federal government's decision to close residential schools. Official policy, laid down by the government, was to encourage the speaking of English on all occasions. The practical advantages of learning English were well understood by many Indigenous people, such as Tomson Highway's father. A student at the Blue Quills School explained that

> Lack of English among the Indians was often very harmful because we have to do business with the white people who do not know our language. In that case, we have to depend upon an interpreter. This often works out badly. For example, he [Mr. Gullion, Indian agent at Saddle Lake] said, Indians often come to him after having made a horse deal, much dissatisfied with the bargain. When it is all explained the Indian often has to say that this was not the way he understood it. If he could have understood English, he would not have made such a deal.[723]

That did not mean the suppression of native languages. The Oblate Fathers for example, made special efforts to learn Blackfoot and Cree, and many times addressed the students in those languages. Even Santa Claus spoke Blackfoot at a Christmas programme at Carlston in 1967! At Onion Lake the students were taught Cree syllabics so that they could write letters home to their families. At the Quills School Father Rheaume came "to teach us how to write in our own language."[724] Some schools also fostered aspects of Indigenous culture. For example at Cluny in 1938, before an audience of 300, "five boys dressed in beaded costumes danced to the rhythm of drums and Indian war songs."[725] Such examples could be multiplied. The children regularly won prizes for their work at exhibitions in Calgary and Edmonton. Donna Feir has also determined that attendance at a residential school actually reduced cultural assimilation. "Those children that lived with and went to school with predominantly non-

---

[723] *Moccasin Telegraph* (vol. 2, no. 2, 1938), pp. 23-4.

[724] Ibid., (vol. 2, no. 1, 1938), p. 15.

[725] See PAA, PR1971.0220/2502, p. 274. Cited by Nina Green, "'Our dear children,'" n. 119.

Aboriginal people were, if anything, more economically and culturally assimilated than those who attended residential schools with their Aboriginal peers."[726]

It has recently been alleged that thousands of children from residential schools went "missing," never to be seen again by their parents. Many were supposedly murdered and buried in unmarked graves. A moment's thought will expose the unlikelihood of this narrative. Most schools were situated on reserves so that students would be as close as possible to their parents, and to facilitate visiting on weekends and holidays. Students were only admitted to a residential school after a parent had submitted a signed application which was forwarded to Ottawa by the local Indian agent, together with a doctor's certificate that the student was in good health. Once admitted, the student's attendance was meticulously followed, and documented in the quarterly returns that the school was obliged to submit to the government. It was very much in the school's interest to hang onto every student in its care, since the grant for that student would be cut off at once if the student stopped attending, for whatever reason.

In addition there was a constant stream of outside visitors to the schools — Indian Agents, police officers, doctors, dentists, nurses, X-ray technicians, dieticians, school inspectors, farm inspectors, business people, and many officials from Ottawa. One reason why the government officials came was to pay the annual treaty money — $5 or $6 —— to which every status Indian was entitled. The absence of any child on Treaty Day would have been noticed and investigated. It thus seems clear that children did not go missing from residential schools. How could they have been, when the schools were watched so closely and visited so regularly by a host of outsiders?

A final bit of evidence that cements the argument of close relations between teachers and students, and the reserve community, is that former students often enrolled their own children in the schools, and returned frequently to the schools for visits.[727]

---

[726] Feir, "The long-term effects of forcible assimilation policy," p. 435.

[727] Nina Green, '"Our dear children": Sisters' Chronicles of Indian Residential Schools', *The Dorchester Review* online, April 1, 2022.

We also have extensive evidence from the archives that the people who administered and taught in the schools cared deeply about the welfare of the children under their charge. This extended to fostering their traditional languages. The First Nations Regional Survey (2015-17), reported that over 60 percent of adults who attended a residential school said they could speak a First Nations language at an intermediate or fluent level.[728] Furthermore, those who attended a residential school were more likely to understand a First Nations language "relatively well" or "fluently" than those who did not attend (74.8 percent vs. 43.6 percent). This is not surprising when it is recalled that several priests who founded residential schools showed their respect and admiration for First Nations culture not only by creating alphabets and dictionaries for a number of their languages, but also by translating various texts into these languages. Yet it is well known that in recent years, well after the abolition of the residential schools, First Nations language fluency has declined precipitously. The First Nations Regional Health Survey (2008-10) found that 87.7 percent of adults who had attended a residential school said that they could understand or speak a First Nations language. In the next report (2015-17), a mere seven years later, the percentage had fallen by nearly 20 percent. It is abundantly clear that the Residential Schools, far from being agents of cultural genocide, fostered the *preservation* of First Nations culture more than any other agency.

In the light of all these testimonials of goodwill towards the residential school students throughout their history, what are we to make of the accusation that the church and government officials who ran the schools were driven by a desire to commit genocide against the native people of Canada? This indictment, though endorsed by no less an authority than the pope, as well as a former Chief Justice of the Supreme Court, numerous First Nations leaders, and apparently the entire membership of the House of Commons, is contradicted by massive evidence from archival and printed sources.

---

[728] *The First Nations Regional Survey (2015-17)*, pp. 164-5.

This chapter originally appeared online as "Not a Genocide" in Quillette, *August 2, 2023. The author wishes to thank Nina Green and Pim Wiebel for their invaluable help with the research.*

Chapter Fifteen

Myths About Attendance at Indian Residential Schools

Brian Giesbrecht and Tom Flanagan, with assistance from Pim Wiebel

In a speech to the United Nations in 2010, Murray Sinclair, who was then Chair of the Truth and Reconciliation Commission, declared: "For roughly seven generations nearly every Indigenous child in Canada was sent to a residential school. They were taken from their families, tribes, and communities, and forced to live in those institutions of assimilation."[729]

Sinclair's false claim is often parroted in academia and other institutions. The First Nations and Indigenous Studies website at the University of British Columbia states that, "In 1920, under the Indian Act, it became mandatory for every Indigenous child to attend a residential school and illegal for them to attend any other educational institution."[730] The Truth and Reconciliation Commission's successor, the National Centre for Truth and Reconciliation, opines, "In 1920, the Indian Act made attendance at Indian Residential Schools compulsory for Treaty-status children between the ages of 7 and 15."[731] This is also what the legacy media, particularly the CBC, has been presenting to Canadians as accurate information for almost a decade.

Canadians, therefore, can hardly be blamed for believing that most Indigenous children attended residential schools, and that they did so because the children's parents were forced to send them there. None of this is true, however. Only a minority of Indigenous children attended residential schools, and competent Indigenous parents who enrolled their children in residential schools did so willingly. They were not forced.

---

[729] Murray Sinclair, speech, April 27, 2010. United Nations Permanent Forum on Indigenous Issues (classactionservices.ca).

[730] Erin Hanson, "The Residential Schools System," https://Indigenousfoundations.arts.ubc.ca/the_residential_school_system/.

[731] NCTR, Residential School History.

The TRC's estimate of the total number of Indigenous children who attended residential schools is at least 150,000.[732] This is more nearly accurate than Murray Sinclair's falsehood, but no one knows exactly how this total was derived because no enumerating or estimating methodology has ever been published. It is also often said that the average term of residence in the schools for those who attended was 4.5 years,[733] but again the source of this number is obscure.

Remember also that the term "Indigenous" embraces not only status Indians, but also non-status Indians, Métis, and Inuit.[734] Canada's residential school program was initiated in 1883 primarily for the Plains Indians, as well as other Indians in western and northern Canada. Although some Métis did attend, the federal government actively discouraged efforts to enrol Métis in residential schools, as it considered the Métis to be a provincial responsibility. The federal government was always conscious of its constitutional responsibility for status Indians as laid down in s. 91(24) of the Constitution Act, 1867, but was determined not to pay for any people for whom there was no legal obligation.

In an article published in *The Dorchester Review*, independent researcher Nina Green demonstrated, using data from the Department of Indian Affairs Annual Reports, that "apart from the years between 1929 and 1940, for almost the entire time residential schools were in operation fewer than one-third of school-age status Indian children were enrolled in them, and even during the years between 1929 and 1940 the percentage was only slightly higher than one-third."[735] Green found that in 1912 only 24% of status children were enrolled, and in 1955, around 30%.

Beginning in the 1960s, the proportion of enrollment of status Indian children in residential schools fell precipitously as the federal government began closing residential schools in favour of sending Indian children to

---

[732] "Your questions answered about Canada's residential school system," CBC News, July 1, 2021.

[733] Frontier Centre for Public Policy, Indian Residential Schools.

[734] "Indigenous" is the new term for "Aboriginal." Section 25 of the Constitution Act, 1982, says that "*Aboriginal peoples of Canada* includes the Indian, Inuit and Métis peoples of Canada."

[735] Nina Green, "Two-Thirds Did Not Attend Residential School," The Dorchester Review online, July 13, 2022.

provincial schools, and as the Indian population underwent a period of historically high growth. By 1969, the percentage of enrollment of Indian children in IRS had fallen to 13%,[736] and from there it declined rapidly until the last residential school closed its doors in 1996. Sinclair's claim that "for seven generations nearly every Indigenous child" attended a residential school is not only wrong, but egregiously wrong. It is a travesty that this misinformation has never been retracted, and that the media continue to repeat it without correction.

The claim that children "were forced to attend" is also a myth. Church-run residential schools had existed in eastern Canada since the 1600s, and Indigenous parents had willingly sent their children to such schools. Some of those early schools had been built by Indigenous people. The most famous example is the Mohawk Institute built by the Canadian Indian leader Joseph Brant. Although no law required Indigenous parents to send their children to these schools, many Indigenous parents chose to do so in the belief that their children would receive a useful education.

In the last quarter of the 19th century, the Plains Indians entered a desperate state, due to the disappearance of game, especially buffalo. The federal government provided relief in various forms, including rations. A related decision was to partner with the churches to operate the existing residential schools, as well as build new ones. The day schools built pursuant to the numbered treaties, 1871-77, were simply not providing the education that had been hoped for.[737] It was hoped that residential schools would provide the education that both Indigenous and non-Indigenous leaders knew was needed.

The false claim is often made that residential schools were created "to kill the Indian in the child," but that phrase was never uttered by a Canadian leader. It came from an American cavalry officer in an entirely different context.[738] Although the language and attitudes of the Canadians who

---

[736] Ibid.

[737] Nicholas Flood Davin, Report on Industrial Schools for Indians and Half-Breeds, March 14, 1879. Report on industrial schools for Indians and half-breeds [microform] (archive.org).

[738] Andrew Stobo Sniderman, "The Man Wrongly Attributed with Uttering 'Kill the Indian in the Child,'" *Maclean's*, November 8, 2013.

began the residential school program would not conform to contemporary sensibilities, the intention from the outset was to provide a modern education for the small minority of Indian children that the federal government could afford to board and educate at the schools. The federal government wanted to create an educated Indian class who could become chiefs and leaders, while the churches were particularly interested in educating future Indian priests, nuns, and ministers. Against this backdrop, the federal government entered the field of educating Indian children long before provincial governments on the prairies assumed responsibility for educating other children. Education for children was not made compulsory until 1916 in Saskatchewan and Alberta and 1917 in Manitoba.[739]

The year 1883 is usually given as the date when the federal government started funding the existing residential schools that had hitherto been wholly run by the churches. This is not completely accurate, because the federal government had given grants to some of the churches prior to 1883 to assist them in the operation of the schools. However, it is true that in 1883 the federal government did begin building new industrial residential schools, while contracting with the churches to have them continue to operate existing schools, with federal government oversight.

In 1892 the federal government formally established a per diem payment system, whereby a church operating a school would be reimbursed for expenses by a dollar figure per day for each of the students enrolled at the school. This payment system endured until 1996 when the last residential school closed. That per diem amount varied from time to time according to the ability of federal coffers to pay. For example, during the Depression of the 1930s per diems were reduced.

The per diem amount allowed for the industrial residential schools was almost twice the amount paid to other church-run schools. The explanation given is that the industrial schools were more expensive to operate, but this explanation doesn't seem to stand up to scrutiny. What is more likely is that the churches were always subsidizing expenses. In fact, the federal government's decision to operate the schools in tandem with the churches was largely based on cost. The residential school program was always a

---

[739] Philip Oreopoulos, "The Compelling Effects of Compulsory Schooling: Evidence from Canada (utoronto.ca)," *Canadian Journal of Economics* 39 (2006), pp. 29-39.

very expensive one for a nation huge in geography, but small in population and revenue.

In 1894 the Indian Act was amended to allow the cabinet to enact regulations requiring Indian children to attend school. However, the regulations as adopted required attendance only at day schools on the reserves where Indians lived. If there was no day school on a reserve, or if Indians did not live on a reserve, compulsory attendance did not apply. One clause allowed for children not being properly cared for or educated to be sent to IRS, but that regulation was rarely if ever enforced in practice. Numerous documents testify to the Department's reluctance to use compulsion to send children to IRS, though persuasion by Indian Agents, missionaries, and the NWMP was endorsed.[740]

In 1920 the law was changed to require status Indian parents to send their children to a school. It is true that a 1920 amendment to the Indian Act made school attendance for Indian children mandatory, bringing Indian school attendance regulations in line with general Canadian compulsory school attendance law.[741] The amendment, however, did not require attendance at a *residential* school. Rather, it stated, "Every Indian child between the ages of seven and fifteen years who is physically able shall attend such day, industrial *or* [emphasis added] boarding school as may be designated by the Superintendent General…provided, however, that such school shall be the nearest available school of the kind required." The Indian Act Amendment, further, applied only to status Indians, and not to Métis or Inuit children.

If the parents lived in an area that had both a day school and a residential school, the parents could choose to send their children to either one. It was only in the more remote areas where there were no day schools that status Indian parents were required by law to send their children to residential schools. And the fact that so many Indian children attended no school at all suggests there was little enforcement of the attendance laws.

---

[740] Nina Green, Brian Giesbrecht, and Tom Flanagan, "They Were Not Forced," *The Dorchester Review* (2023), vol 13, no. 1, pp. 51-56.

[741] Report of the Deputy Superintendent General of Indian Affairs, 1920, p. 13.

How attendance worked can best be seen in Tomson Highway's remarkable book, *Permanent Astonishment*, his personal account of his residential school experience, which he described as "nine of the best years of my life."[742] Tomson and his family loved their traditional lifestyle of living off the land in northern Saskatchewan and Manitoba, where they mainly fished for a living. However, half of Tomson's siblings died of pneumonia as babies, because they were born in such harsh conditions, which convinced his parents that the surviving children must attend a residential school if they were to have a chance at a better future. They were sent to Guy Hill Indian Residential School, a Catholic school near The Pas, Manitoba. There, Tomson learned to play classical piano, and acquired the skills that made him one of Canada's foremost writers and playwrights.

One important point here is that Tomson's parents were under no legal compulsion to send their children to residential school. They did so of their own accord because they thought it best for their children. Another important point is that the Highway family was Roman Catholic, as were many northern Indigenous families. They wanted Tomson and his siblings to have a Catholic education. There was no "cultural genocide" involved. The parents had long ago decided to adopt the Catholic faith. They knew what was taught at the school, and they could have removed their children from the school at any time. They were Catholics who wanted their children educated in Catholic schools. And, of course, they wanted their children to learn to speak, read, and write English.

The procedure by which parents sought their children's admission to a residential school involved filling out a simple application form. Copies of signed application forms can be found at Nina Green's website entitled, "Indian Residential School Records: Native Residential Schools of Canada Researched,"[743] or by searching government records, where thousands of such forms are archived. Some of the parents signed the forms with an "X" because they were illiterate (meaning they had not attended residential school or day school). Presumably, what they were signing was explained to them by an Indian Agent, or other official, or perhaps their chief or

---

[742] Tomson Highway, *Permanent Astonishment: Growing Up Cree in the Land of Snow and Sky* (Toronto: Doubleday, 2021).

[743] Applications – Indian Residential School Records online at indianresidentialschoolrecords.com.

priest. However, most of the applications were signed in the normal way by parents who were obviously literate to varying degrees.

The signing of an application form by a parent didn't guarantee the acceptance of a child into a residential school. The records reveal numerous examples of applications being refused because the school was full, and unable to accommodate more students.

It can be seen by reviewing these applications and refusals that the claim that "nearly all Indigenous children were forced to attend" residential schools is false. Not all applications were successful. The parents were not "forced" to go through this application process. Most parents chose not to send their children to residential schools, but—as detailed above—some parents did decide to do so.

But were some parents "forced" to send their children to residential schools? The answer can be "yes" only by twisting the meaning of "forced." Of course, it can be mischievously argued that all children sent to school by their parents are "forced" to attend school. However, that is not a serious argument. The real argument is whether Indian parents were "forced" to send their children to a residential school by coercion or threats of coercion. In this connection, we must discuss child welfare systems.

Provinces have formal child welfare systems that allow them to lawfully apprehend children who are not receiving adequate care at home. In cases where parents are unable or unwilling to provide a proper home for their children, a child welfare worker apprehends the children and finds a safe placement or foster home. That also includes enrolling the child in a school.

In the years when residential schools existed, the federal government never had a formal child welfare system for the status Indian children for whom it is responsible under Section 91(24) of the Constitution Act, 1867. Rather, the federal government relied on the Indian Agent, who performed a variety of tasks, to identify homes where children were not receiving the proper care (often because the parents were debilitated by alcohol), remove the children, and place them in residential schools. In this way, residential schools served as de facto child welfare institutions, just as they served as de facto orphanages for the many Indian orphans. So, in these cases, where an Indian agent—usually in consultation with others, such as the chief, the NWMP, or the local missionary—removed the child from the home against the parents' will, it might be said—by twisting words—that these parents were "forced" to send their children to a residential school.

However, in child welfare situations, where a child must be removed from the parents' home for the safety of the child, the parents have already lost their right to make decisions for their child. It is not a correct use of words, therefore, to say that unfit parents were "forced" to send their children, because they had already surrendered their parental rights by virtue of neglect or abuse.

How many of the children who attended residential schools between 1883 and 1996 were in this child welfare category, and how many were sent freely by competent, willing parents? We don't know, because the Truth and Reconciliation Commission chose not to examine this vitally important subject. What we do know is that the number of orphans and neglected Indigenous children was considerable. In fact, there were so many children in that category that the law had to be changed to accommodate them. 1920 is not only notable because it was the year when compulsory school attendance was introduced for Indian children (at least nominally) but also because the residential school entrance admittance policy had to be formally changed to accommodate the many Indigenous children who had been orphaned by the deadly Spanish Flu pandemic of 1918-20.

In summary, during the period when IRS operated, fewer than 1/3 of Indian children attended them, and the average length of residence was only a few years. The only children who were "forced" in any sense were orphans and children whose parents were thought to be abusive or neglectful. The large majority of those who attended IRS were sent voluntarily by their parents or other guardians.

It is important to keep these basic facts in mind because IRS have become an all-purpose explanation for all the ills that afflict Indigenous people, including poverty, family breakdown, poor health, alcohol and drug abuse, elevated crime rates, and violence against women. But if only a minority of Indians ever attended IRS (and an even smaller minority of Indigenous people overall), and if the average length of attendance was only a few years, it is hard to see how the schools can be an all-encompassing explanation for anything.

Indigenous people continue to face massive challenges in today's world, and government policies often make things worse rather than better. But seizing on IRS as a universal explanation cannot be correct, and therefore will not point the way to future improvements in Indigenous quality of life.

This chapter was written especially for this book.

Chapter Sixteen

The Tainted Milk Murder Mystery

Mark DeWolf, Rodney A. Clifton, and Hymie Rubenstein

It is a national scandal that Canadians are subjected to a constant stream of allegations regarding historical misdeeds at Indian Residential Schools without any apparent concern for facts, proof, or coherence. Abundant evidence of this tendency can be found in the pages of this book. Examples of allegations with regard to medical practices in the schools are included in a report released on January 24, 2023, claiming that unpasteurized milk was responsible for the deaths of "many" Indigenous children at the Blue Quills Indian Residential School on Alberta's Saddle Lake Indian Reserve,[744] a claim that was cited as evidence of "genocide."[745] Another unfounded allegation, made by an academic, was that "medical experiments" were carried out on children at the schools by introducing differing Vitamin D levels to the milk supply — implying a connection to experiments carried out on concentration camp inmates by Nazi doctors.

The fact that apparently healthy native children arrived at the Blue Quills school and later became ill and, in some cases, died of TB or other diseases is seen by Leah Redcrow, executive director of the First Nation's Acimowin Opaspiw Society, as proof of a grand conspiracy. "We feel that these children were being deliberately infected with tuberculosis," Redcrow told the CBC. "It appears as though people like to accept the fact that these children just died of tuberculosis because First Nations people are natural carriers of tuberculosis and that is a farce." Redcrow heads an investigative team that previously claimed hundreds of the First Nation's children went missing during the residential school era and presumably died.[746] Now she's levelling the even more incendiary charge of mass

---

[744] Emily Mertz, "Children died from drinking unpasteurized raw milk at Saddle Lake residential school: advocacy group," Global News, January 24, 2023.

[745] Sean Amato, "'Evidence of a genocide' found during search of Alta. residential school: First Nation investigators," CTV News, January 24, 2023.

[746] Paige Parsons, "Human remains found near Alberta residential school site likely children, First Nation says," CBC News, May 17, 2022.

murder by the deliberate feeding of tainted milk to innocent Indigenous children.

So farcical was this claim that even the typically credulous CBC showed signs of scepticism in its coverage of the Blue Quills allegations. The broadcaster interviewed Keith Warriner, a professor of food safety at the University of Guelph, who explained that the adoption of pasteurized milk "was a hard sell" throughout the early part of the 20th century and its ability to prevent TB was often contested in public.[747] So it remained common to consume unpasteurized — and potentially infected — milk. Even if these alleged deaths could be traced back to tainted milk, why would anyone have deliberately poisoned it? What motivation would administrators and stuff have for deliberately introducing a highly-infectious disease into the school where they worked?

Were IRS Students Used in Medical Experiments?

There is a dubious academic backstory to the tainted milk controversy. In 2013, Ian Mosby, professor in the Department of History at Metropolitan Toronto University (the former Ryerson Polytechnic), published an article in a peer-reviewed academic journal that — owing to its ostensible accuracy and topicality — was reported in many Canadian news outlets.[748] Mosby, who has a Ph.D. in history from York University, purported to demonstrate that nutritional "experiments" involving milk and added Vitamin D had been carried out by government medical doctors and scientists on children in Indian residential schools.[749]

---

[747] Stephen Cook, "Tainted milk led to deaths of Alberta residential school children, group says," CBC News, January 24, 2023.

[748] Cf. Zoe Tennant, "The dark history of Canada's Food Guide: How experiments on Indigenous children shaped nutrition policy," CBC News, April 19, 2021; Allison Daniel, "Nutrition researchers saw malnourished children at Indian Residential Schools as perfect test subjects," The Conversation, June 28, 2021; André Picard, "Experiments on Aboriginal children were awful, and they have not stopped," *Globe and Mail*, July 24, 2013.

[749] Ian Mosby, "Administering Colonial Science: Nutrition Research and Human Biomedical Experimentation in Aboriginal Communities and Residential Schools, 1942-1952," *Social History*, XLVI (May 2013), pp. 615-642.

As it happens the same subject is taken up by the Truth and Reconciliation Commission Report. At the end of the section on medical experimentation, some of which involved "adding certain vitamins to flour," the authors compare such tests to "a long medical history of questionable research ... without patients' having provided their consent" including the horrific experiments carried out by Nazi doctors in the German death camps during the Second World War.[750]

Mosby too implies the connection to Nazi experimentation in his work. He writes:

> Although it is often assumed that the revelation of the atrocities committed by Nazi doctors and scientists during the Nuremberg Doctors Trials led to an immediate rethinking of how scientific research on human beings was conducted, recent research in the North American context has shown that, in fact, the Nuremberg Doctors Trials – which ended in 1947 and whose verdict included the 10 principles that would later become known as the Nuremberg Code – received little coverage in the popular press and seem to have had little effect on mainstream medical research practices. As Jay Katz has shown, moreover, even scientists who were aware of the Nuremberg Code tended to view it "as a code for barbarians and not for civilized physician investigators."[751]

In short, Canadian doctors seeking to improve the vitamin-D intake of Indigenous children were barbarians hiding behind the Nuremberg Code without realizing it, and Canadians weren't to know anything about that until Professor Mosby arrived to enlighten them.

Their claim is so serious, and has so widely been taken seriously, that we have spent a considerable amount of effort examining it for any distortions that the TRC Report itself may not have identified. If Mosby's assertion were true, it would represent a clear violation of the fiduciary

---

[750] TRC Final Report, Volume 1, *Canada's Residential Schools: The History, Part 2, 1939 to 2000* (McGill-Queen's University Press, 2015), p. 285.

[751] Mosby, loc. cit.

responsibility that government officials and school administrators had for the children under their care.

Some background is necessary. In the 1940s, Indian Affairs instructed school administrators to be much more careful in assessing the health of prospective students before enrolling them in residential schools;[752] and by the 1950s, a doctor's certificate accompanied a parent's application to enrol a child in a school. As a result, from the 1940s onward, medical doctors increasingly visited the residential schools and hostels to examine the children's physical, mental, and emotional health.

During their visits, doctors would treat children without securing parents' informed consent, although they would have had the consent of the institution's administrators.[753] The *Indian Act* gave IRS administrators the power to act in the absence of parents, and in the case of some children whose parents did not speak English, were in hospital, or resided far from the schools or hostels, it would have been very difficult, if not impossible, to secure parental consent in a reasonable length of time.

In the 1940s and early 1950s, a government official thought that residential school students were not getting enough Vitamin D in their diets. Consequently, Indian Affairs provided students in some schools with cod liver oil and standard vitamin pills and, in order to see if there was any positive effect, they did not supply cod liver oil or vitamins to students in other schools and hostels.

By 1966, Vitamin D and other vitamins and minerals were being used to fortify milk powder, and the medical services branch at Indian Affairs proposed that the students in one school switch from vitamin pills to fortified milk powder.

In the so-called "experimental" schools — one could equally, and perhaps more fairly, have applied the term "added Vitamin D trial schools" or "nutritional dairy test cohorts" — the amount of milk consumed before and after the introduction of fortified milk was assessed, and the results

---

[752] TRC Report, Volume 1, *The History, Part 2*, loc. cit., 198 ff.

[753] Ibid., p. 192.

showed that there had been an increase in the milk consumed.[754] Therefore, it was determined, these students were getting more Vitamin D and other vitamins and minerals in their diets.

In examining this issue, the TRC was concerned because neither the students nor their parents gave informed consent for the change in the children's diets.[755] But to anyone giving the matter some thought, this relatively small change in diet would appear to be something that most reasonable parents (and school administrators acting *in loco parentis*) would probably have considered routine, beneficial, and not requiring parental consent. And had the students learned of the study through their parents, that knowledge might have influenced their mealtime behaviour, thus skewing the results. Nevertheless, both Mosby and the TRC report authors *chose* to interpret this minor change as a shady "medical research" study in which the proper and ethical protocol was not followed.

However, contradicting themselves, the TRC commissioners conclude that:

> The study was relatively non-intrusive: the consumption of two products, both deemed to be safe, was being monitored to make sure that the use of an enriched product did not lead to a reduction in consumption and a deterioration, rather than an improvement, in student health.[756]

In other words, the TRC itself recognized that the Vitamin D trial was not, even in a loose sense, a malevolent research study. Rather, the change in diet was simply an attempt to increase the vitamins and minerals the students consumed in order to determine how to improve children's nutrition across the system. Most Canadian parents, as they became more aware of nutrition, made improvements like this in their children's diets all the time.[757]

---

[754] Ibid., p. 228.

[755] Ibid.

[756] Ibid.

[757] Franca Iacovetta, Marlene Epp, Valerie J. Korinek, eds. *Edible Histories, Cultural Politics: Towards a Canadian Food History* (University of Toronto Press, 2012).

In another medical intervention completed by the mid-1960s, 28 students who had contracted amoebic dysentery at Saint Barnabas Anglican Residential School in Onion Lake, Saskatchewan, were treated by Dr. R.D.F. Eaton from the Fort Qu'Appelle Indian Hospital.[758] Eaton used Furamide to treat the students' infection. Some students were treated for 10 days, while others were treated for five days. Eaton reported that two of the students in the five-day group did not recover immediately, while all the students in the 10-day group recovered reasonably quickly. The two students who were still suffering from dysentery continued to receive treatment and both of them soon recovered.

In commenting on this "study," the TRC Report says:

> There is nothing in the records reviewed by the Truth and Reconciliation Commission of Canada to indicate that either the students or the parents were consulted about the use of two different treatment approaches. The conclusion that the study did not involve a sufficient number of students to justify reaching a conclusion raises questions as to whether the research was justified in the first place.[759]

But in fact more information would be needed to understand the treatment protocol that Eaton followed. To characterize efforts to try different treatment methods on sick children as "medical research" (with the intended negative connotations) may be going too far. The TRC should at least have provided more information to show that Eaton's treatment of the children with dysentery was improper or unprofessional at the time.

Similarly, the TRC Report claims there were at least seven other "research studies" conducted on residential school students that did not meet normal standards of informed consent. These claims are as ambiguous as the two studies discussed above. Perhaps it would be more truthful to call them "good emergency medical practices" rather than "research studies." But perhaps saying that would be less newsworthy in the eyes of the CBC, the *Globe and Mail*, and Professor Ian Mosby. Given the implied or direct

---

[758] Report, Volume 1, *The History, Part 2*, p. 228.

[759] Ibid., p. 229.

comparison to Nazi doctors and concentration camps, a more careful examination of such so-called medical "experimentation" would certainly seem necessary.

Looking at the matter reasonably, it is a considerable distortion to equate a lack of "informed consent" with regard to vitamins — in schools to which parents were free to send or not send their children[760] — with the involuntary confinement, mistreatment, and murder of the Nazis' victims. The comparison could, under normal intellectual conditions, be considered far-fetched and absurd — if it were not obviously simplistic, tendentious, and malicious.

The claim that these "experiments" were similar to the crimes of Nazi doctors weakens the credibility of the TRC Report and disparages the work of medical professionals who are no longer alive to defend the harmless procedures they were following. It also undermines the credibility of the quasi-scholarship underpinning a considerable amount of negative news coverage. Arguably, doctors travelling to Indian Residential Schools were trying to do the best job they could under difficult conditions, with a view to improving the nutrition of Indigenous children in their care. In its Final Report, the Commission itself concludes that because of improved medical treatment that residential students received, "the reduction in the student death rate" in the post-1940 period "was dramatic."[761]

This chapter was written especially for this book.

[760] Nina Green, Brian Giesbrecht, Tom Flanagan, "They Were Not Forced," *The Dorchester Review* online, April 21, 2022.

[761] In Final Report, Vol. 1, *The History, Part 2*, p. 234.

Chapter Seventeen

Did Indian Residential Schools Cause Intergenerational Trauma?

Tom Flanagan

"Trauma" is a Greek word meaning wound or injury. Its original and still current use in medicine is to describe physical injuries, such as whiplash after a car accident. More recently, it has been widely used to describe psychological stress caused by wars and natural catastrophes, i.e., Post-Traumatic Stress Syndrome. An even further and more recent extension has applied the concept of trauma to whole peoples or nations, as in the phrase "historical trauma."

Historical trauma is not a bad way to describe what happened to the original peoples of what is now Canada. The coming of the Europeans brought killer diseases against which they had no inherited immunity.[762] It eroded their traditional way of life and made them a small demographic minority in a new nation. Of course, this did not happen all at once. The fur trade was a boon to the Indians and Inuit in much of Canada. By bringing new technologies and opportunities for trade, it raised their standard of living, even though possession of new weapons also touched off new wars. But in the long run the advance of European civilization was devastating for the natives, as agriculture, resource exploitation, and industrial production became the motors of the new economy. Indians found themselves pushed into Indian reserves, where they were protected from extermination but were also made remote from economic progress.

So, there is no question that history dealt the First Nations a bad hand. But it is another question whether residential schools are particularly responsible for their plight. It is commonly asserted today that residential schools are responsible for the "intergenerational trauma" of Indigenous people by having cut them off from their traditional languages and cultures. It is further said that the schools, by removing children from their parents, damaged their sense of family life, so that they were unable to

---

[762] Jared Diamond, *Guns, Germs, and Steel* (New York: W.W. Norton, 1997).

become good parents when it was their turn to marry and raise families. Thus, the damage was passed from generation to generation, resulting in the ills that plague Indigenous people today: lower life expectancy, higher disease morbidity, alcohol and drug abuse, unemployment, crime, and so on.

The legacy media routinely present the thesis of intergenerational trauma from the residential school experience as if it were an established fact. A typical example is a 2021 CBC story entitled "How residential school trauma of previous generations continues to tear through Indigenous families: Trauma can have physical and mental effects for six generations, Indigenous health experts say."[763] The format of such stories has become stylized: a brief, highly torqued portrait of residential schools, a few quotes from "experts," and a couple of personal accounts. But at least one of the CBC stories is far from heart-rending. It concerns a woman who is now a tenured professor of public health at the University of Toronto. She says her parents went to residential school, and she was largely raised in foster homes. "My kids have to deal with this sort of, sometimes crazy, sometimes unstable mom, because I didn't have parents because they went to residential school," she says, adding that she didn't like to go to parent-teacher conferences for her four children because they "evoked negative feelings."

But by any reasonable standard, this woman's life ought to be considered an inspiration, not a disaster. After a difficult childhood, she earned a Ph.D. in child psychology, now holds a tenured position at a prestigious university, and seems to have successfully (she doesn't say otherwise) mothered four children. She would be a viable candidate for super-woman! Whatever intergenerational traumas she claims to have suffered, they haven't kept her from achieving extraordinary success.

Behind these superficial stories in the media lies a body of academic research, the findings of which need to be scrutinized more carefully. There are numerous methodological reasons to be cautious about what is reported in this literature.

---

[763] How residential school trauma of previous generations continues to tear through Indigenous families | CBC News.

First, with a tip of the deer hunter hat to Sherlock Holmes, there is a dog that didn't bark. The obvious first step in research should have been to compare the life outcomes of those who attended residential school to those who did not. Were there differences in variables such as income, employment history, educational attainment, quality of housing, family stability, use of drugs and alcohol, obesity, and other objectively diagnosable medical conditions? Among those who attended residential school, a further investigation, on the dose-response model in medicine, would be to see if a longer period of attendance was correlated with more negative outcomes, as would be predicted by the standard indictment of the schools.

Unfortunately, not enough of this research has been done. A golden opportunity was missed in the *First Nations Regional Health Survey (RHS)*, carried out in the years 2008-2010.[764] In this major effort funded by a consortium of government agencies, researchers carried out more than 21,000 interviews on Indian reserves across Canada. Reserves and individuals were randomly selected in a two-stage sampling framework. The survey included questions about residential school attendance as well as the objective life-outcome variables mentioned above. Yet the researchers published few comparisons of objective outcomes of IRS attendees against others, even though the report is critical of residential schools in several places.

They did say that those who attended residential school were more likely to report having been diagnosed with at least one chronic health condition,[765] but that finding means little because attendees were much older on average than other respondents,[766] and age is notoriously associated with chronic health problems. To its credit, the report did show that those who attended residential school had better educational outcomes than those who did not, though without controlling for age the numbers are

---

[764] First Nations Information Governance Centre (FNIGC) (2012). First Nations Regional Health Survey (RHS) 2008/10: National report on adults, youth and children living in First Nations communities. Ottawa: FNIGC, pp. 15-17.

[765] Ibid., p. 118.

[766] Ibid., p. 203.

hard to interpret.[767] Similar results about educational attainment were found in a survey taken in the years 2015-17. That survey also found higher levels of native language retention among those who attend IRS, though again age would be a confounding factor.[768] These fragmentary findings illustrate what might have been achieved if researchers had focussed on objective outcomes.

Unfortunately, neglect of objective outcomes has typified most Canadian research on the alleged IRS factor in intergenerational trauma. A comprehensive literature review published in 2017 listed 67 published studies on the subject.[769] This research, carried out almost entirely by social workers, psychologists, psychiatrists, physicians, and nurses, reported virtually nothing about the income, employment, education, and other objectively measurable characteristics of ISR attendees. There was little work by economists, sociologists, and political scientists, who might have been more interested in objective outcomes. That dog simply didn't bark.

One exception is the work of Simon Fraser University economist Donna Feir, who found that Indian mothers who attended IRS had a similar socio-economic status to those who did not.[770] More recently, she and a colleague showed in a highly sophisticated analysis that, at least from the 1950s onward, those who attended residential school tended to experience an increase in height, decrease in obesity, and lesser prevalence of diabetes, in comparison to those who went to non-residential schools. Substantial statistical acrobatics were required to tease out these results because children sent to residential school in this period tended to be shorter, fatter,

---

[767] Ibid., p. 205, Table 17.3.

[768] Pim Wiebel comments, Did Indian Residential Schools Cause Intergenerational Trauma? The Dorchester Review online, August 31, 2022.

[769] Residential schools and the effects on Indigenous health and well-being in Canada—a scoping review | Public Health Reviews | Full Text (biomedcentral.com), Table 2.

[770] Donna L. Feir, "The Intergenerational Effect of Forcible Assimilation Policy on Education," DDP1501.pdf (uvic.ca), p. 3.

and in poorer health than those who went elsewhere because the schools served in effect as refuges for abused and neglected children.[771]

Apart from Feir's work, published research deals almost exclusively with subjective variables such as self-reported health and happiness among residential school attendees and their children (and grandchildren). The latter is an increasingly important part of the research. Almost all the schools were shut down by the 1980s, so most who attended are deceased or at least aged. Researchers, therefore, are focussing on their children or even grandchildren, on the assumption that negative effects of IRS attendance might be passed down across generations. Respondents to questionnaires and interviews are sorted as to whether they had at least one parent, or perhaps one grandparent, who attended IRS.

It is an interesting approach, but it neglects other factors of family life that are politically incorrect to mention today but that are obviously important from a common-sense viewpoint. For example, did the child come from a stable, two-parent family? Was there a mixed marriage in which a non-Indian parent and relatives could provide additional opportunities for children?

The authors of the review article summarize some of the results of the 67 articles they collected:

> Twelve papers used self-reported health or general quality of life as an outcome measure and found that people who had attended residential schools generally felt as though their health or quality of life had been negatively impacted.... However, while the studies reveal negative effects in relation to the residential school system, this cannot be said for everyone who attended. For example, some studies have found better overall reported health among those with family members who attended.... Physical health problems, namely chronic health conditions and infectious diseases, were also apparent in the literature. Thirteen papers related specific physical health conditions to residential school attendance. These included conditions such as HIV/AIDS, chronic

---

[771] Idem and M. Christopher Auld, "Indian Residential Schools: Height and Body-mass post 1930," *Canadian Journal of Economics* 54 (2021), pp. 126-163.

conditions (e.g., diabetes, obesity), tuberculosis (TB), Hepatitis C
virus (HCV), chronic headaches, arthritis, allergies, and sexually
transmitted infections (STIs).... [M]any First Nations people who
had personally attended residential schools reported suffering from
physical ailments including chronic headaches, heart problems,
and arthritis.

Mental health, and particularly emotional well-being, was the area
of health most commonly identified as affected by residential
school attendance. Forty-three studies reviewed found that
personal or intergenerational residential school attendance was
related to mental health issues such as mental distress, depression,
addictive behaviours and substance misuse, stress, and suicidal
behaviours.... Familial residential school attendance has been
associated with lower self-perceived mental health and a higher
risk of distress and suicidal behaviours.... Intergenerational effects
were found [by one researcher] among women who had parents or
grandparents attend residential schools, with women reporting that
familial attendance at residential school had had an enduring
impact on their lives and mental health.

Substance abuse and addictive behaviours have also been
identified as common among those impacted by residential
schools....

Suicide and suicidal thoughts and attempts were associated with
personal and familial residential school attendance in several
papers.... Youth (12–17 years) participating in the on-reserve First
Nations Regional Health Survey who had at least one parent who
attended residential school reported increased suicidal thoughts
compared to those without a parent that attended.

There are some obvious problems with these findings that can be stated by
anyone familiar with statistical research in the social sciences. An
inventory of such problems can be found in the famous article by Stanford
medical researcher John Ioannidis, "Why Most Published Research
Findings are False,"[772] so I draw on Ioannidis for the following critique.

---

[772] Why Most Published Research Findings Are False (plos.org).

These studies were all carried out in the first two decades of the 21ˢᵗ century, after the Report of the Royal Commission on Aboriginal Peoples (1996) condemned Indian Residential Schools.[773] After that, the government of Canada negotiated the Indian Residential Schools Settlement Agreement (2006), leading to compensation payments of about $5 billion to those who had attended the schools.[774] Then the Truth and Reconciliation Commission held widely publicized hearings from 2010 to 2015, at which thousands of people who had attended residential schools were encouraged to testify about their experiences, without much balancing testimony solicited from those who had taught or otherwise worked in the schools. So, for more than two decades, former attendees heard over and over that the schools were the worst thing that ever happened to them, priming them to tell researchers that residential schools were a major contributor to whatever problems they experienced in their own lives. And a great deal of money was at stake. As Ioannidis puts it, "The greater the financial and other interests and prejudices in a scientific field, the less likely the research findings are to be true."[775]

Another problem is the design of these studies. When multiple researchers start with a single factor—in this case, attendance at Indian residential schools—and then look for association with a range of variables, some positive correlations are bound to show up. The problem is magnified when dealing with self-reported social and psychological variables such as stress, anxiety, suicidal thoughts, general good health, drug and alcohol abuse, depression, self-esteem, fear, resentment, shame, and troubled relationships, which are often defined by different researchers in varying ways. The lack of rigorous, universally accepted definitions makes it easier to squeeze positive results out of ambiguous data. To quote Ioannidis again, "The greater the flexibility in designs, definitions, outcomes, and

---

[773] Report of the Royal Commission on Aboriginal Peoples - Library and Archives Canada (bac-lac.gc.ca).

[774] Statistics on the Implementation of the Indian Residential Schools Settlement Agreement (rcaanc-cirnac.gc.ca).

[775] Ioannidis, op. cit., corollary 5.

analytical modes in a scientific field, the less likely the research findings are to be true."[776]

The problem is even further magnified when researchers divide their samples into small subsamples, as was sometimes done in these studies, proclaiming that a result holds true for only one sex, or only for certain age groups. The finding may be interesting, but the methodology makes it tentative at best. Subsamples in quantitative research seldom exactly mirror the larger sample, and their smaller size gives rise to larger error variance.

The underlying problem can be illustrated by a simple thought experiment. Picture an unweighted coin. The chances of flipping five heads in a row are 0.5 to the fifth power, or approximately 0.03. That is more demanding than the level of statistical significance of 0.05 used in much research. Yet if you flip the coin a hundred times, you will not be surprised to have a run of five (or even more) heads somewhere along the line. Improbable things almost always happen if there are a lot of trials. Similarly, if you run correlations of one variable against many others, you will get some correlations that are chance phenomena, even if the computer says the finding is statistically significant because the probability of it happening by chance is $p < .05$. This problem plagues all statistical research and can be overcome only by replication of studies using different samples.

Further false results arise when researchers are seeking positive correlations and expect to find them, which is overwhelmingly true of the literature on the effects of attendance at residential schools. All the publications start by giving a negative portrait of the schools, which leaves no doubt where the sympathies of the researchers lie. This is not to say that they are dishonest in the way they carry out their work, but they are human beings whose sympathies can influence the way they interpret and report ambiguous findings.

Another issue is that a number of these studies are based on small samples that do not allow comparative findings. As Ioannidis puts it, "The smaller the studies conducted in a scientific field, the less likely the research

---

[776] Ibid., Corollary 4.

findings are to be true."[777] Fourteen of the 67 studies summarized in the review article mentioned above were based on sample sizes of fewer than 100, and several others were not much larger. Researchers in most of these small studies interviewed only residential school attendees without a control group. If you talk only to attendees, you may find that many of them mention various social and psychological problems, but that doesn't prove that such problems are more prevalent among them than among those who attended reserve day schools, or public schools in town, or no school at all.

The medical and social problems of Indigenous people are certainly real, but should residential schools be indicted as the chief or even a major cause? Beyond the methodological issues highlighted above, several factual obstacles to accepting the thesis are apparent. Careful tabulations by independent researcher Nina Green show that at most one third of Indian children ever attended IRS, and in most years the percentage was considerably less.[778] There were always more students in day schools on Indian reserves, plus some who attended residential schools on a daily basis while continuing to live at home, or who went to public or Catholic schools in nearby towns, or did not go to any school at all. And of those who did go to residential schools, many were there only briefly; the average period of attendance has been estimated at 4.5 years.[779] Particularly for those whose time of attendance was below the mean, was that enough to destroy children's bonds with their family and traditional culture? Other influences upon First Nations seem more important, such as the confinement to Indian reserves, which impeded economic progress, followed by extension of the welfare state, which undermined previously strong Indigenous families.

In any case, the past is over and cannot be changed. Canada has profusely apologised, especially for residential schools but for other forms of

---

[777] Ibid., Corollary 1.

[778] Two-Thirds Did Not Attend Residential School – The Dorchester Review.

[779] Rodney A. Clifton and Mark DeWolf, "Putting the TRC Report into Context," in Clifton and DeWolf, eds., *From Truth Comes Reconciliation* (Winnipeg: Frontier Centre for Public Policy, 2021), p. 37.

education, too.[780] Cash compensation totalling many billions of dollars has been paid out or promised to First Nations individuals for the alleged sins of the past,[781] and more will probably be forthcoming. Indigenous people can now do more for themselves and their children by focusing on things they can change, such as low educational achievement, family disintegration, and governance on reserves, rather than rehearsing the past.

This chapter was originally published in The Dorchester Review *online, August 31, 2022.*

---

[780] Fiscal Explosion: Federal Spending on Indigenous Programs, 2015–2022 (fraserinstitute.org).

[781] From Reconciliation to Reparations: Exploiting a Noble Idea (fraserinstitute.org).

Chapter Eighteen

My Life in Two Indian Residential Schools

Rodney A. Clifton

Over the last couple of years, countless reports have been published about missing children and mass, unmarked graves at Canadian Indian Residential Schools (IRS). The first news report from the Kamloops Residential School was published at the end of May 2021.[782] Since then, many others have claimed that hundreds, if not thousands, of Indigenous children died, or were murdered, and their bodies were secretly buried, often in the dead of night, on school property. The *New York Times* called its first story "'Horrible History': Mass Graves of Indigenous Children Reported in Canada."[783]

Readers may be surprised to learn that these reports were *not* the first time that children were said to have been murdered in Canada's Indian Residential Schools. A horrific claim was made by Doris Young on June 22, 2012, during the Truth and Reconciliation Commission (TRC) hearings. Ms Young had been a student at the Elkhorn Anglican School in Manitoba, and the Commission reported that she "recalled *a child being killed* in this residential school." [Emphasis added] In the TRC Report, Doris Young is quoted as saying:

> I remember was, there was all these screams, and there was blood over the, the walls. [Crying] … and we were told that if we, if we ever told, or tried to run away, we would, the same thing would happen to us. [Crying] So, it was a dangerous time for, for children, and for me at that, those days. [Crying] We never really

---

knew who would be next to be murdered because we witnessed one already. [Crying][784]

Let me explain why the response to Ms Young's testimony is strange. The Commission included two lawyers, Chief Wilton Littlechild and Justice Murray Sinclair, and one would assume that they thought Ms Young's testimony was true before including it in the final TRC Report. But if the commissioners were convinced that the testimony was true, why did they not refer the alleged murder to the RCMP to be investigated? Of course if Elkhorn school employees murdered a young child, they should have been charged, and if they were guilty, they should have been convicted and punished. Finally, why did the news media wait nine years until the Kamloops revelation before reporting the possibility that Indigenous children were being murdered and buried in residential schoolyards?

Even with the ambiguous public record, the highest Canadian government officials, both the Prime Minister and the Governor General, have talked as if the claims of murdered Indigenous children buried in schoolyards were unquestionably true.[785] Since the Kamloops announcement, the federal government has made over $130 million available to exhume bodies.[786] But so far, no verified remains of residential school students have been exhumed at any of the residential schools that were included in the Indian Residential School Settlement Agreement.[787]

On the other hand, in the thousands of pages of news reports on IRS in the mainstream media, there have been few, if any, stories about the experiences of IRS employees, Indigenous or non-Indigenous. Surely, their experiences are worthy of consideration because their integrity is being maligned by the news reports, and because they may have relevant

---

[784] The Truth and Reconciliation Commission of Canada, *Canada's Residential Schools: The Legacy*, Vol. 5, (Montreal; McGill-Queen's University Press, 2015), 189.

[785] Justin Trudeau, "Trudeau Offers Apology, No Concrete Commitments During Visit to Tk'emlups te Secwepepemic Nation," *Global News*, October 18, 2021; Maclean's, "Governor General Mary Simon's 2021 Throne Speech: Full Transcript," *Maclean's*, November 23, 2021.

[786] See CBC News, "Ottawa Pledges $320 Million to Search for Residential School Graves and Support Survivors," *CBC News*, August 10, 2021.

[787] Brian Giesbrecht, "Unmarked Graves Claim Reach Farce Levels," *Western Standard*, February 5, 2023.

information to share. I will briefly tell my story, knowing that my integrity will be scrutinized.

My Experience at Siksika

In 1966, I was a second-year student in the Faculty of Education at the University of Alberta, and I was enrolled in a "Cross Cultural Education" program designed to prepare teachers to work on Indian reserves and Métis colonies. A summer internship was required, and I was assigned to the Blackfoot Reserve (now called Siksika First Nation), 100 km east of Calgary.

So, beginning in early May, I spent four months in the Agency Office as a "go-for-it" (a "swamper" as the older employees called me). The program's aim was that I would do a variety of jobs so I would become familiar with Siksika culture, language, and people. My personal aim was to finish my B.Ed. degree and find a teaching position on a Reserve (First Nation) or Métis colony.

During those four months, I lived in the teachers' wing of Old Sun, the Anglican residential school. Readers may be surprised to learn that the school was named after a famous Siksika chief who signed Treaty 7, and the Roman Catholic Residential School was named after another famous chief, Crowfoot, who also signed Treaty 7.[788] At the time, students were still in residence, some were taking classes in the school, and some were bused to public schools off the reserve. In most cases, these students went home on weekends, which was common in many southern Canadian residential schools.

My responsibilities in the Agency Office were to greet people who came for information, answer the telephone, type correspondence and reports,

---

[788] If people read the names of the schools and hostels in the Truth and Reconciliation Commission Report, they will see that approximately 35 percent of the 159 institutions had, at one time, Indigenous names. Surprisingly, more residences had Indigenous names than saints' names. Why, one wonders, would the churches call their institutions by Indigenous names if they were trying to eradicate Indigenous cultures and languages? See The Truth and Reconciliation Commission of Canada, *Canada's Residential Schools: Missing Children and Unmarked Burials*, Vol. 4, (Montreal: McGill-Queen's University Press, 2015), pp. 141-151.

and file them. After a few days, I realized that about 50 percent of the Agency employees were Siksika, and the Siksika language was routinely spoken in the Office. The Siksika employees and visitors were, in fact, eager to teach me their language.

When the farming instructor went to consult with farmers and ranchers, I would often go with him. On these trips, I met many ranchers and farmers, and later I helped a few of them brand calves and bale hay. I even ate "prairie oysters," which tasted like pepperoni, and I didn't mind getting cow manure on my jeans as I helped wrestle calves to the ground in preparation for branding, dehorning, castration, and vaccination. I grew up in a small working-class community, so activities like these were somewhat familiar. Later in the summer, I helped a group of Siksika men set up the tipis for the annual Sun Dance. People came from as far away as Saskatchewan and Montana to take part in this important cultural and religious ceremony.

I also helped the Indian Agent and the RCMP officers record the names of people who received "treaty money" during "treaty days." If the children were not with their parents, the family did not receive money for those children. At that time, no one reported that children who had attended Old Sun Anglican Residential School or Crowfoot Roman Catholic Residential School were missing. I had never heard of any missing residential school children until the publishing of the 2021 news report on the Kamloops school.

Before the end of June, Mr. Muir, the guidance counsellor, and I travelled around the reserve to register children for the next school year. We registered a few hundred children, and their parents signed registration forms agreeing to have their children attend specific schools. These forms were filed at the Agency Office, and Indian Affairs paid for the students' education if they went to either a residential school or a public school. At that time, school inspectors were assessing the teaching and learning, and if children were missing, the inspectors would have quickly noticed. Some children were bussed to off-reserve schools by Siksika bus drivers, and no doubt they would have reported any children who were missing to the Agency office, the Chief, and Band Councillors.

While living in Old Sun, I attended church services in the chapel. It was common that the school chapel was also the parish church. I also attended a couple of funerals and saw burials at Canon Stockham Anglican cemetery, which is a couple of kilometres from the school. At the time, between 80 and 90 percent of the graves were unmarked, and the percentage of unmarked graves is about the same today. It is worth noting that only with Christianity were any Siksika graves marked. For over 15,000 years, the Siksika did not mark graves or keep records of where bodies were placed.

It is also important to know that the first Church of England priest on the Blackfoot reserve, Rev. J.W. Tims, published a *Grammar and Dictionary of the Blackfoot Language* in 1889, a mere twelve years after the signing of Treaty 7.[789] During my time, the children spoke Blackfoot in the playrooms and on the playground. They also spoke Blackfoot when their parents came to pick them up to take them home for weekends and holidays.

During that summer, I dated a young Siksika woman, Elaine Ayoungman. We were married in 1968 and have been together for over five decades. Elaine attended Old Sun for ten years and when we were young and she was asked if she went to a residential school, she would often say "No, I went to a private Anglican school."[790] Elaine's parents, Arthur and Nora, attended the same school for eight years, and so did her grandmother, Rosie Ayoungman.

Neither Elaine nor her parents had heard of children going to school and not returning home. I am sure that if this had happened, the parents would have reported the names of missing children to the school principal, the Indian Agent, the Chief and Band Council, and the RCMP without delay.

I heard about an incident about 40 years ago that will give readers an idea of the care and respect shown towards parents by an Old Sun principal. In the early 1950s, Elaine's older sister, Rosella, was in grade three or four.

---

[789] J.W. Tims, *Grammar and Dictionary of the Blackfoot Language in the Dominion of Canada for the Use of Missionaries, School-teachers, and Others* (London: Society for Promoting Christian Knowledge, 1889).

[790] Today Elaine does not want to talk about her residential school experiences, and she does not want me to talk about my experiences either.

One morning she vomited into her bowl of cereal, and the junior girls' supervisor told her that she had to eat the cereal. On Friday when Rosella went home, she told her parents what had happened. Her father, Arthur, told his father, Anthony, who did not speak English, and they met with the principal/priest on Sunday when they went to Old Sun to attend the Anglican church service and to return the children to school. The principal listened to Arthur's account of Rosella's treatment, and on Tuesday morning, less than a week after the incident, the junior girls' supervisor was on the train returning her to Ontario where she had lived. This story illustrates that at least some school administrators respected Indigenous parents and their children and did not tolerate abusive behaviour from staff.

Returning to my experiences, by the middle of August, I still had not been paid the stipend that Indian Affairs had promised, and I did not have enough money to return to university for the next academic year. I eventually received the stipend in October or November, and finally I could pay the bill for my room and board at Old Sun.

The young men who would soon become my brothers-in-law teased me that I was learning why the Siksika were not keen on Indian Affairs: "The 'Nabegoone (white people, including me) in the Office are fair, but terribly slow in getting things done." Their words included the notion, not directly said of course, that the Blackfoot work on "Indian time." That was a typical Siksika joke that young Blackfoot men use to tease each other. When I got the hang of the ribbing, I could tease them as they had teased me, all of us laughing at the developing relationship. Occasionally, they would include Siksika words, so I continued learning the language. "Sakum," for example, is used to show you are joking or telling a "white lie" to a friend or relative.[791]

At the beginning of August, I had seen an advertisement in *The Anglican Journal* that a Senior Boys' Supervisor was needed at Stringer Hall, the Anglican residence in Inuvik, Northwest Territories. I applied for the job and got it. So, at the end of August, I boarded a DC-4 at the Edmonton

---

[791] Of course "white lie" does not mean a lie told by a white person. It is English usage thought to date from a 1567 letter by R. Adderley, meaning "a harmless or trivial lie, esp. one told in order to avoid hurting another person's feelings." Oxford English Dictionary online.

Municipal Airport, and flew to Inuvik, which took about eleven hours because the plane stopped at many communities in Northern Alberta and the Northwest Territories.

My Experience at Inuvik

The Rev. Leonard Holman, the Anglican administrator of the residence, met me at the airport and drove me to Stringer Hall, the hostel for children who were attending Sir Alexander Mackenzie school, the public school in Inuvik. At that time, I knew I was going to be paid $300 a month and I would pay $50 for room and board, but I did not know my responsibilities. The next day, I learned that I would be on duty for 22 hours a day, six days a week, supervising 85 Senior Boys, between the ages of twelve and 21, in three dorms. When these 85 boys were in school, I did not need to look after them, but I was responsible for boys who were too ill to go to school but not sick enough to be in the hostel's infirmary or the local hospital.

Soon I realized that there were 285 students living in Stringer Hall, of whom 73 percent were Inuit, 16 percent were Dene, and 11 percent were Caucasian and Métis. It is important to know that in the North, all children from small communities and traplines lived in residences when they attended school. The Church of England missionaries had evangelized the coast where the Inuit lived, while the Roman Catholic missionaries had evangelized the Mackenzie River valley and woodland where the Dene lived. As such, Grollier Hall, the Roman Catholic hostel, also enrolled about 285 students with about 75 percent being Dene.

I also learned that parents sent their children to one of the hostels because of their family's religious affiliation. Some students who were expected to arrive did not show up because they were needed at home or on the traplines. At that time, it was impossible to find the children if their parents did not want them to be found. Families travelled by dog-sled during the winter and by boat during the summer, and they could easily disappear on the tundra or in the bush. Of course, the RCMP and truant officers would not be able to find them. As a result, no one tried to force

331

these Northern children to attend school, and it was clear the children came to school because their parents wanted them to receive a formal education.

During the year, I kept detailed notes, records, and photos of the children, parents, staff, and administrators in the hostel.[792] Fortunately, John and Irma Honigmann, two cultural anthropologists from North Carolina, were in Inuvik studying the integration of the Eskimo (Inuit) into the community. I worked with them in examining the integration of the Inuit, Dene, Métis, and Caucasian students into the hostel and school.[793] A few years later, they published *Arctic Townsmen: Ethnic Backgrounds and Modernization*.[794]

Throughout the winter, parents who trapped furs in the Mackenzie Delta would come by dog-sled to Inuvik to trade pelts, purchase supplies, and visit their children. Even in the middle of winter, when the temperature was well below −30 and the sun did not rise above the horizon, some parents stayed in tents close to the hostel, and some were put up in rooms in the residence. The parents staying in Stringer Hall would eat meals in the staff dining room with their children. During meals they would speak their native languages, and Indigenous staff, who spoke the same language, would often take part in the conversations.

On occasion, I would see a couple of junior girls walking down the hall speaking Inuktitut. I would point my finger at them in a playful scolding, and they would giggle with their black eyes twinkling with glee, hold tight to each other's arms, turn around and walk the opposite direction continuing to talk in Inuktitut. After a couple of steps, they would look back at me with big grins on their faces. No disrespect was intended, but this was the "cat and mouse" game of teaching English that they enjoyed as much as I did. As with modern immersion language programs, my aim was to help the children develop their English language ability. All

---

[792] I gave all my material to the National Centre for Truth and Reconciliation so that it could be used by any interested person.

[793] Rodney. A. Clifton, "The Social Adjustment of Native Students in a Northern Hostel," *Canadian Review of Sociology and Anthropology*, 9 (1972), pp. 163-166.

[794] John J. and Irma Honigmann, *Arctic Townsmen: Ethnic Backgrounds and Modernization* (Ottawa: Canadian Research Centre for Anthropology, Saint Paul University, 1970).

employees encouraged the students to speak English, but I never saw any students being punished for speaking their mother tongue.

In Stringer Hall, about 50 percent of the staff members were Indigenous, including two young Inuk women, Annie, and Lucy, who supervised the junior boys and girls. As expected, they spoke Inuktitut to the Inuit children when the language was needed. The Dene and Métis children often spoke English when they first arrived at Stringer Hall, so they could communicate with most of the other students and the English-speaking employees.

At that time, I made an agreement with some of the young Inuit children that I would help them learn English if they would teach me Inuktitut. By Christmas time, they could speak basic English, but all I could say was a few sentences in Inuktitut that were inappropriate for people, especially adults, to say in public.

On Saturdays, the young children would often come to get Rosalind Malack, the 23-year-old nurse who came from London, England, and me for walks on the Mackenzie River when it was frozen or up the riverbank behind the hostel to go sliding on cardboard. On these walks, the children would encourage me to say the naughty phrases I had learned from them. "Say it Mr. Clifton! Say it," they would plead. When I said the phrases, the children would laugh and say "Funny, funny Mr. Clifton." The boys would laugh openly, but the girls would put their hands over their mouths, clutch each other, and giggle.

Interestingly, there were murals painted on the walls of the dining room, stairwells, and dorms of Stringer Hall. Many of the murals were of Inuit people, dog teams, seal hunts, and caribou. Most interesting, in the chapel, there was a large mural of Jesus and his disciples. All the people, including Christ, were depicted as Inuit.

At that time, the Inuit used specific facial expressions to show agreement or disagreement with a speaker. All the hostel employees, both Indigenous and non-Indigenous, used these facial expressions no matter the language they were speaking. No one thought that this was strange just as no one thought that Indigenous students wearing jeans and western shirts, playing a guitar, or speaking English was strange.

John and Irma Honigmann's careful study clearly shows that Sir Alexander Mackenzie School was, in fact, preparing students for the modern world. According to my wife, Elaine, Old Sun was doing the same. For example, Elaine's grade four teacher, Miss King, drilled her Siksika students in English spelling and grammar every week. For over 20 years, Elaine and I played thousands of games of Scrabble, and she won over 60 percent of the games. Miss King would have been immensely proud of Elaine's English language ability, and she would have surely told her affectionately, "You've done well, my dear."

When Tragedy Happened

Overall, the students in both Old Sun and Stringer Hall seemed to be reasonably well adjusted and happy. The only time junior children wet their beds in Stringer Hall, which could show a degree of distress or trauma, was when they stayed up late on Saturday nights watching movies and drinking soft drinks. More importantly, no children went missing or died at either Old Sun or Stringer Hall when I was living in those residences. Yet, I know about four children from these two residencies who died. The deaths were indeed tragic and need an explanation.

On March 8, 1962, three young girls ran away from Old Sun during a blizzard. They made their way to a house where one of the girls lived at a place called "Four Corners," which was about a kilometre from the school. The parents told the girls that they had to walk back to Old Sun while the blizzard was raging. The girls went out into the storm, and two of them, Mabel Crane Bear and Belinda Raw Eater, froze to death.[795] Ten years later, on June 23, 1972, six years after I left Inuvik, three young boys ran away from Stringer Hall, trying to walk to Tuktoyaktuk, about 150 kilometres to the north. Two of the boys, Dennis Dick and Jack Elanik, died.[796]

---

[795] Tim Fontane, "TRC Report: 5 Stories of Residential School Escapees Who Died," *CBC News*, December 14, 2015.

[796] Brandi Morin, "Residential School Runaway Remembers Harrowing Journey that Killed Two Friends," *CBC News*, September 21, 2017.

For people who have spent time in the North, it seems strange that these children tried to walk to Tuktoyaktuk at a time when the muskeg would be soft and soggy, making walking exceedingly difficult, very cold, and wet, even if they were wearing rubber boots. Of course, the boys knew that hordes of Arctic insects would be swarming over their unprotected bodies. Most astonishingly, they ran away only a few days before they would have been flown home for summer holidays.

In both these tragic cases, I heard that the other students, family members, school employees, and teachers were both shocked and upset about what happened. Many people were heartbroken by these deaths at a time when grief counselling was not available to help either children or adults deal with their emotional trauma. Again, this reaction shows the close relationship that often developed between some school employees and the students.

All the residential schools I have visited had cemeteries close by, again because the school chapel was the parish church. As a result, both Indigenous and non-Indigenous parishioners were interred in these cemeteries. Over the last 50 years, I have seen that Indigenous parishioners often leave the graves of family members unmarked except for wooden crosses which, of course, deteriorate over time. As a result, cemeteries close to residential schools often have unmarked graves.

Time for a Reassessment

Should you think that my experiences in Old Sun and Stringer Hall are true of all the schools and hostels that existed from 1883 when the Federal government began paying for the students' education, to 1996 when the last one closed?

Of course, one should not overgeneralize from my experiences. But one should realize that at least in these two schools, Indigenous languages and cultures were not being eradicated, and children were not being abused. In fact, they were being supported and encouraged, at least during the time I was there.

As a result of my experiences, I wonder if it is true that hundreds or thousands of children died at residential schools and were buried in schoolyards without proper funerals and without official documentation. In fact, a group of researchers have found the death certificates for a substantial number of children who were reported as missing by the National Centre for Truth and Reconciliation. In many cases, these certificates were signed by medical doctors and parents.[797] The claims of missing children have already cost Indigenous people considerable anguish and trauma, and the attempt to discover if children were buried in IRS schoolyards has cost Canadian taxpayers millions of dollars.[798] If we keep going the way we are going now, the claims will likely cost much more, both psychologically and monetarily.

I am afraid that when the evidence is finally published, and if no IRS students are confirmed to have been secretly buried in unmarked graves with no official documentation, the gulf between Indigenous and non-Indigenous Canadians will widen and become more difficult to breach. If this happens, Canada will have drifted further from — rather than closer to — reconciliation. This is contrary to what the Truth and Reconciliation Commission said it expects.

The TRC said that truth is necessary for reconciliation, but the recent, questionable claims show that transparency and verification are also important. If these claims are true, then surely criminal charges should be laid against both those who were responsible and those who did not report the crimes to the proper authorities. Unfortunately, the few school employees who are still alive are aging and there is a limited amount of time to record their histories and to decide their innocence or guilt in abusing residential school children. Canadians should be pushing the authorities to have these claims carefully assessed as soon as possible so that justice is achieved for both the children and the school employees.

I doubt that any Canadian believes that people, Indigenous or non-Indigenous, who abused or murdered residential school children should

---

[797] Personal correspondence from Nina Green, and independent researcher. See also Terry Glavin, "The Year of the Graves: How the World's Media got it Wrong on Residential School Graves," *National Post*, May 26, 2022.

[798] As of the summer of 2023, none had actually been uncovered.

escape punishment. I also doubt that any Canadian believes that innocent people should be condemned and punished. Our justice system is based on the presumption of innocence until proven guilty, but this presumption is being denied to hundreds of IRS employees, most of whom cannot speak for themselves.

It is time for Canadian governments and the churches, especially those who managed residential schools — the Roman Catholic, Anglican, United, Mennonite, and Baptist churches — to speak about the decent work that many of their members did by taking care of and educating these children at a time when few people would do that work. Many of these people, who worked extremely hard with little sleep and extremely poor compensation, are now being condemned without any way of defending themselves. Yet in their lifetime they were the only Canadians providing many Indigenous children with options to live a decent life in the real world.

Of course, it is sad that Indigenous children died at residential schools, but during those times many children died of communicable diseases.[799] Indigenous children were probably less immune to infectious diseases than other Canadian children. Even so, the death of any child is heart-breaking, but today our sadness must be tempered by considering the circumstances of the times. We cannot honestly judge the past by the values and resources we have today. Now it is extremely easy to be virtuous without thinking carefully about the hardships that both students and residential school employees experienced many years ago.

Finally, the mainstream news media should confirm the claims of missing and possibly murdered Indigenous children *before* publishing such stories about Indian Residential Schools. Similarly, Canadian officials, especially the Prime Minister and the Governor General, should verify what was claimed *before* lowering the Canadian flag and proclaiming that these claims are true. A democracy cannot function without a commitment to truth by governments, their officials, and the news media. Truth, and its verification, must be re-established as a fundamental value for Canada. Without truth, I fear that we will not have an honest and fair reconciliation.

---

[799] See, for example, George Jasper Wherrett, *The Miracle of the Empty Beds: A History of Tuberculosis in Canada* (Toronto:University of Toronto Press, 1977).

A version of this chapter was originally published online by C2C Journal *as "My Life in Two Indian Residential Schools" September 5, 2022.*

Postscript: Reconciliation and Truth

C.P. Champion and Tom Flanagan

Reconciliation: "a situation in which two people or groups of people become friendly again after they have argued" (Cambridge Dictionary).[800]

Truth: "the real facts about a situation, event, or person" (Cambridge Dictionary).[801]

"Reconciliation" became a talismanic word in the 1990s, above all with the appointment of South Africa's Truth and Reconciliation Commission in 1996. The word also figured prominently in the report of Canada's Royal Commission on Aboriginal Peoples (1998). Part of the agreement negotiated under Prime Minister Paul Martin and executed by Prime Minister Stephen Harper was the appointment of a Canadian Truth and Reconciliation Commission (TRC), chaired initially by Justice Harry Laforme and subsequently by Murray Sinclair. Canada's TRC reported in 2015.

The Canadian Reconciliation process has evolved over time towards one-way reparations rather than the common-sense definition cited above of mutual rapprochement. It is striking that every single one of the TRC's 94 recommendations is a demand for the federal government, or occasionally some other organization such as the Catholic Church, to provide some benefit to First Nations. The TRC uttered no calls for First Nations to offer anything to Canadians or indeed to do anything for themselves. For example, the TRC could have recommended to First Nations to express gratitude to Canada for the benefits of literacy and scientific medicine. It could also have suggested that First Nations try to address social pathologies that are at least partly under their own influence, such as violence against women; heavy consumption of tobacco, drugs, and

---

[800] RECONCILIATION | English meaning - Cambridge Dictionary.

[801] TRUTH | English meaning - Cambridge Dictionary.

339

alcohol; and lack of family support for education. A spirit of mutual cooperation seems more appropriate to Reconciliation rather than one-sided recrimination and demands for redress.

If the concept of Reconciliation has been distorted in recent years, truth has suffered even more grievously.

In its formal report, the TRC made some effort to point out the positive aspects of residential schools and refrained from using toxic terminology such as "genocide," preferring instead the more ambiguous term "cultural genocide." But in the wake of the pseudo-discoveries at Kamloops and elsewhere, many politicians, Indigenous leaders, and media commentators have thrown aside balance, restraint, and caution, turning truth into a casualty.

Public discussion of residential schools and related issues is filled with the following assertions, all of which are either totally false or grossly exaggerated:

- Thousands of "missing children" went away to residential schools and were never heard from again.

- These missing children are buried in unmarked graves underneath or around mission churches and schools.

- Many of these missing children were murdered by school personnel after being subjected to physical and sexual abuse, even outright torture.

- The carnage is appropriately defined as genocide.

- Many human remains have already been located by ground-penetrating radar, and many more will be found as government-funded research progresses.

- Most Indian children attended residential schools.

- Those who attended residential schools did not go voluntarily but were compelled to attend by federal policy and enforcement.

- Attendance at residential school has traumatized Indigenous people, creating social pathologies that descend across generations.

- Residential schools destroyed Indigenous languages and culture.

The flight from truth makes true Reconciliation impossible. Why will Canadians want to extend the hand of friendship to Indigenous people who continue to call them criminals and murderers? Why will Indigenous people want to engage in mutual cooperation with people whom they have been led to regard as criminals and murderers?

Recovering a more balanced picture of residential schools is the only road to genuine Reconciliation. We hope this book, and the earlier essays on which it is based, will be a step in that direction.

Author Biographies

C.P. Champion is author of *The Strange Demise of British Canada* (McGill-Queen's University Press, 2010) and *Relentless Struggle: Saving the Army Reserve 1995-2019* (Durnovaria, 2019), and edits *The Dorchester Review*.

Rodney A. Clifton is Professor Emeritus at the University of Manitoba and a Senior Fellow at the Frontier Centre for Public Policy. He is co-editor with Mark DeWolf of *From Truth Comes Reconciliation: An Assessment of the Truth and Reconciliation Commission Report* (Frontier Centre for Public Policy, 2021).

Mark DeWolf taught English at secondary schools for 35 years and is co-editor with Rodney Clifton of *From Truth Comes Reconciliation: An Assessment of the Truth and Reconciliation Commission Report* (Frontier Centre for Public Policy, 2021).

Tom Flanagan is professor emeritus at the University of Calgary.

Ian Gentles is professor of history and global studies at Tyndale University.

Brian Giesbrecht is a retired Manitoba Provincial Court Judge.

Jonathan Kay is Canadian editor of *Quillette*.

D. Barry Kirkham KC practised as a barrister for over 50 years, retiring in 2019.

Michael Melanson is a skilled tradesman and writer living in Winnipeg.

James Pew is an independent writer and entrepreneur. He edits The Turn and Woke Watch Canada Newsletter on Substack.

Greg Piasetzki is a Toronto-based intellectual property lawyer with an interest in Canadian history.

Jacques Rouillard is professor emeritus in the Department of History at the Université de Montréal.

Hymie Rubenstein edits The REAL Indigenous Report on Substack. As Professor of Anthropology at the University of Manitoba, he wrote about the lifeways of Indigenous and other cultures for 31 years.

Frances Widdowson was an Associate Professor, in the Department of Economics, Justice, and Policy Studies at Mount Royal University in Calgary from 2008 to 2021. She is currently working on a manuscript entitled *The Woke Academy: How Advocacy Studies Murder Academic Disciplines and Effective Policy Development.*

Pim Wiebel (a pseudonym) worked for over three decades in Indigenous community development and refugee resettlement and is a former Indian Residential School teacher.

The authors and editors would like to thank independent researcher Nina Green for her extraordinary work on this subject.